RSF: The Russell Sage Foundation Journal of the Social Sciences

Anti-poverty Policy Initiatives for the United States

VOLUME 4, NUMBER 2, FEBRUARY 2018

RSF: The Russell Sage Foundation Journal of the Social Sciences   ISSN 2377-8261

The Russell Sage Foundation

The Russell Sage Foundation, one of the oldest of America's general purpose foundations, was established in 1907 by Mrs. Margaret Olivia Sage for "the improvement of social and living conditions in the United States." The foundation seeks to fulfill this mandate by fostering the development and dissemination of knowledge about the country's political, social, and economic problems. While the foundation endeavors to assure the accuracy and objectivity of each book it publishes, the conclusions and interpretations in Russell Sage Foundation publications are those of the authors and not of the foundation, its trustees, or its staff. Publication by Russell Sage, therefore, does not imply foundation endorsement.

Board of Trustees

Claude M. Steele, *Chair*
Larry M. Bartels
Karen S. Cook
Sheldon H. Danziger
Kathryn Edin
Michael Jones-Correa
Lawrence F. Katz
David Laibson
Nicholas Lemann
Sara S. McLanahan
Martha Minow
Peter R. Orszag
Mario Luis Small
Shelley E. Taylor
Hirokazu Yoshikawa

Mission Statement

RSF: The Russell Sage Foundation Journal of the Social Sciences is a peer-reviewed, open-access journal of original empirical research articles by both established and emerging scholars. It is designed to promote cross-disciplinary collaborations on timely issues of interest to academics, policymakers, and the public at large. Each issue is thematic in nature and focuses on a specific research question or area of interest. The introduction to each issue will include an accessible, broad, and synthetic overview of the research question under consideration and the current thinking from the various social sciences.

RSF Journal Editorial Board

Elizabeth O. Ananat, Duke University
Karen S. Cook, Stanford University
Sheldon H. Danziger, Russell Sage Foundation
Mesmin Destin, Northwestern University
Janet C. Gornick, The CUNY Graduate Center
Jennifer Hochschild, Harvard University
Mary E. Pattillo, Northwestern University
Becky Pettit, University of Texas at Austin
James Sidanius, Harvard University
Miguel S. Urquiola, Columbia University
Mary C. Waters, Harvard University

Copyright © 2018 by Russell Sage Foundation. All rights reserved. Printed in the United States of America. No part of this publication may be reproduced, stored in a retrieval system, or transmitted in any form or by any means, electronic, mechanical, photocopying, recording, or otherwise, without the prior written permission of the publisher. Reproduction by the United States Government in whole or in part is permitted for any purpose.

Opinions expressed in this journal are not necessarily those of the editors, editorial board, trustees, or the Russell Sage Foundation.

We invite scholars to submit proposals for potential issues through the *RSF* application portal: https://rsfjournal.onlineapplicationportal.com/. Submissions should be addressed to Suzanne Nichols, Director of Publications.

To view the complete text and additional features online please go to **www.rsfjournal.org**.

Open Access Policy

RSF: The Russell Sage Foundation Journal of the Social Sciences is an open access journal. It is published under a Creative Commons Attribution-NonCommercial-No Derivs 3.0 Unported License.

Russell Sage Foundation
112 East 64th Street
New York, NY 10065

ISSN (print):   2377-8253
ISSN (electronic): 2377-8261
ISBN: 978-0-87154-779-8

Robin Hood

Robin Hood, New York's largest poverty-fighting organization, finds, funds, and creates over 200 of the most effective programs, to help 1.8 million New Yorkers learn and earn their way out of poverty. Each year, Robin Hood reduces barriers to opportunities for nearly half a million New York City residents. From keeping more than 200,000 New Yorkers from going hungry, to helping more than 10,000 people secure jobs, to educating more than 55,000 students, to helping nearly 11,000 remain stably housed, Robin Hood is there for those in need.

While Robin Hood's primary focus is on New York, its impact extends beyond the city. The organization's metrics-based approach has been adopted by other charities around the nation, and the programs Robin Hood funds are often replicated in other cities.

Anti-poverty Policy Initiatives for the United States

ISSUE EDITORS
Lawrence M. Berger, University of Wisconsin–Madison
Maria Cancian, University of Wisconsin–Madison
Katherine Magnuson, University of Wisconsin–Madison

CONTENTS

Anti-poverty Policy Innovations: New Proposals for Addressing Poverty in the United States **1**
Lawrence M. Berger, Maria Cancian, and Katherine Magnuson

Part I. Tax and Transfer Programs

A Universal Child Allowance: A Plan to Reduce Poverty and Income Instability Among Children in the United States **22**
H. Luke Shaefer, Sophie Collyer, Greg Duncan, Kathryn Edin, Irwin Garfinkel, David Harris, Timothy M. Smeeding, Jane Waldfogel, Christopher Wimer, and Hirokazu Yoshikawa

Cash for Kids **43**
Marianne P. Bitler, Annie Laurie Hines, and Marianne Page

A Targeted Minimum Benefit Plan: A New Proposal to Reduce Poverty Among Older Social Security Recipients **74**
Pamela Herd, Melissa Favreault, Madonna Harrington Meyer, and Timothy M. Smeeding

Reforming Policy for Single-Parent Families to Reduce Child Poverty **91**
Maria Cancian and Daniel R. Meyer

Reconstructing the Supplemental Nutrition Assistance Program to More Effectively Alleviate Food Insecurity in the United States **113**
Craig Gundersen, Brent Kreider, and John V. Pepper

A Renter's Tax Credit to Curtail the Affordable Housing Crisis **131**
Sara Kimberlin, Laura Tach, and Christopher Wimer

The Rainy Day Earned Income Tax Credit: A Reform to Boost Financial Security by Helping Low-Wage Workers Build Emergency Savings **161**
Sarah Halpern-Meekin, Sara Sternberg Greene, Ezra Levin, and Kathryn Edin

Anti-poverty Policy Innovations: New Proposals for Addressing Poverty in the United States

LAWRENCE M. BERGER, MARIA CANCIAN, AND KATHERINE MAGNUSON

The 2016 presidential election has brought to the fore proposals to fundamentally restructure the U.S. anti-poverty safety net. Even though much of the current debate centers on shrinking or eliminating federal programs, we believe it is necessary and useful to explore alternatives that represent new approaches and significant innovations to existing policy and programs. This double issue of *RSF: The Russell Sage Foundation Journal of the Social Sciences* builds on and extends the scholarly conversation on the state of current U.S. anti-poverty policy by highlighting a collection of related innovative and specific policy proposals for the United States. Well before the election, the authors of the articles in this volume were explicitly tasked with proposing substantially new policies solidly grounded in social science evidence that have the potential to transform anti-poverty policy. Assuming the goal to be reducing poverty among the U.S. population, we asked what new ideas should be seriously considered. The authors responded with carefully crafted proposals that tackle poverty from a variety of perspectives. Some of these proposals are more of a departure from existing policies than others, some borrow from other countries or revive old ideas, some are narrow in focus and others much broader, but all seek to move anti-poverty efforts into new territory.

BACKGROUND

Just over fifty years ago, the War on Poverty marked a significant expansion of the scope and scale of anti-poverty programs, as well as a considerable change in their financing and

---

Lawrence M. Berger is Vilas Distinguished Achievement Professor in the School of Social Work and director of the Institute for Research on Poverty at the University of Wisconsin–Madison. **Maria Cancian** is professor of public affairs and social work and former director of the Institute for Research on Poverty at the University of Wisconsin–Madison. **Katherine Magnuson** is Vilas Distinguished Achievement Professor and doctoral program chair at the University of Wisconsin–Madison School of Social Work.

© 2018 Russell Sage Foundation. Berger, Lawrence M., Maria Cancian, and Katherine Magnuson. 2018. "Anti-poverty Policy Innovations: New Proposals for Addressing Poverty in the United States." *RSF: The Russell Sage Foundation Journal of the Social Sciences* 4(2): 1–19. DOI: 10.7758/RSF.2018.4.2.01. We are grateful for intellectual contributions by Judith Bartfeld, Marcia Carlson, J. Michael Collins, Eric Grodsky, Robert Haveman, Julia Isaacs, Thomas Kaplan, Sarah Halpern-Meekin, Michael Massoglia, Daniel Meyer, John Karl Scholz, Timothy Smeeding, James Walker, and Barbara Wolfe, from which this work greatly benefited. Direct correspondence to: Lawrence M. Berger at lmberger@wisc.edu, 3420 Social Sciences Building, 1180 Observatory Dr., Madison, WI 53706; Maria Cancian at maria.cancian@wisc.edu, 3436 Social Sciences Building, 1180 Observatory Dr., Madison, WI 53706; and Katherine Magnuson at kmagnuson@wisc.edu, 3432 Social Sciences Building, 1180 Observatory Dr., Madison, WI 53706.

Open Access Policy: *RSF: The Russell Sage Foundation Journal of the Social Sciences* is an open access journal. This article is published under a Creative Commons Attribution-NonCommercial-NoDerivs 3.0 Unported License.

administration. The federal government required, and fully or substantially funded, new entitlement programs—including Food Stamps and Medicaid—and a broad range of related programs and services such as Head Start, Legal Services, and Job Corps. From the 1960s until the mid-1990s, most changes to anti-poverty programs were arguably incremental, although there were notable exceptions including the establishment and major expansions of the Earned Income Tax Credit (EITC) and the development of the child support enforcement system. Passed in 1996, the Personal Responsibility and Work Opportunity Reconciliation Act (PRWORA), along with accompanying expansions in the EITC and childcare subsidies (administered through the Child Care Development Block Grant, CCDBG), represented a significant redirection for anti-poverty policy. Perhaps most notably, it eliminated the entitlement to cash assistance provided by Aid to Families with Dependent Children (AFDC) and replaced it with Temporary Assistance for Needy Families (TANF), a time-delimited benefit contingent on meeting work requirements. It also decoupled Food Stamps and Medicaid from cash welfare.

Advocates suggested that the 1996 welfare reform, by eliminating the entitlement to cash assistance and freeing states to substantially restructure their welfare program, would lead to fifty active laboratories of innovation—states experimenting with different approaches to helping low-income families, and the best models being disseminated and adopted. Although clearly variation in state program characteristics is greater under TANF than AFDC, the most striking result of the change in rules and funding may be the shrinking proportion of poor families who participate in TANF and the declining share of program funds spent on cash assistance and employment services, despite stubbornly persistent levels of poverty among vulnerable populations as assessed by the official poverty measure, which includes only pretax cash income. As we write this introduction in the first months of the Trump administration, attention has turned away from expansive proposals for new government programs toward greater reliance on market-oriented approaches to poverty, an approach embraced by the Clinton administration in the 1990s. The Republican-controlled Congress and recent cabinet appointees advocate dismantling the Affordable Care Act and are considering restrictions or block grants to replace the Supplemental Nutrition Assistance Program (SNAP, or Food Stamps), and Medicaid.

It is not only federal policy that shapes poverty policy. State- and local-level support for government anti-poverty programs and market-oriented interventions varies considerably. The variation across states in the character of many major programs is significant—from the expansion of Medicaid eligibility (Rose 2015; Courtemanche et al. 2017; Buettgens, Holahan, and Recht 2015), to the availability of a state EITC (Williams 2017; Cooper, Lutz, and Palumbo 2015), to variation in the scope and generosity of cash benefits under TANF (Schott, Pavetti, and Floyd 2015; Floyd 2017). Major increases in the minimum wage (Autor, Manning, and Smith 2016; Neumark 2015), as well as paid sick leave (Isaacs, Healy, and Peters 2017; Ahn 2016), and fair scheduling (National Women's Law Center 2017) continue to garner support in many states and localities. In addition, some states have invested more heavily in supporting low-income students who attend postsecondary education or training (Barr and Turner 2013; U.S. Department of Education 2016; McLendon and Perna 2014), as well as providing support for the youngest learners through universal or targeted prekindergarten programs (Bartik and Hershbein 2017; Friedman-Krauss, Barnett, and Nores 2016).

The fractious nature of national and state politics—reflecting stark differences in world views between the politicians in our major political parties—makes even modest policy changes that require legislative approval challenging. Nonetheless, given the clear need for better policy options, we believe that it is worthwhile—and, indeed, necessary—to propose, develop, and refine innovative anti-poverty policies. The early months of the Trump administration illustrate the challenges of major social policy innovation, even when one party controls the White House and both houses of Congress. On the other hand, signals are clear that states will be given more latitude, along with the risks and potential for innovation that implies. For example, President Trump has ordered that all agencies consider "whether some or all of the functions of an agency . . . are appropriate for the federal government or would be better left to state or local governments or to the private sector" (White House 2017), and the administration has signaled enthusiasm for state waivers, for example, related to Medicaid.

The current political uncertainty makes it difficult to judge the scope and most likely context for potential change. We argue that this is an appropriate juncture to again consider innovations in anti-poverty policy that push beyond marginal changes to existing programs to consider new and different approaches to the major challenges that persist despite fifty years of focused anti-poverty policy. This is what the articles in this volume aim to do. Not even a double issue can hope to touch on all the critical components of a comprehensive anti-poverty strategy, and many issues—including issues related to immigration, incarceration, and health care, for example—are not systematically addressed here. A range of innovative policies addressing income support, employment, housing, and education and training, among other topics, are included, however. Before turning to the specific policy proposals, we provide context by reviewing current and expected poverty-related trends, evidence on the causes and consequences of poverty, and evidence on existing anti-poverty policies.

DEFINING POVERTY

The word *poverty* brings to mind many differing images, and has been used to describe a variety of contexts of scarcity. In public conversations, poverty typically refers to a lack of economic resources; sometimes, however, it is defined more broadly as social exclusion (particularly in the European context). For some, it evokes images of poor children and families from economically developing countries, who struggle to meet their most basic needs. Yet, even in a nation as wealthy as the United States, the word characterizes the living conditions of a substantial share of the population. The overall economic conditions in the United States have cycled between growth and recession, but even the extensive economic expansion of the past seventy-five years has failed to lift millions of citizens out of poverty.

Measuring poverty with economic resources is complicated because it requires defining both which types of resources should be counted and the minimum threshold below which individuals and families should be deemed to have insufficient resources. For poverty scholars, the term *poverty* in the United States has a very specific meaning. In the 1960s, the U.S. federal government developed a method for generating a dollar amount of pre-tax cash income that, if not exceeded, could be used to designate an individual or family as poor. The resulting poverty thresholds, which differ according to family size, are used for tracking trends in poverty rates. They also inform the poverty guidelines issued each year by the U.S. Department of Health and Human Services, which are used for determining social program eligibility. The poverty thresholds have been updated annually using the Consumer Price Index (CPI) to track inflation. In 2016, the official poverty guideline was just over $24,000 for a family of two parents and two children, and just under $12,000 for an individual adult living alone (U.S. Department of Health and Human Services 2016).

Concern that the official poverty measure (OPM) was outdated—because it fails to account for contemporary family expenses and in-kind public benefits and tax transfers, which have increasingly become the primary means of combatting poverty, and because it does not take into account geographic differences in the cost of living—led the Census Bureau to create a supplemental poverty measure (SPM). The SPM differs in several ways from the OPM, including the measure of resources, the measure of need, the household members whose resources and needs are considered, and adjustments for geographic differences (Renwick and Fox 2016). Perhaps most importantly for this discussion, the SPM considers post-tax income, and includes noncash benefits. Thus, unlike the official measure, the SPM accounts for income from the EITC and the Child Tax Credit, as well as the value of SNAP and Special Supplemental Nutrition Program for Women, Infants, and Children (WIC) benefits, in addition to direct cash assistance (such as TANF and Social

Security). Especially for low-income families with children, who increasingly receive assistance from tax credits and SNAP rather than from TANF, the SPM provides a better indicator of poverty and the effectiveness of current policy—as well as of the potential effects of the proposals in this volume that center on tax credits and in-kind benefits. In addition, the SPM accounts for work-related expenses, out-of-pocket medical expenses, and child support paid to other households. It also takes into account the incomes of spouses and cohabiting partners, and considers all resident children regardless of their relationships to the household head or heads. It therefore provides a more complete accounting of household resources than the OPM. Moreover, it uses poverty thresholds that are updated to reflect the current cost of a basic set of necessities, with different thresholds for different living arrangements, for renters versus owners, and for different cost of living levels across geographic areas (Garner 2010; see also Fox et al., "Waging Wars," 2015; Wimer et al. 2016). Given these advantages, this double issue's final article by Christopher Wimer, Sophie Collyer, and Sara Kimberlin (2018), which estimates the effects of many of the proposals on poverty, relies principally on the SPM. However, here and in other articles, we also reference the OPM, given its continued prominence and importance for policy.

POVERTY TRENDS

The official poverty rate fell precipitously during the 1960s. Since the 1960s, it has fluctuated between about 11 percent and 15 percent, increasing during economic downturns, and decreasing during times of economic expansion. In 2015, about 43.1 million individuals (13.5 percent) lived in poverty, as measured by the OPM (Proctor, Semega, and Kollar 2016); this was a decline from the peak of the Great Recession in 2010 (15.1 percent). The supplemental poverty rate indicated that 45.7 million people were poor in 2015, a rate slightly higher than the official measure (14.3 percent), reflecting, among other things, that SPM thresholds are generally higher than the official poverty thresholds.

Average poverty rates, however, mask considerable variation in poverty across populations of interest. Reflecting historical and current experiences of oppression and discrimination, African Americans and Hispanics face considerably higher rates of poverty than non-Hispanic whites (26.2 percent and 23.1 percent, respectively, compared with 10.1 percent). Moreover, children have significantly higher rates of poverty (21.1 percent) than adults (13.5 percent) or the elderly (age sixty-five or older; 10.0 percent). Poverty also differs by nativity (14.2 percent for native born, 18.5 percent for foreign born), family structure (28.2 percent for single female-headed households compared with 6.2 percent for households headed by a married couple), and educational attainment (28.9 percent for those without a high school degree compared with 5.0 percent for those with at least a bachelor's degree) (Proctor, Semega, and Kollar 2016). Finally, official poverty rates differ by location. Poverty is higher in the South and West compared to the rest of the United States, and in urban and rural areas, compared to suburban areas.

Most individuals and families who experience poverty do so for a short time. Data from 2009 to 2012 suggest that more than 30 percent of the population experienced a spell of poverty lasting two or more months during this period (Proctor, Semega, and Kollar 2016). However, many poverty spells are short lived; less than 3 percent of the population experienced poverty in all forty-eight months of this period. Of course, persistence of poverty differs across sociodemographic groups too. For example, whereas only about 10 percent of all children experience persistent poverty throughout childhood (for half or more years from birth to age eighteen), 37 percent of African American children do (Ratcliffe and McKernan 2013).

Finally, some scholars and policymakers argue for more attention on those at the very bottom of the U.S. income distribution—the highly disadvantaged. This group received attention following welfare reform in the 1990s, with a focus on welfare-leaving families who did not find stable work and had limited public supports available to them. Since then, the highly disadvantaged groups of interest have broadened to include individuals and families in "deep poverty" (below 50 percent of the poverty line), as well as those experiencing "disconnection" from employment, schooling, and public assistance, low food security, other forms of severe material hardship (such as housing instability, eviction), and the $2-a-day poor (Edin and Shaefer 2015). These populations may face economic hardship that is acute, compounded across dimensions, and persistent over the life course or even generations (Desmond 2015; Seefeldt 2016). Estimates of the size and growth of this population differ depending on the measures used (DeNavas-Walt and Proctor 2015; Sherman and Trisi 2015; Short 2015). However, the bulk of research suggests a growth in deep poverty in the past twenty years as measured by the official federal poverty measure (Fox et al., "Trends in Deep Poverty," 2015; Shaefer and Edin 2013; Shaefer, Edin, and Talbert 2015; but, for a substantially different conclusion, see also Winship 2016). Although additional research is required to refine estimates of the size of the highly disadvantaged population, it is clear that a significant number of Americans are living on very little cash income.

CAUSES AND CONSEQUENCES OF POVERTY

Two key institutions that shape economic fortunes—the labor market and the family—have dramatically changed over the last half-century in ways that leave large segments of the population increasingly vulnerable to poverty and its effects. The low-wage labor market has been characterized by stagnation with little growth in wages and few opportunities for advancement (Osterman 2014). At the same time, young adults with low levels of education have increasingly transitioned into parenthood in the context of unmarried romantic partnerships that often dissolve shortly after their child's birth. We discuss these important and related changes and what it means for the next generation of children born into vulnerable economic conditions.

For many, falling into or avoiding poverty largely turns on success in the labor market (Fox et al., "Trends in Deep Poverty," 2015; Shaefer, Edin, and Talbert 2015). Employment challenges faced by less-educated workers are both structural and cyclical (Autor 2010; Farber 2011). Changes in the structure of the economy have diminished the importance of the manufacturing sector, traditionally a source of relatively high-wage jobs for men with low levels of education (Autor 2010) and, more recently, the housing crisis during the Great Recession diminished the construction industry as a source of new jobs (Glaeser 2010). Globalization, skill-biased technical change, and changes in union influence have also reduced employment and wage-growth opportunities for less-educated workers. Job growth for workers without a college education is now concentrated in the low-wage personal service sector (Damme 2011). These changes have resulted in stagnant earnings for less-educated workers and limited their ability to earn their way out of poverty.

Between 1990 and 2005, poverty was characterized more by low wages than by joblessness, but the picture has changed since 2007 (Smeeding 2006). Although low wages are still an important factor, unemployment and unstable work are primary causes of non-elderly poverty today (Levy and Kochan 2012). In 1998, about 67 percent of the U.S. population sixteen years of age or older was participating in the labor force; this rate declined significantly during the Great Recession, and has not increased much since, rates remaining no higher than 63 percent since 2014. Furthermore, nearly 19 percent of adults between the ages of twenty-five and fifty-four were not participating in the labor force in 2016, again reflecting an incomplete recovery to levels prior to the Great Recession (Bureau of Labor Statistics 2017).

As is the case for poverty more generally, labor market experiences are crucial determinants of falling into or avoiding deep poverty (Fox et al., "Trends in Deep Poverty," 2015; Shaefer, Edin, and Talbert 2015). Notably, unstable employment, combined with low hours and wages, rather than a total disconnection from employment, appears to be driving deep poverty for many families (Shaefer, Edin, and Talbert 2015). Irregular or unpredictable hours, split shifts, and contingent labor arrangements leave many low-wage workers with variable and inadequate incomes (Lambert, Fugiel, and Henly 2014). The increase in precarious employment is characterized by decreased job tenure and increases in long-term unemployment, nonstandard work hours, and contingent employment in which workers are temporary or work on limited contracts (Lambert 2008; Kalleberg 2009). Low-skill workers have been especially affected by these trends, resulting in high levels of job insecurity (Kalleberg 2009; Lambert, Fugiel, and Henly 2014) and income instability (Morduch and Schneider 2017).

Challenges to sustained employment, including physical and mental illness and disability, addiction, and lack of transportation, are widespread in deep poor populations (Fox et al., "Trends in Deep Poverty," 2015; Turner, Danziger, and Seefeldt 2006). Whereas the majority of families in deep poverty are headed by a single parent, a substantial proportion of the deep poor (now nearly 40 percent) are unemployed working-age adults without dependent children (Fox et al., "Trends in Deep Poverty," 2015). Less-educated men, particularly those of color and who have criminal justice histories, are disproportionately likely to experience deep poverty as a result of low levels of labor force participation and high unemployment (Cuddy, Venator, and Reeves 2015; Holzer, Raphael, and Stoll 2006; Jacobs 2015; Council of Economic Advisers 2014) and limited access to income supports.

Whereas the economy is likely to continue to recover from the recession, and unemployment will decrease as a result, the fundamental polarization between high- and low-skill jobs is not expected to end (Autor 2010; Manyika et al. 2011). The wages received by those entering the formal labor market with modest levels of human capital are low. Although men continue to have higher earnings than women, less-educated men have seen much sharper declines in compensation than women (Blank 2009a; Bureau of Labor Statistics 2015). In addition, no evidence indicates that earnings growth alone will be enough to raise incomes above poverty for those with low human capital. Even with the exceptionally strong economy and rapid job creation in the 1990s, real wage growth among families leaving welfare was estimated to range between 2.0 percent and 4.5 percent per year (Card, Michalopoulos, and Robins 2001; Pavetti and Acs 2001). The challenge now is to support sustained labor market participation, increase opportunities for workers to improve skills, encourage earnings growth among all low-skilled workers, and effectively assist low-wage workers who remain poor.

Several determinants of labor market outcomes—related to the structure of employment opportunities as well as to workers' skills—are key to understanding the labor market. First, whereas higher returns to education are expected to spur less-educated workers to greater human capital investments, growth in educational attainment has been meager (Goldin and Katz 2008). As a result, too few young people, particularly males, are acquiring the degrees and skills required to succeed in the labor market. Demographic shifts in immigration patterns also affect the skill level of the workforce. Over the past forty years, legal immigrants have increasingly arrived from countries with lower levels of human capital and higher rates of poverty, such as Mexico, Central America, and Asia (Raphael and Smolensky 2009). Moreover, the population of undocumented immigrants, who have especially low levels of skills, has grown by more than 300 percent since 1990, though growth declined sharply after 2001 (Warren and Warren 2013).

Finally, incarceration is a key poverty-relevant issue. Nearly 1.6 million individuals were in a prison facility at the end of 2012, the majority of whom were black males younger than forty (Carson and Golinelli 2013). The substantial variation in imprisonment rates by race and gender has been well established. For example, in 2012, incarceration rates for black and white adult males were 2.84 percent and 0.46 percent, respectively, compared to 0.12 percent and 0.05 percent for black and white adult females (Carson and Golinelli 2013). Indeed, incarceration—and criminal justice involvement more generally—is particularly common for black males. Evidence suggests that about half of all black men will be arrested by age twenty-three (Brame et al. 2012; Brame et al. 2014) and that 68 percent of black men without a high school degree will experience incarceration between the ages of twenty and thirty-four, which is true for about 28 percent of white men without a high school degree and 21 percent of black men with a high school degree (Pettit 2012). High rates of incarceration raise important unresolved questions about the implications for labor market opportunities, both for those with incarceration histories and those in affected communities (Holzer, Raphael, and Stoll 2004). Evidence suggests that having a criminal background creates substantial barriers to employment when individuals return to their communities. Criminal history has been identified as the biggest barrier to employment, even more so than failing to complete high school (Peterangelo and Henken 2016). Yet, recidivism is strongly related to whether former inmates get jobs quickly and maintain steady work (Council of Economic Advisers 2016).

Against this backdrop of a difficult labor market for low-skilled adults, major demographic transitions related to family formation have also occurred. First, young adults are now more likely to partner with individuals of comparable education, contributing to greater household income inequality by increasing the pairing of higher (and lower) earners (Schwartz 2013). Second, whereas marriage rates have stabilized for more educated adults, they have declined among the less educated. Of particular consequence, unmarried births among disadvantaged families are now common, representing 57 percent of births to women with less than a high school degree, but only 9 percent of births to women with at least a bachelor's degree (Shattuck and Kreider 2013). Moreover, nearly three-quarters of unmarried births are unplanned (Sawhill 2014).

The so-called drift into parenthood by low-income young adults (Sawhill 2014) is particularly problematic because their romantic and parental relationships are often short lived. The majority of cohabiting parents break up within a few years of their child's birth. Many low-income children are then raised with limited involvement with and financial support from their fathers. Whereas child support contributions from noncustodial parents (NCPs) have the potential to reduce poverty, a large proportion of low-income custodial parents receive only partial or no support, often because NCPs have low incomes themselves (Cancian, Meyer, and Han 2011; Smeeding, Garfinkel, and Mincy 2011). Over time, mothers and fathers repartner and have additional children, creating *complex families* that are likely to remain socially and economically disadvantaged. Children in complex families are then disproportionately likely to experience ongoing family instability, low income, and poverty; moreover, public benefit programs are challenged in designing supports and services that meet the needs of these complex families (Carlson and Meyer 2014).

Addressing the increasing divergence in the fortunes and life trajectories of advantaged and disadvantaged groups (defined by socioeconomic factors such as education, income, race, and wealth) is a fundamental challenge. Sara McLanahan describes the resulting "diverging destinies" as especially consequential for individual well-being and economic mobility (2004; see also McLanahan and Jacobsen 2015). Higher-income individuals have advantages in nearly every relevant institution—the family, neighborhoods, schools, and the labor market (where they encounter primarily other higher-income individuals)—whereas low-income individuals face compounding disadvantages in all of these domains. Economic resources and parental investments are increasing for advantaged children and youths, whereas their disadvantaged counterparts experience comparatively fewer investments.

Parents' economic disadvantage plays a formative role in shaping children's opportunities for success and acquisition of skills. The degree of intergenerational transmission of poverty and inequality varies across studies, but the correlation between parent and child income is typically estimated to be about 0.5 (Corak 2006; Jäntti 2009; for recent estimates suggesting higher persistence, see Mitnik et al. 2015). Such persistence in economic positions across generations, coupled with strong theory about why poor children fare worse than their more advantaged peers and accumulating empirical evidence about how poverty affects families and children's daily experiences, implies that poverty may be determinative in children's life chances.

Theoretical models of how poverty affects children encompass both what money can buy and how poverty harms relationships. Economic models view families with greater economic resources as being better able to purchase or produce important "inputs" into their children's development, such as books and educational materials at home, high-quality childcare settings and schools, and safe neighborhoods (Becker 1991). Economically disadvantaged parents may also have less time to invest in children, owing to higher rates of single parenthood, nonstandard work hours, and less flexible work schedules (Smolensky and Gootman 2003). Psychologists and sociologists point to the quality of family relationships and stress to explain poverty's detrimental effects on children. These theoretical models posit that higher income may improve parents' psychological well-being and family processes, in particular the quality of parents' interactions with their children. A long line of research has found that low income is associated with more punitive and less nurturing, stimulating, and responsive parenting. Finally, sources of everyday stress that poor children encounter outside of their family relationships, such as violent or polluted neighborhoods, may also have far-reaching negative consequences in their development (Evans 2001, 2004).

Research on the effects of poverty have focused largely on children's academic achievement and educational attainment, perhaps because these are strong predictors of subsequent economic well-being. Income gaps and associated socioeconomic status-based gradients in academic skills are present when children enter school and persist through adolescence (Magnuson, Waldfogel, and Washbrook 2012). Poor children complete a year less of schooling than those who have family incomes between one and two times the federal poverty line, and two years less than those who have family incomes more than twice the federal line (Duncan, Ziol-Guest, and Kalil 2010). As described, far too many young adults are entering the labor market without the skills needed to secure stable employment at wages high enough to keep themselves and their family out of poverty.

Despite debate about whether and how much of the estimated associations between poverty and achievement outcomes are causal, several quasi-experimental studies point to substantively meaningful effects (Akee et al. 2010; Dahl and Lochner 2012; Morris, Duncan, and Rodrigues 2011; Milligan and Stabile 2011; see also Duncan, Magnuson, and Votruba-Drzal 2015). Deep and early poverty is particularly strongly associated with lower levels of educational achievement and attainment, holding constant other family advantages (Brooks-Gunn and Duncan 1997). Emerging research in neuroscience and developmental psychology suggests that poverty early in a child's life may be particularly harmful (Miller and Chen 2013). Not only does the astonishingly rapid development of young children's brains leave them sensitive (and vulnerable) to environmental conditions, but the family context (as opposed to schools or peers) dominates their everyday lives.

Increasingly, scholars have recognized the importance of appropriate behavior, self-regulation, and mental health in determining labor market and other important adult outcomes, such as criminal activity (Cunha et al. 2006). Many of the same environmental factors and resource constraints that contribute to differential educational attainment may also limit social and emotional development. Low-income children demonstrate less self-regulation, poorer mental health, and more problem behaviors than their higher-income counterparts in childhood and throughout adolescence (Magnuson and Votruba-Drzal 2009). These factors may contribute to criminal activity and incarceration, further compounding lower levels of education and job skills, thus limiting low-income children's later labor market prospects (Cunha et al. 2006).

In short, a myriad of factors, including changes in labor market opportunities that disadvantage less-skilled workers, demographic trends that increase disparities in the family resources available to children of more- and less-advantaged parents, and changes in public policy, have converged in ways that are creating and exacerbating inequality in many aspects of contemporary American life. These factors have widespread implications with respect to both the current causes and consequences of poverty and for the intergenerational transmission thereof. They suggest the need to review current policies and consider new alternatives that are responsive to the twin challenges of poverty and inequality. In the following section, we review the effectiveness of current policies to provide context for the innovations developed in the articles that follow.

THE EFFECTIVENESS OF CURRENT ANTI-POVERTY POLICIES
Over the past twenty-five years, anti-poverty policies and related social welfare benefits have

largely shifted from a system of guaranteed income support to a work-based safety net. These changes were solidified in PRWORA, which reflected a long-standing debate about the adverse effects of income transfers and the effectiveness of job training programs and work supports, as well as a shift toward a cultural norm of parental employment, even for mothers of young children. In addition to emphasizing work, PRWORA also included provisions to encourage marriage and bolster child support enforcement. The shift during the 1990s to work-conditioned benefits reallocated public benefits from nonworking to working households. Those with the lowest market incomes (less than 50 percent of the poverty line) once received substantially more in benefits than those with higher incomes (Moffitt 2015). This, however, is no longer the case: for single-parent families under 50 percent of the poverty line, increases in earnings now result in larger public benefit transfers; moreover, families that are near or just above the poverty line receive substantially larger transfers than in the past (Scholz, Moffitt, and Cowan 2009). Whereas low-income working families have benefited, the shift has left families increasingly vulnerable to periodic unemployment; it also coincides with an increase in the proportion of families that experience very little cash income, deep poverty, or high rates of material hardship—because families without income from formal employment are ineligible for many forms of public assistance, and cash assistance in particular (Sherman and Trisi 2014; Ziliak 2016).

State policies regarding work requirements, lifetime limits on program participation, family caps, and time-limited cash benefits, as well as diversionary tactics for applicants, appear to have affected rates of deep poverty (Hetling, Kwon, and Saunders 2015) or, at the very least, resulted in a considerable segment of the poor population having very little access to cash income (Shaefer and Edin 2013; Shaefer, Edin, and Talbert 2015). At the same time, funding for work supports, such as childcare subsidies, subsidized health insurance, nutrition assistance, and wage supplements (in the form of the EITC) grew extensively. Income support programs thus now function as complements to, rather than substitutes for, formal employment.

The policy changes associated with the 1996 welfare reform have been studied extensively, although much of the evidence was collected during a period of economic expansion. On the whole, welfare "reform generally raised earnings, although not by amounts that are likely to raise many poor families out of poverty" (Grogger and Karoly 2005, 153). Specific aspects of TANF's work-based safety net have also been evaluated and generally been found to be associated with anticipated labor market effects, though effects on poverty are less evident. For example, mandatory work requirements (or requirements to participate in work-related activities) are associated with reduced welfare use and increased employment (Blank 2002, 2009b; Grogger, Karoly, and Klerman 2002), as are family caps, sanctions, and time limits. More generous childcare subsidies have also been found to promote maternal employment (Dunifon 2010; Grogger and Karoly 2005).

Although, on average, employment increased and there were limited improvements in economic well-being in the wake of welfare reform, as noted above, limited cash support may have increased economic hardship and deepened poverty for those who were not able to find steady work. Moreover, welfare sanctions and reduced access to cash welfare were associated with other negative outcomes, including child welfare involvement (Slack, Lee, and Berger 2007). There are also concerns that the end of the entitlement to cash assistance has contributed to disparities in access to economic support, for example, by race and ethnicity (Fording, Soss, and Schram 2011). Finally, the limited effectiveness of TANF as a safety net program was made clear during the Great Recession, when unemployment rates rose sharply, but TANF participation did not. As a result, trends in poverty and especially deep poverty are now more closely aligned with the business cycle than in the past (Bitler and Hoynes 2016).

Of course, patterns of public program participation look very different today than they did twenty years ago. Specifically, TANF has become much less salient, whereas SNAP, subsidized health insurance, and the EITC have grown dramatically in importance. Indeed, the largest social welfare expenditures today are for means-tested entitlements from Medicaid and SNAP, as well as the EITC. In 2015, the EITC program paid approximately $67 billion (U.S. Department of the Treasury 2017) and SNAP paid over $74 billion (U.S. Department of Agriculture 2017) in benefits to low-income families, versus total spending of $29 billion for TANF and its related childcare components, including state maintenance of effort spending (U.S. Department of Health and Human Services 2017, table A1). Whereas TANF caseloads dropped considerably in the wake of welfare reform and saw limited growth during the Great Recession, SNAP participation expanded significantly, real expenditures increasing over 200 percent between 1980 and 2010. SNAP also assisted the poor much more than TANF during the Great Recession. If counted as an income equivalent, SNAP benefits have reduced the depth and severity of poverty substantially over the last two decades (Shaefer and Edin 2013; Tiehen, Jolliffe, and Smeeding 2016). Likewise, EITC participation and expenditures have grown dramatically over the past several decades and were instrumental for working families during the Great Recession. Liana Fox and her colleagues estimate that the EITC and SNAP reduced child poverty by approximately 8 percentage points, leading them to argue that anti-poverty programs have been more effective in reducing poverty than previously thought ("Waging War," 2015). Finally, Medicaid and subsidies for health insurance expanded for children as a result of federal funding for State Child Health Insurance Program beginning in 1997, and for adults significantly as a result of state options to expand Medicaid under the Affordable Care Act of 2010.

As first conceived, work-based welfare benefits were created as a way to push (and pull) welfare-dependent single mothers into the labor market. Yet, the increasingly apparent limitations and volatility of the low-wage labor market raise the question of how a work-based safety net can effectively bolster the employment and economic well-being of all workers, both those with and without families to support. Of additional concern, many disadvantaged men, who have in recent decades all but lost their earnings advantage relative to women, often do not have co-resident dependent children and are therefore ineligible for programs limited to resident parents. Disadvantaged nonresident fathers may have few connections to agencies outside of the penal and child support systems, suggesting that reforms to leverage these systems to increase employment and responsible fatherhood may hold promise. Policymakers continue to confront questions about the right mix of policies to increase the availability of family-supporting employment, enable low-wage workers to support their families when working, encourage reemployment when work is scarce, and provide an adequate safety net for those not currently able to work.

WHY INNOVATE NOW?

The challenges are clear. The United States has experienced significant economic growth, yet the fruits of productivity and labor market participation are not being experienced by a large proportion of our population. Inter- and intragenerational inequalities in both opportunities and outcomes by socioeconomic status and race-ethnicity are significant across a wide range of social institutions, spanning neighborhoods, housing, education, the labor market, and the criminal justice system. Less-educated workers face low (and stagnant) wages, instability in employment and hours, minimal employer-provided benefits, and limited opportunities for advancement. The large population of disadvantaged individuals with criminal justice histories—particularly black men—faces substantial labor market barriers and has little access to public benefits. Assortative mating and differences in family formation, fertility, and stability between advantaged and disadvantaged groups have contributed to diverging patterns of family life, with striking implications for the next generation. In particular, children born to disadvantaged parents are highly likely to spend time in a single-mother household and to experience parental multi-partner fertility and associated family instability and fluidity. Low-income children continue to experience lower-quality neighborhoods, housing, and schools. Within this context, anti-poverty policy has increasingly offered work-conditioned benefits and, particularly for nonworking individuals and families, has increasingly offered in-kind rather than cash assistance. Thus, a considerable portion of the low-income population relies on little cash income. Taken together, these factors suggest that anti-poverty innovations are warranted.

The current political divides may undercut the potential for bipartisan initiatives to address poverty. And, the early days of the Trump administration suggest more support for limiting or dismantling programs designed to address poverty, than for expanding their reach. On the other hand, class divides have received new attention, and there remains some bipartisan support for evidence-based policy change. Social science scholars have developed a significant base of research to inform what more could be done and what the effects of new innovations might be. Social science theory and empirical evidence have continued to accumulate and point to key ways in which policy innovations could better support the current generations of workers, both those who struggle to find steady employment and earn a family-sustaining wage, as well as those completing their education, starting to work and, often, also starting their families. Such evidence further points to how to help the younger generation—the children of low-income adults—who may be harmed by the experience of deep and persistent economic hardship, and who often miss out on experiences they will need to thrive later in their lives. Finally, it points to innovative ways to build on the current safety net to better assist low-income individuals and families, both those who are strongly and those who are weakly attached to the labor market.

INNOVATIVE ANTI-POVERTY APPROACHES

With policymakers' need for evidence-based solutions in mind, each article in this volume focuses on a specific social problem or population and presents a detailed, actionable response. The articles leverage the best available theoretical and empirical social science research to present evidence-based arguments for implementing a set of novel and potentially transformational policy innovations. The proposals span a wide range of policy domains, including cash transfers, employment-related policies, postsecondary education, housing support, food security, family planning, and two-generation human capital development. Despite this range, the proposals do not explicitly address several important policy topics: for example, immigration, incarceration, childcare, child welfare, transportation, subsidized health care, and Medicaid.

As Wimer, Collyer, and Kimberlin discuss in detail in the last article in this double issue (2018), the costs and impact of these proposals vary widely. So do the scale and ambition of the innovations, and the authors' attention to details of policy implementation and the organizational contexts of programmatic implementation. Some call for wholesale transformation of programs or institutions, such as establishing a universal child allowance (Bitler, Hines, and Page 2018; Shaefer et al. 2018), or guaranteeing universal access to an above-poverty wage job (Paul et al. 2018). Others leverage existing programs to address key challenges facing the poor, for example, a minimum benefit to reduce elderly poverty (Herd et al. 2018), and a renter's tax credit (Kimberlin, Tach, and Wimer 2018) to address housing costs. Others advocate for expanding investments to improve education and training—whether for children and their parents (Sommer et al. 2018), or adult workers (Holzer 2018; Strumbos, Linderman, and Hicks 2018). Many of the proposals respond to the needs of families with children, or to the particular vulnerability of children in single-parent families. However, only Lawrence Wu and Nicholas D. E. Mark (2018) consider an effort to directly alter family structure. They review evidence on the potential for improved access to contraception—specifically long-acting reversible contraceptives (LARCs)—to reduce unintended and nonmarital pregnancy and improve economic and social well-being. In contrast to most of the other articles in this double issue, Wu and Mark call for a pilot to test the impact of their proposal.

Whereas all the proposals address concerns with poverty, they vary substantially in their proximate goals, and at least implicitly, in their theory of poverty or anti-poverty policy. Mark Paul and his colleagues (2018), who propose a federal job guarantee whereby all American adults would be assured of full-time employment in a "public works" job with above-poverty wages and benefits, is the most costly, and also the most transformative. By assuring employment—with adequate wages and benefits—the authors argue that the need for many other programs would be eliminated. The proposal may have limited policy relevance, but it provides an important counterpoint to other articles in this double issue, which implicitly assume the current structure of the labor market, with a low minimum wage and limited required benefits.

A number of the proposals aim to reduce the proportion of workers relying on low-wage jobs by improving education and training in an effort to provide access to better jobs. Teresa Eckrich Sommer and her colleagues (2018) propose redesigning the Head Start program to more fully serve the needs of both parents and children by combining parental education, training, and employment opportunities with the existing early childhood education components of the program. Diana Strumbos, Donna Linderman, and Carson C. Hicks (2018) argue for a national community college model based on the CUNY ASAP model, which provides students with extensive advising, academic, career, and financial supports while requiring full-time enrollment in a highly structured degree program. Harry Holzer (2018) lays out a competitive grant program to states to implement performance-based community college programs to improve academic and employment outcomes for disadvantaged populations. Indivar Dutta-Gupta and his colleagues (2018) argue for a national on-the-job training and subsidized employment program for low-skilled workers.

Other proposals aim to supplement the earnings of low-wage workers in ways that generally improve the returns to work, and target particular challenges. For example, Jennifer Romich and Heather Hill (2018) describe a plan to "couple" minimum wage hikes with changes in existing benefit programs to avoid high marginal tax rates and benefit cliffs and, thereby, to offer a package of increased wages and sustained benefit (particularly SNAP and EITC) receipt. Sarah Halpern-Meekin and colleagues (2018) propose enabling workers to defer 20 percent of their EITC refund—with a 50 percent savings match—for a six-month period to encourage emergency saving among low-wage workers.

In contrast, this issue also includes a range of proposals to directly support individuals and families with insufficient resources, regardless of work status. Three proposals target families with children through new cash transfer mechanisms: both Marianne Bitler, Annie Laurie Hines, and Marianne Page (2018) and H. Luke Shaefer and his colleagues (2018) propose an unconditional child allowance, albeit in very different forms; Maria Cancian and Daniel Meyer (2018) propose a public guarantee of private child support payments available to all children not living with both parents. Sara Kimberlin, Laura Tach, and Christopher Wimer (2018) also propose a new transfer program that would provide a refundable renter's tax credit for families facing high rental costs relative to their income; Pamela Herd and her colleagues (2018) argue for a targeted minimum benefit plan that would provide a guaranteed benefit through the Social Security system to bring the income of poor elderly individuals to the poverty threshold, regardless of their work history. Other proposals build off and expand existing programs. For example, Craig Gundersen, Brent Kreider, and John V. Pepper (2018) present a plan to change the SNAP benefit formula to increase benefits and substantially reduce food insecurity among SNAP recipients.

In short, the proposals highlighted in this double issue all aim to reduce poverty, but they offer markedly different solutions, in many ways solving different problems. If the problem is insufficient resources, the solution may be to make more money available to families with limited earnings, though the authors here have very different ideas about who should get what, and under what conditions. A few would not require work, but would provide support only to resident parents with children (child allowance proposals of Bitler, Hines, and Page 2018 and of Shaefer et al. 2018), or with children living apart from a parent (child support assurance proposal of Cancian and Meyer 2018). These authors highlight the needs of children and the returns to public investments to reduce their vulnerability to poverty. The child allowance proposals offer a universal benefit. The child support assurance proposal emphasizes the need to support nonresident parents' contributions—children receive government support not when their custodial parent (usually their mother) is poor, but when their nonresident parent (usually their father) has inadequate earnings or otherwise is unable or unwilling to meet parental obligations.

Other proposals target the inadequacy of work and earnings—but the various proposals are based on very different assumptions about the nature of the problem. If work is not available, and earnings are the preferred resource, then providing jobs is a logical solution. But, should there be a universal and unlimited guarantee of government work at above-poverty wages, as Paul and colleagues (2018) propose, or time-limited, targeted subsidized jobs, paying minimum wages and often provided by private-sector employers, as Dutta-Gupta and colleagues (2018) propose? The answer depends in part on whether low wages reflect the structure of the labor market and of workers in today's economy—which argues for a job guarantee to change workers' options—or a skills mismatch that can be addressed with investment in human capital, at least in the medium to long run.

The articles in this double issue respond to a call for innovative policy proposals intended to reduce poverty and improve economic well-being. The individual responses differ across many dimensions and, as Wimer, Collyer, and Kimberlin (2018) stress in the final article, these differences can make comparisons challenging. At the same time, the range of approaches is instructive in highlighting the scope and diversity of potential innovations. In the face of continued high rates of poverty, growing inequality, and significant dissatisfaction with current efforts, there are reasons to substantially broaden the range of policies under discussion. The proposals that follow offer an important set of options to seed the debate.

REFERENCES

Ahn, Thomas. 2016. *The Labor Market Impacts of Paid Sick Leave: Evidence from Connecticut*. Washington, D.C.: Employment Policies Institute.

Akee, Randall K. Q., William E. Copeland, Gordon Keeler, Adrian Angold, and Elizabeth J. Costello. 2010. "Parent's Incomes and Children's Outcomes: A Quasi-Experiment with Casinos on American Indian Reservations." *American Economic Journal: Applied Economics* 2(1): 86–115.

Autor, David. 2010. *The Polarization of the Job Opportunities in the U.S. Labor Market: Implications for Employment and Earnings*. Washington, D.C.: Center for American Progress and the Hamilton Project.

Autor, David H., Alan Manning, and Christopher L. Smith. 2016. "The Contribution of the Minimum Wage to U.S. Wage Inequality over Three Decades: A Reassessment." *American Economic Journal: Applied Economics* 8(1): 58–99.

Barr, Andrew, and Sarah E. Turner. 2013. "Expanding Enrollments and Contracting State Budgets: The Effect of the Great Recession on Higher Education." *Annals of the American Academy of Political and Social Science* 650(1): 168–93.

Bartik, Timothy J., and Brad Hershbein. 2017. "Pre-K in the Public Schools: Evidence from Within All States." Paper presented to the Summer Research Workshop, Institute for Research on Poverty, University of Wisconsin–Madison. Madison (June 19–22, 2017).

Becker, Gary S. 1991. *A Treatise on the Family*. Cambridge, Mass.: Harvard University Press.

Bitler, Marianne P., Annie Laurie Hines, and Marianne Page. 2018. "Cash for Kids." *RSF: The Russell Sage Foundation Journal of the Social Sciences* 4(2): 43–73. DOI: 10.7758/RSF.2018.4.2.03.

Bitler, Marianne, and Hilary Hoynes. 2016. "The More Things Change, the More They Stay the Same? The Safety Net and Poverty in the Great Recession." *Journal of Labor Economics* 34(S1): S403–44.

Blank, Rebecca M. 2002. "Evaluating Welfare Reform in the United States." *Journal of Economic Literature* 40(4): 1105–66.

———. 2009a. "Economic Change and the Structure of Opportunity for Less-Skilled Workers." In *Changing Poverty, Changing Policies*, edited by Maria Cancian and Sheldon Danziger. New York: Russell Sage Foundation.

———. 2009b. "What We Know, What We Don't Know, and What We Need to Know About Welfare Reform." In *Welfare Reform and Its Long-Term Consequences for America's Poor*, edited by James P. Ziliak. Cambridge: Cambridge University Press.

Brame, Robert, Shawn D. Bushway, Ray Paternoster, and Michael G. Turner. 2014. "Demographic Patterns of Cumulative Arrest Prevalence by Ages 18 and 23." *Crime & Delinquency* 60(3): 471–86.

Brame, Robert, Michael G. Turner, Raymond Paternoster, and Shawn D. Bushway. 2012. "Cumulative Prevalence of Arrest from Ages 8–23 in a National Sample." *Pediatrics* 129(1): 21–27.

Brooks-Gunn, Jeanne, and Greg J. Duncan. 1997. "The Effects of Poverty on Children." *Future of Children* 7(2): 55–71.

Buettgens, Matthew, John Holahan, and Hannah Recht. 2015. *Medicaid Expansion, Health Coverage, and Spending: An Update for the 21 States that Have Not Expanded Eligibility*. Policy Brief. Washington, D.C.: Henry J. Kaiser Family Foundation.

Bureau of Labor Statistics. 2015. "Women's Earnings Compared to Men's Earnings in 2014." *TED: The Economics Daily*, November 20, 2015. Accessed February 19, 2017. https://www.bls.gov/opub/ted/2015/womens-earnings-compared-to-mens-earnings-in-2014.htm.

———. 2017. "Labor Force Statistics from the Current Population Survey." U.S. Department of Labor. Accessed September 20, 2017. https://www.bls.gov/cps/.

Cancian, Maria, and Daniel R. Meyer. 2018. "Reforming Policy for Single-Parent Families to Reduce Child Poverty." *RSF: The Russell Sage Foundation Journal of the Social Sciences* 4(2): 91–112. DOI: 10.7758/RSF.2018.4.2.05.

Cancian, Maria, Daniel R. Meyer, and Eunhee Han. 2011. "Child Support: Responsible Fatherhood and the Quid Pro Quo." In "Young Disadvantaged Men: Fathers, Families, Poverty, and Policy." Special issue, *Annals of the American Academy of Political and Social Science* 635(1): 140–62.

Card, David, Charles Michalopoulos, and Philip K. Robins. 2001. "The Limits to Wage Growth: Measuring the Growth Rate of Wages for Recent Welfare Leavers." NBER working paper no. 8444. Cambridge, Mass.: National Bureau of Economic Research.

Carlson, Marcia J., and Daniel R. Meyer, eds. 2014. "Family Complexity, Poverty, and Public Policy." Special issue, *Annals of the American Academy of Political and Social Science* 654(1).

Carson, E. Ann, and Daniela Golinelli. 2013. "Prisoners in 2012: Trends in Admissions and Releases, 1991–2012." Bulletin no. NCJ 243920. Washington: U.S. Department of Justice, Bureau of Justice Statistics.

Cooper, Daniel H., Byron F. Lutz, and Michael G. Palumbo. 2015. "The Role of Taxes in Mitigating Income Inequality Across the U.S. States." *National Tax Journal* 68(4): 943–74.

Corak, Miles. 2006. "Do Poor Children Become Poor Adults? Lessons from a Cross Country Comparison of Generational Earnings Mobility." In *Dynamics of Inequality and Poverty* (Research on Economic Inequality, volume 13), edited by John Creedy and Guyonne Kalb. Bingley, West Hampshire: Emerald Group Publishing.

Council of Economic Advisers. 2014. "The Labor Force Participation Rate Since 2007: Causes and Policy Implications." Washington: Government Printing Office.

———. 2016. "Economic Perspectives on Incarceration and the Criminal Justice System." Washington: Government Printing Office.

Courtemanche, Charles, James Marton, Benjamin Ukert, Aaron Yelowitz, and Daniela Zapata. 2017. "Impacts of the Affordable Care Act on Health Insurance Coverage in Medicaid Expansion and Non-Expansion States." *Journal of Policy Analysis and Management* 36(1): 178–210.

Cuddy, Emily, Joanna Venator, and Richard V. Reeves. 2015. "In a Land of Dollars: Deep Poverty and Its Consequences." *Social Mobility Papers*. Washington, D.C.: Brookings Institution (May 7).

Cunha, Flavio, James J. Heckman, Lance Lochner, and Dimitriy V. Masterov. 2006. "Interpreting the Evidence on Life Cycle Skill Formation." In *Handbook of the Economics of Education*, vol. 1, edited by Eric A. Hanushek and Finis Welch. New York: Elsevier.

Dahl, Gordon B., and Lance Lochner. 2012. "The Impact of Family Income on Child Achievement: Evidence from the Earned Income Tax Credit." *The American Economic Review* 102(5): 1927–56.

Damme, Lauren. 2011. "A Future of Low-Paying, Low-Skill Jobs?" Policy Brief 23. Washington, D.C.: New America Foundation. Accessed September 20, 2017. https://www.newamerica.org/economic-growth/policy-papers/a-future-of-low-paying-low-skill-jobs/.

DeNavas-Walt, Carmen, and Bernadette D. Proctor. 2015. "Income and Poverty in the United States: 2014." *Current Population Reports*, series P60, no. 252. Washington: U.S. Government Printing Office.

Desmond, Matthew. 2015. "Severe Deprivation in America: An Introduction." *RSF: The Russell Sage Foundation Journal of the Social Sciences* 1(1): 1–11. DOI: 10.7758/RSF.2015.1.1.01.

Duncan, Greg J., Katherine Magnuson, and Elizabeth Votruba-Drzal. 2015. "Children and Socioeconomic Status." In *Ecological Settings and Processes.* Vol. 4 of *Handbook of Child Psychology and Developmental Science,* edited by Richard M. Lerner. New York: John Wiley & Sons.

Duncan, Greg J., Kathleen M. Ziol-Guest, and Ariel Kalil. 2010. "Early-Childhood Poverty and Adult Attainment, Behavior, and Health." *Child Development* 81(1): 306–25.

Dunifon, Rachel E. 2010. "Welfare Reform and Intergenerational Mobility." Report for the Economic Mobility Project. Washington, D.C.: The Pew Charitable Trusts.

Dutta-Gupta, Indivar, Kali Grant, Julie Kerksick, Dan Bloom, and Ajay Chaudry. 2018. "Working to Reduce Poverty: A National Subsidized Employment Proposal." *RSF: The Russell Sage Foundation Journal of the Social Sciences* 4(3): 64–83. DOI: 10.7758/RSF.2018.4.3.04.

Edin, Kathryn J., and H. Luke Shaefer. 2015. *$2.00 a Day: Living on Almost Nothing in America.* New York: Houghton Mifflin Harcourt.

Evans, Gary W. 2001. "Environmental Stress and Health." In *A Handbook of Health Psychology,* edited by Andrew Baum, Tracey A. Revenson, and Jerome E. Singer. Mahwah, N.J.: Lawrence Erlbaum.

———. 2004. "The Environment of Childhood Poverty." *American Psychologist* 59(2): 77–92.

Farber, Henry S. 2011. "Job Loss in the Great Recession: Historical Perspective from the Displaced Workers Survey, 1984–2010." NBER working paper no. 17040. Cambridge, Mass.: National Bureau of Economic Research.

Floyd, Ife. 2017. *TANF Cash Benefits Have Fallen by More Than 20 Percent in Most States and Continue to Erode.* Washington, D.C.: Center on Budget and Policy Priorities.

Fording, Richard C., Joe Soss, and Sanford F. Schram. 2011. "Race and the Local Politics of Punishment in the New World of Welfare." *American Journal of Sociology* 116(5): 1610–57.

Fox, Liana, Christopher Wimer, Irwin Garfinkel, Neeraj Kaushal, and Jane Waldfogel. 2015. "Waging War on Poverty: Poverty Trends Using a Historical Supplemental Poverty Measure." *Journal of Policy Analysis and Management* 34(3): 567–92.

Fox, Liana, Christopher Wimer, Irwin Garfinkel, Neeraj Kaushal, JayHyun Nam, and Jane Waldfogel. 2015. "Trends in Deep Poverty from 1968 to 2011: The Influence of Family Structure, Employment Patterns, and the Safety Net." *RSF: The Russell Sage Foundation Journal of the Social Sciences* 1(1): 14–34. DOI: 10.7758/RSF.2015.1.1.02.

Friedman-Krauss, Allison, W. Steven Barnett, and Milagros Nores. 2016. *How Much Can High-Quality Universal Pre-K Reduce Achievement Gaps?* Washington, D.C.: Center for American Progress.

Garner, Thesia. 2010. "Supplemental Poverty Measure Thresholds: Laying the Foundation." Washington: Bureau of Labor Statistics.

Glaeser, Edward. 2010. "Children Moving Back Home and the Construction Industry." *Economix* (blog). *New York Times,* February 16. Accessed September 20, 2017. http://economix.blogs.nytimes.com/2010/02/16/kids-moving-back-home-and-the-construction-industry/.

Goldin, Claudia, and Lawrence F. Katz. 2008. *The Race Between Education and Technology.* Cambridge, Mass.: Harvard University Press.

Grogger, Jeffrey, and Lynn A. Karoly. 2005. *Welfare Reform: Effects of a Decade of Change.* Cambridge, Mass.: Harvard University Press.

Grogger, Jeffrey, Lynn A. Karoly, and Jacob Alex Klerman. 2002. *Consequences of Welfare Reform: A Research Synthesis.* DRU-2676-DHHS. Santa Monica, Calif.: RAND.

Gundersen, Craig, Brent Kreider, and John V. Pepper. 2018. "Reconstructing the Supplemental Nutrition Assistance Program to More Effectively Alleviate Food Insecurity in the United States." *RSF: The Russell Sage Foundation Journal of the Social Sciences* 4(2): 113–30. DOI: 10.7758/RSF.2018.4.2.06.

Halpern-Meekin, Sarah, Sara Sternberg Greene, Ezra Levin, and Kathryn Edin. 2018. "The Rainy Day Earned Income Tax Credit: A Reform to Boost Financial Security by Helping Low-Wage Workers Build Emergency Savings." *RSF: The Russell Sage Foundation Journal of the Social Sciences* 4(2): 161–76. DOI: 10.7758/RSF.2018.4.2.08.

Herd, Pamela, Melissa Favreault, Madonna Harrington Meyer, and Timothy M. Smeeding. 2018.

"A Targeted Minimum Benefit Plan: A New Proposal to Reduce Poverty Among Older Social Security Recipients." *RSF: The Russell Sage Foundation Journal of the Social Sciences* 4(2): 74–90. DOI: 10.7758/RSF.2018.4.2.04.

Hetling, Andrea, Jinwoo Kwon, and Correne Saunders. 2015. "The Relationship Between State Welfare Rules and Economic Disconnection Among Low-Income Single Mothers." *Social Service Review* 89(4): 653–85.

Holzer, Harry J. 2018. "A 'Race to the Top' in Public Higher Education to Improve Education and Employment Among the Poor." *RSF: The Russell Sage Foundation Journal of the Social Sciences* 4(3): 84–99. DOI: 10.7758/RSF.2018.4.3.05.

Holzer, Harry J., Steven Raphael, and Michael A. Stoll. 2004. "Will Employers Hire Former Offenders? Employer Preference, Background Checks and Their Determinants." In *Imprisoning America: The Social Effects of Mass Incarceration*, edited by David Weiman, Bruce Western, and Mary Pattillo. New York: Russell Sage Foundation.

———. 2006. "Perceived Criminality, Criminal Background Checks, and the Racial Hiring Practices of Employers." *The Journal of Law and Economics* 49(2): 451–80.

Isaacs, Julia B., Olivia Healy, and H. Elizabeth Peters. 2017. "Paid Family Leave in the United States: Time for a New National Policy." Washington, D.C.: Urban Institute.

Jacobs, Elisabeth. 2015. "The Declining Labor Force Participation Rate: Causes, Consequences, and the Path Forward." Testimony given before the United States Joint Economic Committee, July 15. Washington, D.C.: Washington Center for Equitable Growth.

Jäntti, Markus. 2009. "Mobility in the U.S. and in Comparative Perspective." In *Changing Poverty, Changing Policies*, edited by Maria Cancian and Sheldon Danziger. New York: Russell Sage Foundation.

Kalleberg, Arne L. 2009. "Precarious Work, Insecure Workers: Employment Relations in Transition." *American Sociological Review* 74(1): 1–22.

Kimberlin, Sara, Laura Tach, and Christopher Wimer. 2018. "A Renter's Tax Credit to Curtail the Affordable Housing Crisis." *RSF: The Russell Sage Foundation Journal of the Social Sciences* 4(2): 131–60. DOI: 10.7758/RSF.2018.4.2.07.

Lambert, Susan J. 2008. "Passing the Buck: Labor Flexibility Practices That Transfer Risk onto Hourly Workers." *Human Relations* 61(9): 1203–27.

Lambert, Susan J., Peter J. Fugiel, and Julia R. Henly. 2014. "Precarious Work Schedules Among Early-Career Employees in the U.S.: A National Snapshot." EINet Research Brief. Chicago: University of Chicago.

Levy, Frank, and Thomas Kochan. 2012. "Addressing the Problem of Stagnant Wages." *Comparative Economic Studies* 54(4): 739–64.

Magnuson, Katherine, and Elizabeth Votruba-Drzal. 2009. "Enduring Influences of Childhood Poverty." In *Changing Poverty, Changing Policies*, edited by Maria Cancian and Sheldon Danziger. New York: Russell Sage Foundation.

Magnuson, Katherine, Jane Waldfogel, and Elizabeth Washbrook. 2012. "SES Gradients in Skills During the School Years." In *From Parents to Children: The Intergenerational Transmission of Advantage*, edited by John Ermisch, Marcus Jantti, and Timothy Smeeding. New York: Russell Sage Foundation.

Manyika, James, Michael Chui, Brad Brown, Jacques Bugin, Richard Dobbs, Charles Roxburgh, and Angela Hung Byers. 2011. *Big Data: The Next Frontier for Innovation, Competition, and Productivity*. New York: McKinsey Global Institute.

McLanahan, Sara. 2004. "Diverging Destinies: How Children Are Faring Under the Second Demographic Transition." *Demography* 41(4): 607–27.

McLanahan, Sara, and Wade Jacobsen. 2015. "Diverging Destinies Revisited." In *Families in an Era of Increasing Inequality*, edited by Susan M. McHale, Paul R. Amato, Alan Booth, and Jennifer Van Hook. New York: Springer International.

McLendon, Michael K., and Laura W. Perna, eds. 2014. "The Role of State Policy in Promoting College Access and Success." Special issue, *Annals of the American Academy of Political and Social Science* 655(1).

Miller, Gregory E., and Edith Chen. 2013. "The Biological Residue of Childhood Poverty." *Child Development Perspectives*. 7(2): 67–73.

Milligan, Kevin, and Mark Stabile. 2011. "Do Child Tax Benefits Affect the Wellbeing of Children? Evidence from Canadian Child Benefit Expansions." *American Economic Journal: Economic Policy* 3(3): 175–205.

Mitnik, Pablo A., Victoria Bryant, Michael Weber, and David B. Grusky. 2015. "New Estimates of Intergenerational Mobility Using Administrative

Data." *Statistics of Income* working paper. Washington: Internal Revenue Service.

Moffitt, Robert A. 2015. "The Deserving Poor, the Family, and the U.S. Welfare System." *Demography* 52(3): 729–49.

Morduch, Jonathan, and Rachel Schneider. 2017. *The Financial Diaries: How American Families Cope in a World of Uncertainty*. Princeton, N.J.: Princeton University Press.

Morris, Pamela A., Greg J. Duncan, and Christopher Rodrigues. 2011. "Does Money Really Matter? Estimating Impacts of Family Income on Young Children's Achievement with Data from Random-Assignment Experiments." *Developmental Psychology* 47(5): 1263–79.

National Women's Law Center. 2017. "Recently Enacted and Introduced State and Local Fair Scheduling Legislation." Washington, D.C.: National Women's Law Center.

Neumark, David. 2015. "The Effects of Minimum Wages on Employment." *Federal Reserve Bank of San Francisco Economic Letter* (2015): 37.

Osterman, Paul. 2014. "Career Ladders in the Low-Wage Labor Market." In *What Works for Workers? Public Policies and Innovative Strategies for Low-Wage Workers*, edited by Stephanie Luce, Jennifer Luff, Joseph A. McCartin, and Ruth Milkman. New York: Russell Sage Foundation.

Paul, Mark, William Darity Jr., Darrick Hamilton, and Khaing Zaw. 2018. "A Path to Ending Poverty by Way of Ending Unemployment: A Federal Job Guarantee." *RSF: The Russell Sage Foundation Journal of the Social Sciences* 4(3): 44–63. DOI: 10.7758/RSF.2018.4.3.03.

Pavetti, LaDonna, and Gregory Acs. 2001. "Moving Up, Moving Out, or Going Nowhere? A Study of Employment Patterns of Young Women and the Implications for Welfare Mothers." *Journal of Policy Analysis and Management* 20(4): 721–36.

Peterangelo, Joe, and Rob Henken. 2016. "Who Are Milwaukee's Unemployed Jobseekers?" Presentation at Federal Reserve Bank of Chicago Economic Development Forum: Eliminating Barriers to Employment in Wisconsin's Most Distressed Communities—Expungement. Milwaukee, Wisc. (May 12, 2016).

Pettit, Becky. 2012. *Invisible Men: Mass Incarceration and the Myth of Black Progress*. New York: Russell Sage Foundation.

Proctor, Bernadette D., Jessica L. Semega, and Melissa A. Kollar. 2016. "Income and Poverty in the United States: 2015." *Current Population Reports*, series P60, no. 256(RV). Washington: U.S. Government Printing Office.

Raphael, Steven, and Eugene Smolensky. 2009. "Immigration and Poverty in the United States." In *Changing Poverty, Changing Policies*, edited by Maria Cancian and Sheldon Danziger. New York: Russell Sage Foundation.

Ratcliffe, Caroline, and Signe-Mary McKernan. 2013. "Child Poverty and Its Lasting Consequence." *Low-Income Families* working paper 21. Washington, D.C.: Urban Institute.

Renwick, Trudi, and Liana Fox. 2016. "The Supplemental Poverty Measure: 2015." *Current Population Reports*, series P60, no. 258. Washington: U.S. Government Printing Office for U.S. Bureau of the Census.

Romich, Jennifer, and Heather D. Hill. 2018. "Coupling a Federal Minimum Wage Hike with Public Investments to Make Work Pay and Reduce Poverty." *RSF: The Russell Sage Foundation Journal of the Social Sciences* 4(3): 22–43. DOI: 10.7758/RSF.2018.4.3.02.

Rose, Shanna. 2015. "Opting In, Opting Out: The Politics of State Medicaid Expansion." *The Forum* 13(1): 63–82.

Sawhill, Isabel V. 2014. *Generation Unbound: Drifting into Sex and Parenthood Without Marriage*. Washington, D.C.: Brookings Institution Press.

Scholz, J. Karl, Robert Moffitt, and Benjamin Cowan. 2009. "Trends in Income Support." In *Changing Poverty, Changing Policies*, edited by Maria Cancian and Sheldon Danziger. New York: Russell Sage Foundation.

Schott, Liz, LaDonna Pavetti, and Ife Floyd. 2015. *How States Use Federal and State Funds under the TANF Block Grant*. Washington, D.C.: Center on Budget and Policy Priorities.

Schwartz, Christine R. 2013. "Trends and Variation in Assortative Mating: Causes and Consequences." *Annual Review of Sociology* 39: 451–70.

Seefeldt, Kristin S. 2016. *Abandoned Families: Social Isolation in the Twenty-First Century*. New York: Russell Sage Foundation.

Shaefer, H. Luke, Sophie Collyer, Greg Duncan, Kathryn Edin, Irwin Garfinkel, David Harris, Timothy M. Smeeding, Jane Waldfogel, Christopher Wimer, and Hirokazu Yoshikawa. 2018. "A Universal Child Allowance: A Plan to Reduce Poverty and Income Instability Among Children in the

United States." *RSF: The Russell Sage Foundation Journal of the Social Sciences* 4(2): 22–42. DOI: 10.7758/RSF.2018.4.2.02.

Shaefer, H. Luke, and Kathryn Edin. 2013. "Rising Extreme Poverty in the U.S. and the Response of Federal Means-Tested Transfer Programs." *Social Service Review* 87(2): 250–68.

Shaefer, H. Luke, and Kathryn Edin, and Elizabeth Talbert. 2015. "Understanding the Dynamics of $2-a-Day Poverty in the United States. *RSF: The Russell Sage Foundation Journal of the Social Sciences* 1(1): 120–38. DOI: 10.7758/RSF.2015.1.1.07.

Shattuck, Rachel M., and Rose M. Kreider. 2013. "Social and Economic Characteristics of Currently Unmarried Women with a Recent Birth: 2011." ACS-21. Washington: U.S. Government Printing Office.

Sherman, Arloc, and Danilo Trisi. 2014. *Deep Poverty Among Children Worsened in Welfare Law's First Decade*. Washington, D.C.: Center on Budget and Policy Priorities.

———. 2015. *Safety Net More Effective Against Poverty than Previously Thought*. Washington, D.C.: Center on Budget and Policy Priorities.

Short, Kathleen. 2015. "The Supplemental Poverty Measure: 2014." *Current Population Reports*, series P60, no. 254. Washington: U.S. Government Printing Office.

Slack, Kristen S., Bong Joo Lee, and Lawrence M. Berger. 2007. "Do Welfare Sanctions Increase Child Protective Services Involvement? A Cautious Answer." *Social Service Review* 81(2): 207–28.

Smeeding, Timothy M. 2006. "Poor People in Rich Nations: The United States in Comparative Perspective." *Journal of Economic Perspectives* 20(1): 69–90.

Smeeding, Timothy M., Irwin Garfinkel, and Ronald B. Mincy. 2011. "Introduction to Young Disadvantaged Men: Fathers, Families, Poverty, and Policy." *Annals of the American Academy of Political and Social Science* 635(1): 6–23.

Smolensky, Eugene, and Jennifer A. Gootman, eds. 2003. *Working Families and Growing Kids: Caring for Children and Adolescents*. Washington, D.C.: National Academies Press.

Sommer, Teresa Eckrich, Terri J. Sabol, Elise Chor, William Schneider, P. Lindsay Chase-Lansdale, Jeanne Brooks-Gunn, Mario L. Small, Christopher King, and Hirokazu Yoshikawa. 2018. "A Two-Generation Human Capital Approach to Anti-poverty Policy." *RSF: The Russell Sage Foundation Journal of the Social Sciences* 4(3): 118–43. DOI: 10.7758/RSF.2018.4.3.07.

Strumbos, Diana, Donna Linderman, and Carson C. Hicks. 2018. "Postsecondary Pathways Out of Poverty: City University of New York Accelerated Study in Associate Programs and the Case for National Policy." *RSF: The Russell Sage Foundation Journal of the Social Sciences* 4(3): 100–17. DOI: 10.7758/RSF.2018.4.3.06.

Tiehen, Laura, Dean Jolliffe, and Timothy M. Smeeding. 2016. "The Effect of SNAP on Poverty." In *Snap Matters: How Food Stamps Affect Health and Well-Being*, edited by Judith Bartfeld, Craig Gundersen, Timothy M. Smeeding, and James P. Ziliak. Palo Alto, Calif.: Stanford University Press.

Turner, Lesley J., Sheldon Danziger, and Kristin S. Seefeldt. 2006. "Failing the Transition from Welfare to Work: Women Chronically Disconnected from Employment and Cash Welfare." *Social Science Quarterly* 87(2): 227–49.

U.S. Department of Agriculture. 2017. "Supplemental Nutrition Assistance Program Participation and Costs." Accessed February 26, 2017. https://www.fns.usda.gov/sites/default/files/pd/SNAPsummary.pdf.

U.S. Department of Education. 2016. *Fulfilling the Promise, Serving the Need: Advancing College Opportunity for Low-Income Students*. Washington: U.S. Department of Education.

U.S. Department of Health and Human Services. 2016. "Annual Update of the HHS Poverty Guidelines." *Federal Register* 81(15): 4036–37.

———. 2017. "FY2015 Federal TANF & State MOE Financial Data." Accessed February 26, 2017. https://www.acf.hhs.gov/sites/default/files/ofa/tanf_financial_data_fy_2015.pdf.

U.S. Department of the Treasury. 2017. "About EITC." Accessed February 26, 2017. https://www.eitc.irs.gov/EITC-Central/abouteitc.

Warren, Robert, and John R. Warren. 2013. "Unauthorized Immigration to the United States: Annual Estimates and Components of Change, by State, 1990 to 2010." *International Migration Review* 47(2): 296–329.

White House. 2017. "Presidential Executive Order on a Comprehensive Plan for Reorganizing the Executive Branch." Executive Order No. 13781. Washington: Office of the Press Secretary.

Williams, Erica. 2017. *States Can Adopt or Expand Earned Income Tax Credits to Build a Stronger Future Economy.* Washington, D.C.: Center on Budget and Policy Priorities.

Wimer, Christopher, Sophie Collyer, and Sara Kimberlin. 2018. "Assessing the Potential Impacts of Innovative New Policy Proposals on Poverty in the United States." *RSF: The Russell Sage Foundation Journal of the Social Sciences* 4(3): 167–83. DOI: 10.7758/RSF.2018.4.3.09.

Wimer, Christopher, Liana Fox, Irwin Garfinkel, Neeraj Kaushal, and Jane Waldfogel. 2016. "Progress on Poverty? New Estimates of Historical Trends Using an Anchored Supplemental Poverty Measure." *Demography* 53(4): 1207–18.

Winship, Scott. 2016. *Poverty After Welfare Reform.* New York: Manhattan Institute for Policy Research.

Wu, Lawrence L., and Nicholas D. E. Mark. 2018. "Could We Level the Playing Field? Long-Acting Reversible Contraceptives, Nonmarital Fertility, and Poverty in the United States." *RSF: The Russell Sage Foundation Journal of the Social Sciences* 4(3): 144–66. DOI: 10.7758/RSF.2018.4.3.08.

Ziliak, James P. 2016. "Temporary Assistance for Needy Families." In *Economics of Means-Tested Transfer Programs in the United States*, volume 1, edited by Robert A. Moffitt. Chicago: University of Chicago Press.

PART I
Tax and Transfer Programs

A Universal Child Allowance: A Plan to Reduce Poverty and Income Instability Among Children in the United States

H. LUKE SHAEFER, SOPHIE COLLYER, GREG DUNCAN, KATHRYN EDIN, IRWIN GARFINKEL, DAVID HARRIS, TIMOTHY M. SMEEDING, JANE WALDFOGEL, CHRISTOPHER WIMER, AND HIROKAZU YOSHIKAWA

To reduce child poverty and income instability, and eliminate extreme poverty among families with children in the United States, we propose converting the Child Tax Credit and child tax exemption into a universal, monthly child allowance. Our proposal is based on principles we argue should undergird the design of such

H. Luke Shaefer is associate professor of social work and public policy and director of Poverty Solutions at the University of Michigan. **Sophie Collyer** is a research analyst at the Center on Poverty and Social Policy at the Columbia University School of Social Work. **Greg Duncan** is distinguished professor in the School of Education at University of California, Irvine. **Kathryn Edin** is Bloomberg Distinguished Professor at the Zanvyl Krieger School and Bloomberg School of Public Health at Johns Hopkins University. **Irwin Garfinkel** is Mitchell I. Ginsberg Professor of Contemporary Urban Problems and interim dean of the Columbia University School of Social Work. **David Harris** is president of Children's Research and Education Institute and an associate of the Columbia Population Research Center. **Timothy M. Smeeding** is Lee Rainwater Distinguished Professor of Public Affairs and Economics at the University of Wisconsin–Madison. **Jane Waldfogel** is Compton Foundation Centennial Professor for the Prevention of Children's and Youth Problems at Columbia University School of Social Work. **Christopher Wimer** is co-director of the Center on Poverty and Social Policy at the Columbia University School of Social Work. **Hirokazu Yoshikawa** is Courtney Sale Ross Professor of Globalization and Education and professor at New York University.

© 2018 Russell Sage Foundation. Shaefer, H. Luke, Sophie Collyer, Greg Duncan, Kathryn Edin, Irwin Garfinkel, David Harris, Timothy M. Smeeding, Jane Waldfogel, Christopher Wimer, and Hirokazu Yoshikawa. 2018. "A Universal Child Allowance: A Plan to Reduce Poverty and Income Instability Among Children in the United States." *RSF: The Russell Sage Foundation Journal of the Social Sciences* 4(2): 22–42. DOI: 10.7758/RSF.2018.4.2.02. Direct correspondence to: H. Luke Shaefer at lshaefer@umich.edu, University of Michigan, Gerald R. Ford School of Public Policy, 735 South State St., Ann Arbor, MI 48104; Sophie Collyer at smc2246 @columbia.edu, Center on Poverty and Social Policy, Columbia University School of Social Work, 1255 Amsterdam Ave., New York, NY 10027; Greg Duncan at gduncan@uci.edu, School of Education, University of California, Irvine, 3200 Education, Irvine, CA 92697; Kathryn Edin at kathy_edin@jhu.edu, Zanvyl Krieger School, Johns Hopkins University, Department of Sociology, 533 Mergenthaler Hall, 3400 N. Charles St., Baltimore, MD 21218; Irwin Garfinkel at ig3@columbia.edu, Columbia University School of Social Work, 1255 Amsterdam Ave., New York, NY 10025; David Harris at davidbharris@mac.com, Columbia Population Research Center, 1255 Amsterdam Ave., New York, NY 10027; Timothy M. Smeeding at smeeding@wisc.edu, University of Wisconsin-Madison, 3464 SSSB, 1180 Observatory Dr., Madison, WI 53706; Jane Waldfogel at jw205@columbia.edu, Columbia University School of Social Work, 1255 Amsterdam Ave., New York, NY 10027; Christopher Wimer at cw2727 @columbia.edu, Columbia University School of Social Work, 1255 Amsterdam Ave., 7th Floor, New York, NY 10027; and Hirokazu Yoshikawa at hiro.yoshikawa@nyu.edu, New York University, 726 Broadway, 5th Floor, New York, NY 10003.

Open Access Policy: *RSF: The Russell Sage Foundation Journal of the Social Sciences* is an open access journal. This article is published under a Creative Commons Attribution-NonCommercial-NoDerivs 3.0 Unported License.

policies: universality, accessibility, adequate payment levels, and more generous support for young children. Whether benefits should decline with additional children to reflect economies of scale is a question policymakers should consider. Analyzing 2015 Current Population Survey data, we estimate our proposed child allowance would reduce child poverty by about 40 percent, deep child poverty by nearly half, and would effectively eliminate extreme child poverty. Annual net cost estimates range from $66 billion to $105 billion.

Keywords: child poverty, child tax credit, income instability, social welfare policy

The child poverty rate in the United States remains stubbornly high—particularly among families with young children—and is much higher than in other affluent countries. This rate is not just the product of our demographics or labor market conditions; it also reflects our nation's social policy choices. Most notably, the bulk of the benefits from two large policies providing income support for families with children is based on the federal income tax system. The $1,000 per child per year Child Tax Credit and a $4,000 per child per year tax exemption (often referred to as the child deduction) mostly go to families with incomes well above the poverty line, at a combined annual cost of $97 billion (Tax Policy Center 2016).

To be sure, the United States has significantly expanded its work-based social safety net over the past two decades, with impressive results. In fact, the United States now spends more on poor families with children than ever before (Moffitt 2015). In particular, the Earned Income Tax Credit (EITC) and Child Tax Credit (CTC), which are refundable and paid to wage earners, play a vital anti-poverty role by encouraging work and providing increased assistance to poor parents who earn low wages but are able to maintain steady employment.[1] Together, the EITC and CTC lift more children out of poverty than any other federal program (Marr et al. 2015).

Despite these policy successes, one particularly vulnerable group of children has fallen through the cracks—children whose parents are unable to maintain regular work (Moffitt 2015). Relying on a number of different metrics and numerous sources of data, researchers find evidence of worsening conditions and highly volatile incomes among America's poorest families (Edin and Shaefer 2015; Jencks 2016; Moffitt 2015). What aid is available to families at the very bottom increasingly comes in the form of in-kind benefits, rather than cash (Fox et al. 2015). While such benefits are crucial for bolstering the living standards of the poor, a number of scholars argue that a core dilemma facing America's extreme poor is the absence of accessible cash income (Edin and Shaefer 2015, 2016). Thus, America's transition to a work-based social safety net, begun in the 1990s, remains incomplete because it has failed to ensure a stable base-level source of cash income for all children.

A stable source of cash income could reduce material hardship among families by increasing the overall dependable cash resources available to cover core expenses. Moreover, a growing body of evidence from rigorous studies suggests that income transfers—even relatively small ones—can improve child health and development. Poverty-reducing income transfers to families with children may also reduce social costs in the long term by furthering education attainment, reducing crime, reducing homelessness, and increasing labor market productivity (Evans, Sullivan, and Wallskog 2016; Holzer et al. 2008; Hoynes and Patel 2015; Almond, Currie, and Duque 2017).

Embedded in the U.S. tax code—at a combined cost of $95.6 billion in 2014—the Child Tax Credit and child tax exemption recognize that families incur significant expenses when raising children. But because their benefits are based on earnings, they leave out many of America's youngest children who are the most likely to be living in families too poor to be eligible for the full credit (Harris 2012). Moreover, both are provided annually, at tax time,

---

1. In statutory law, the Child Tax Credit refers to the nonrefundable credit. The Additional Child Tax Credit (ACTC) refers to the refundable portion of the CTC. When we use CTC, we refer to both the nonrefundable component (the CTC) and the refundable component (the ACTC), as is common when discussing the policy.

Figure 1. Federal Expenditures on Children by Major Cash and Near-Cash Programs, 2015 (in Billions)

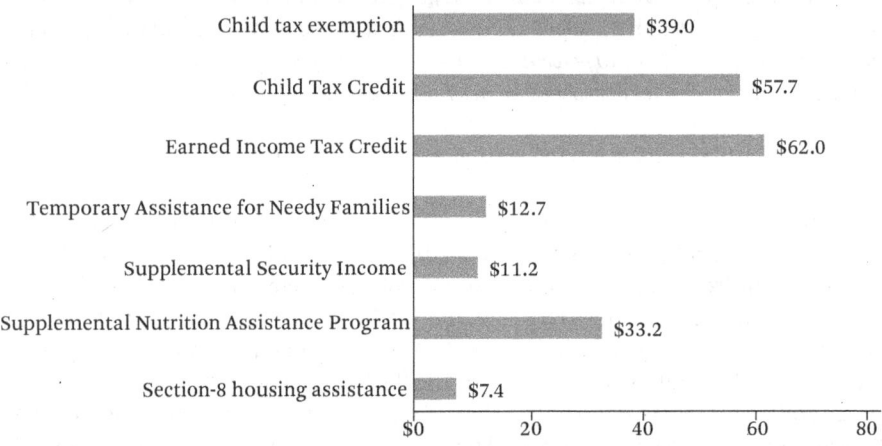

Source: Authors' compilation based on Tax Policy Center 2016 and Isaacs et al. 2016.
Note: Data on child tax exemption and Child Tax Credit come from the Center for Tax Policy. Other data are adapted from Isaacs et al. 2016. Data are based on outlays, rather than appropriated or authorized levels. Child Tax Credit and Earned Income Tax Credit amounts include both tax expenditure and refundable portions of the credits. Child Tax Credit amount includes the Additional Child Tax Credit.

making it difficult for families struggling with income instability to provide a consistent level of support for their children throughout the year. All in all, the Child Tax Credit and child tax exemption are not well designed to meet the ongoing and emergency needs of families with children in the United States.

Our proposed universal monthly child allowance replaces these U.S. tax code provisions with a regular, dependable, monthly cash benefit—an income floor—for all families with children, including the most vulnerable. It is designed to complement our nation's work-based safety net. Also, because it would be available to all children, a universal child allowance would avoid the stigma attached to existing means-tested, income transfer programs.

Such a child allowance would also benefit children whose parents are continuously engaged in the labor market by providing a reliable monthly income stream, an important advantage given the significant, and growing, inter- and intra-year income and expense volatility American families are experiencing (Sandstrom and Huerta 2013; Jacob and Hacker 2008; Morduch and Schneider 2017). Finally, it would also provide assistance to children in middle-class families, most of whose incomes have barely budged in the last twenty years. The richest fifth of families, which include nearly seventeen million children, spend nearly $10,000 per child per year on child enrichment expenditures alone, leaving children in both low- and middle-income families behind (Duncan and Murnane 2011).

BACKGROUND

The United States has increased its financial commitment to fighting poverty substantially over the past half century by introducing refundable tax credits and expanding the Supplemental Nutrition Assistance Program (SNAP), formerly the Food Stamp Program (for 2015 cost data, see figure 1). Estimates using the supplemental poverty measure (SPM), which more fully accounts for in-kind aid and refundable tax credits than the official poverty measure, show that child poverty fell by 35 percent between 1967 and 2012, and virtually all of that reduction was due to increased means-tested public benefits (Wimer et al. 2016). Research using data from the Consumer Expenditure Survey also finds falling consumption-based poverty in the past few decades (Meyer and Sullivan 2012).

In particular, the EITC, CTC, and SNAP have expanded significantly since the mid-1990s. When counted as income, they lift more children out of poverty than any other federal programs, demonstrating how government policies can work to help poor families with children (Short 2015). Even after counting in-kind benefits, however, approximately 17 percent of children still live in families with incomes below the poverty line, and an additional 25 percent live in families with net incomes between 100 percent and 200 percent of the SPM poverty line (Short 2015).

But what about families that cannot find work, or whose work is not enough for them to benefit substantially from work-related tax credits? The only income benefits available to nonworking families with children are SNAP and what is left of Temporary Assistance for Needy Families (TANF). SNAP provides a critical floor of support for eligible families, especially those with children. But recent benefit cuts and the fact that SNAP recipients can use their benefits only to buy food impose major limits on the extent to which the program can help low-income families provide adequate support for their children. Paying for housing, for instance, has become increasingly challenging for low-income families. Yet housing assistance programs currently help only about one in four eligible households (Desmond 2016).

Although means-tested aid to poor families with children has increased during the past few decades, research finds that aid—particularly in the form of cash aid—to the very poorest among them has declined (Edin and Shaefer 2015; Moffitt 2015; Jencks 2016). For families with children, this is related to the declining resources allocated to TANF, the cash assistance program established by the welfare reform of 1996. According to the TANF-to-poverty ratio—a measure of program access—the number of families receiving cash assistance per 100 families in poverty has declined from sixty-eight in 1996 to twenty-three in 2015 (Floyd, Pavetti, and Schott 2017). Researchers have also found that TANF failed to respond to the rise in poverty and unemployment that accompanied the Great Recession (Garfinkel, McLanahan, and Wimer 2016).

Comparison with Peer Countries
If poverty is defined based only on pre-tax, pre-transfer (mostly earned) income, then the U.S. poverty rate differs little from the rates of other Organization for Economic Co-operation and Development (OECD) countries. The United States is unique, however, in its high rate of post-tax, post-transfer poverty. Numerous reports suggest that using a definition of after-tax and after-benefit income that includes refundable tax credits, SNAP, public housing, and other near-cash benefits produces a child relative poverty rate—based on a poverty line defined as half of median income—of 21 percent (see figure 2) (OECD 2016; Smeeding and Thevenot 2016). This is the fifth-highest rate of all OECD countries and surpassed only by many far poorer countries.[2]

Part of the reason that other nations have fewer poor children than the United States is that they provide what the OECD terms a *universal child benefit*—a cash grant that goes to all families with children. Austria, Canada, Denmark, Finland, France, Germany, Ireland, Luxembourg, the Netherlands, Norway, Sweden, and the UK have all implemented a version of a child benefit (Matthews 2016; Garfinkel et al. 2016). Some call their measures *child allowances* (CA). Others implement their CA through the tax code as universal *child tax credits*. A notable feature of these universal child benefit plans is that they are accessible to all: families with children receive them regardless

---

2. Christopher Wimer and Timothy Smeeding show that the SPM poverty line is about 40 percent of median income; here again the United States does poorly according to LIS and the SPM, which cite a poverty rate of 16 to 18 percent (Wimer and Smeeding 2016, figure 3). Children are deemed poor in Europe if their total household net incomes fall below 60 percent of a given year's median, a poverty line that is more than half again as high as the SPM line. By that definition, child poverty is about 26 to 27 percent in the United States and far lower in the EU (Wimer and Smeeding 2016, figure 4).

Figure 2. Child Income Poverty Rates, 2012

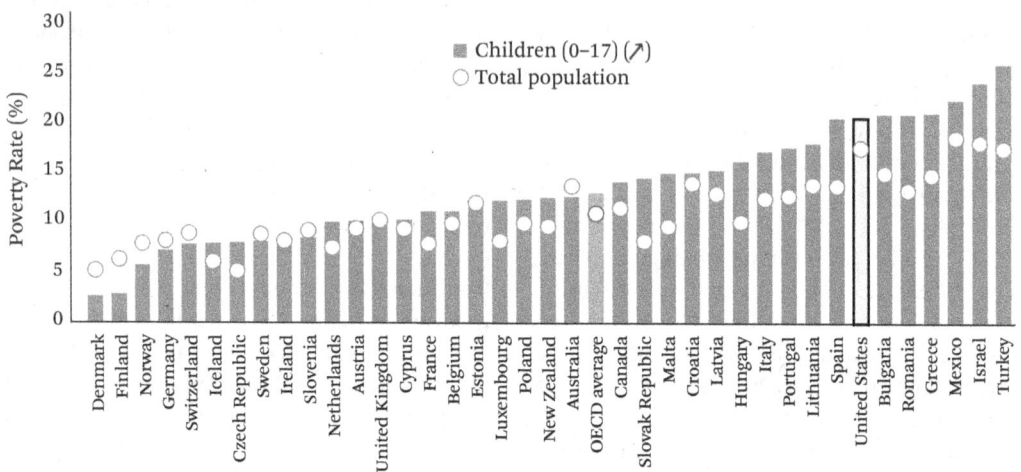

Source: Authors' compilation based on OECD 2016.
Note: Percentage of children (0–17) that live in households with an equivalized post-tax and transfer income of less than 50 percent of the national annual median equivalized post-tax and transfer household income. Data for Canada refer to 2011.

of whether parents work and whatever their income.

The level of these child benefits varies by country. The benefit in U.S. dollars for two children in Belgium and Germany is about $5,600 per year; in Ireland $4,000, and in the Netherlands $2,400 (Matthews 2016). Canada has a base child allowance, in U.S. dollars, of roughly $5,000 per child under six and $4,300 per child age six to seventeen, but with variation by province and income.[3] As with the Canadian program, our proposed U.S. child allowance would recognize the greater income needs of families with young children. It is important that these nations have universal health-care programs and heavily subsidized, low-cost, high-quality childcare and early childhood education. Thus, families with children in these countries need less money to buy these critical supports for child development than in the United States.

Income and Child Health and Development

Three major pathways have been proposed through which a child allowance and other sources of family income may affect child health and development: investments in children's learning, positive effects on biological and stress processes, and improvements in cognitive bandwidth and decision-making processes. With their *investment perspective*, economists argue that time and money are the two basic resources parents draw upon to invest in their children. Such investments as high-quality childcare and education, housing in good neighborhoods, and rich learning experiences enhance children's development, as do investments of parents' time.

Gary Becker's household production theory suggests that children from poor families lag behind their economically advantaged counterparts in part because their parents have fewer resources to invest in them (1991). Compared with more affluent parents, poor parents are less able to purchase inputs for their children, such as books and educational materials at home, high-quality child care settings and schools, and safe neighborhoods (Kaushal, Magnuson, and Waldfogel 2011).

Evidence suggests that the level of cognitive stimulation in the home environment varies

---

3. The amounts are gradually reduced with income. Thus, it is not a true universal system, but near universal.

with family income (Votruba-Drzal 2006). Economically disadvantaged parents may also have less time to invest in their children, owing to higher rates of single parenthood, nonstandard work hours, and less flexible work schedules. This too may have negative consequences for children. In sum, the investment perspective contends that family income matters to children because it enables parents to buy a variety of things that support learning and healthy development.

As formulated by developmental psychologists and neuroscientists, the *family and environmental stress perspective* holds that low-resourced families face significant economic pressure as they struggle to make ends meet. Given high levels of intra-year income volatility, such pressures may even be felt by families with annual incomes above poverty, who experience such negative shocks as illness, layoff, or seasonal fluctuations in work hours during the year. For poor parents, economic pressure creates high levels of psychological distress, including depressive and hostile feelings (Kessler and Cleary 1980; Gennetian and Shafir 2015), and leads to increased stress and worse mental health (Evans and Garthwaite 2014).

Psychological distress, in turn, spills over into marital and co-parenting relationships. As couples struggle to make ends meet, their interactions may become more hostile and conflicted, leading to parenting practices that are on average more punitive, harsh, inconsistent, and detached, as well as less nurturing, stimulating, and responsive to children's needs (McLoyd 1990). Such lower-quality parenting is likely to elevate children's physiological stress responses, and ultimately harms children's development (Conger et al. 2002).

Stress processes linked to poverty include detrimental changes in the body's hormonal responses to prolonged stress (HPA axis processes), as well as alterations in immune and aging processes linked to adversity (Shonkoff, Garner, et al. 2012). Evidence also exists that brain activity and even early brain volume are associated with socioeconomic status, although the existing studies are correlational (Noble, Engelhardt, et al. 2015; Noble, Houston, et al. 2015; Hair et al. 2015). These changes in turn are linked to poorer health as well as worse learning outcomes in adolescence and later adulthood (Ziol-Guest et al. 2012).

Finally, as discussed in the context of income instability, poverty conditions can compromise *parents' cognitive resources (bandwidth)* and have detrimental consequences for cognitive tasks and financial and other decision making (Gennetian and Shafir 2015). All told, the conceptual linkages between family income and the developmental needs of children and adolescents suggest that the kind of completely dependable base-level monthly income support provided by our proposed universal child allowance would have substantial benefits, especially for children with family incomes below or near the poverty line.

Evidence on Income Effects

A large body of nonexperimental literature finds that poverty is associated with perinatal problems and reductions in children's cognitive skills, academic achievement, educational attainment, and earnings (Aizer et al. 2016; Duncan and Brooks-Gunn 1997; Ziol-Guest et al. 2012; Almond, Currie, and Duque 2017; and others summarized in Butcher 2016). Evidence also links family income poverty with a range of poor health outcomes, both communicable and noncommunicable diseases in adulthood, for example (Marmot et al. 2008). Associations with child socioemotional outcomes and mental health are smaller, but also consistent in this literature (Yoshikawa, Aber, and Beardslee 2012).

Fewer causal studies have been conducted, and clearly more research is needed, especially in the U.S. context. Two coordinated sets of income maintenance and welfare reform experiments spanning the 1970s through the 1990s show mixed effects of boosts to family income during adolescence (Morris, Duncan, and Clark-Kauffman 2005; Maynard 1977; Maynard and Murnane 1979). However, experimentally induced boosts to family income when children are making the transition to formal schooling appear to raise levels of academic achievement. On average, these latter experiments showed that a boost of $4,000 per year for two to three years is associated with a 0.18 standard deviation increase in academic achievement (Duncan, Morris, and Rodrigues 2011).

A quasi-experimental literature has investigated relatively exogenous sources of variation in tax benefits such as the U.S. EITC and Canadian child allowance (referred to as a child tax credit), finding improvement in birth outcomes (Strully, Rehkopf, and Xuan 2010), improved health among adults and children, and increased school achievement in middle childhood (Dahl and Lochner 2012; Milligan and Stabile 2011; Nichols and Rothstein 2016). Casino windfall cash disbursements have also been linked to higher achievement and educational attainment, reduced incidence of risk behaviors in adolescence, and improved health outcomes (Akee et al. 2010; Costello et al. 2003; Wolfe et al. 2012). A recent randomized control trial of conditional cash transfers for families with children in two U.S. cities found that the program led to increased income and savings, reduced poverty and material hardship, improvements in some health outcomes, and increased life satisfaction among parents. It did not lead to academic improvements among participating children, and did lead to a reduction in employment, mostly driven by one site—Memphis (Miller et al. 2016).

The theoretical case for the positive effects of income transfers is strongest for very young children because the developing brain is more sensitive to environmental influences, both enrichment and adversity, in the first years of life (Center on the Developing Child 2016; Duncan, Magnuson, and Votruba-Drzal 2014). A recent study of an unconditional prenatal income supplement in Canada found it to be associated with a number of positive outcomes at birth (Brownell et al. 2016). Further evidence comes from a study matching the timing of the rollout of the Food Stamp Program across U.S. counties in the 1960s and 1970s to data from the Panel Study of Income Dynamics, which finds an association between food stamp availability and reduced risk of ill health in adulthood as well as positive impacts (for females only) on educational attainment and other indicators of economic self-sufficiency (Hoynes, Schanzenbach, and Almond 2016). The largest adult impacts were associated with the availability of food stamps prior to birth, and the outcomes gradually declined as the age at food stamp introduction increased from birth to age five.

Anna Aizer and her colleagues also find long-run improvements in children's health associated with maternal receipt of social benefits early in life—in this case from the Mother's Pension program established in the early part of the twentieth century (2016).

Although some forms of in-kind benefits have also been shown to improve the lives of poor families, cash transfers may be more effective because cash is fungible, allowing families more freedom to efficiently allocate benefits to address their specific needs (Hammond and Orr 2016; Muennig et al. 2016; Edin and Shaefer 2015). In-kind transfers may lead to unintended changes in behavior as families overconsume based on what benefits are available (Hammond and Orr 2016).

In sum, a number of evaluations using a variety of associational and quasi-experimental methods suggest that cash or near-cash transfers in a variety of forms can be an effective and cost-effective way to improve the health and material well-being of poor families across a number of domains (Akee et al. 2010; Brownell et al. 2016; Butcher 2016; Halpern-Meekin et al. 2015; Muennig et al. 2016; Wolfe et al. 2012). Added to this is experimental evidence from developing countries that find cash transfer can be an effective method of social support (Banerjee et al. 2015; Haushofer and Shapiro 2016).

Income Stability
Evidence indicates that economic instability and income and expenditure volatility both within and across years have increased over the past two decades (Sandstrom and Huerta 2013; Jacobs and Hacker 2008). These frequently result from excessive reliance on short-term employment, unexpected major expenses, unreliable work schedules, depletion and loss of capital and assets, and increased difficulty in saving money (Morduch and Schneider 2017; Sandstrom and Huerta 2013). Family income instability can also result from changes in the composition of members who contribute income to the family (Sandstrom and Huerta 2013).

Income instability is associated with higher rates of marital hardship, financial uncertainty, poorer adolescent school behaviors, eviction, psychological distress, and increased health problems (Morduch and Schneider 2017; Sandstrom and Huerta 2013; Choi 2009; Brown 2006; Desmond 2016; Gennetian and Shafir 2015). Research also finds that income instability is associated with reduced parenting quality. Studies show that low-income individuals direct a disproportionate amount of their time and mental capacity to addressing monthly ongoing poverty-related concerns (Mani et al. 2013). This means that when families experience economic hardship, parents are limited in their psychological ability to engage in activities that may enrich their children's lives (Osborne, Berger, and Magnuson 2012).

Instability may further compound the physiological and mental effects of poverty as families who experience economic instability show more parenting stress and depression (Osborne, Berger, and Magnuson 2012; Meadows, McLanahan, and Brooks-Gunn 2008). Such instability exacerbates stress and clinical depression in poor families, increasing the likelihood that they will make bad decisions in difficult situations. In their work examining the negative toll of scarcity, Sendhil Mullainathan and Eldar Shafir argue that income and expense volatility is a source of stress in and of itself, with detrimental effects on poor families (2013). In fact, literature in the natural sciences finds that unpredictability or instability early in life may be even more harmful than chronic low income (Rosenblum and Andrews 1994; Rosenblum and Paully 1984). Some literature in psychology has linked unpredictability in early childhood to adverse outcomes later in life (Doom, Vanzomeren-Dohm, and Simpson 2016).

BASING POLICY ON EVIDENCE AND PRINCIPLES

Although the work-based safety net in the United States is successful in many respects, our broader look at the nation's policies for providing economic support for its children has shown that much of the aid is directed toward middle- and high-income families, and very little cash support is available to the nation's poorest children. Furthermore, the disbursement of much of this economic support is lumpy, which can create intra-year boom-and-bust cycles for families.

To counteract these shortcomings, we propose a universal monthly child allowance that would replace our country's existing Child Tax Credit and child tax exemption. We have based our design on a set of core analytic principles intended to inform policy discussions. Agreement on core principles can support consensus about the general design of any policy, in this case income-based policies that support families with children. We propose five core principles and three policy alternatives based on them. Our simple policy alternative draws on principles one through three; our tiered alternative draws on one through four; and our tiered and equalized option draws on all five:

1. The child allowance should be universal because all families incur substantial expenses on behalf of their children and the healthy development of all children is in the nation's interest.

2. The allowance should be readily accessible and of sufficient frequency to meet short-run cash needs. This would be accomplished through a monthly electronic benefit transfer and help address the growing problem of income instability.

3. Payment levels should be adequate for a family to address the basic needs of its children, which research suggests is in the range of $250 per month per child.

4. Families with younger children should be eligible for larger payments because early childhood is when children's developmental needs are greatest, the costs of child rearing are highest, and family incomes tend to be lowest.

5. Policymakers should consider whether per child payment levels should decline with additional children, reflecting economies of scale present in larger families.

Three proposed versions of a child allowance include simple (monthly payments of $250 per child per month for all children under age eighteen), tiered (monthly payments of $300 per child under age six, $250 per child age six through seventeen); tiered and equivalized (monthly payments of $300 for the first child under age six and $250 for the first child age six through seventeen, with a reduction in these benefit levels as the number of children in the household increases). In each case, payments would be taxed at the marginal income tax rate of the unit claiming the child.

Universal Child Allowance

Universality is appropriate because resource needs increase universally with additional children in the household, and we all have a common interest in our nation's children. Children need to be fed, clothed, and housed, but parents' desires to promote the future well-being of their children lead them to spend an additional $3,586 per child per year on enrichment items such as childcare, lessons, and summer camps (Kaushal, Magnuson, and Waldfogel 2011).[4] A universal child allowance would help to support both basic needs and enrichment.

The better children in our country do, the more they can contribute economically, socially, and culturally to our country throughout their lifetimes. Providing a universal child benefit is a material and symbolic expression of our common interest in their welfare. Local and state governments in the United States recognized this common interest by leading the world throughout most of the nineteenth and twentieth centuries in the public provision of universal elementary and secondary education. These investments in the education of all of our nation's children—done through a universal mechanism—is one reason the United States is now the richest large nation on earth (Garfinkel, Rainwater, and Smeeding 2010; Goldin and Katz 2009).

Recognizing that raising children is a costly endeavor for families, the U.S. federal income tax system already allows parents—except for those with the lowest and highest incomes—to receive a credit of $1,000 per child from their taxes owed. Families may further deduct up to $4,000 per child from their taxable income, but again families with very low incomes do not benefit. For recipient families, this tax credit and exemption are economically equivalent to a child allowance consisting of a single annual payment. Our proposed child allowance payments would be more generous, would be paid monthly and would include families from both the poorest and the wealthiest families.

Some argue that benefits should be focused only on children in poor families, excluding those with higher incomes. The poorest families are clearly the neediest. Programs limited to the poor, like SNAP and TANF, relieve poverty and prevent hardship. But they also create labor disincentives by reducing benefits as incomes increase, a problem that would be muted with a universal child allowance because it does not impose a marginal tax rate other than standard income tax rates. Stigma associated with means-testing also leads some in need to decline benefits, and may have unintended negative effects on those who participate (Halpern-Meekin et al. 2015). Furthermore, the process of means-testing requires an expensive administrative apparatus to certify and recertify need. Determinations must be made on who is in need and how often need should be assessed. In contrast, relying on a universal benefit that is taxed as income would circumvent all these issues, as well as the need for administrative structures to impose means-tests in favor of systems that already exist.

In the United States today, near-poor, lower middle-income and even middle-income families with children struggle to meet their child rearing expenses, and would benefit from a universal child allowance. By providing benefits to all children, a universal child allowance would provide a solid income floor that would reduce poverty, integrate the poor into mainstream society, and increase the economic security of all children. Universal programs also enjoy more popularity than safety net programs targeting only poor families.

Readily Accessible and Frequent Allowance

Intra-year income instability is a large and growing problem for poor and working-class families with children. Refundable tax benefits paid as a lump sum at tax time allow families to pay for large expenses at that time, but make it difficult for them to make ends meet across lean months of the year (Nichols and Rothstein 2016). A better policy would disperse benefits with sufficient frequency to moderate the

---

4. This figure is based on the 1996 to 2007 Consumer Expenditure Surveys and has been inflated to 2015 dollars.

boom-and-bust cycle built into the low-wage labor market, today's family dynamics, and even the safety net. We propose a monthly approach. The U.S. Social Security system currently pays monthly cash benefits to a large number of aged, disabled and survivor recipients in an efficient manner. Our child allowance could work in the same way.

Adequate Payment Levels
We propose that a child allowance be designed to help families fill the gap between their available resources and the costs of their basic needs. Detailed accounts comparing the incomes and expenditures of poor families with children find that the average poor family experiences a significant monthly shortfall, usually on the order of a few hundred dollars (Halpern-Meekin et al. 2015; Lugo-Gil and Yoshikawa 2006; Edin and Lein 1997). Qualitative research shows that families at the bottom use a variety of survival strategies in efforts to fill that gap. Recent research (conducted by some of us) finds that low-income families perceive that an infusion of even a small amount of cash income can make a big difference in family well-being, even if it is not enough to meet the basic needs of children on its own (Edin and Shaefer 2015; Rojas et al. forthcoming). Research suggests that an annual benefit in the amount of $1,000 or more could impact a range of outcomes (Duncan, Morris, and Rodrigues 2011; Dahl and Lochner 2012; see also Bitler, Hines, and Page 2018).

More research is needed to understand precisely where a child allowance benefit level should be set. Both resources needed by low-income families, as well as parameters of child development spending for families higher up the income spectrum should be considered. For the purposes of this analysis, we set our baseline payment level at $250 per child per month, which would place it within the range of existing child benefit levels in other countries, and large enough that existing research would suggest the benefit could have a meaningful impact.

Larger Payments for Younger Children
Early childhood presents a perfect storm of difficult conditions, which could be addressed by a child allowance. First, it is a time of astonishingly rapid development, when children's brains are acquiring critical neural function and structures that serve as the foundation for future cognitive, social, emotional, and health outcomes (Nelson and Sheridan 2011). Evidence reviewed in the previous section suggests that the development of young children may be most responsive to increases in household income. Second, early childhood is the time when key child enrichment expenditures—in particular childcare—are highest. Data from the Consumer Expenditure Survey show that although total expenditures on child enrichment tend to be higher for school-age than preschool children, key expenditures on child care tend to be much higher ($1,438 versus $240 per child per year) for families with only preschoolers relative to families with only school-age children (Kaushal, Magnuson, and Waldfogel 2011). Childcare for infants and toddlers is particularly expensive because infants and toddlers require much closer adult contact than older preschoolers do.

Third, parents of young children tend to have lower family incomes than parents of older children. Census Bureau data for 2014 show that nearly one-quarter (23.5 percent) of children under age six live in families with cash incomes below the official poverty line, versus less than one-fifth (19.4 percent) of children age six and older. More than 2.5 million infants, toddlers, and older preschoolers live in deep poverty, defined as income less than one-half of the official poverty line (Jencks 2016). These considerations argue in favor of higher child allowance payments to families with young rather than older children, which we operationalize as an additional $50 per month per child under the age of six. At the same time, however, we note that an undifferentiated payment has the virtue of simplicity and constitutes a symbolic and practical expression of the ethical belief that all children are equally deserving.

Payments and Additional Children
Whether benefits should decline with additional children to reflect economies of scale is a question policymakers should consider. A common practice in studies of family well-being is to adjust income for family size, reflect-

ing a less-than-proportional increase in expenses as the number of family members increases. Consensus on exactly what those adjustments should look like (see, for example, Anyaegbu 2010), however, has not been reached and so we do not include such an adjustment in two of our three proposed policy versions. At one extreme is the assumption that all family members add the same amount to a family's need for income, for example, families with four members generate twice the need for income as families with only two members. This is almost certainly not always the case—despite the fact that childcare expenses increase directly with the number of children—given that expenditures on, say, heating or cooling a home hardly change with additional family members. Also, younger children can double up in bedrooms, reducing the need for more expensive housing. Carried to an extreme, this argument suggests that additional members add nothing to family needs; but this is clearly not the case, given the importance of expenditures such as food, which do increase. A critical question is how exactly families would allocate child allowance benefits. Economies of scale will apply in some cases but not others.

One can express the spectrum of possible adjustments with the exponent X in the following simple equation:

$$\text{Needs} = (\text{Number of children})^X$$

where $X=1$ in the case of equal needs for all family members and $X=0$ if needs do not increase at all with increases in family size (Buhmann et al. 1988).

When the National Research Council issued its recommendations for a new poverty measure, it proposed that X be set in the range of 0.65 to 0.75 (Citro and Michael 1995, 162). We adopted a 0.70 value, which effectively assumes that two children generate needs for income that are 62 percent more than one, and that three children generate 2.2 times the needs of one.

UNIVERSAL CHILD ALLOWANCE AND ITS IMPACTS ON POVERTY

We simulate three potential universal child allowance models. In our simple proposal, based on principles one through three, every child, regardless of age, receives $250 per month. Payments would be taxed back at marginal tax rates and would replace the existing Child Tax Credit, the Additional Child Tax Credit, and the child exemption. In our tiered version based on principles one through four, the benefit varies by age, with children under age six receiving $300 per month instead of $250, and all else being the same as in the first model. Finally, in our tiered and equivalized model, we apply an equivalence scale to the second model, allowing benefits to be reduced for each additional child in the family (based on principles one through five).

Impacts on Poverty

To assess the likely effects of a universal child allowance on poverty among children in the United States, we simulated the addition of child allowance payments to total family income for 2015 in the Current Population Survey's (CPS) Annual Social and Economic Supplement (ASEC), the same dataset used to compute annual official and supplemental poverty statistics (see the appendix for technical details; the simulations build on analyses presented in Garfinkel et al. 2016). For poverty and deep poverty estimates, we use the supplemental poverty measure. We report on impacts on child poverty rates (defined as total resources falling under 100 percent of the supplemental poverty threshold), deep poverty rates (defined as total resources falling under 50 percent of the poverty threshold), and a variation on the Shaefer and Edin extreme ($2 per day) poverty rate, defined here as annual cash incomes falling under a $2 per person, per day threshold (Shaefer and Edin 2013; Edin and Shaefer 2016).[5]

The core results of our simulations are shown in figure 3. The leftmost columns in figure 3 show child poverty, deep poverty, and ex-

---

5. In the CPS microdata, a small number of cases are recorded as having negative total SPM family income. This is a result of negative values that can result from business or farm losses or from the SPM's subtraction of expenses from income. We set these negative values to zero before beginning our simulations.

Figure 3. Child Poverty Falls Dramatically with a Universal Child Allowance

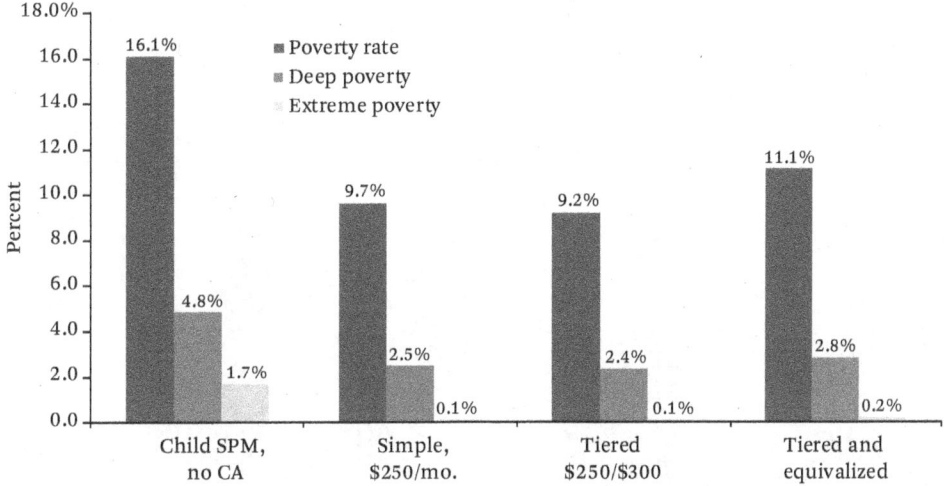

Source: Authors' calculations based on CPS ASEC data (Flood et al. 2017).

treme poverty rates as they stood in 2015. Under current anti-poverty policy, child poverty stands at 16.1 percent, deep poverty at 4.9 percent, and annual extreme poverty at 1.7 percent.

The remaining bars in figure 3 show the effects of a universal child allowance on various poverty metrics after we conduct the steps outlined above. Under our simple model, if we were to adopt a universal $250 per month child benefit regardless of age, our estimates show that child poverty would fall by approximately 40 percent, from 16.1 percent to 9.7 percent. Deep poverty would be cut nearly in half, from 4.9 percent to 2.5 percent. And extreme poverty would be virtually eliminated (down to 0.1 percent). If younger children were granted $50 more per month, as shown in the tiered model (model 2), child poverty would fall even more, to 9.3 percent. Deep poverty would not be reduced much further, while extreme poverty for children would again be effectively eliminated.

In the rightmost set of bars (model 3), we show the effect of a benefit that is tiered and equivalized (that is, adjusted for family size). Shrinking the benefit amount for additional children would result in a drop in child poverty from 16.1 percent to "only" 11.1 percent, in contrast to the unequivalized mixed-age benefit, which would reduce poverty to 9.7 percent.

Deep poverty, too, would not be reduced as much, while extreme poverty would still be virtually eliminated.

Figure 4 repeats the analyses from figure 3, but displays results for children under the age of six. This exercise illustrates the extent to which the mixed model, with enhanced payments for those under six, results in greater reductions in poverty (and deep poverty) for those children targeted by the enhancements. We do not show results for extreme poverty here because of the limited size of the sample and also because we know that such benefits would eliminate extreme poverty for all children.

Comparing the results in figures 3 and 4, we can see that child poverty is higher among younger children (17.3 percent) than all children (16.1 percent), which is well known. As it does for all children, a simple universal child allowance of $250 a month reduces young-child poverty by about 38 percent, from 17.3 percent to 10.7 percent. It also reduces young-child deep poverty by nearly 50 percent. The tiered model, with enhanced payments, results in a slightly larger decline in young-child poverty (44 percent) than for child poverty overall (40 percent). The equivalized benefit yields less reduction in poverty and in deep poverty among young children, as it does for all children.

Figure 4. Young Child Poverty Falls Dramatically with a Universal Child Allowance

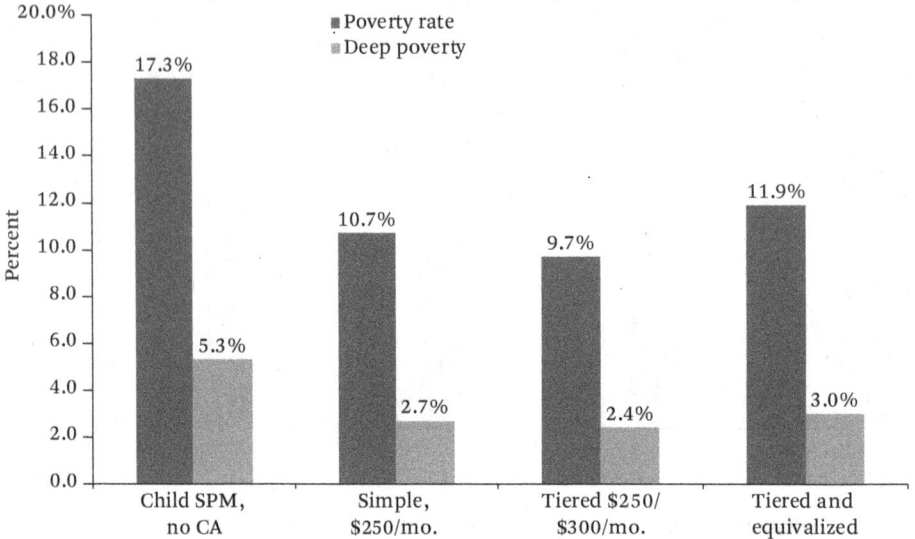

Source: Authors' calculations based on CPS ASEC data (Flood et al. 2017).

Figure 5. Poverty Rates for Children Within Demographic Groups

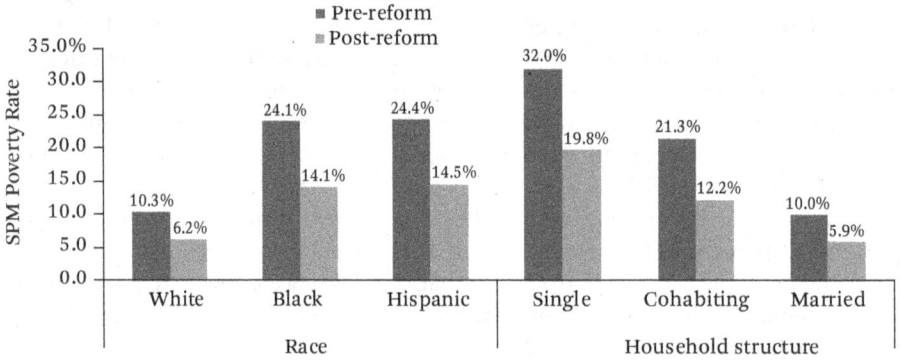

Source: Authors' calculations based on CPS ASEC data (Flood et al. 2017).

In figure 5, we take our simple child allowance version and estimate the policy's differential effects on poverty (using the SPM) by race and ethnicity and household structure. We find that the proportional change in poverty caused by a child allowance is relatively similar across race and ethnicity, even as the underlying starting rates of poverty pre-reform are starkly different. The poverty rate of black and Hispanic children both fall from a little above 24 percent to just over 14 percent (a bit more than a 40 percent drop), and that among non-Hispanic white children from 10.3 percent to 6.2 percent.

When examining the changes by household structure, the poverty rate among children living in single-mother household living alone falls from 32.0 percent to 19.8 percent (a 38.1 percent drop), slightly less than among children in married families (41.2 percent), the biggest drop being among families with unmarried co-habiting partners (from 21.3 percent to 12.2 percent).

Finally, figure 6 explores the net benefit of our proposed policy reforms for recipient families, again using our baseline, simple child allowance version. On the vertical axis is the net

Figure 6. Net Gain in SPM Resources for Recipient Families

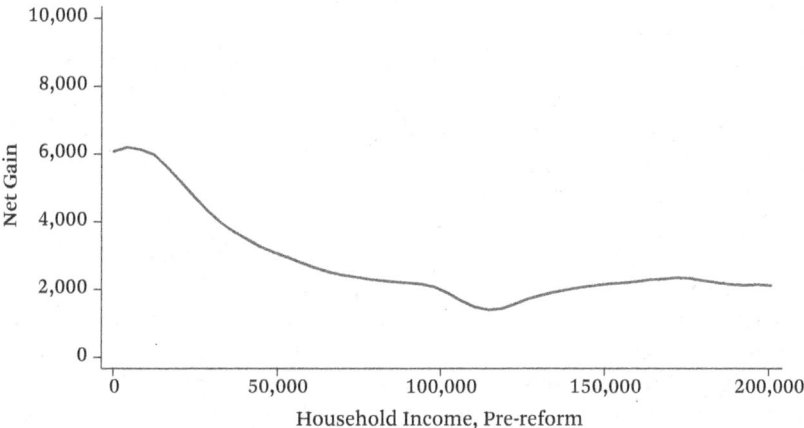

Source: Authors' calculations based on CPS ASEC data (Flood et al. 2017).
Note: The net gain in does not account for the $93 billion additional cost of the child allowance, only the net gain of the child allowance subtracting the CTC and child exemption.

Table 1. Cost Estimates of Universal Child Allowance Proposals (in Billions)

	Total Direct Cost	Cost Savings[a]	Net Cost of CA
Universal $250/mo. CA	$190	$97	$93
Tiered $250/$300/mo. CA	202	97	105
Tiered and equivalized CA	163	97	66

Source: Authors' compilation based on Tax Policy Center 2016.
[a]Cost savings are the estimated results of eliminating the CTC, ACTC, and also the child exemption under federal tax law.

benefit families receive after adding the child allowance and subtracting expected lost benefits from the refundable component of the CTC and child exemption. (Net benefit does not reflect additional funding changes needed to raise the revenue to cover the full child allowance benefit at this level. Net costs are discussed in more detail in the next section.) The horizontal axis plots total income of families with children. At a $250 per child benefit, all families across the income spectrum benefit. However, the net benefit of the policy reform declines smoothly as income rises until annual family income level reaches just over $100,000, where it dips slightly, and then essentially levels out over the remainder of the distribution. This chart suggests that the net benefit of the policy change would be positive, even at lower benefit levels.

Estimating the Cost of Our Universal Child Allowance

Estimates of the likely annual costs of our proposals are shown in table 1. Our simple plan would generate $190 billion in total direct costs (in the form of benefits paid); the tiered model would add $12 billion to this sum. Reducing benefits for additional children to reflect economies of scale reduces costs to a still-substantial $163 billion.

These figures overestimate net costs of our proposed policy reform, however, because they do not account for savings from the elimination of the $4,000 per child tax exemption and the Child Tax Credit and Additional Child Tax Credit (ACTC) now available to families with children under the federal tax code. Results provided by the Urban Institute's Tax Policy Center indicate that the joint cost of these three benefits (the CTC, ACTC, and child tax exemption) in 2015 was approximately $97 billion. The net costs of a universal child allowance are therefore considerably smaller than the total costs, though still substantial. The net cost of a universal $250 per month benefit would be $93 billion, the tiered model $105 billion, and the net cost of a tiered and equivalized model about $66 billion.

The net costs of our proposal are higher than those that Marianne Bitler, Annie Laurie Hines, and Marianne Page propose in this issue (2018) because we propose a higher benefit more in line with existing child allowances, and do not repurpose funding from the child-related parts of the EITC to pay for our proposed benefit so that it continues to provide an incentive for employment. The Bitler, Hines, and Page proposal focuses on what is possible to even out the safety net while being revenue neutral. In terms of the added net cost of our proposal, though substantial, it could be paid for in a variety of ways, such as increasing marginal income tax rates or increasing taxes on investment income. One could tax benefits back for high-income earners at a higher rate, similar in effect to how the current CTC and child exemption phase out with higher earnings. Such measures would reduce or eliminate the net benefit of the policy reform to upper income taxpayers.

Further Considerations
What would it take for our proposal to be revenue neutral, that is, zero net cost to the federal budget? As an exercise in budget balancing, we calculated that the cost of a $125 monthly child allowance or a $150 equivalized monthly allowance would roughly match savings from the $97 billion elimination of the Child Tax Credit and child tax exemption (Tax Policy Center 2016). This calculation shows the inherent fiscal feasibility of a U.S. child allowance, although research suggests that a family's need for monthly cash income per child exceeds $150, and this benefit level combined with our proposed reforms would lead to some net losers among middle-income families. For this reason, we prefer to set the amount at $250 per child and consider ways to raise the needed revenue.

In our plan, the EITC remains unchanged as an incentive for employment and annual income supplement. TANF could remain as is, and funds could be used to promote employment, training, and childcare as states see fit. Although we would consider our child allowance to be taxable income, our proposal does not consider it as countable income in determining benefits from programs like SNAP, as is true of the current Child Tax Credit. Doing so would clearly reduce the costs of those programs and in turn reduce the net cost of our proposed CA. With expenditures on children through SNAP, TANF, low-income housing assistance, and child benefits in Supplemental Security Income (SSI) totaling roughly $52 billion in 2015 (figure 1), savings resulting from considering our CA as countable income might reduce its cost by around $16 billion. Even in this case, research suggests families would benefit from the fact that our CA would substitute flexible cash for a portion of the in-kind benefits they received from SNAP and housing assistance programs (Edin and Shaefer 2015). However, reducing other benefits would reduce the overall value of the new child allowance and for that reason we do not propose it here.

CONCLUSION
Through its child tax exemption and Child Tax Credit, our nation recognizes the value of assisting parents in paying for the costs of raising children. At nearly $100 billion per year, these tax-based benefits represent, in effect, sizable annual child allowance payments to middle-income families. We have argued that the structure of these two programs is not in keeping with a principled approach to supporting our nation's children. They omit the lowest (and highest) income families and, in the case of the child tax exemption, benefits generally increase with income. Their once-yearly payment schedule is poorly suited to the growing number of families with month-to-month income instability.

Transforming the Child Tax Credit and child tax exemption into a universal child allowance for all American children would reflect the implicit recognition embedded in the tax code that families incur significant expenses when raising children. In addition, our universal child allowance would provide a base-level source of cash support—an income floor—for our most vulnerable families, and indeed all families with children. It would complement our nation's work-based safety net because the child allowance would not be reduced as earnings increase. And because it would be available to all children, its benefits would not suffer the stigma attached to existing means-tested income transfer programs or the hassle of recertification of benefits, except at tax time.

Our simulations of a universal child allowance show that child poverty would be cut by over 40 percent over current levels, and deep child poverty would be cut by half. Extreme, $2 per day, poverty among children would be eliminated. To be sure, the costs involved would be substantial. But this investment would lead to large and direct reductions in child poverty, and might also have a significant effect on the poverty and well-being of future generations.

APPENDIX: SIMULATION PROCEDURES
We based our simulation on the CPS ASEC, a nationally representative household survey conducted each year and containing detailed information on the demographics, incomes, and other characteristics of approximately two hundred thousand Americans. We begin by using data from the 2016 CPS ASEC, which is the most recent available dataset as of this writing. The data were extracted from the University of Minnesota's Integrated Public Use Microdata Series (Flood et al. 2017).

The basis for our simulations is the Supplemental Poverty Measure released by the Census Bureau and the Bureau of Labor Statistics. The SPM is the result of decades of scholarly work designed to improve the measurement of income poverty in the United States (Citro and Michael 1995; Short 2015). Details of the measure can be found elsewhere (for the latest detailed methodology, see Short 2015); briefly, the SPM is an improvement over official statistics in at least four key respects: its poverty thresholds are based on contemporary patterns of living standards and expenditures on a core basket of necessities; it uses a broader definition of the family unit that includes cohabiters, foster children, and some unrelated children alongside family members related by blood, marriage, or adoption; it uses poverty thresholds that vary by housing status and geographic differences in the cost of living; and it uses a broader definition of resources, which accounts for after-tax income, the value of in-kind benefits like food stamps and housing assistance, and the deduction of out-of-pocket expenses on necessities like work, childcare, and medical care. This last improvement is most critical for the current analysis because it is the foundation of our child poverty estimates that more fully account for the total resources available to families with children. This is because official statistics simply ignore resources coming from anti-poverty programs that work through the tax system or take the form of near-cash (or in-kind) benefits.

To simulate the effects of a universal child allowance, we first assign annual child allowance income values to all children meeting key age criteria. For example, under a universal $250 per month child allowance, we would assign $3,000 to every child in the microdata up to age seventeen. Under a mixed model, children under age six receiving $300 per month and older children $250, we assign all children age six through seventeen $3,000 and all children from birth to age five $3,600. We then total this income within SPM family units and assign it to all members of the SPM family. Because we envision that the child allowance would replace the CTC and ACTC, we also zero out the total values of both programs.

We then assume that income from the child allowance, which is universal, would be taxed like any other source of income. To accomplish this in the microdata, we apply the marginal tax rate of the tax filer provided by the census tax calculator to the new income assigned to the family. We then recalculate family income by adding the value of the taxed-back child allowance and subtracting the old values of the CTC and ACTC, and compare this recalculated family income to the SPM poverty thresholds in the data. In one of our simulations, we also apply an equivalence scale to the benefit before taxing it back and recalculating poverty rates. The equivalence scale we adopt is: (number of children in the SPM unit)^07.

REFERENCES

Aizer, Anna, Shari Eli, Joseph Ferrie, and Adriana Lleras-Muney. 2016. "The Long Run Impact of Cash Transfers to Poor Families." *American Economic Review* 106(4): 935–71.

Akee, Randall K. Q., William E. Copeland, Gordon Keeler, Adrian Angold, and E. Jane Costello. 2010. "Parents' Incomes and Children's Outcomes: A Quasi-Experiment Using Transfer Payments from Casino Profits." *American Economic Journal: Applied Economics* 2(1): 86–115.

Almond, Douglas, Janet Currie, and Valentina Duque. 2017. "Childhood Circumstances and Adult Outcomes: Act II." *NBER* working paper no. 23017. Cambridge, Mass.: National Bureau of Economic Research. Accessed September 22, 2017. http://www.nber.org/papers/w23017.

Anyaegbu, Grace. 2010. "Using the OECD Equivalence Scale in Taxes and Benefits Analysis." *Labour Gazette* 4(1): 49–54.

Banerjee, Abhijit, Esther Duflo, Nathanael Goldberg, Dean Karlan, Robert Osei, William Parienté, Jeremy Shapiro, Bram Thuysbaert, and Christopher Udry. 2015. "A Multifaceted Program Causes Lasting Progress for the Very Poor: Evidence from Six Countries." *Science* 348(6236). doi: 1260799.

Becker, Gary S. 1991. *A Treatise on the Family*. Cambridge, Mass.: Harvard University Press.

Bitler, Marianne P., Annie Laurie Hines, and Marianne Page. 2018. "Cash for Kids." *RSF: The Russell Sage Foundation Journal of the Social Sciences* 4(2): 43–73. DOI: 10.7758/RSF.2018.4.2.03.

Brown, Susan L. 2006. "Family Structure Transitions and Adolescent Well-Being." *Demography* 43(3): 447–61.

Brownell, Marni D., Mariette J. Chartier, Nathan C. Nickel, Dan Chateau, Patricia J. Martens, Joykrishna Sarkar, Elaine Burland, Douglas P. Jutte, Carole Taylor, Robert G. Santos, and Alan Katz. 2016. "Unconditional Prenatal Income Supplements and Birth Outcomes." *Pediatrics* 137(6): 1–11.

Buhmann, Brigitte, Lee Rainwater, Guenther Schmaus, and Timothy M. Smeeding. 1988. "Equivalence Scales, Well-Being, Inequality, and Poverty: Sensitivity Estimates Across Ten Countries Using the Luxembourg Income Study (LIS) Database." *Review of Income and Wealth* 34(2) (June): 115–42.

Butcher, Kristin F. 2016. "Assessing the Long-Run Benefits of Transfers to Low-Income Families." Paper presented at the Hutchins Center event "From Bridges to Education: Bet Bets for Public Investment," Brookings Institution, Washington, D.C. (January 9, 2016). Accessed September 20, 2017. https://www.brookings.edu/research/assessing-the-long-run-benefits-of-transfers-to-low-income-families/.

Center on the Developing Child. 2016. Harvard University. Accessed November 17, 2017. http://developingchild.harvard.edu.

Choi, Laura. 2009. "Financial Stress and Its Physical Effects on Individuals and Communities." *Community Development Investment Review* 5(3): 120–22.

Citro, Constance F., and Robert T. Michael, eds. 1995. *Measuring Poverty: A New Approach*. Washington, D.C.: National Academy Press.

Conger, Rand D., Lora E. Wallace, Yumei Sun, Ronald L. Simons, Vonnie C. McLoyd, and Gene H. Brody. 2002. "Economic Pressure in African American Families: A Replication and Extension of the Family Stress Model." *Developmental Psychology* 38(2): 179–93.

Costello, E. Jane, Scott N. Compton, Gordon Keeler, and Adrian Angold. 2003. "Relationship Between Poverty and Psyschopathology: A Natural Experiment." *Journal of the American Medical Association* 290(15): 2023–29.

Dahl, Gordon B., and Lance Lochner. 2012. "The Impact of Family Income on Child Achievement: Evidence from the Earned Income Tax Credit." *American Economic Review* 102(5): 1927–56.

Desmond, Matthew. 2016. *Evicted: Poverty and Profit in the American City*. New York: Crown.

Doom, Jenalee R., Adrienne Vanzomeren-Dohm, and Jeffry A. Simpson. 2016. "Early Unpredictability Predicts Increased Adolescent Externalizing Behaviors and Substance Use: A Life History Perspective." *Development and Psychopathology* 28(4): 1505–16.

Duncan, Greg J., and Jeanne Brooks-Gunn, eds. 1997. *Consequences of Growing Up Poor*. New York: Russell Sage Foundation.

Duncan, Greg J., Katherine Magnuson, and Elizabeth Votruba-Drzal. 2014. "Boosting Family Income to

Promote Child Development." *Future of Children* 24(1): 99–120.

Duncan, Greg J., Pamela A. Morris, and Chris Rodrigues. 2011. "Does Money Really Matter? Estimating Impacts of Family Income on Young Children's Achievement with Data from Random-Assignment Experiments." *Developmental Psychology* 47(5): 1263–79.

Duncan, Greg J., and Richard J. Murnane, eds. 2011. *Whither Opportunity?: Rising Inequality, Schools, and Children's Life Chances: Rising Inequality, Schools, and Children's Life Chances*. New York: Russell Sage Foundation/Spencer Foundation.

Edin Kathryn, and Laura Lein. 1997. "Work, Welfare, and Single Mothers' Economic Survival Strategies." *American Sociological Review* 62(2): 253–66.

Edin, Kathryn, and H. Luke Shaefer. 2015. *$2.00 a Day: Living on Almost Nothing in America*. Boston, Mass.: Houghton Mifflin Harcourt.

———. 2016. "Q&A on $2.00 a Day." *$2 a Day*. Accessed September 22, 2017. http://www.twodollarsaday.com/resources/.

Evans, William N., and Craig L. Garthwaite. 2014. "Giving Mom a Break: The Impact of Higher EITC Payments on Maternal Health." *American Economic Journal: Economic Policy* 6(2): 258–90.

Evans, William N., James X. Sullivan, and Melanie Wallskog. 2016. "The Impact of Homelessness Prevention Programs on Homelessness." *Science* 353(6300): 694–99.

Flood, Sarah, Miriam King, Steven Ruggles, and J. Robert Warren. 2017. Integrated Public Use Microdata Series, Current Population Survey: Version 5.0. [dataset]. Minneapolis: University of Minnesota. DOI: 10.18128/D030.V5.0.

Floyd, Ife, LaDonna Pavetti, and Liz Schott. 2017. "TANF Reaching Few Poor Families." Washington, D.C.: Center on Budget and Policy Priorities. Accessed November 17, 2017. http://www.cbpp.org/sites/default/files/atoms/files/6-16-15tanf.pdf.

Fox, Liana, Christopher Wimer, Irwin Garfinkel, Neeraj Kaushal, and Jane Waldfogel. 2015. "Waging War on Poverty: Poverty Trends Using a Historical Supplemental Poverty Measure." *Journal of Policy Analysis and Management* 34(3): 567–92.

Garfinkel, Irwin, David Harris, Jane Waldfogel, and Christopher Wimer. 2016. "Doing More for Our Children: Modeling a Universal Child Allowance or More Generous Child Tax Credit." New York: The Century Foundation, Bernard L. Schwartz Rediscovering Government Initiative. Accessed September 22, 2017. https://s3-us-west-2.amazonaws.com/production.tcf.org/app/uploads/2016/03/16013632/DoingMoreForOurChildren_Final.pdf.

Garfinkel, Irwin, Sara McLanahan, and Christopher Wimer. 2016. *Children of the Great Recession*. New York: Russell Sage Foundation.

Garfinkel, Irwin, Lee Rainwater, and Timothy M. Smeeding. 2010. *Wealth and Welfare States: Is America a Laggard or Leader?* Oxford: Oxford University Press.

Gennetian, Lisa A., and Eldar Shafir. 2015. "The Persistence of Poverty in the Context of Financial Instability: A Behavioral Perspective." *Journal of Policy Analysis and Management* 34(4): 904–36.

Goldin, Claudia D., and Lawrence F. Katz. 2009. *The Race Between Education and Technology*. Cambridge, Mass.: Harvard University Press.

Hair, Nicole L., Jamie L. Hanson, Barbara L. Wolfe, and Seth D. Pollak. 2015. "Association of Child Poverty, Brain Development, and Academic Achievement." *JAMA Pediatrics* 169(9): 822–29.

Halpern-Meekin, Sarah, Kathryn Edin, Laura Tach, and Jennifer Sykes. 2015. *It's Not Like I'm Poor: How Low Income Parents Make Ends Meet in a Post Welfare World*. Berkeley: University of California Press.

Hammond, Samuel, and Robert Orr. 2016. "Toward a Universal Child Benefit." Washington, D.C.: Niskanen Center. Accessed September 22, 2017. https://niskanencenter.org/wp-content/uploads/2016/10/UniversalChildBenefit_final.pdf.

Harris, David B. 2012. "The Child Tax Credit: How the United States Underinvests in Its Youngest Children in Cash Assistance and How Changes to the Child Tax Credit Could Help." Ph.D. diss., Columbia University School of Social Work. Accessed November 17, 2017. http://academiccommons.columbia.edu/catalog/ac%3A175200.

Haushofer, Johannes, and Jeremy Shapiro 2016. "The Short-Term Impact of Unconditional Cash Transfers to the Poor: Experimental Evidence from Kenya." *Quarterly Journal of Economics* 131(4): 1973–2042.

Holzer, Harry J., Diane W. Schanzenbach, Greg J. Duncan, and Jens Ludwig. 2008. "The Economic Costs of Childhood Poverty in the United States." *Journal of Children and Poverty* 14(1): 41–61.

Hoynes, Hilary, and Ankur J. Patel. 2015. "Effective Policy for Reducing Inequality? The Earned Income Tax Credit and the Distribution of Income." *NBER* working paper no. 21340. Cambridge, Mass.: National Bureau of Economic Research.

Hoynes, Hilary, Diane Whitmore Schanzenbach, and Douglas Almond. 2016. "Long-Run Impacts of Childhood Access to the Safety Net." *American Economic Review* 106(4): 903–34.

Isaacs, Julia, Sara Edelstein, Heather Hahn, Ellen Steele, and C. Eugene Steuerle. 2016. "Kids' Share 2016: Report on Federal Expenditures on Children in 2015 and Future Projections." Washington, D.C.: Urban Institute.

Jacobs, Elisabeth, and Jacob Hacker. 2008. "The Rising Instability of American Family Income, 1969–2004." *EPI* briefing paper no. 213. Washington, D.C. Economic Policy Institute. Accessed September 22, 2017. http://www.epi.org/publication/bp213/.

Jencks, Christopher. 2016. "Why Have the Very Poor Become Poorer?" *New York Review of Books*, June 9. Accessed September 22, 2017. http://www.nybooks.com/articles/2016/06/09/why-the-very-poor-have-become-poorer/.

Kaushal, Neeraj, Katherine Magnuson, and Jane Waldfogel. 2011. "How Is Family Income Related to Investments in Children's Learning?" In *Whither Opportunity*, edited by Greg J. Duncan and Richard J. Murnane. New York: Russell Sage Foundation/Spencer Foundation.

Kessler, Ronald C., and Paul D. Cleary. 1980. "Social Class and Psychological Distress." *American Sociological Review* 45(3): 463–78.

Lugo-Gil, Julieta, and Hirokazu Yoshikawa. 2006. "Assessing Expenditures on Children in Low-Income, Ethnically Diverse and Immigrant Families." National Poverty Center Working Paper Series no. 06–36. Ann Arbor: University of Michigan.

Mani, Anandi, Sendhil Mullainathan, Eldar Shafir, and Jiaying Zhao. 2013. "Poverty Impedes Cognitive Function." *Science* 341(6149): 976–80.

Marmot, Michael Sharon Friel, Ruth Bell, Tanja A. Houweling, and Sebastian Taylor. 2008. "Closing the Gap in a Generation: Health Equity Through Action on the Social Determinants of Health." *The Lancet* 372(9650): 1661–69.

Marr, Chuck, Chye-Ching Huang, Arloc Sherman, and Brandon Debot. 2015. "EITC and Child Tax Credit Promote Work, Reduce Poverty, Support Children's Development, Research Finds." Washington, D.C.: Center on Budget and Policy Priorities. Accessed September 22, 2017. https://www.cbpp.org/sites/default/files/atoms/files/6-26-12tax.pdf.

Matthews, Dylan 2016. "Sweden Pays Parents for Having Kids—And It Reaps Huge Benefits. Why Doesn't the US?" *Vox*, May 23. Accessed September 22, 2017. https://www.vox.com/2016/5/23/11440638/child-benefit-child-allowance.

Maynard, Rebecca A. 1977. "The Effects of the Rural Income Maintenance Experiment on the School Performance of Children." *American Economic Review* 67(1): 370–75.

Maynard, Rebecca A., and Richard J. Murnane. 1979. "The Effects of a Negative Income Tax on School Performance: Results of an Experiment." *Journal of Human Resources* 14(4): 463–76.

McLoyd, Vonnie C. 1990. "The Impact of Economic Hardship on Black Families and Children: Psychological Distress, Parenting, and Socioemotional Development." *Child Development* 61(2): 311–46.

Meadows, Sarah O., Sara S. McLanahan, and Jeanne Brooks-Gunn. 2008. "Stability and Change in Family Structure and Maternal Health Trajectories." *American Sociological Review* 73(2): 314–34.

Meyer, Bruce D., and James X. Sullivan. 2012. "Identifying the Disadvantaged: Official Poverty, Consumption Poverty, and the New Supplemental Poverty Measure." *Journal of Economic Perspectives* 26(3): 111–36.

Miller, Cynthia, Rhiannon Miller, Nandita Verma, Nadine Dechausay, Edith Yang, Timothy Rudd, Jonathan Rodriguez, and Sylvie Honig. 2016. *Effects of a Modified Conditional Cash Transfer Program in Two American Cities: Findings from Family Rewards 2.0*. New York: MDRC. Accessed September 22, 2017. http://www.mdrc.org/sites/default/files/CEOSIF_Family_Rewards%20Report-Web-Final_FR.pdf.

Milligan, Kevin, and Mark Stabile. 2011. "Do Child Tax Benefits Affect the Well-Being of Children? Evidence from Canadian Child Benefit Expansions." *American Economic Journal: Economic Policy* 3(3): 175–205.

Moffitt, Robert A. 2015. "The Deserving Poor, the Family, and the U.S. Welfare System." *Demography* 52(3): 729–49.

Morduch, Jonathan, and Rachel Schneider. 2017. *How American Families Cope in a World of Un-*

certainty. Princeton, N.J.: Princeton University Press.

Morris, Pamela, Greg J. Duncan, and Elizabeth Clark-Kauffman. 2005. "Child Well-Being in an Era of Welfare Reform: The Sensitivity of Transitions in Development to Policy Change." *Developmental Psychology* 41(2005): 919–32.

Muennig, Peter A., Babak Mohit, Jinging Wu, Haomiao Jia, and Zohn Rosen. 2016. "Cost Effectiveness of the Earned Income Tax Credit as a Health Policy Investment." *American Journal of Preventive Medicine* 51(6): 874–81.

Mullainathan, Sendhil, and Eldar Shafir. 2013. *Scarcity: Why Having Too Little Means So Much*. New York: Henry Holt and Company.

Nelson, Charles A., and Margaret A. Sheridan. 2011. "Lessons from Neuroscience Research for Understanding Causal Links Between Family and Neighborhood Characteristics and Educational Outcomes." In *Whither Opportunity*, edited by Greg J. Duncan and Richard J. Murnane. New York: Russell Sage Foundation/Spencer Foundation.

Nichols, Austin, and Jesse Rothstein. 2016. "The Earned Income Tax Credit." In *Economics of Means-Tested Transfer Programs in the United States*, vol. 1, edited by Robert A. Moffitt. Chicago: University of Chicago Press.

Noble, Kimberly G., Laura E. Engelhardt, Natalie H. Brito, Luke J. Mack, Elizabeth J. Nail, Jyoti Angal, Rachel Barr, William P. Fifer, and Amy J. Elliott. 2015. "Socioeconomic Disparities in Neurocognitive Development in the First Two Years of Life." *Developmental Psychobiology* 57(5): 535–51.

Noble, Kimberly G., Suzanne M. Houston, Natalie H. Brito, Hauke Bartsch, Eric Kan, Joshua M. Kuperman, Natacha Akshoomoff, et al. 2015. "Family Income, Parental Education and Brain Structure in Children and Adolescents." *Nature Neuroscience* 18(5): 773–78.

Organization for Economic Co-operation and Development (OECD). 2016. "Income Distribution Database (IDD): Gini, Poverty, Income, Methods and Concepts." Accessed September 22, 1017. http://www.oecd.org/social/income-distribution-database.htm.

Osborne, Cynthia, Lawrence M. Berger, Katherine Magnuson. 2012. "Family Structure Transitions and Changes in Maternal Resources and Well-Being." *Demography* 49(1): 23–47.

Rojas, Neerja, Hirokazu Yoshikawa, Mayra L. Rangel, S. Melvin, Lisa A. Gennetian, Kimberly Noble, Greg J. Duncan, and Katherine Magnuson. forthcoming. "The Experiences of an Unconditional Cash Transfer Among Low-Income Mothers of Infants: An Experimental, Mixed-Methods Study." Manuscript under review.

Rosenblum, Leonard A., and Michael W. Andrews. 1994. "Influences of Environmental Demand on Maternal Behavior and Infant Development." *Acta Paediatrica* 83(s397): 57–63.

Rosenblum, Leonard A., and Gayle S. Paully. 1984. "The Effects of Varying Environmental Demands on Maternal and Infant Behavior." *Child Development* 55(1): 305–14.

Sandstrom, Heather, and Sandra Huerta. 2013. "The Negative Effects of Instability on Child Development: A Research Synthesis." Washington, D.C.: Urban Institute.

Shaefer, H. Luke, and Kathryn Edin. 2013. "Rising Extreme Poverty in the United States and the Response of Federal Means-Tested Transfers." *Social Service Review* 87(2): 250–68.

Shonkoff, Jack P., Andrew S. Garner, Benjamin S. Siegel, Mary I. Dobbins, et al. 2012. "The Lifelong Effects of Early Childhood Adversity and Toxic Stress." *Pediatrics* 129(1): e232–46.

Short, Kathleen. 2015. "The Supplemental Poverty Measure: 2014." *Current Population Reports*, series P60, no. 254. Washington: Government Printing Office for U.S. Census Bureau.

Smeeding, Timothy M., and C. Thevenot. 2016. "Addressing Child Poverty: How Does the United States Compare with Other Nations?" *Academic Pediatrics* (3 Suppl): S67–75.

Strully, Kate W., David H. Rehkopf, and Ziming Xuan. 2010. "Effects of Prenatal Poverty on Infant Health: State Earned Income Tax Credits and Birth Weight." *American Sociological Review* 75(4): 534–62.

Tax Policy Center. 2016. "Options to Repeal the Child Tax Credit and Exemption for Dependents (July 2016)." Washington, D.C.: Urban Institute and Brookings Institution. Accessed November 17, 2017. http://www.taxpolicycenter.org/simulations/options-repeal-child-tax-credit-and-exemption-dependents-july-2016.

Votruba-Drzal, Elizabeth. 2006. "Economic Disparities in Middle Childhood Development: Does Income Matter?" *Developmental Psychology* 42(6): 1154–67.

Wimer, Christopher, Liana Fox, Irwin Garfinkel,

Neeraj Kaushal, and Jane Waldfogel. 2016. "Progress on Poverty? New Estimates of Historical Trends Using an Anchored Supplemental Poverty Measure." *Demography* 53(4): 1207–18.

Wimer, Christopher, and Timothy M. Smeeding. 2016. "U.S.A. Child Poverty: The Impact of the Great Recession." In *Children of Austerity: Impact of the Great Recession on Child Poverty in Rich Countries*, edited by Bea Cantillon, Yekaterina Chzhen, Sudhanshu Handa, and Brian Nolan. Oxford: Oxford University Press.

Wolfe, Barbara, Jessica Jakubowski, Robert Haveman, and Marissa Courey. 2012. "The Income and Health Effects of Tribal Casino Gaming on American Indians." *Demography* 49(2): 499–524.

Yoshikawa, Hirokazu, J. Lawrence Aber, and William R. Beardslee. 2012. "The Effects of Poverty on the Mental, Emotional, and Behavioral Health of Children and Youth: Implications for Prevention." *American Psychologist* 67(4): 272–84.

Ziol-Guest, Kathleen. M., Greg J. Duncan, Ariel Kalil, and W. Thomas Boyce. 2012. "Early Childhood Poverty, Immune-Mediated Disease Processes, and Adult Productivity." *Proceedings of the National Academy of Sciences* 109 Suppl.: 17289–93.

Cash for Kids

MARIANNE P. BITLER, ANNIE LAURIE HINES, AND MARIANNE PAGE

Although a growing number of studies suggest that providing poor families with income supplements of as little as $1,000 per year will improve children's well-being, many poor children miss important sources of income support provided through the tax system because their parents either do not work or do not file taxes. Accessing assistance through means-tested programs is also challenging. We propose replacing the complicated array of benefits provided through the tax system with a universal child benefit of $2,000 per child that would be available regardless of parents' work status. Our reform would ensure that all children receive enough assistance to make a difference and it would be simpler and more equitable than the current array of child benefits that are provided through the tax code.

Keywords: poverty, universal income, tax expenditures, children, EITC, CTC, exemptions

It is well known that children who live in poor families are at a substantially higher risk of growing up to be poor adults than those who grow up in more advantaged families. Wagmiller and Adelman for example, document that adults who experienced at least one year of poverty during childhood are more than ten times as likely to be poor at age thirty-five as those whose families were never poor (2009). Moreover, there are worrying signs that poor children's chances for long-run success are worsening: recent studies indicate that educational achievement gaps between poor and non-poor children have been widening over time (Reardon 2011; Bailey and Dynarski 2011). For example, Sean Reardon documents that in the forty years between 1968 and 2008, the achievement gap between high- and low-income children increased by about 50 percent. Academic performance is an important

---

Marianne P. Bitler is professor of economics at the University of California, Davis, and research associate at the National Bureau of Economic Research. **Annie Laurie Hines** is a graduate student in economics at the University of California, Davis. **Marianne Page** is professor of economics and director of the Center for Poverty Research at the University of California, Davis, and research associate at the National Bureau of Economic Research.

© 2018 Russell Sage Foundation. Bitler, Marianne P., Annie Laurie Hines, and Marianne Page. 2018. "Cash for Kids." *RSF: The Russell Sage Foundation Journal of the Social Sciences* 4(2): 43–73. DOI: 10.7758/RSF.2018.4.2.03. We thank Hilary Hoynes and Elira Kuka for sharing code from joint work with Marianne P. Bitler related to use of SOI and CPS data (Bitler, Hoynes, and Kuka 2017). Direct correspondence to: Marianne P. Bitler at bitler@ucdavis.edu, Department of Economics, University of California, Davis, One Shields Ave., Davis, CA 95616; Marianne Page at mepage@ucdavis.edu, Department of Economics, University of California, Davis, One Shields Ave., Davis, CA 95616; and Annie Laurie Hines at ahines@ucdavis.edu, Department of Economics, University of California, Davis, One Shields Ave., Davis, CA 95616.

Open Access Policy: *RSF: The Russell Sage Foundation Journal of the Social Sciences* is an open access journal. This article is published under a Creative Commons Attribution-NonCommercial-NoDerivs 3.0 Unported License.

predictor of future economic success, so these trends point toward higher levels of immobility in the future, particularly when coupled with the increases in income inequality that current generations of parents have experienced.

Although evidence is long-standing that family income during childhood predicts adult income, it is only recently that we have begun to understand the causal mechanisms behind this correlation. The increasing availability of large administrative datasets and the adoption of creative natural experiment analysis approaches have allowed social scientists to come closer to emulating randomized control experimental designs, which are the gold standard for causal inference but have been rare in the study of income disparities. These advances are critical to the development of effective anti-poverty policies: without them, it is impossible to know how much of the difference in children's outcomes is driven by differences in monetary resources versus other family background characteristics or circumstances that are correlated with parental income. Careful quasi-experimental studies consistently show that providing low-income families with sustained financial aid improves both short-run measures of children's well-being and their eventual labor market and health outcomes. The studies include analyses that exploit negative shocks to income, such as those precipitated by unanticipated job loss, and analyses that harness positive boosts to family income that are generated through the U.S. safety net and tax system.

The rapidly expanding evidence that "money matters" suggests that we may be able to improve poor children's opportunities by increasing existing levels of cash assistance. Providing higher levels of cash assistance may also be an economically sensible investment because the ensuing improvements in children's later labor market and health outcomes are likely to reduce later public expenditures on welfare and health care. Moreover, economic theory asserts that direct cash aid should dominate many other forms of government assistance because cash aid maximizes poor families' flexibility in choosing child investments that will have the highest payoff to the family.

Twenty years after the passage of the Personal Responsibility and Work Opportunity Reconciliation Act (PRWORA), however, the majority of means-tested cash assistance to the nondisabled is delivered only to families in which an adult is employed. As discussed in the introduction to this issue, cash benefits provided through the Temporary Assistance for Needy Families (TANF) program have declined dramatically, and are now frequently tied to parental work effort. Furthermore, approximately half of the financial assistance that is available to able-bodied parents is generated through their tax returns, and tied to positive earnings. Children whose parents are unable or unwilling to find work cannot receive the refundable part of the Child Tax Credit (CTC) or the earnings subsidies that are provided through the Earned Income Tax Credit (EITC). Moreover, many low-income parents who do work and are eligible for these credits do not receive them because they have difficulties navigating the tax code or fail to file taxes altogether. Families who do not file taxes also fail to receive assistance that is available through the tax code's dependent exemptions. In addition, many families who are eligible for near-cash benefits available through programs like the Supplemental Nutrition Assistance Program (SNAP) do not take them up because of difficulties or stigma associated with accessing welfare programs. Taken together, this means that a nontrivial number of children who would gain from additional monetary resources are not currently receiving them. For example, in data from the 2014 calendar year Current Population Survey (CPS) Annual Social and Economic Supplement (ASEC), 10 percent of families with children under eighteen received no benefits from tax exemptions, the EITC, or the CTC. Six percent of families also did not get benefits through either the tax system or SNAP.

In this article, we review the rapidly expanding evidence on the causal relationship between family income and children's short and long-term well-being. We then propose a new lump-sum child benefit that does not require a family to file taxes and would be available to all families with citizen children, regardless of their parents' work status. Our proposal targets citizen children because they are easy to track through existing administrative systems.[1] As we describe later, however, the child benefit could be extended to some noncitizen children through the same systems. Current research suggests that an annual benefit of approximately $2,000 per child would generate meaningful improvements in children's well-being and life chances, and may have multiple advantages over the current array of cash assistance programs. It could also be implemented so as to be revenue neutral by replacing the child-related credits and exemptions that are part of the tax code. This would enable policymakers to avoid political economy challenges associated with funding new programs and would have the added benefit of separating the goals of equalizing children's life chances from the goal of incentivizing adults' participation in the labor market. One concern with our approach might be that a fixed grant would reduce work effort. Therefore, we discuss how variants of our proposal with different expected effects on parental work effort would be likely to affect the distribution of income across poor and near-poor children.

FAMILY INCOME AND CHILDREN'S SHORT- AND LONG-TERM WELL-BEING

Fifteen years ago, we knew that poor children were at relatively greater risk of experiencing a host of negative outcomes that include lower levels of educational attainment, higher rates of criminal involvement, and higher rates of mental illness (see, for example, Brooks-Gunn and Duncan 1997; Moore et al. 2009). We have also long known that poor children show notable compromises in the development of their cognitive and social-emotional skills (Bradley and Corwyn 2002; Brooks-Gunn and Duncan 1997; Farah et al. 2006; Noble, McCandliss, and Farah 2007; Evans and Cassells 2014; Yoshikawa, Aber, and Beardslee 2012). These outcomes in turn predict lower likelihood of labor market success and higher likelihood of poverty in adulthood. Consistent with these predictions, some studies have documented high rates of intergenerational income and poverty persistence (Solon 1992; Zimmerman 1992; Chetty et al. 2014). The article by Luke Shaefer and his colleagues in this issue (2018) also describes many other studies that have linked family income with a variety of measures of children's short and longer-term well-being.

Until recently, however, we knew less about why these relationships existed. It has been unclear, for example, how much of the persistence in poverty across generations reflects the causal effect of growing up in a family with compromised monetary resources versus the effect of family background characteristics or neighborhood environments that are often correlated with low income. Fortunately, recent research developments have allowed social scientists to pinpoint important pathways that were previously difficult to identify with any clarity. Researchers have become increasingly adept at applying statistical and econometric methods that help separate causal effects from potentially confounding correlations. Moreover, improved access to large administrative datasets has provided opportunities to successfully apply these methods yet maintain statistical precision. Careful quasi-experimental and experimental studies harnessing these research advances show that changing the amount of money consistently available to families can directly affect child well-being and children's later life success.

One set of studies uses unanticipated parental job displacements generated by mass layoffs and firm closures to examine the effects on children of a plausibly exogenous decline in family income. Mass layoffs are determined at the firm level, so job losses that are precipitated by such events are unlikely to be related to individual characteristics that independently affect children.[2] Moreover, as is well known, these types of job displacements lead to substantial, persistent earnings declines (for a review of the literature, see von Wachter 2010). Steven Davis and Till von Wachter, for example, find that

---

1. Roughly 97 percent of children in the United States are citizens.

2. Recent work by Nathaniel Hilger questions this assumption (2016). Using an identification strategy that further accounts for individual characteristics, he still finds evidence that parental job loss has a small effect on children's educational attainment, however.

men with more than three years of prior job tenure at larger firms, who lose their jobs in a mass layoff, experience annual present value earnings reductions of about 12 percent in an average year (2011).[3]

Studies that compare children whose parents experienced an unanticipated job loss with similar children whose parents were able to maintain their jobs find that those with displaced parents have worse measures of early life health (Lindo 2010) and academic achievement (Coelli 2005; Stevens and Schaller 2011; Hilger 2016). Moreover, there is evidence that these impacts persist to later life labor market success. Using Canadian tax data, Philip Oreopoulos, Marianne Page, and Ann Stevens find that children whose fathers experienced a job displacement have adult earnings that are about 9 percent lower than children whose fathers did not experience an employment shock (2008). They are also more likely to receive social assistance. Importantly, these effects are driven by individuals whose parents were at the bottom of the income distribution: among those children whose father's earnings were initially in the lowest quartile, subsequent earnings are 17 percent lower than predicted if their father had not been displaced.[4]

These impacts on short- and long-term measures of child well-being may result directly from parents' compromised ability to invest in their children, but another potential pathway is through increases in family stress. Psychologists, neuroscientists, and economists have documented that economic stress has deleterious effects on mental health and family functioning, which may in turn affect children's outcomes (Aizer, Stroud, and Buka 2016; Conger, Conger, and Elder 1997; Conger et al. 1994; Cutrona et al. 2003; McLoyd 1998; Conger 2011; Evans and Garthwaite 2014; Reeb, Conger, and Martin 2013; Santiago, Wadsworth and Stump 2011). Recent work by Mullainathan and Shafir 2013 also documents that income volatility combined with scarcity can have psychological impacts that make it difficult for parents to escape poverty and to parent effectively.

Fortunately, evidence is also strong that the negative effects of income deprivation can be counteracted by policies that provide cash or near-cash assistance. Leveraging variation in family income generated by the 1990s welfare-reform experiments, Greg Duncan, Pamela Morris, and Chris Rodriques find that a $1,000 increase in family income increases children's achievement test scores by around 5 percent of a standard deviation (2011). Aletha Huston and her colleagues examine the New Hope experiment, which provided wage subsidies to full-time workers that were sufficient to raise family income above the poverty threshold along with childcare subsidies and health insurance (2001). They find that this combination of factors led to substantive improvements in both school performance and social outcomes that were concentrated among boys.

Perhaps most encouraging is what we have learned from careful quasi-experimental studies of the two primary cash and near-cash assistance programs currently available to children in the United States: the Earned Income Tax Credit, which provides cash refunds to working families through the tax system, and the Supplemental Nutrition Assistance Program formerly known as Food Stamps, which provides vouchers that can be redeemed for food.[5] The EITC was created in 1975 and currently provides a refundable tax credit to low-income working families through the tax system. Adults twenty-five and older without children are eligible for a small transfer, but a larger credit is available to families with children. Following a substantial expansion that took effect from 1993 to 1995, the maximum value of EITC benefits roughly doubled. In 2013, the EITC reached more than 21.6 million families with children, providing over $66 billion in benefits. These transfers are substantive: the

---

3. Mass layoffs have also been found to negatively affect adult health (Sullivan and von Wachter 2009); parental health may in turn affect children's outcomes.

4. Although Nathaniel Hilger does not find significant effects on later life earnings, his analyses focus on very young men, those under age twenty-five (2016).

5. Vouchers are currently provided through electronic benefit cards.

average EITC benefit received by a family with two children in 2013 was $3,667.[6]

Several studies exploit the mid-1990s expansions of the Earned Income Tax Credit to create treatment and control groups of children who were living in otherwise similar families but received different income boosts because of when and where they were living or the size of the family in which they lived. Hilary Hoynes, Douglas Miller, and David Simon find that a $1,000 increase in income reduces the probability that a newborn is below the low birth weight threshold (2,500 grams) by 2 to 3 percent (2015). Kate Strully, David Rehkopf, and Ziming Xuan find that in states that adopted EITCs during the 1990s, the average birthweight of infants born to unmarried women with a high school degree or less increased by about sixteen grams (2010). These findings are important in part because birthweight predicts later life economic success: Sandra Black, Paul Devereux, and Kjell Salvanes estimate that a 10 percent increase in birthweight increases later life earnings by 1 percent (2007). A related study using variation across years in predicted EITC income finds that a $1,000 increase in family income raises a child's math and reading test scores by 6 percent of a standard deviation (Dahl and Lochner 2012.[7] Test score increases of this magnitude are also associated with substantive improvements in later life labor market outcomes: based on their review of the literature on the returns to school achievement, Patrick Kline and Christopher Walters suggest that one standard deviation increase in test scores likely generates an increase in earnings of at least 10 percent (2016).[8] Indeed, a related study finds that adolescent exposure to the EITC improves later life education, employment and earnings outcomes (Bastian and Michelmore 2016). In their article in this issue, Shaefer and his colleagues (2018) also provide a review of the EITC literature.

The SNAP program provides vouchers to families that can be used to purchase food in grocery stores. In 2014, vouchers were received by 46.5 million people at a cost of $74.1 billion and average monthly benefits were $257 per household (Hoynes and Schanzenbach 2016). The amount of the voucher is intentionally low enough that it does not fully cover food purchases in most households; as a result, many argue that it should be thought of as a program that effectively provides low-income families with near-cash assistance because most families would spend at least as much on food as their SNAP benefit.[9]

In a series of studies, Hoynes and Diane Schanzenbach (and often Douglas Almond) make use of geographic variation in the timing of the initial rollout of the Food Stamp Program in the 1960s and early 1970s to compare outcomes among similar children with differential exposure to the program because of when and where they were born. Almond, Hoynes and Schanzenbach find that prenatal exposure to the Food Stamp Program leads to higher average birth weight and lower neo-natal mortality (2011).[10] Relative to infants who did not have prenatal access, the incidence of low birth weight among exposed infants was about 7 percent lower for whites and 5 to 11 percent lower

6. Our calculations are based on tables 2.3, 2.5 and 3.3 of the Statistics of Income Individual Tax Tables (2013a).

7. Samuel Lundstrom finds a coding error in their study; fixing this reduces the magnitude of their findings by one-third (2017).

8. For a list of studies and their associated estimates, see Kline and Walters 2016, table A.IV. Their numbers are based on these assumptions: childhood family income at the poverty line is about 26 percent of average family earnings, average discounted lifetime earnings are $522,000 in 2010 dollars (Chetty et al. 2014), and the discount rate is 3 percent.

9. Some studies suggest that the marginal propensity to consume food out of SNAP benefits is higher than it would be if cash benefits were increased. For example, Beatty and Tuttle 2015 examine the ARRA-funded increase in SNAP benefits and find that recipients do not respond to increases in benefits in the way the neoclassical model predicts. Using roll out of the Food Stamp program, however, Hilary Hoynes and Diane Schanzenbach find evidence that Food Stamp benefits are treated by recipients like cash (2009).

10. Neo-natal mortality estimates are not often statistically significant.

for blacks. Using the same research design in a later study, Hoynes, Schanzenbach, and Almond also examined longer-term outcomes and find that disadvantaged children with full access to the Food Stamp program from conception to age five experienced a 0.3 standard deviation reduction in metabolic syndrome (2016).[11] Disadvantaged girls who were fully exposed during the first five years of life were also 0.2 standard deviations more likely to be self-sufficient in adulthood than those who did not have access (p-value was .14). Hoynes and her colleagues conclude that the increase in self-sufficiency and decrease in metabolic syndrome are largely driven by the effect of early life Food Stamp access on educational attainment (2016). Using the Continuous Work History Sample and rollout dates from Hoynes and Schanzenbach (2009), Marianne Bitler and Theodore Figinski find that for women born between 1955 and 1980, early life exposure to Food Stamps leads to small but statistically significant increases in earnings at age thirty-two (2017).

Using more recent program variation, Chloe East exploits changes in immigrant parents' eligibility for Food Stamps across states and over time that followed passage of PRWORA (2016). She focuses on U.S.-born children of immigrants whose mothers had at most a high school degree. She finds that an additional year of parental eligibility in early childhood reduces the chance that the child is reported to be in poor, fair or good health (versus very good or excellent health) by 6 percent.

These studies make it clear that the benefits of cash and near-cash assistance may go well beyond short-term improvements in early childhood well-being. The long-term benefits are also widespread and include improvements in both adult health and economic success. Cash assistance interventions may also have a higher return than a simple accounting exercise would suggest because the associated improvements in later life health and earnings will be associated with later reductions in public expenditures on health care and welfare.

CASH AND NEAR-CASH ASSISTANCE IN THE UNITED STATES

Despite evidence that cash and near-cash benefits that are provided through our existing safety net improve poor children's outcomes, a significant number of poor children do not receive them. Figure 1 plots household participation in TANF, the EITC and SNAP as a function of the ratio of private income to poverty thresholds, using a sample of non-elderly families from the Current Population Survey.[12] The figure makes clear that only families at the very bottom of the private income to poverty threshold distribution are getting cash assistance from TANF, and that even among the lowest income households, participation rates are very low: the TANF participation rate is below 15 percent in households with private income that is 50 percent of the poverty line, for example. SNAP and EITC participation rates are much higher and extend much further up the income to poverty distribution, yet even among the poorest households, SNAP participation rates do not exceed 60 percent.[13] The EITC is the only program for which participation among families with incomes near the poverty threshold

---

11. Their index of self-sufficiency is based on the individual's levels of education, earnings, poverty status and participation in public-assistance programs. Their index of metabolic syndrome is based on measures of obesity, high blood pressure, diabetes, heart attack, and heart disease.

12. Estimates are based on the 2010 March CPS. Private income includes all earnings and unearned private income but excludes all government transfers and net taxes. Participation estimates are based on local linear regressions where an indicator for household participation is regressed on the ratio of private income to poverty. Bruce Meyer, Wallace Mok, and James Sullivan document that underreporting of transfers in the CPS and other household surveys has worsened over time (2009). As a result, the figure might understate true participation rates. However, unless underreporting is higher at lower levels of income, the figure should be informative about the distribution of program spending across the income to poverty distribution. If underreporting is higher at the bottom, the differences across the distribution should be even starker.

13. This participation estimate includes families who are not eligible for SNAP, and is therefore lower than estimates of take-up rates. It is also possible, given recent increases in underreporting, that these values are some-

Figure 1. Kernel Density Plot, Program Participation

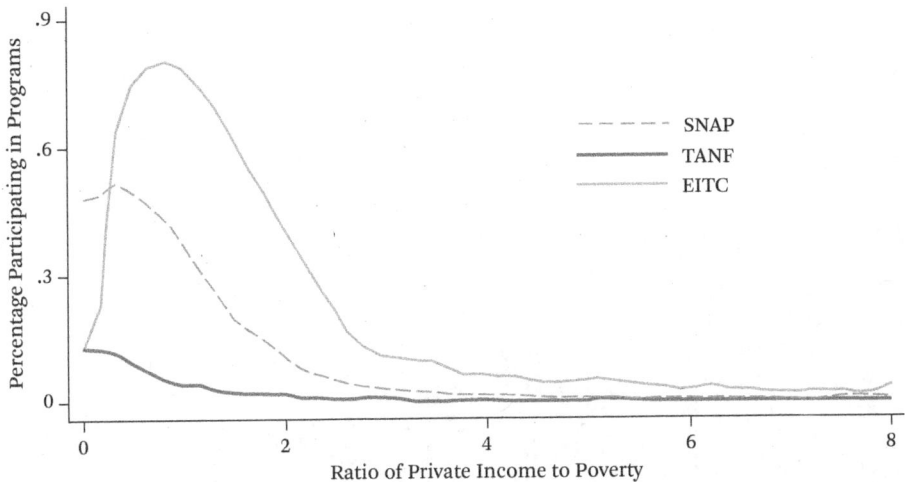

Source: Authors' compilation based on 2010 CPS ASEC data (U.S. Department of Commerce, Bureau of the Census, and U.S. Department of Labor, Bureau of Labor Statistics 2010).
Note: Local linear regressions of participation in various safety-net programs are presented as a function of the ratio of private income in the household to the household-level poverty threshold for the sample of non-elderly headed households, using the 2010 March CPS. Participation is depicted for the 2010 survey year, income having been reported for 2009. The bandwidth is 1/20 of the range of the private income to poverty threshold for those between 0 percent and 800 percent of poverty (as measured with private income).

exceeds 60 percent. The EITC also reaches many near-poor households, including many with private income to poverty ratios that exceed 200 percent, but program benefits are largely missed by those at the very bottom of the income distribution.[14]

Figure 2 shows the distribution of families with children whose private income is below 600 percent of the poverty line, across the private income-to-needs distribution. When combined with figure 1, figure 2 makes clear that a nontrivial fraction of children live in families who are at substantial risk of falling through the cracks in our current safety net. In particular, more than 8 percent of these families have private incomes that are less than 20 percent of the poverty line, and almost 13 percent have incomes that are less than 50 percent. It is also important to notice that the distribution of families with children is not uniform across the distribution of income to needs, and there is a large point mass at zero. Figures 4 through 7 and figures A3 and A4 and A8 through A10 show similar distributions for subgroups defined by race of household head, family size, and parents' marital status.

Together, these figures make clear that our major cash and near-cash assistance programs miss a nontrivial number of poor children, particularly those children living in the poorest families. This results from several factors. First, the EITC is tied to employment, so children whose parents are unable (or unwilling) to work cannot receive the substantial income

---

what low. One study reports that for those eligible for SNAP, the participation rate among eligibles in 2011 was 77 percent (Cunnyngham, Sukasih, and Castner 2016).

14. It may seem strange that the EITC and SNAP are both received higher up in the income distribution than where their eligibility levels, as determined by poverty guidelines, end. But, the x-axis measures private income at the household level, divided by household poverty thresholds, and may accurately not represent the income and poverty thresholds of households with multiple family units. It also pools income across family units, and poverty is typically lower for big family units.

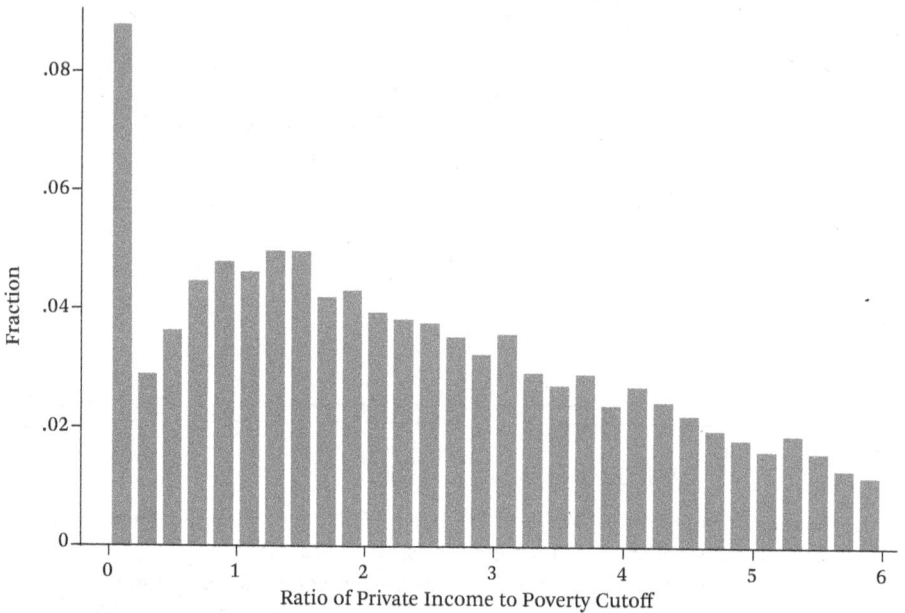

Figure 2. Distribution of Families with Children

Source: Authors' compilation based on 2015 CPS ASEC data (U.S. Department of Commerce, Bureau of the Census, and U.S. Department of Labor, Bureau of Labor Statistics 2015).
Note: Figure presents the distribution of families with children, including noncitizen children, in the Current Population Survey, 2015 survey year, by the ratio of private income to the poverty cutoff.

boost that it provides. Second, even children whose parents have positive earnings cannot receive EITC benefits unless their parents file a tax return. Previous studies indicate that approximately 16 percent of those who are eligible for the EITC may be in this nonfiler category, and that two-thirds of EITC-eligible nonparticipants do not file taxes (Plueger 2009). Low take-up of EITC benefits may result from lack of information regarding eligibility (Bhargava and Manoli 2015). Moreover, it is well known that the tax code is complicated and difficult to understand (Chetty, Friedman, and Saez 2013; Chetty and Saez 2013; Feldman, Katuscak, and Kowano 2016; Liebman and Zeckhauser 2004).

Without access to EITC benefits, the primary source of near-cash assistance available to poor children without disabled parents is SNAP, which provides an average monthly benefit of about $125 per person. As with the EITC, however, some eligible children do not receive SNAP benefits, at least in part because negative identity cues and stigma often accompany participation in means-tested programs (Bertrand, Mullainathan, and Shafir 2004; Moffitt 1983). Less than universal SNAP take-up may also result from the difficulties that low-income families face when they attempt to navigate the larger set of U.S. welfare programs and their varying rules, which in turn depend on different income concepts and family-unit definitions, and induce a dizzying host of marginal tax rates. There are also substantive "hassle" costs associated with participating in the safety net because families are often required to visit a variety of offices to register for different programs, and must know where to go and what information to bring along. Receipt of SNAP benefits sometimes requires fingerprints, and SNAP applications can be as long as thirty-six pages.[15] Taken together, these factors may push the stress and cognitive-load limits of many would-be participants (Bertrand, Mullainathan

---

15. The literature on the administrative burden of public-benefit programs is extensive (see, for example, Aizer 2007; Brien and Swann 1999; Brodkin and Majmundar 2010; Heinrich 2016; Herd et al. 2013; Klerman and

and Shafir 2004). In the face of these challenges, individuals' "bandwidth" for optimal decision making may be seriously constrained (Schilbach, Schofield, and Mullainathan 2016). Finally, as with the EITC, many families may simply be unaware that they are eligible for SNAP (Daponte, Sanders, and Taylor 1999).

A BROADER AND SIMPLER CASH ASSISTANCE PROGRAM

We propose a broader and simpler cash assistance program that reaches more children. Our program would track all citizen children under eighteen (through their Social Security numbers or birth certificates), and all of their families would automatically be sent a monthly, nontaxable, lump-sum benefit based on the number of children in the family.[16] We focus on citizen children for administrative simplicity because noncitizen children are less easily identified and tracked with existing administrative systems. The universal child benefit would not depend on any other parameters and it would not be counted against other means-tested benefits. An income supplement of this type would be devoid of stigma because it would be provided to all citizen children, and would substantially reduce informational burdens and hassle costs.[17] Families would not need to file a tax return or be evaluated for eligibility by a social worker. It would be vastly simpler than the current patchwork system of tax credits and deductions, making it easier for needy families to participate and would eliminate confusion associated with different definitions of children across credits. The lump-sum benefit would be distributed on a monthly basis to provide stability and help families accommodate unanticipated shocks that are far removed in time from the disbursement of one annual benefit.

Existing studies suggest than an annual benefit of $2,000 per child would be more than enough to provide meaningful impacts.[18] This would also yield an increase in family income comparable to the average assistance currently provided to two-child families through the EITC. As described, a $1,000 increase in EITC income is associated with a 2 to 3 percent reduction in the probability that a newborn is below the low birth weight threshold (Hoynes, Miller, and Simon 2015). An additional $1,000 raises a child's achievement scores by about 5 percent of a standard deviation (Duncan, Morris, and Rodrigues 2011; Dahl and Lochner 2012). Existing studies also find that improvements in children's health and academic achievement of this magnitude are predictive of economically meaningful increases in later life economic success (for example, Kline and Walters 2016).

A frequent concern with government income transfers is that they reduce work incentives. Evidence suggests that a universal child benefit would be unlikely to generate large reductions in parental work effort, however. Recent work by Ben-Shalom, Moffitt, and Scholz 2012, for example, finds that most major means-tested transfer programs do not meaningfully reduce hours of work.[19] Programs that do appear to reduce labor supply are generally associated with either a high earnings tax rate or

---

Danielson 2009; Moynihan, Herd, and Harvey 2015; Schanzenbach 2009; Schwabish 2012; Wolfe and Scrivner 2005).

16. For simplicity of design, we propose that the benefit be nontaxable. Taxing the universal child benefit would work against its main purpose by reducing its full value. Progressivity and cost savings could be built into the benefit by phasing it out for families with very high income.

17. Another body of literature shows that some children who are eligible for some government benefits but live in families with immigrant members do not participate in these programs because of concerns that claiming benefits will lead to difficulties with becoming naturalized citizens (for example, Watson 2014).

18. To maintain its real value over time, the universal benefit would be indexed using the CPI or PCE.

19. Exceptions are SSI, TANF, and housing assistance programs, which include significantly larger work disincentives. Of course, our universal credit might be expected to have negative effects on labor force participation in the range of the current EITC phase-in, but the magnitude of any negative effects would be reduced by leaving the current no-child EITC in place, or expanding the generosity of the no-child EITC credit.

with sharp discontinuities that cause complete elimination of benefits with an additional dollar of earnings. In contrast, Hoynes and Schanzenbach estimate quite modest earnings reductions in conjunction with rollout of the Food Stamp program, which had a nontrivial benefit reduction rate (2012).[20] The universal child benefit would not impose an earnings tax. Moreover, as noted, many beneficiaries would be children whose parents are not currently working.

A $2,000 per child lump-sum benefit would cost the federal government approximately $142 billion per year and would reach the 24.5 percent of families with children under eighteen who have private incomes below the poverty line but currently receive no support through the tax system or from SNAP.[21] The cost of providing this income supplement could be reduced by phasing it out among high-income families.

An income transfer of this magnitude could also be sustained without substantially increasing the level of government expenditures by repurposing funds currently devoted to the CTC (and Additional Child Tax Credit, ACTC), the child dependent exemption, and the *child-related* parts of the EITC.[22] This would have the clear political advantage of maintaining revenue neutrality (and allow the Congressional Budget Office or Joint Committee on Taxation to score it accordingly), and would redirect government assistance from higher-income families toward children living in the most disadvantaged families. The long-standing child exemption—which currently provides families with approximately $600 per child, per year—is not available to non–tax filers, and largely benefits families with incomes above the poverty line.[23] Moreover, the magnitude of the benefits received through the child exemption is larger for families who face higher marginal tax rates. The CTC (nonrefundable) and ACTC (refundable) jointly provide qualifying families with benefits of up to $1,000 per child under age seventeen. Like the child exemption, the CTC primarily benefits middle-income families.[24] The ACTC and EITC do play a substantive role in poverty alleviation (Hoynes and Rothstein 2016), but for families with two children the maximum benefits allowed through these combined programs are comparable to the value of the lump-sum transfer that would replace it.

We document our proposal's feasibility by leveraging 2013 Internal Revenue Service (IRS) Statistics of Income (SOI) tax data (2013a, 2013b). Details behind our calculations are described in the online appendix and shown in online table A1. Approximately $27.2 billion would be available from repurposing the CTC,

---

20. The roll-out was associated with an annual reduction of about three hundred hours for participating households, but had no evident effect on family earnings (Hoynes and Schanzenbach 2012).

21. For comparability with estimates in Christopher Wimer, Sophie Collyer, and Sara Kimberlin's article in this double issue (2018), our estimate is based on calculations from the Current Population Survey. We use the 2015 CPS because at the time of this writing, the imputed tax items in the 2016 CPS were not available. CPS estimates will differ somewhat from estimates elsewhere in this article that are based on the SOI data because the CPS does not survey all groups who file taxes (such as some military families). The SOI data also exclude nonfilers but may include individual claims that will later be disallowed (such as after an audit). Another difference between the datasets is that the CPS distinguishes citizens from noncitizens, which is relevant to our proposal. Citizenship status cannot be determined in the SOI, although filing for children lacking a SSN or Taxpayer Identification Number is not allowed.

22. Using funds from the CTC, Additional CTC and child-dependent exemption to fund a universal child benefit is similar to the proposal put forward by Shaefer and his colleagues in this issue (2018). A critical difference between our proposal and theirs is that our proposal would also harness funds from the EITC and comes closer to being revenue neutral.

23. The estimated value of the child exemption is based on the amount of the dependent exemption in 2013, which was $3,900. We multiply this amount by the average marginal tax rate of 14.7 percent.

24. For example, a married couple with two children and adjusted gross income of $150,000 is still eligible for the credit.

and another $27.9 billion from the ACTC. We do not propose repurposing child exemptions that are currently available for disabled dependents or for older children away at college. Funds from the child exemptions would, therefore, yield about $42 billion. Together, funds repurposed from the CTC, the Additional CTC, and the child exemptions total $97 billion.

We also calculate how much would be available if we repurposed the child-related portion of the EITC without eliminating the part of the EITC earnings subsidy currently provided to families without children. This part of the EITC would continue to be available to *all* working adults. As before, our proposal would hold constant all EITC funds that go to families with disabled dependents or with older children in college. We calculate that the child-related part of the EITC would yield $54 billion of available funding. Combining these sources, the total amount repurposed for our child benefit would be $151 billion. We divide this estimated funding amount by the total number of children, and inflate to 2015 dollars, yielding an estimated annual benefit of approximately $2,000 per child. Our estimate of the average EITC benefit received by a family with two children is $3,667. Our estimate of the average EITC benefit received by a family with three or more children is $4,022. Thus, our alternative cash assistance program would provide *all* families with two children additional income similar to or larger than the amount they currently receive (on average) from the EITC. Families with more children would receive larger benefits. One-child families would, on average, receive less than they do under the current system. These static estimates are based on the assumption that there would be no accompanying changes in parents' labor force participation or earnings.

Figures 3 through 12 show how our revenue neutral proposal would change the distribution of government income support across families. The figures are based on data from the 2015 Current Population Survey ASEC, and plot the average benefit amount received by families with different (private) income-to-needs ratios under both the current system, and under our proposal. One can see immediately from figure 3 that repurposing funds from the EITC, CTC and child exemptions would increase government income support to children at the lowest end of the income distribution, and reduce support for many families with private incomes between 100 and 200 percent of the poverty line. Among those families (approximately 19 percent of those with children), the average cost of replacing the current array of tax benefits with a $2,000 universal benefit would be $1,203. This cost is balanced, however, by increases to families whose income is less than 50 percent of the poverty line (approximately 12 percent,). For very poor families, the average income gain would be $3,047.

Figures 4 through 7 show that subsidizing the most economically disadvantaged children under our proposal would produce similar distributional effects within race and ethnic groups. What is not evident in the figures, however, is that children with different racial or ethnic identities tend to be located in different parts of the income-to-needs distribution. Figures 8 through 11 present histograms showing the fraction of families with different levels of income to needs by the race-ethnicity of the family head. It is clear that, relative to white non-Hispanic headed families, children in families headed by black non-Hispanics are much more likely to live in families with no private income. More than 15 percent of families with a black parent and a child under eighteen have no private income. The comparable statistic for the other demographic groups is 9 percent. Similarly, relative to non-Hispanic whites, many more Hispanic children live below the median of the private income-to-needs distribution.

Thus, because black and Hispanic families are so much poorer than non-Hispanic white families, they are relatively more likely to gain from the repurposed funds. Figures A1 through A4 show that children living in single-parent-headed families would similarly benefit more than children in married-couple families: even though our proposal's distributional effects are similar within marital groups, children living in single-parent families are disproportionately likely to have low income to needs.[25] The first

25. We also analyzed the proposal's distributional effects by family size (see figures A5 through A7).

(*Text continues on p. 58.*)

Figure 3. Distribution of Universal Child Benefit, All Families

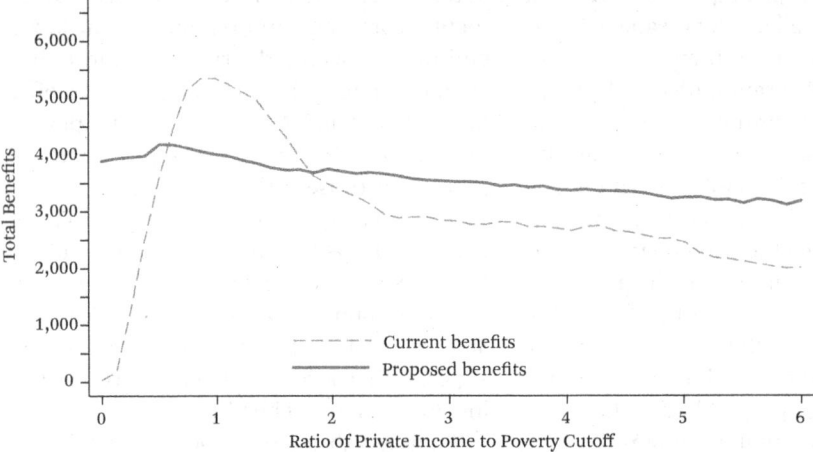

Source: Authors' compilation based on 2015 CPS ASEC data (U.S. Department of Commerce, Bureau of the Census, and U.S. Department of Labor, Bureau of Labor Statistics 2015).
Note: Figures show the distribution of the value of combined child exemptions (multiplied by the marginal tax rate), child-related parts of the EITC, and Child Tax Credit and Additional Child Tax Credit by the ratio of private income to the poverty level, using microdata from Current Population Survey, 2015 survey year (income from the 2014 calendar year). The sample for both calculations is all families, including noncitizen children, with at least one child under age eighteen. Although our main proposal does not extend benefits to noncitizen children, noncitizen children are only 2.5 percent of all children in the United States and 1.2 percent of children under five. We exclude families with a reported negative private income (0.06 percent of the families), and those at or above six times the ratio of private income to poverty threshold (14.39 percent).

Figure 4. Distribution of Universal Child Benefit, White Non-Hispanic Household Head

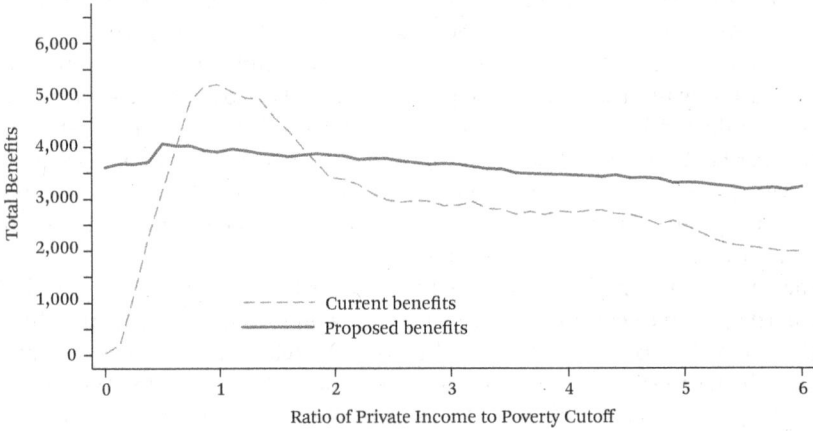

Source: Authors' compilation based on 2015 CPS ASEC data (U.S. Department of Commerce, Bureau of the Census, and U.S. Department of Labor, Bureau of Labor Statistics 2015).
Note: Figures show the distribution of the value of combined child exemptions (multiplied by the marginal tax rate), child-related parts of the EITC, and Child Tax Credit and Additional Child Tax Credit by the ratio of private income to the poverty level, using microdata from Current Population Survey, 2015 survey year. The sample for both calculations is all families with a white, non-Hispanic household head, with at least one child under age eighteen, including noncitizen children. We exclude families with a reported negative private income, and those at or above six times the ratio of private income to poverty threshold.

Figure 5. Distribution of Universal Child Benefit, Black Non-Hispanic Household Head

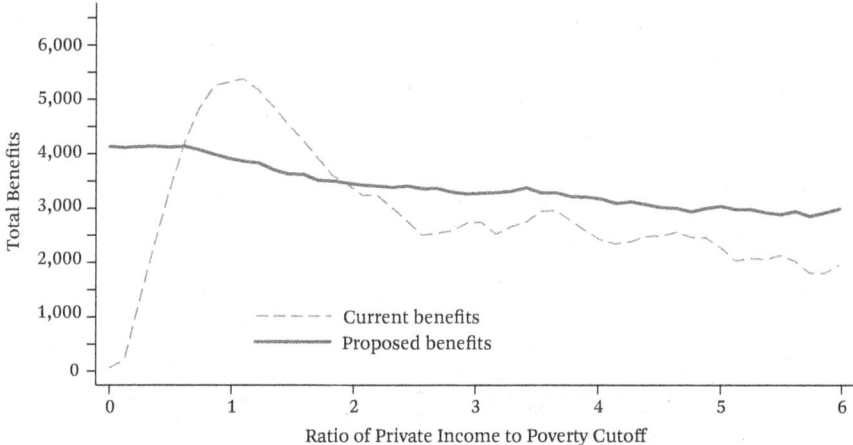

Source: Authors' compilation based on 2015 CPS ASEC data (U.S. Department of Commerce, Bureau of the Census, and U.S. Department of Labor, Bureau of Labor Statistics 2015).
Note: Figures show the distribution of the value of combined child exemptions (multiplied by the marginal tax rate), child-related parts of the EITC, and Child Tax Credit and Additional Child Tax Credit by the ratio of private income to the poverty level, using microdata from Current Population Survey, 2015 survey year. The sample for both calculations is all families with a black, non-Hispanic household head, with at least one child under age eighteen, including noncitizen children. We exclude families with a reported negative private income, and those at or above six times the ratio of private income to poverty threshold.

Figure 6. Distribution of Universal Child Benefit, Hispanic Household Head

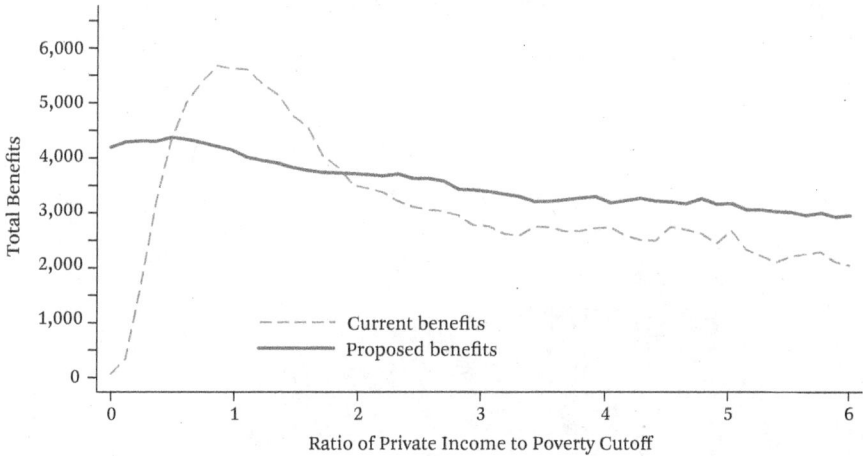

Source: Authors' compilation based on 2015 CPS ASEC data (U.S. Department of Commerce, Bureau of the Census, and U.S. Department of Labor, Bureau of Labor Statistics 2015).
Note: Figures show the distribution of the value of combined child exemptions (multiplied by the marginal tax rate), child-related parts of the EITC, and Child Tax Credit and Additional Child Tax Credit by the ratio of private income to the poverty level, using microdata from Current Population Survey, 2015 survey year. The sample for both calculations is all families with a Hispanic household head, with at least one child under age eighteen, including noncitizen children. We exclude families with a reported negative private income, and those at or above six times the ratio of private income to poverty threshold.

Figure 7. Distribution of Universal Child Benefit, Other Non-Hispanic Household Head

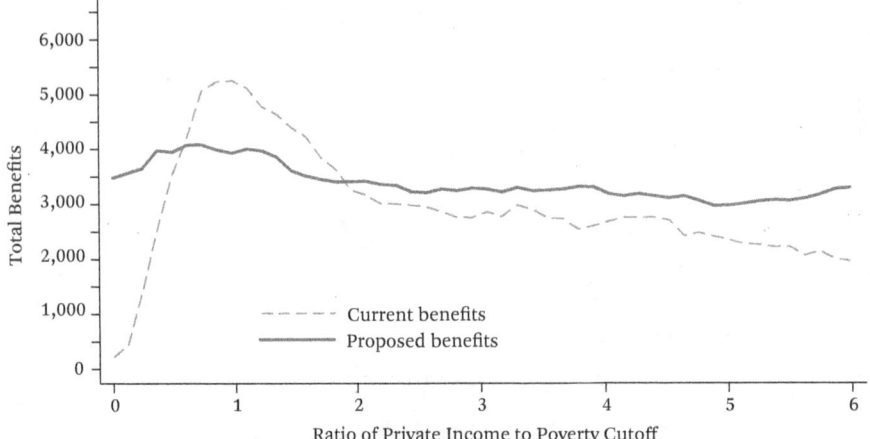

Source: Authors' compilation based on 2015 CPS ASEC data (U.S. Department of Commerce, Bureau of the Census, and U.S. Department of Labor, Bureau of Labor Statistics 2015).
Note: Figures show the distribution of the value of combined child exemptions (multiplied by the marginal tax rate), child-related parts of the EITC, and Child Tax Credit and Additional Child Tax Credit by the ratio of private income to the poverty level, using microdata from Current Population Survey, 2015 survey year. The sample for both calculations is all families with an other, non-Hispanic household head, with at least one child under age eighteen, including noncitizen children. We exclude families with a reported negative private income, and those at or above six times the ratio of private income to poverty threshold.

Figure 8. Distribution of Families, White Non-Hispanic Household Head

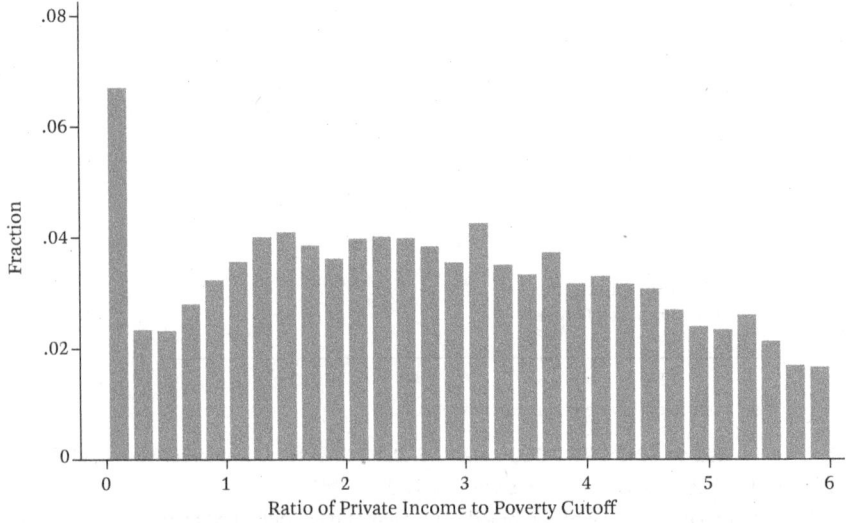

Source: Authors' compilation based on 2015 CPS ASEC data (U.S. Department of Commerce, Bureau of the Census, and U.S. Department of Labor, Bureau of Labor Statistics 2015).
Note: Figure presents the distribution of families with children with a white non-Hispanic household head, including noncitizen children, in the Current Population Survey, 2015 survey year, by the ratio of private income to the poverty cutoff.

Figure 9. Distribution of Families, Black Non-Hispanic Household Head

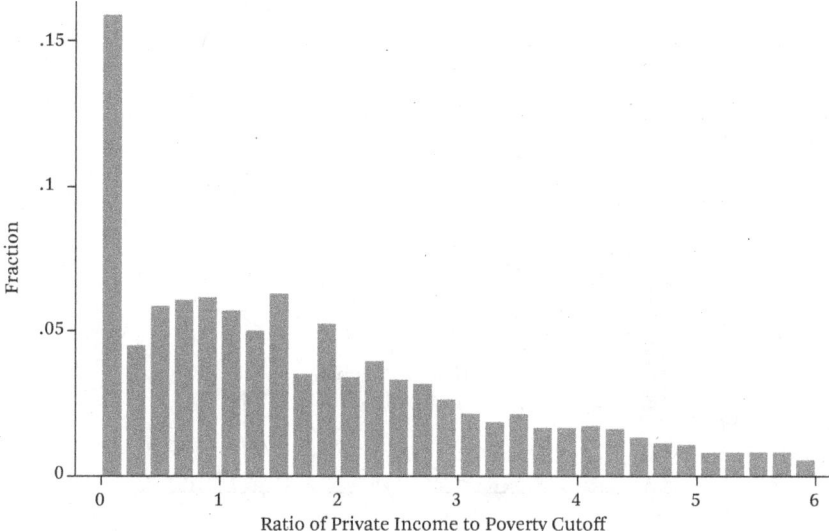

Source: Authors' compilation based on 2015 CPS ASEC data (U.S. Department of Commerce, Bureau of the Census, and U.S. Department of Labor, Bureau of Labor Statistics 2015).
Note: Figure presents the distribution of families with children with a black non-Hispanic household head, including noncitizen children, in the Current Population Survey, 2015 survey year, by the ratio of private income to the poverty cutoff.

Figure 10. Distribution of Families, Hispanic Household Head

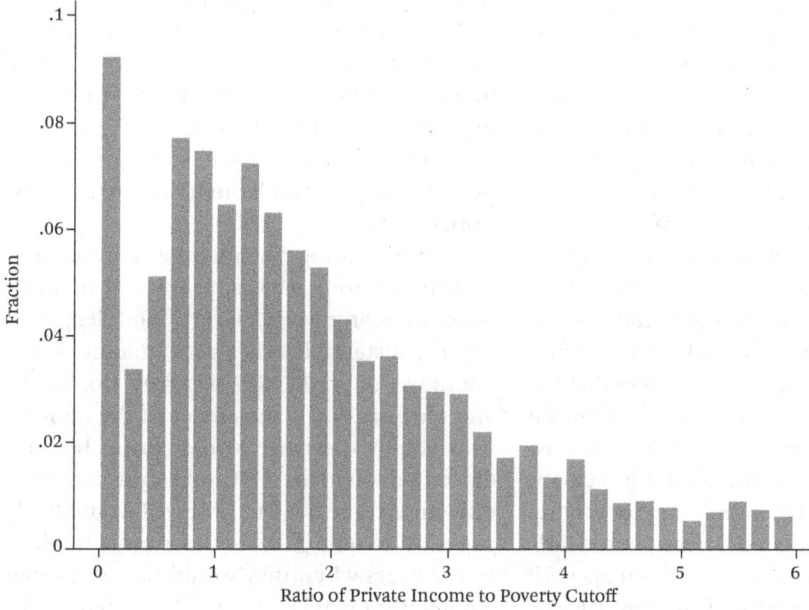

Source: Authors' compilation based on 2015 CPS ASEC data (U.S. Department of Commerce, Bureau of the Census, and U.S. Department of Labor, Bureau of Labor Statistics 2015).
Note: Figure presents the distribution of families with children with a Hispanic household head, including noncitizen children, in the Current Population Survey, 2015 survey year, by the ratio of private income to the poverty cutoff.

Figure 11. Distribution of Families, Other Non-Hispanic Household Head

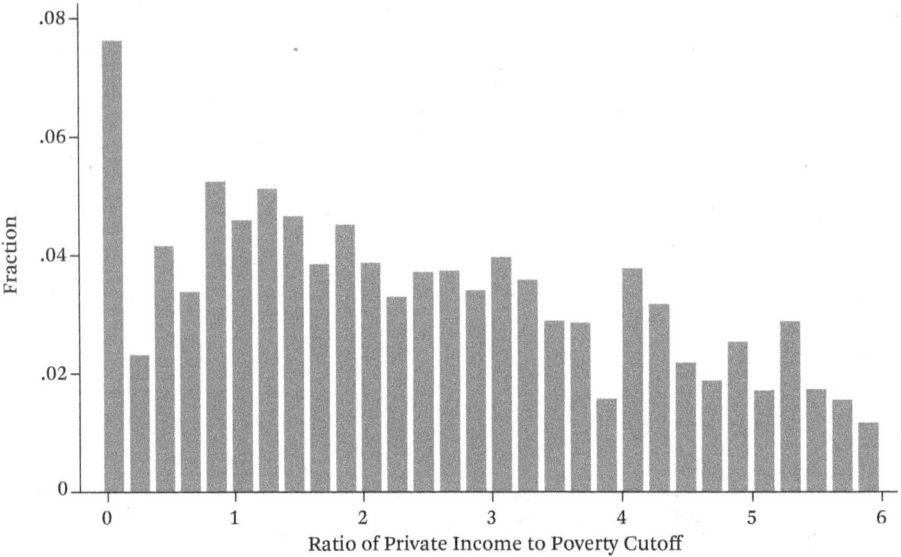

Source: Authors' compilation based on 2015 CPS ASEC data (U.S. Department of Commerce, Bureau of the Census, and U.S. Department of Labor, Bureau of Labor Statistics 2015).
Note: Figure presents the distribution of families with children with an other non-Hispanic household head, including noncitizen children, in the Current Population Survey, 2015 survey year, by the ratio of private income to the poverty cutoff.

article in this issue also provides estimates, using a number of different metrics, of how our proposal would affect poverty.

Most of the income loss that near-poor families would experience under this revenue-neutral proposal is driven by our repurposing of the child-related parts of the EITC. If the feasibility of implementing a universal benefit requires that the government hold constant its current level of child-related tax expenditures, then we would support the replacement of the child-related component of the EITC with a universal child benefit because we believe that the cost to "less poor" children would be balanced by the gains to children whose families are even more disadvantaged. Rates of food insecurity, for example, are substantially higher among the very poor relative to the near-poor: nearly 25 percent of children living in families with incomes below 50 percent of the poverty line experience low food security, versus 16 percent of children whose family incomes are between 100 and 150 percent (Wight et al. 2014). Julie Siebens also documents a significant income gradient in material hardship (2013). As described earlier, the replacement of the current array of tax benefits with a universal child benefit would also ensure a fairer distribution of the government's current monetary investment in children. Equality of opportunity cannot be achieved through government programs that tie the level of child benefits to the parents' work effort.

Finally, among low-income families, the "churning" from one year to the next between states of near-poverty, poverty, and deep poverty is substantial, as is a concomitant churning in use of the EITC (Ackerman, Holtzblatt, and Masken 2009). Thus many of the families who would experience income losses because of a reduction in the EITC subsidy would do so only in some years. Our proposal would likely generate income gains to those same families in the years when they would not have been eligible for tax related benefits. Moreover, for families who experience high income volatility, the dependability of the income received through the universal child benefit could generate important psychological benefits.

Our cost estimates are based on the assump-

Figure 12. Distribution of Universal Child Benefit, One-Child Option

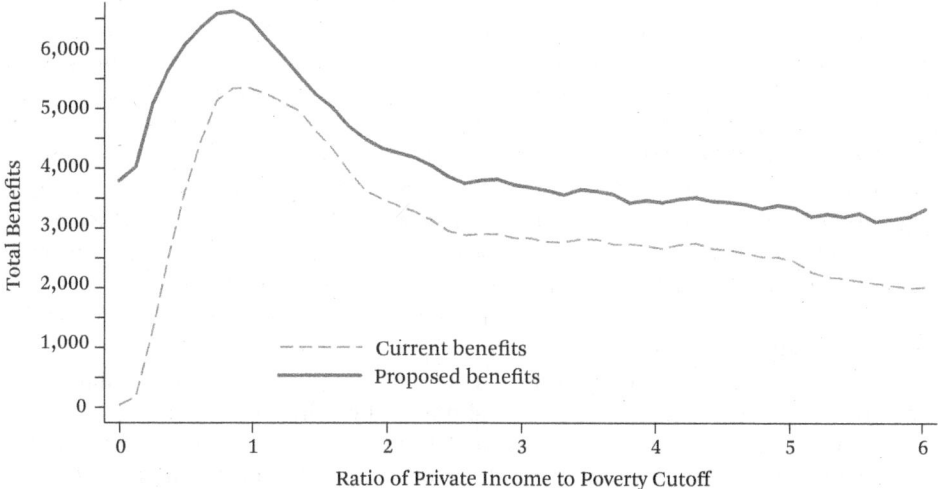

Source: Authors' compilation based on 2015 CPS ASEC data (U.S. Department of Commerce, Bureau of the Census, and U.S. Department of Labor, Bureau of Labor Statistics 2015).
Note: The distribution is of the value of combined child exemptions (multiplied by the marginal tax rate), child-related parts of the EITC, and Child Tax Credit and Additional Child Tax Credit by the ratio of private income to the poverty level, using microdata from Current Population Survey, 2015 survey year (2014 calendar year). The sample for both calculations is all families with children, including non-citizen children, with at least one child under age eighteen. We exclude families with a reported negative private income (0.06 percent of the families), and those at or above six times the ratio of private income to poverty threshold (14.39 percent).

tion that reducing the EITC earnings subsidy to the level currently available to childless adults would not affect parents' labor force participation or earnings. A potential concern with any proposal that reduces the EITC subsidy is that the EITC is known to be effective at inducing individuals to either enter the labor force or to spend more time working. Because the EITC wage subsidy is substantially higher for families with children than for those without children, repurposing child-related EITC funds would likely reduce some parents' incentives to work. This could be accommodated by altering the income span of the no-child EITC's flat and phase-out ranges. It is also important that most studies that causally link income to poor children's success are based on natural experiments that simultaneously alter parents' labor force participation (for example, studies of job loss or of changes in EITC generosity). It may be that part of the documented resulting improvements in child well-being result from other changes in family dynamics that accompany changes in parental work.

To maintain the work incentives inherent in the current tax system, our preferred policy would be to simply divorce the government provision of child-related income support, which should be made on the grounds that all children are entitled to a basic standard of living, from government wage subsidies that are currently provided by the EITC but vary with family size. Figure 12 shows what would happen to the distribution of income support if we were to replace the child exemptions and ACTC with our $2,000 universal child benefit, while maintaining the EITC for all families (including those without children) at the same subsidy and phase-out rates that are currently applied to families with one child (see also Shaefer et al. 2018). Under this proposal, average benefits would increase throughout the entire distribution. Using the CPS, we estimate that this proposal would cost an additional $74 billion.[26] Approximately $9 billion would be recouped by repurposing the EITC benefits that currently go to families with more than one child, but it would cost an additional $83 billion to increase the small EITC wage subsidy currently provided to families with no children up to the level of the one-child EITC.[27] The additional cost of this proposal could be covered by phasing out the universal child benefit for high-income families. The CTC currently phases out when families' adjusted gross income exceeds $75,000.

Figures A11 through A16 show the distributional effects of this alternative proposal for different demographic groups. Once again, conditional on families' income to needs, the effects across groups of providing the universal benefit plus the one-child EITC are similar, but because black, Hispanic, and single-head families are disproportionately at the bottom of the income-to-needs distribution, children in these families benefit more than white non-Hispanic children living with married parents. Obviously, providing low-income childless adults an EITC subsidy equivalent to the current one-child EITC would generate enormous gains for this group.

An alternative proposal that would preserve much of the EITC's positive work incentives but would still cost less than the current system of benefits would be to provide all eligible families *with dependents* the one-child EITC wage subsidy, while maintaining the current EITC wage subsidy for those without dependents. This proposal would cost an additional $34 billion. From our perspective, a disadvantage of this proposal would be that it would continue to conflate the goal of providing work incentives with the goal of providing for children's needs.

A few additional notes here are warranted. First, the simplest way of disbursing universal benefits would be through the Social Security system, because social security numbers are typically assigned to children shortly after birth. The only additional step that would be required would be to link parents' information to their children. The Social Security Administration (SSA) already obtains address, employer, and earnings data from the IRS, which could be used to help track parents. It also currently distributes other benefits to children via the Social Security and Supplemental Security Income programs. We suggest that the mother (assuming one is present) be the default parental link to the child, because this would easily be determined at birth. When necessary, due to divorce or changes in custody, the reference parent could be changed at local SSA offices.

During the initial transition period, the tax system could be used to help identify eligible children and pass necessary information to the SSA. Eligibility for low-income children whose parents are nonfilers, or who are not in the Social Security system, could be determined via systems that assess eligibility for programs serving broad populations, such as Medicaid and SNAP. The provision of benefits to tax nonfilers could also be made automatically by providing information from state agencies and the IRS to the SSA, or by allowing families to register the link with their children at local SSA offices. Families who do not currently sign up for these programs or who file taxes could also obtain the benefit by voluntarily filing a tax return.[28]

SUMMARY

Although the United States provides cash assistance to low-income children through a variety of tax and transfer programs, the current system fails to reach many children. Income

---

26. This assumes no increase in take-up among no-child families.

27. In contrast, if we provide all families with children the EITC wage subsidy currently available to families without children (as in our revenue-neutral proposal) then we are able to repurpose a net amount of $43 billion toward the universal child benefit using the SOI numbers.

28. Some challenges would be associated with distributing benefits to children whose parents split custody. One option would send the benefit to the parent the child is living with most of the time. Over time, however, benefits might be capitalized into child-support agreements.

support for children whose parents are unable to work is particularly limited, yet children of poor, nonworking parents may be among our most vulnerable. Moreover, complexities associated with the current set of assistance programs that are available in the United States ensure that even many low-income children with working parents do not receive the support for which they are eligible. We propose that the United States should increase the financial resources available to poor children by providing an annual, universal, $2,000 per child benefit. We also argue that the case for a child benefit is distinct from that for incentivizing low-income adults' labor supply: government investments in children should be made on the grounds of equality of opportunity, whereas programs such as the EITC should reward the same level of work effort equally across all adults irrespective of their family composition. The current system clearly mixes these goals while imposing many hurdles that make it difficult for low-income parents to make optimal investments. Our reform would address these challenges, and could be provided at limited cost by harnessing the dollars that are currently spent on the more complicated set of child benefits that are provided through the tax code.

APPENDIX

Figure A1. Distribution of Universal Child Benefit by Marital Status, Single Household Head

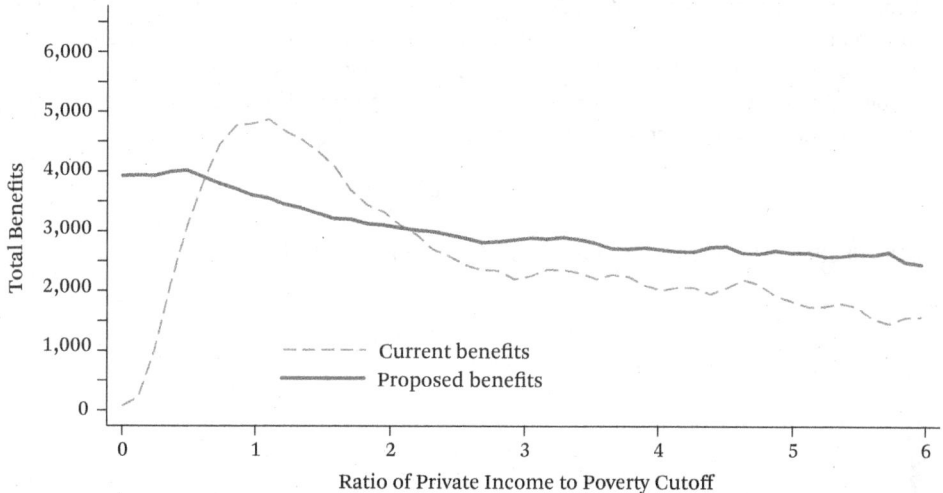

Source: Authors' compilation based on 2015 CPS ASEC data (U.S. Department of Commerce, Bureau of the Census, and U.S. Department of Labor, Bureau of Labor Statistics 2015).
Note: The distribution is of the value of combined child exemptions, child-related parts of the EITC, and Child Tax Credit and Additional Child Tax Credit by the ratio of private income to the poverty level, using microdata from Current Population Survey, 2015 survey year. The sample for both calculations is all families with a single household head with children, including noncitizen children, with at least one child under age eighteen. We exclude families with a reported negative private income, and those at or above six times the ratio of private income to poverty threshold.

Figure A2. Distribution of Universal Child Benefit by Marital Status, Married Household Head

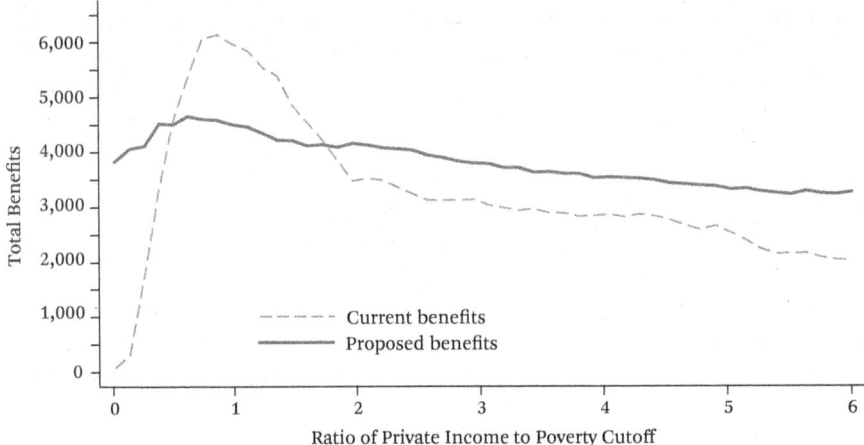

Source: Authors' compilation based on 2015 CPS ASEC data (U.S. Department of Commerce, Bureau of the Census, and U.S. Department of Labor, Bureau of Labor Statistics 2015).
Note: The distribution is of the value of combined child exemptions, child-related parts of the EITC, and Child Tax Credit and Additional Child Tax Credit by the ratio of private income to the poverty level, using microdata from Current Population Survey, 2015 survey year. The sample for both calculations is all families with a married household head with children, including noncitizen children, with at least one child under age eighteen. We exclude families with a reported negative private income, and those at or above six times the ratio of private income to poverty threshold.

Figure A3. Distribution of Families by Marital Status, Single Household Head

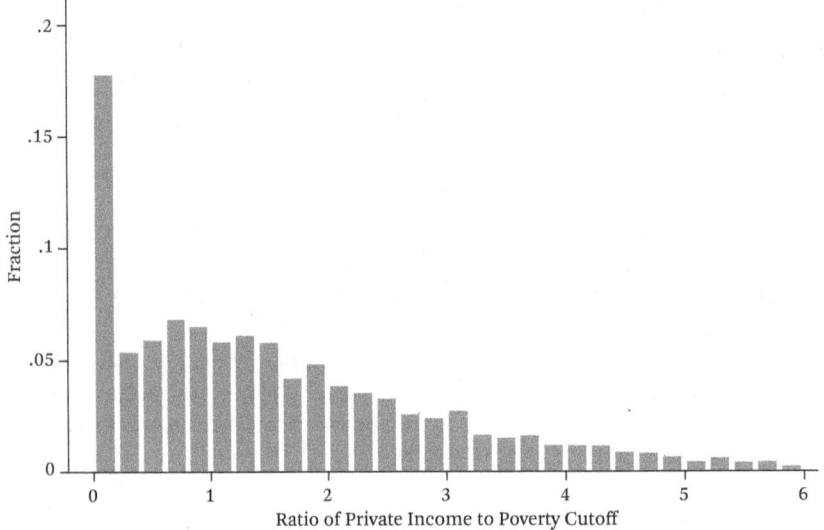

Source: Authors' compilation based on 2015 CPS ASEC data (U.S. Department of Commerce, Bureau of the Census, and U.S. Department of Labor, Bureau of Labor Statistics 2015).
Note: Figure presents the distribution of families with children with a single household head, including noncitizen children, in the Current Population Survey, 2015 survey year, by the ratio of private income to the poverty cutoff.

Figure A4. Distribution of Families by Marital Status, Married Household Head

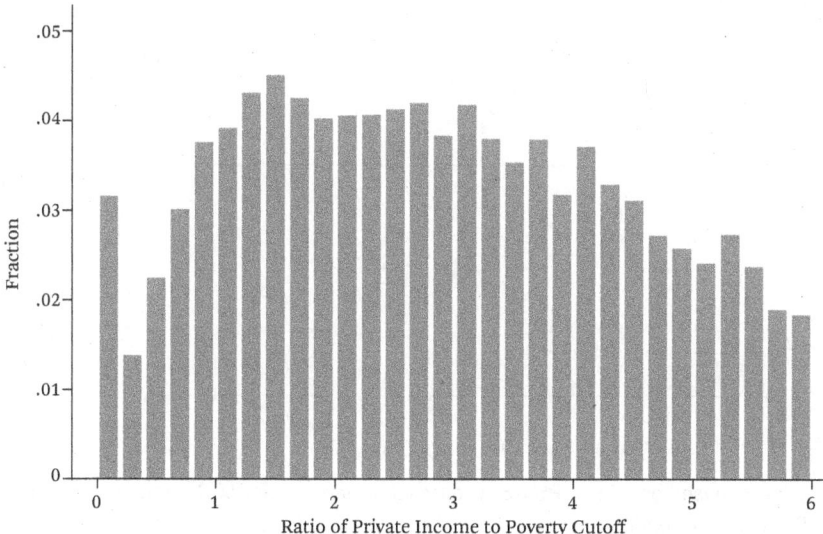

Source: Authors' compilation based on 2015 CPS ASEC data (U.S. Department of Commerce, Bureau of the Census, and U.S. Department of Labor, Bureau of Labor Statistics 2015).
Note: Figure presents the distribution of families with children with a married household head, including noncitizen children, in the Current Population Survey, 2015 survey year, by the ratio of private income to the poverty cutoff.

Figure A5. Distribution of Benefits by Family Size, One-Child Families

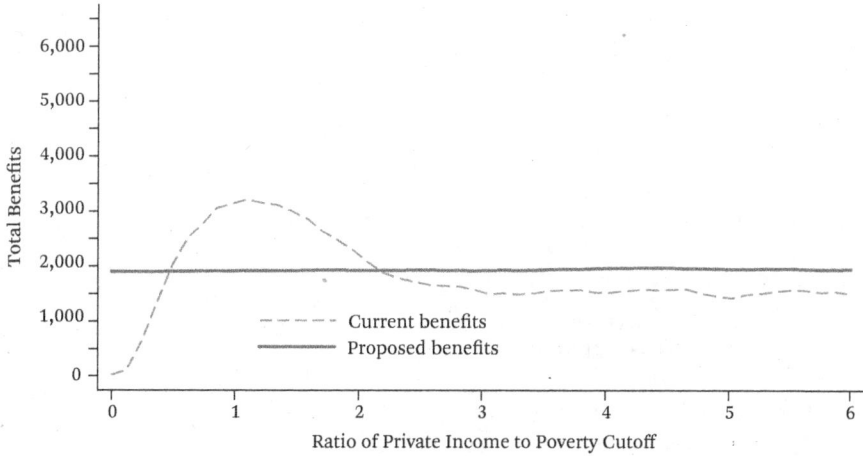

Source: Authors' compilation based on 2015 CPS ASEC data (U.S. Department of Commerce, Bureau of the Census, and U.S. Department of Labor, Bureau of Labor Statistics 2015).
Note: The distribution is of the value of combined child exemptions, child-related parts of the EITC, and Child Tax Credit and Additional Child Tax Credit by the ratio of private income to the poverty level, using microdata from Current Population Survey, 2015 survey year. The sample for both calculations is all families with one child under age eighteen, including noncitizen children. We exclude families with a reported negative private income, and those at or above six times the ratio of private income to poverty threshold.

Figure A6. Distribution of Benefits by Family Size, Two-Child Families

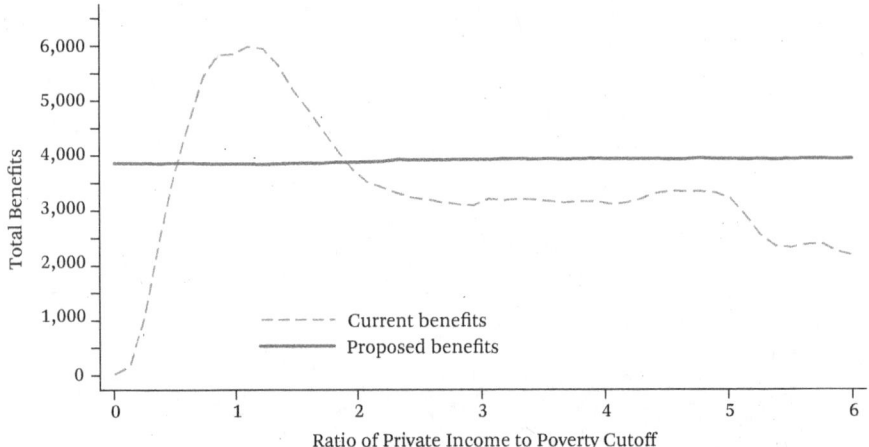

Source: Authors' compilation based on 2015 CPS ASEC data (U.S. Department of Commerce, Bureau of the Census, and U.S. Department of Labor, Bureau of Labor Statistics 2015).
Note: The distribution is of the value of combined child exemptions, child-related parts of the EITC, and Child Tax Credit and Additional Child Tax Credit by the ratio of private income to the poverty level, using microdata from Current Population Survey, 2015 survey year. The sample for both calculations is all families with two children, including noncitizen children. We exclude families with a reported negative private income, and those at or above six times the ratio of private income to poverty threshold.

Figure A7. Distribution of Benefits by Family Size, Three-Child Families

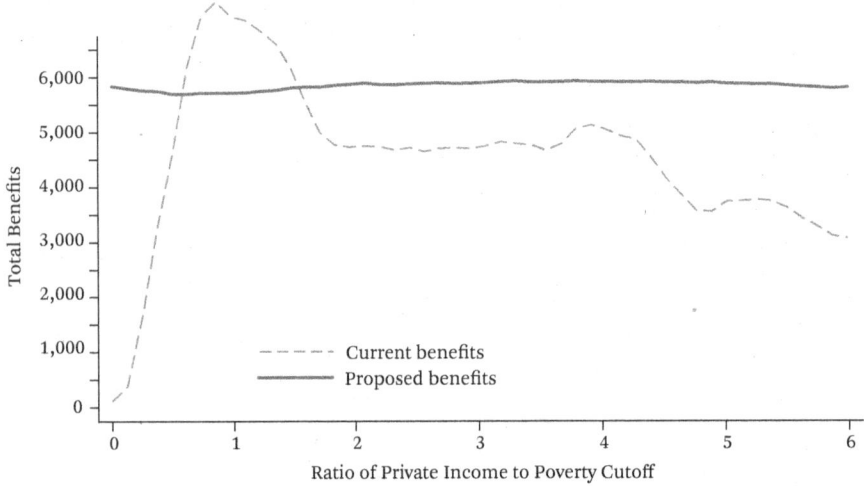

Source: Authors' compilation based on 2015 CPS ASEC data (U.S. Department of Commerce, Bureau of the Census, and U.S. Department of Labor, Bureau of Labor Statistics 2015).
Note: The distribution is of the value of combined child exemptions, child-related parts of the EITC, and Child Tax Credit and Additional Child Tax Credit by the ratio of private income to the poverty level, using microdata from Current Population Survey, 2015 survey year. The sample for both calculations is all families with three children or more, including noncitizen children. We exclude families with a reported negative private income, and those at or above six times the ratio of private income to poverty threshold.

Figure A8. Distribution of Families, One-Child Families

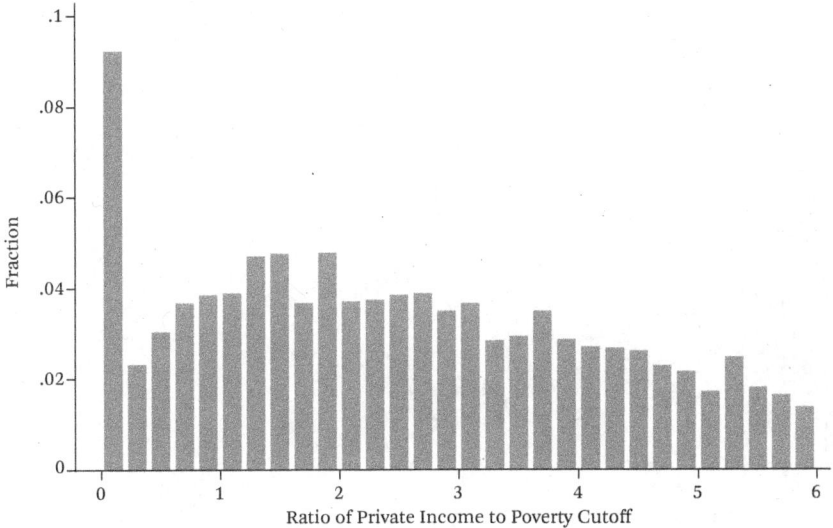

Source: Authors' compilation based on 2015 CPS ASEC data (U.S. Department of Commerce, Bureau of the Census, and U.S. Department of Labor, Bureau of Labor Statistics 2015).
Note: Figure presents the distribution of families with one child, including noncitizen children, in the Current Population Survey, 2015 survey year, by the ratio of private income to the poverty cutoff.

Figure A9. Distribution of Families, Two-Child Families

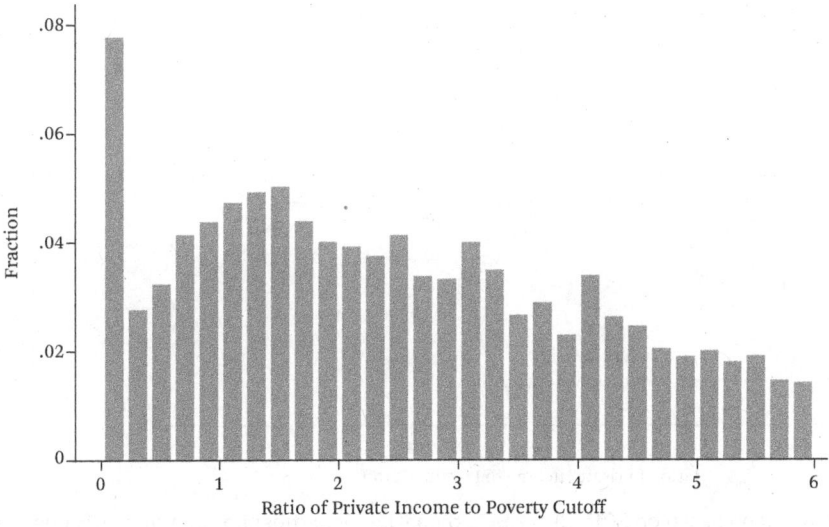

Source: Authors' compilation based on 2015 CPS ASEC data (U.S. Department of Commerce, Bureau of the Census, and U.S. Department of Labor, Bureau of Labor Statistics 2015).
Note: Figure presents the distribution of families with two children, including noncitizen children, in the Current Population Survey, 2015 survey year, by the ratio of private income to the poverty cutoff.

Figure A10. Distribution of Families, Three-Child Families

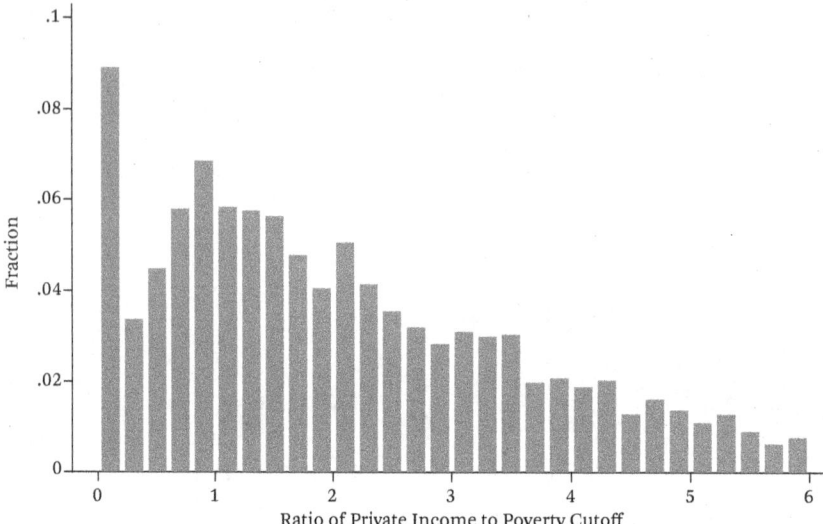

Source: Authors' compilation based on 2015 CPS ASEC data (U.S. Department of Commerce, Bureau of the Census, and U.S. Department of Labor, Bureau of Labor Statistics 2015).
Note: Figure presents the distribution of families with three or more children, including noncitizen children, in the Current Population Survey, 2015 survey year, by the ratio of private income to the poverty cutoff.

Figure A11. Distribution of Benefits by Race-Ethnicity, White Non-Hispanic Household Head, One-Child Option

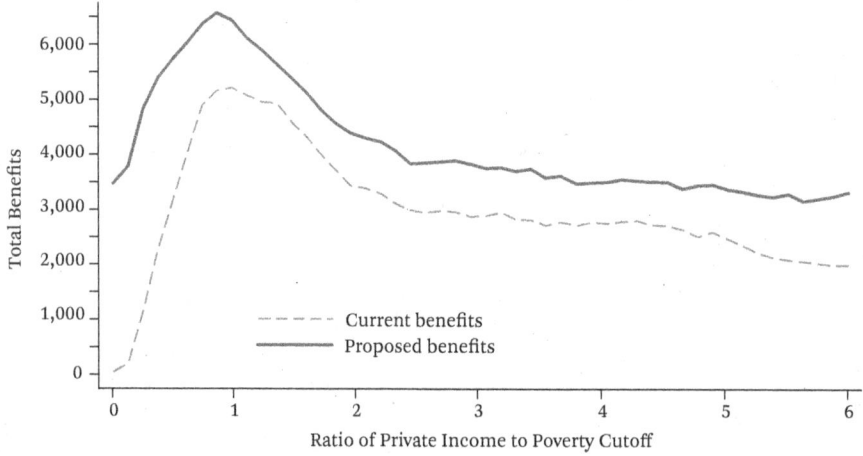

Source: Authors' compilation based on 2015 CPS ASEC data (U.S. Department of Commerce, Bureau of the Census, and U.S. Department of Labor, Bureau of Labor Statistics 2015).
Note: The distribution is of the value of combined child exemptions, child-related parts of the EITC, and Child Tax Credit and Additional Child Tax Credit by the ratio of private income to the poverty level, using microdata from Current Population Survey, 2015 survey year. The sample for both calculations is all families with children, including noncitizen children, with at least one child under age eighteen and a white, non-Hispanic household head. We exclude families with a reported negative private income, and those at or above six times the ratio of private income to poverty threshold.

Figure A12. Distribution of Benefits by Race-Ethnicity, Black Non-Hispanic Household Head, One-Child Option

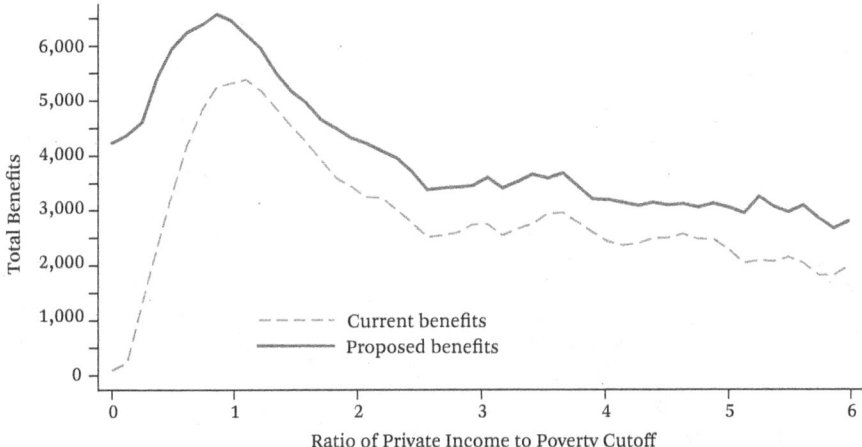

Source: Authors' compilation based on 2015 CPS ASEC data (U.S. Department of Commerce, Bureau of the Census, and U.S. Department of Labor, Bureau of Labor Statistics 2015).
Note: The distribution is of the value of combined child exemptions, child-related parts of the EITC, and Child Tax Credit and Additional Child Tax Credit by the ratio of private income to the poverty level, using microdata from Current Population Survey, 2015 survey year. The sample for both calculations is all families with children, including noncitizen children, with at least one child under age eighteen and a black, non-Hispanic household head. We exclude families with a reported negative private income, and those at or above six times the ratio of private income to poverty threshold.

Figure A13. Distribution of Benefits by Race-Ethnicity, Hispanic Household Head, One-Child Option

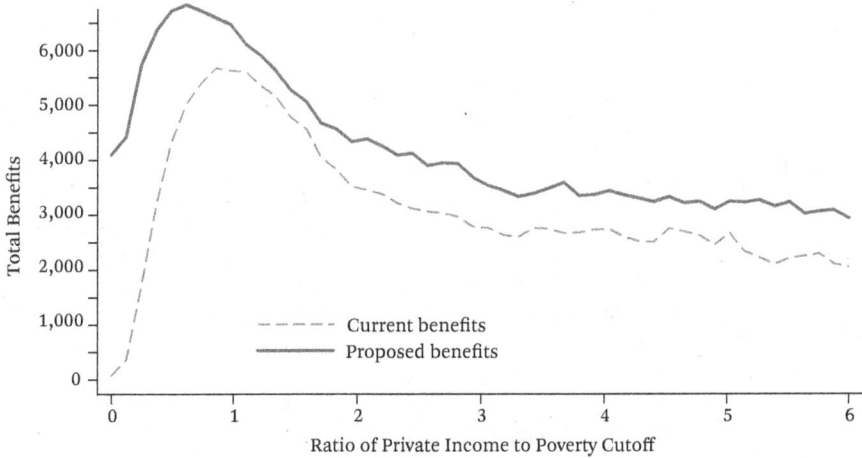

Source: Authors' compilation based on 2015 CPS ASEC data (U.S. Department of Commerce, Bureau of the Census, and U.S. Department of Labor, Bureau of Labor Statistics 2015).
Note: The distribution is of the value of combined child exemptions, child-related parts of the EITC, and Child Tax Credit and Additional Child Tax Credit by the ratio of private income to the poverty level, using microdata from Current Population Survey, 2015 survey year. The sample for both calculations is all families with children, including noncitizen children, with at least one child under age eighteen and a Hispanic household head. We exclude families with a reported negative private income, and those at or above six times the ratio of private income to poverty threshold.

Figure A14. Distribution of Benefits by Race-Ethnicity, Other Non-Hispanic Household Head, One-Child Option

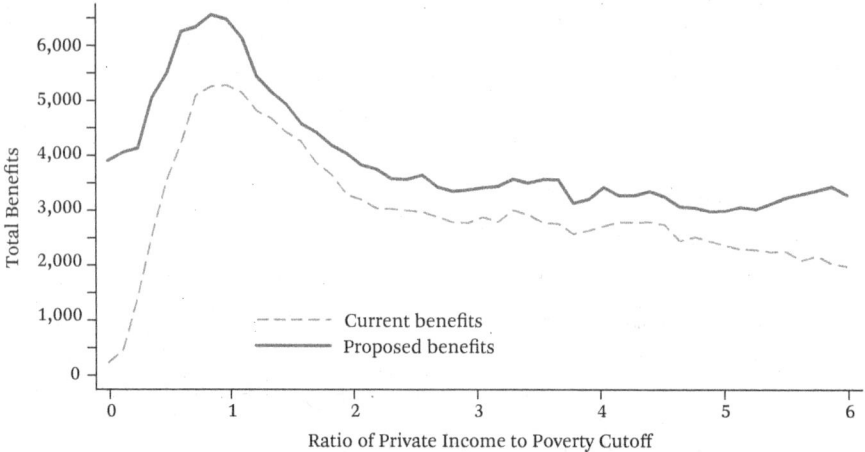

Source: Authors' compilation based on 2015 CPS ASEC data (U.S. Department of Commerce, Bureau of the Census, and U.S. Department of Labor, Bureau of Labor Statistics 2015).
Note: The distribution is of the value of combined child exemptions, child-related parts of the EITC, and Child Tax Credit and Additional Child Tax Credit by the ratio of private income to the poverty level, using microdata from Current Population Survey, 2015 survey year. The sample for both calculations is all families with children, including noncitizen children, with at least one child under age eighteen and an other, non-Hispanic household head. We exclude families with a reported negative private income, and those at or above six times the ratio of private income to poverty threshold.

Figure A15. Distribution of Benefits by Marital Status, Single Household Head, One-Child Option

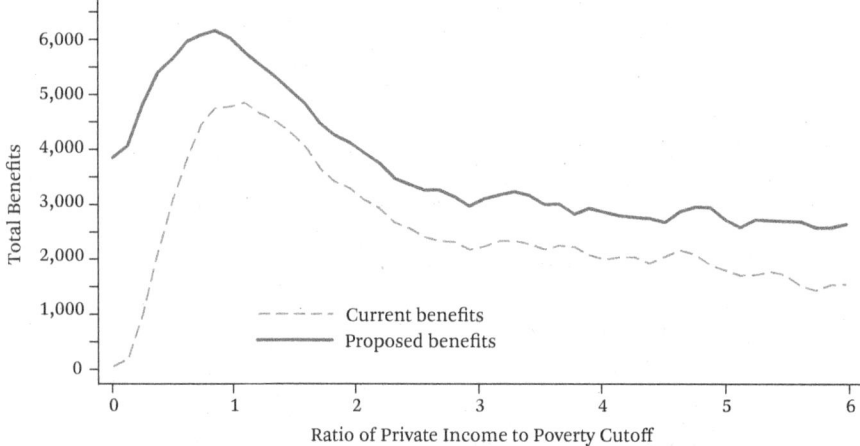

Source: Authors' compilation based on 2015 CPS ASEC data (U.S. Department of Commerce, Bureau of the Census, and U.S. Department of Labor, Bureau of Labor Statistics 2015).
Note: The distribution is of the value of combined child exemptions, child-related parts of the EITC, and Child Tax Credit and Additional Child Tax Credit by the ratio of private income to the poverty level, using microdata from Current Population Survey, 2015 survey year. The sample for both calculations is all families with children, including noncitizen children, with at least one child under age eighteen and a single household head. We exclude families with a reported negative private income, and those at or above six times the ratio of private income to poverty threshold.

Figure A16. Distribution of Benefits by Marital Status, Married Household Head, One-Child Option

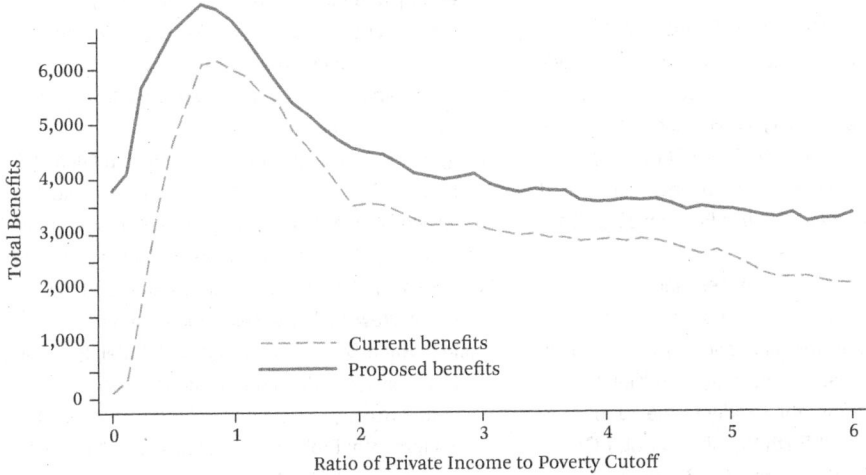

Source: Authors' compilation based on 2015 CPS ASEC data (U.S. Department of Commerce, Bureau of the Census, and U.S. Department of Labor, Bureau of Labor Statistics 2015).
Note: The distribution is of the value of combined child exemptions, child-related parts of the EITC, and Child Tax Credit and Additional Child Tax Credit by the ratio of private income to the poverty level, using microdata from Current Population Survey, 2015 survey year. The sample for both calculations is all families with children, including noncitizen children, with at least one child under age eighteen and a married household head. We exclude families with a reported negative private income, and those at or above six times the ratio of private income to poverty threshold.

REFERENCES

Ackerman, Deena, Janet Holtzblatt, and Karen Masken. 2009. "The Pattern of EITC Claims over Time: A Panel Data Analysis." Washington: U.S. Department of the Treasury, Internal Revenue Service.

Aizer, Anna. 2007. "Public Health Insurance, Program Take-Up, and Child Health." *Review of Economics and Statistics* 89(3): 400–15.

Aizer, Anna, Laura Stroud, and Stephen Buka. 2016. "Maternal Stress and Child Outcomes: Evidence from Siblings." *The Journal of Human Resources* 51(3): 523–55.

Almond, Douglas, Hilary W. Hoynes, and Diane Whitmore Schanzenbach. 2011. "Inside the War on Poverty: The Impact of Food Stamps on Birth Outcomes." *Review of Economics and Statistics* 93(2): 387–403.

Bailey, Martha J., and Susan M. Dynarski. 2011. "Inequality in Postsecondary Education." In *Whither Opportunity? Rising Inequality, Schools, and Children's Life Chances*, edited by Greg J. Duncan and Richard J. Murnane. New York: Russell Sage Foundation.

Bastian, Jacob, and Katherine Michelmore. 2016. "The Long Term Impact of the Earned Income Tax Credit on Children's Education and Employment Outcomes." Working paper. Ann Arbor: University of Michigan.

Beatty, Timothy K. M., and Charlotte J. Tuttle. 2015. "Expenditure Response to Increases in In-Kind Transfers: Evidence from the Supplemental Nutrition Assistance Program." *American Journal of Agricultural Economics* 97(2): 390–404.

Ben-Shalom, Yonatan, Robert A. Moffitt, and John Karl Scholz. 2012. "An Assessment of the Effectiveness of Antipoverty Programs in the United States." In *Oxford Handbook of the Economics of Poverty*, edited by Phillip Jefferson. Oxford: Oxford University Press.

Bertrand, Marianne, Sendhil Mulllainathan, and Eldar Shafir. 2004. "A Behavioral Economics View of Poverty." *American Economic Review Papers and Proceedings* 94(2): 419–23.

Bhargava, Saurabh, and Dayanand Manoli. 2015. "Psychological Frictions and Incomplete Take-up of Social Benefits: Evidence from an IRS Field

Experiment." *American Economic Review* 105(11): 3489–529.
Bitler, Marianne, and Theodore Figinski. 2017. "Understanding the Effects of the War on Poverty." Working paper. Davis: University of California.
Bitler, Marianne, and Hilary W. Hoynes. 2016. "The More Things Change, the More They Stay the Same? The Safety Net and Poverty in the Great Recession." *Journal of Labor Economics* 34(S1): S403–44.
Bitler, Marianne, Hilary W. Hoynes, and Elira Kuka. 2017. "Do In-Work Tax Credits Serve as a Safety Net?" *Journal of Human Resources* 52(2): 319–50.
Black, Sandra E., Paul J. Devereux, and Kjell G. Salvanes 2007. "From the Cradle to the Labor Market? The Effect of Birth Weight on Adult Outcomes." *Quarterly Journal of Economics* 122(1): 409–39.
Bradley, Robert H., and Robert F. Corwyn. 2002. "Socioeconomic Status and Child Development." *Annual Review of Psychology* 53: 371–99.
Brien, Michael J., and Christopher A. Swann. 1999. "Prenatal WIC Participation and Infant Health: Selection and Maternal Fixed Effects." Working paper. Charlottesville: University of Virginia Department of Economics.
Brodkin, Evelyn Z. and Malay Majmundar. 2010. "Administrative Exclusion: Organizations and the Hidden Costs of Welfare Claiming." *Journal of Public Administration Research and Theory* 20(4): 827–48.
Brooks-Gunn, Jeanne, and Greg J. Duncan. 1997. "The Effects of Poverty on Children." *Children and Poverty* 7(2): 55–71.
Chetty, Raj, John N. Friedman, and Emmanuel Saez. 2013. "Using Differences in Knowledge to Uncover the Impacts of the EITC on Earnings." *American Economic Review* 103(7): 2683–721.
Chetty, Raj, Nathaniel Hendren, Patrick Kline, and Emmanuel Saez. 2014. "Where Is the Land of Opportunity: The Geography of Intergenerational Mobility in the United States." *Quarterly Journal of Economics* 129(4): 1553–623.
Chetty, Raj, and Emmanuel Saez. 2013. "Teaching the Tax Code: Earnings Responses to an Experiment with EITC Recipients." *American Economic Journal: Applied Economics* 5(1): 1–31.
Coelli, Michael B. 2005. "Parental Income Shocks and the Education Attendance of Youth." Working Paper. Melbourne: University of Melbourne, Department of Economics.
Conger, Katherine J. 2011. "Economic Hardship, Parenting, and Family Stability in a Cohort of Rural Adolescents." In *Economic Restructuring and Family Wellbeing in Rural America*, edited by K. Smith and A. Tickamyer. State College: Pennsylvania State University.
Conger, Rand D., Katherine J. Conger, and Glen H. Elder. 1997. "Family Economic Hardship and Adolescent Adjustment: Mediating and Moderating Processes." In *Consequences of Growing Up Poor*, edited by Greg J. Duncan and Jeanne Brooks-Gunn. New York: Russell Sage Foundation.
Conger, Rand D., Xiaojia Ge, Glen H. Elder, Frederick O. Lorenz, and Ronald L. Simons. 1994. "Economic Stress, Coercive Family Process, and Developmental Problems of Adolescents." *Child Development* 65(2): 541–61.
Cunnyngham, Karen, Amang Sukasih, and Laura Castner. 2016. "Empirical Bayes Shrinkage Estimates of State Supplemental Nutrition Assistance Program Rates in Fiscal Year 2011 to 2013 for All Eligible People and the Working Poor." Washington, D.C.: Mathematica Policy Research.
Cutrona, Carolyn E., Daniel W. Russell, W Todd. Abraham, Kelli A. Gardner, Janet N. Melby, Chalandra Bryant, and Rand D. Conger. 2003. "Neighborhood Context and Financial Strain as Predictors of Marital Interaction and Marital Quality in African American Couples." *Personal Relationships* 10(3): 389–409.
Dahl, Gordon B., and Lance Lochner. 2012. "The Impact of Family Income on Child Achievement: Evidence from the Earned Income Tax Credit." *American Economic Review* 102(5): 1927–56.
Daponte, Beth Osborne, Seth Sanders, and Lowell Taylor. 1999. "Why Do Low-Income Households Not Use Food Stamps: Evidence from an Experiment." *Journal of Human Resources* 34(3): 612–28.
Davis, Steven J., and Till M. von Wachter. 2011. "Recessions and the Costs of Job Loss." *Brookings Papers on Economic Activity* 43(2): 1–72.
Duncan, Greg J., Pamela A. Morris, and Chris Rodrigues. 2011. "Does Money Really Matter? Estimating Impacts of Family Income on Young Children's Achievement with Data from Random-Assignment Experiments." *Developmental Psychology* 47(5): 1263–79.
East, Chloe N. 2016. "The Effect of Food Stamps on Children's Health: Evidence from Immigrants' Changing Eligibility." Job Market Paper. Denver:

University of Colorado. Accessed October 3, 2017. http://www.sole-jole.org/17153.pdf.

Evans, Gary W., and Rochelle C. Cassells. 2014. "Childhood Poverty, Cumulative Risk Exposure, and Mental Health in Emerging Adults." *Clinical Psychological Science* 2(3): 287–96.

Evans, William N., and Craig L. Garthwaite. 2014. "Giving Mom a Break: The Impact of Higher EITC Payments on Maternal Health." *American Economic Journal: Economic Policy* 6(2): 258–290.

Farah, Martha J., David M. Shera, Jessica H. Savage, Laura Betancourt, Joan M. Giannetta, Nancy L. Brodsky, Elsa K. Malmud, and Hallam Hurt. 2006. "Childhood Poverty: Specific Associations with Neurocognitive Development." *Brain Research* 1110(1): 166–74.

Feldman, Naomi E., Peter Katuscak, and Laura Kowano. 2016. "Taxpayer Confusion: Evidence from the Child Tax Credit." *American Economic Review* 106(3): 807–35.

Heinrich, Carolyn J. 2016. "The Bite of Administrative Burden: A Theoretical and Empirical Investigation." *Journal of Public Administration and Research Theory* 26(3): 403–20.

Herd, Pamela, Thomas DeLeire, Hope Harvey, and Donald Moynihan. 2013. "Shifting Administrative Burden to the State: The Case of Medicaid Take-Up." *Public Administration Review* 73(s1)(September/October): S69–81.

Hilger, Nathaniel G. 2016. "Parental Job Loss and Children's Long-Term Outcomes: Evidence from 7 Million Fathers' Layoffs." *American Economic Journal: Applied Economics* 8(3): 247–83.

Hoynes, Hilary W., Douglas L. Miller, and David Simon. 2015. "Income, the Earned Income Tax Credit, and Infant Health." *American Economic Journal: Economic Policy* 7(1): 172–211.

Hoynes, Hilary W., and Jesse Rothstein. 2016. "Tax Policy Toward Low-Income Families." *NBER* Working Paper no. 22080. Cambridge, Mass.: National Bureau of Economic Research.

Hoynes, Hilary W., and Diane Whitmore Schanzenbach. 2009. "Consumption Responses to In-Kind Transfers: Evidence from the Introduction of the Food Stamp Program." *American Economic Journal: Applied Economics* 1(4): 109–39.

———. 2012. "Work Incentives and the Food Stamp Program." *Journal of Public Economics* 96(1): 151–62.

———. 2016. "U.S. Food and Nutrition Programs." In *Economics of Means-Tested Transfer Programs in the United States*, vol. 1, edited by Robert A. Moffitt. Chicago: University of Chicago Press.

Hoynes, Hilary W., Diane Whitmore Schanzenbach, and Douglas Almond. 2016. "Long Run Impacts of Childhood Access to the Safety Net." *The American Economic Review* 106(4): 903–34.

Huston, Aletha C., Greg J. Duncan, Robert Granger, Johannes Bos, Vonnie McLoyd, Rashmita Mistry, Danielle Crosby, Christina Gibson, Katherine Magnuson, Jennifer Romich, and Ana Ventura. 2001. "Work-Based Antipoverty Programs for Parents Can Enhance the School Performance and Social Behavior of Children." *Child Development* 72(1): 318–36.

Klerman, Jacob, and Caroline Danielson. 2009. "Determinants of the Food Stamp Program Caseload." Contractor and Cooperator Report no. 50. Washington: U.S. Department of Agriculture, Economic Research Service and Food and Nutrition Assistance Research Program.

Kline, Patrick M., and Christopher R. Walters. 2016. "Evaluating Public Programs with Close Substitutes: The Case of Head Start." *Quarterly Journal of Economics* 131(4): 1795–848.

Liebman, Jeffrey, and Richard Zeckhauser. 2004. "Schmeduling." Mimeo. Boston, Mass.: Harvard Kennedy School.

Lindo, Jason M. 2010. "Are Children Really Inferior Goods? Evidence from Displacement-Driven Income Shocks." *Journal of Human Resources* 45(2): 301–27.

Lundstrom, Samuel M. 2017. "The Impact of Family Income on Child Achievement: Evidence from the Earned Income Tax Credit: Comment." *American Economic Review* 107(2): 623–28.

McLoyd, Vonnie C. 1998. "Socioeconomic Disadvantage and Child Development." *American Psychologist* 53(2): 185–204.

Meyer, Bruce D., Wallace K. C. Mok, and James X. Sullivan. 2009. "The Under-Reporting of Transfers in Household Surveys: Its Nature and Consequences. *NBER* Working Paper no. 15181. Cambridge, Mass.: National Bureau of Economic Research.

Moffitt, Robert. 1983. "An Economic Model of Welfare Stigma." *American Economic Review* 73(5): 1023–35.

Moore, Kristin Anderson, Zakia Redd, Mary Burkhauser, Kassim Mbwana, and Ashleigh Collins. 2009. "Children in Poverty: Trends, Consequences, and Policy Options." Research Brief no. 2009-11. Bethesda, Md.: Child Trends.

Moynihan, Donald, Pamela Herd, and Hope Harvey. 2015. "Administrative Burden: Learning, Psychological, and Compliance Costs in Citizen-State Interactions." *Journal of Public Administration Research and Theory* 25(1): 43-69.

Mullainathan, Sendhil, and Eldar Shafir. 2013. *Scarcity: Why Having Too Little Means So Much*. New York: Time Books, Henry Holt.

Noble, Kimberly G., Bruce D. McCandliss, and Martha J. Farah. 2007. "Socioeconomic Gradients Predict Individual Differences in Neurocognitive Abilities." *Developmental Science* 10(4): 464-80.

Oreopoulos, Philip, Marianne Page, and Ann H. Stevens. 2008. "The Intergenerational Effects of Worker Displacement." *Journal of Labor Economics* 26(3): 455-83.

Plueger, Dean. 2009. "Earned Income Tax Credit Participation Rate for Tax Year 2005." Research Bulletin. Washington: Internal Revenue Service.

Reardon, Sean F. 2011. "The Widening Academic Achievement Gap between the Rich and the Poor: New Evidence and Possible Explanations." In *Whither Opportunity? Rising Inequality, Schools, and Children's Life Chances*, edited by Greg J. Duncan and Richard J. Murnane. New York: Russell Sage Foundation.

Reeb, Ben T., Katherine J. Conger, and Monica J. Martin. 2013. "Perceived Economic Strain Exacerbates the Effect of Parental Depressed Mood on Hostile Parenting." *Journal of Family Psychology* 27(2): 263-70.

Santiago, Catherine DeCarlo, Martha E. Wadsworth, and Jessica Stump. 2011. "Socioeconomic Status, Neighborhood Disadvantage, and Poverty Related Stress: Prospective Effects on Psychological Syndromes Among Diverse Low-Income Families." *Journal of Economic Psychology* 32(2): 218-30.

Schanzenbach, Diane Whitmore. 2009. "Experimental Estimates of the Barriers to Food Stamp Enrollment." Discussion paper no. 1367-09. Madison, Wisc.: Institute for Research on Poverty.

Schilbach, Frank, Heather Schofield, and Sendhil Mullainathan. 2016. "The Psychological Lives of the Poor." *American Economic Review Papers & Proceedings* 106(5): 435-40.

Schwabish, Jonathan. 2012. "The Impact of Online Food Stamp Applications on Participation." Paper presented at the Annual Meeting of the Association of Public Policy and Management. (November 8, 2012).

Shaefer, H. Luke, Sophie Collyer, Greg Duncan, Kathryn Edin, Irwin Garfinkel, David Harris, Timothy M. Smeeding, Jane Waldfogel, Christopher Wimer, and Hirokazu Yoshikawa. 2018. "A Universal Child Allowance: A Plan to Reduce Poverty and Income Instability Among Children in the United States." *RSF: The Russell Sage Foundation Journal of the Social Sciences* 4(2): 22-42. DOI: 10.7758/RSF.2018.4.2.02.

Siebens, Julie. 2013. "Extended Measures of Well-Being: Living Conditions in the United States 2011." *Household Economic Studies* Series P70, no. 136. Washington: U.S. Census Bureau.

Solon, Gary. 1992. "Intergenerational Income Mobility in the United States." *American Economic Review* 82(3): 393-408.

Statistics of Income. 2013a. "Individual Tax Return Line Item Estimates." Washington: Internal Revenue Service.

———. 2013b. "Individual Income Tax Returns." Washington: Internal Revenue Service.

Stevens, Ann H., and Jessamyn Schaller. 2011. "Short-Run Effects of Parental Job Loss on Children's Academic Achievement." *Economics of Education Review* 30(2): 289-99.

Strully, Kate W., David H. Rehkopf, and Ziming Xuan. 2010. "Effects of Prenatal Poverty on Infant Health: State Earned Income Tax Credits and Birth Weight." *American Sociological Review* 75(4): 534-62.

Sullivan, Daniel, and Till M. von Wachter. 2009. "Job Displacement and Mortality: An Analysis Using Administrative Data." *Quarterly Journal of Economics* 124(3): 1265-306.

U.S. Department of Commerce, Bureau of the Census, and U.S. Department of Labor, Bureau of Labor Statistics. 2010 and 2015. Current Population Survey: Annual Social and Economic (ASEC) Supplement Survey. Washington: U.S. Census Bureau.

von Wachter, Till M. 2010. "Summary of the Literature on Job Displacement in the US and EU: What We Know and What We Would Like to Know." In *Wage Structures, Employment Adjustments and Globalization: Evidence from Linked and Firm-Level Panel Data*, edited by David Marsden and François Rycx. Applied Econometrics Association Series. New York: Palgrave Macmillan.

Wagmiller, Robert Lee, and Robert M. Adelman.

2009. "Childhood and Intergenerational Poverty: The Long-Term Consequences of Growing Up Poor." New York: National Center for Children in Poverty.

Watson, Tara. 2014. "Inside the Refrigerator: Immigration Enforcement and Chilling Effects in Medicaid Participation." *American Economic Journal: Economic Policy* 6(3): 313–38.

Wight, Vanessa, Neeraj Kaushal, Jane Waldfogel, and Irwin Garfinkel. 2014. "Understanding the Link between Poverty and Food Insecurity Among Children: Does the Definition of Poverty Matter?" *Journal of Children and Poverty* 20(1): 1–20.

Wimer, Christopher, Sophie Collyer, and Sara Kimberlin. 2018. "Assessing the Potential Impacts of Innovative New Policy Proposals on Poverty in the United States." *RSF: The Russell Sage Foundation Journal of the Social Sciences* 4(3): 167–83. DOI: 10.7758/RSF.2018.4.3.09.

Wolfe, Barbara, and Scott Scrivner. 2005. "The Devil May Be in the Details: How the Characteristics of SCHIP Programs Affect Take-Up." *Journal of Policy Analysis and Management* 24(3): 499–522.

Yoshikawa, Hirokazu, J. Lawrence Aber, and William R. Beardslee. 2012. "The Effects of Poverty on the Mental, Emotional, and Behavioral Health of Children and Youth: Implications for Prevention." *American Psychologist* 67(4): 272–84.

Zimmerman, David J. 1992. "Regression Toward Mediocrity in Economic Stature." *American Economic Review* 82(3): 409–29.

A Targeted Minimum Benefit Plan: A New Proposal to Reduce Poverty Among Older Social Security Recipients

PAMELA HERD, MELISSA FAVREAULT, MADONNA HARRINGTON MEYER, AND TIMOTHY M. SMEEDING

In recent years, the big news in Social Security reform has been the program's fiscal concerns. In light of concerns about both program costs and benefit adequacy, we propose an effective and relatively inexpensive targeted program to provide a minimally adequate floor to old-age income through the Social Security system. This minimum benefit plan would provide a cost-effective method for reducing elder poverty to very low levels. A key element is that the benefit would not count toward income eligibility thresholds for other social programs. Other aspects include an income-tested benefit that would bring beneficiaries to 100 percent of the poverty threshold; application by filing of a 1040 income tax return; and setting of benefit levels and distribution through the Social Security Administration.

Keywords: elderly, poverty, social security, income guarantee

In recent years, the big news in Social Security reform has been the program's fiscal concerns. Beneath the headlines, however, large pockets of poverty remain, particularly among those who are single, women, and black people. In light of concerns about both program costs and benefit adequacy, we propose an effective and relatively inexpensive targeted program to provide a minimally adequate floor to old-age income through the Social Security system. This proposal would provide a minimum benefit to Social Security beneficiaries that increases their

Pamela Herd is professor in the La Follette School of Public Affairs at the University of Wisconsin–Madison. **Melissa Favreault** is senior fellow in the Income and Benefits Policy Center at the Urban Institute. **Madonna Harrington Meyer** is professor of sociology and senior research associate at the Center for Policy Research at the Maxwell School of Syracuse University. **Timothy M. Smeeding** is professor in the La Follette School of Public Affairs at the University of Wisconsin–Madison.

© 2018 Russell Sage Foundation. Herd, Pamela, Melissa Favreault, Madonna Harrington Meyer, and Timothy M. Smeeding. 2018. "A Targeted Minimum Benefit Plan: A New Proposal to Reduce Poverty Among Older Social Security Recipients." *RSF: The Russell Sage Foundation Journal of the Social Sciences* 4(2): 74–90. DOI: 10.7758/RSF.2018.4.2.04. The opinions expressed herein are those of the authors alone, and should not be construed as representing the opinions or policy of any agency of the federal government nor of any of the educational and research institutions that sponsor their work. This research was supported, in part, by an AARP Innovation Award. Direct correspondence to: Pamela Herd at pherd@lafollette.wisc.edu, 1080 Observatory Dr., University of Wisconsin–Madison, Madison, WI 53706; Melissa Favreault at mfaveau@urban.org, 2100 M Street NW, Income and Benefits Policy Center, Urban Institute, Washington, D.C. 20037; Madonna Harrington Meyer at mhm@maxwell.syr.edu, Syracuse University, 426 Eggers Hall, Syracuse, NY 13244; and Timothy M. Smeeding at smeeding@lafollette.wisc.edu, 3464 Social Science Building, Institute for Research on Poverty, University of Wisconsin–Madison, 1180 Observatory Dr., Madison, WI 53706.

Open Access Policy: *RSF: The Russell Sage Foundation Journal of the Social Sciences* is an open access journal. This article is published under a Creative Commons Attribution-NonCommercial-NoDerivs 3.0 Unported License.

household income to 100 percent of the poverty level. This minimum benefit plan (MBP), modeled after the Canadian minimum benefit for the elderly (the Guaranteed Income Supplement or GIS) with benefit determination akin to the United States' Earned Income Tax Credit (EITC), would provide a cost-effective method for reducing old-age poverty among Social Security recipients to historically low levels.

THE RISK FOR POVERTY AND ECONOMIC SECURITY AMONG THE AGED

Although Social Security has been the United States' most effective anti-poverty policy, reducing elderly cash income poverty rates from nearly 40 percent in the late 1950s to around 9 percent today, problems with income security among older adults remain (Marchand and Smeeding 2016). Social Security provides a guaranteed monthly income for most, but economic insecurity is still a common experience for many older Americans. Approximately 9 percent of older adults fall below the poverty line, though poverty rates that take the costs of medical care into account are closer to 14 percent (Renwick and Fox 2016). Moreover, subgroups face even higher poverty rates. The poverty rate for single older adults is three times as high as for married older adults (Proctor, Semega, and Kollar 2016). For example, 4 percent of married adults versus 15 percent of single older adults fall below the official poverty line. Older women are nearly twice as likely to be poor as are men. Black older adults are three times as likely to be poor as white older adults (18 percent versus 6 percent). Particularly striking is that nearly 30 percent of single black older women live below the poverty line; the rate for comparable white women is 13 percent (Proctor, Semega, and Kollar 2016).

Labor force participation, and therefore earnings, are limited for older people for a wide variety of reasons. Older adults face health problems, both physical and cognitive, that may limit their ability to participate in the labor force (Zajakova, Montez, and Herd 2014). They also face widespread age discrimination. We generally expect older people to exit the labor force, which is part of the reason that Social Security exists in the first place. Social Security recognizes the specific economic vulnerabilities associated with aging (Quadagno 1984). The broader rationale for protecting vulnerable old adults, which formed the justification for the New Deal, is that freedom from economic insecurity is a basic social right in a functioning democracy (Marshall 1950). The question becomes, how best to meet this social right?

CURRENT OLD AGE SOCIAL INSURANCE PROGRAM ANTI-POVERTY ISSUES

Social Security has been extraordinarily successful at protecting older adults from economic insecurity and poverty. Indeed, Social Security is the most successful anti-poverty policy ever implemented in the United States. Poverty rates declined from nearly 40 percent in the 1950s to under 10 percent today among those age sixty-five and older, largely as a function of more generous income protections offered to successive generations by Social Security (Englehart and Gruber 2004; Center for Budget and Policy Priorities 2015). Indeed, poverty rates among older adults today that exclude Social Security income would be about 40 percent (Center for Budget and Policy Priorities 2015). Nonetheless, Social Security is ineffective at protecting certain older Americans from poverty and income insecurity, notably black single women.

Social Security has a dual eligibility structure; recipients may qualify for benefits as either retired workers or as spouses of retired workers. Individuals quality for retired worker benefits, or Old Age Social Insurance (OASI), by having a minimum level of earnings over forty quarters, or a total of ten years of earnings. Benefit size is then based on the highest thirty-five years of earnings over one's work life. Individuals may also qualify for spousal and survivor benefits based on having been married to a qualifying worker for at least ten years. At the full retirement age, they can receive a spousal benefit that is 50 percent of the value of their current or previous partner's benefit. The survivor benefit, should that partner die, is equivalent to 100 percent of the deceased's benefit. Although individuals may be eligible for both benefits, they only receive one, whichever is the larger.

Spousal and survivor benefits are predominantly received by women. Although in more recent cohorts, growing percentages of women qualify for worker benefits (benefits based on their own employment and earnings), they are still just as likely as their mothers were to draw on their spousal and widow benefits because their earnings are generally much lower than their husbands' (Sass 2016). Just as in 1960, nearly two-thirds of women today draw on benefits based on their spouse's earning's record—though a growing faction of these women are dually entitled (Social Security Administration 2015). Dually entitled means that though women qualify for spousal-survivor benefits and worker benefits, they draw on the spousal and widow benefits because these benefits are higher than their worker benefits (Social Security Administration 2015; Herd 2005b).

Women's earnings continue to lag men's because they have lower levels of labor force participation and lower earnings. Gender differences in earnings continue to be linked to gender discrimination in the labor force, chronic shortages of high-quality, affordable, flexible child care, and women's ongoing disproportionate responsibility for providing care for both children and older adults (Budig and England 2001; Kahn, García-Manglano, and Bianchi 2014). About 60 percent of mothers who had a child in the last year were in the labor force (Kaestner, Lubotsky, and Qureshi 2016). Moreover, the trend since 2000 has been upward, especially during the Great Recession, in the fraction of stay-at-home mothers (Cohn, Livingston, and Wang 2014). Although men do more of the housework and childcare than in previous generations, women still spend about twice as much time on childrearing activities as men do (Bianchi, Robinson, and Milkie 2006). The long-term implications for cumulative lifetime earnings—and thus subsequent Social Security benefits earnings linked to earnings—is large. White women earn 82.5 percent of white men, black women earn 89.9 percent of black men and Hispanic women earn 89.0 percent of Hispanic men (Herd 2005b; IWPR 2016).

Accordingly, while the features of spousal and survivor benefits offset risks disproportionately faced by women, this protective feature of the program only helps those who marry—for a minimum of ten years. Historically, these benefits have been less helpful to black and poor women given their greater propensity to be employed and lesser propensity to marry compared to white women. Dramatic changes in marriage trends are further reducing the effectiveness benefits for all women, but especially for black women and women with low educational attainment. The percentage of women born between 1960 and 1964 who will never marry is 5.4 percent for college graduates and about 12 percent for non-college graduates. The race differences are even more striking. Around 7 percent of white women in this cohort will never marry, versus 36 percent of black women (Goldstein and Kenney 2001). Younger cohorts of women are also far more likely to divorce. Divorced women need a ten-year marriage to qualify, but fewer than 50 percent of marriages will meet this criterion in future cohorts (Haider, Jacknowitz, and Schoeni 2003). The result is that among women born in the 1960s, the proportion of white and Hispanic women who reach old age qualified for spouse or widow benefits will hover just above 80 percent, versus 50 percent of black women (Harrington Meyer, Wolf, and Himes 2006).

Spousal and survivor benefits are less progressive than worker benefits and reduce the overall progressivity of the program (Gustman, Steinmeier, and Tabatabai 2011; Harrington Meyer 1996; Herd 2005b). With worker benefits, the lower an individual's average lifetime earnings, the higher the percentage of earnings the benefit replaces. If one person within a married couple earns $6,000 a month across his life, he would have a benefit that replaces 31 percent of this level ($1,866 a month). If his wife had not worked, her spousal benefit would increase the total household replacement rate to 47 percent. In contrast, a couple who each earned an average of $1,000 monthly would have benefits that replace 68 percent of prior earnings (for a household total of $1,258). Although still progressive, the latter couple sees no benefit from spousal benefits despite their greater labor force participation and lower incomes.

Survivor benefits especially penalize dual-earner couples, who now make up the majority of families. In 2015, just over 60 percent of married couples with children under eighteen were both employed, versus less than 33 percent in 1950 (Bureau of Labor Statistics 2016). The problem for dual-earner couples is illustrated in the following example. In one couple, each spouse earns $30,000 a year, for a combined average annual lifetime income of $60,000. The other couple is a one-earner household with a total income of $60,000. The woman in the one-earner household would receive a $1,200 widow benefit. The woman in the two-earner couple, as a widow, would receive only an $800 benefit. Her survivor benefit is $800 and her worker benefit is also $800, but she receives just one of the two benefits.

The dual-earner couple penalty is disproportionately harmful to black families. Historically, black married women have been more likely to work than white women (Goldin 1977). Moreover, black households remain more likely than white households to have more similar earnings between spouses (Winslow-Bowe 2009). The married couples with the more equivalent earnings pay the highest dual-earner penalty.

Social Security is generally understood as one leg of a three-legged stool. The importance of Social Security income has been increasing as the other two legs, private pensions and private savings, have become more wobbly and unequal. Whereas Social Security continues to be based on collective risk, private pensions are increasingly based on individual risk and responsibility (Harrington Meyer and Herd 2007). In the past, both the Social Security leg and the employer-pension leg pooled risk across all beneficiaries, with the government and employers, respectively, assuming responsibility. Today, most employment-related pensions are in the form of defined contributions, which are managed by the employee. In the 1970s, approximately one-quarter of private-sector employees participating in an employer-sponsored pension plan participated in a defined contribution plan—and these individuals were largely concentrated among small employers, with large employers almost exclusively providing defined benefit plans. By 2013, 70 percent of private-sector employees pension participants were in defined contribution plans (EBRI 2015). Employer-provided pensions now place risk almost entirely on individuals. The value of this type of pension, like the value of personal savings, is linked to the ups and downs of the stock market and the individual's ability to invest those resources wisely. Poor decisions or simply poor luck can decimate individuals' retirement income.

Moreover, private pension coverage is on the wane. A mixture of "alternative work engagements," such as contractual labor, the decline in jobs covered by unions, and the growing number of low-wage jobs, has led to a decline in employer pension support (Katz and Kreuger 2016; Harrington Meyer and Herd 2007).[1] The fraction of full-time workers in the public and private sector offered pensions has fallen from 74 percent in the late 1970s to 64 percent in 2012 (Munnell and Bleckman 2014). In the private sector, only 43 percent of all full- and part-time employees are offered pensions and about 37 percent actually participate. Finally, the Great Recession put all forms of savings at risk. Moreover, many participants gut their private pensions. Even with the penalty for early withdrawal, the proportion of individuals taking early withdrawals from defined contribution plans rose from 13.3 to 15.4 percent between 2004 and 2010 (Argento, Bryant, and Sabelhaus 2015).

The third leg of the stool, private savings have always been the most unstable. Private savings, which are organized around individual risk and responsibility, ebb and flow with changes in the economy. Generally, most Americans have more debt than savings, and in recent years private savings have been at record lows (Harrington Meyer and Herd 2007). Workers in jobs with less income, hours, benefits, and stability are least likely to be able to save. Older women, blacks and Hispanics, and single persons find it particularly difficult to save for old age.

Although Social Security still provides some floor, the lack of a more traditional income

---

1. Katz and Kreuger define alternative work arrangements as temporary help agency workers, on-call workers, contract workers, and independent contractors or freelancers (2016). Their data show that the percentage of workers engaged in alternative work rose from 10.1 percent in February 2005 to 15.8 percent in late 2015.

guarantee within the program, which would provide a flat income payment to protect against poverty, weakens the program's ability to provide improved protections against the new financial risks older adults are facing.

ADDRESSING THE POLICY PROBLEM

A new minimum benefit has become one of the most common proposals to address both general poverty among the elderly, as well as the weaknesses of spousal and survivor benefits (Congressional Research Service 2014). Before discussing minimum benefits in the current policy context and our proposed minimum benefit proposal, however, we review some common alternative policy options. We argue that each of these options has important negative features and that an MBP would more effectively reduce old-age poverty.

Earnings Sharing

Periodically, policy analysts renew attention to earnings sharing as a mechanism to address weaknesses with spousal and survivor benefits. Given that decisions about who should work and who should stay home to care for children or frail older parents may be made as a couple, then perhaps rewards via Social Security should be reaped as a couple. Thus, both persons in a marriage should receive credit for half of each year's earnings for Social Security for the duration of the marriage (Iams, Reznik, and Tamborini 2010; Favreault and Steuerle 2007; Congressional Budget Office 1986; Burkhauser 1982). Although these proposals reduce gender inequality within married couples, they do not address poverty for the growing share of women who spend all or most of their adult lives single.

Increasing Survivor Benefits

Currently, spouse beneficiaries receive 50 percent of their spouse or ex-spouse's benefit, while widows receive 100 percent of that benefit. Concerned about poverty among widows, many policy analysts have proposed giving less to the couple while the husband is alive and more to the widow after he is dead (Smeeding, Estes, and Glass 1999; Hurd and Wise 1997; Burkhauser and Smeeding 1994). The U.S. Government Accountability Office (GAO 2007) recently explored giving spouses just 33 percent or giving widows 112.5 percent. Although such proposals show some redistribution of resources to lower-income women, they do not provide any economic security for women who have not met the marriage requirements for spousal and survivor benefits, who are often the women most in need of economic assistance.

Care Credits

Some policy analysts favor care credits as a way to provide an economic reward for those who either take time out of the labor force or have low earnings because of the care they have provided for children, the disabled, or frail older relatives. Early options included adding more drop-out years to the benefit formula, or even permitting caregivers to drop all zero year earnings from the benefit formula, so that those who opted out of work to care for family members could drop more than the currently allowed five years from the thirty-five year earnings benefit calculation (Herd 2006). Such proposals do not take into account those with reduced wages due to care work, thus more recent proposals provide a credit for earnings that were in fact not, or only partially, earned. Some provide credit only for childcare; others include care for older people (Herd 2006; GAO 2007). The main problem with care credit proposals, however, is that they are not particularly effective at targeting the poorest beneficiaries and substantially improving their incomes (Herd 2006), though they are relatively more effective than the prior alternatives already detailed.

WHY CURRENT MINIMUM BENEFITS ARE FAILING OLDER AMERICANS

The United States currently has a means-tested minimum benefit program, Supplemental Security Income (SSI), the benefit has some serious shortcomings that prevent it from effectively protecting the income security of the oldest Americans (Center on Budget and Policy Priorities 2014). In combination with Supplemental Nutrition Assistance Program (SNAP, formerly Food Stamps) benefits and minimal Social Security benefits, SSI would lift a single person with no other income to only 85 percent of the poverty threshold, and a couple to 101.8 percent. However, 80 percent of SSI beneficiaries are single, so most have incomes well below the poverty line (Center on Budget and Policy Priorities 2014). SSI counts all unearned income, including Social Security benefits, interest on savings, and dividend income, at a 100 percent marginal tax rate over and above the $20 per month income exclusion, whereas earned income is subject to a 50 percent tax rate, with additional exclusions for work expenses. SSI also has asset tests. In 1972, when SSI was created, asset limits were set at $1,500 for individuals and $2,250 for couples. In 1989, they were raised to $2,000 for individuals and $3,000 for couples. They have not been raised since. If these guidelines had kept pace with inflation since 1989, they would be more than three times the size of the current levels at $7,652 for individuals and $11,478 for couples (Center on Budget and Policy Priorities 2014).

Additionally, SSI take-up rates are quite low: between 40 percent and 60 percent of those who are eligible do not even apply for benefits (Center on Buget and Policy Priorities 2014; McGarry 2000; McGarry and Schoeni 2015; Smeeding 1999). Overall, just 60 percent of poor elderly Americans receive SSI benefits (U.S. House Ways and Means Committee 2004). Eligible poor older Americans who do not apply are unaware of the benefits, put off by the cumbersome eligibility forms, or too stigmatized by the process. Another reason for low take-up is that older Americans must apply separately for SSI. This additional administrative layer, alongside a complicated application due to factors such as asset tests, reduces take-up (Center on Budget and Policy Priorities 2014; Hubbard, Skinner, and Zeldes 1995). In short, SSI does not provide an effective minimum benefit. The asset guidelines and the complicated administrative structure reduce the program's effectiveness at improving the income security of the poorest older Americans.

Some have argued for the improvement of SSI benefits rather than the creation of a minimum benefit within Social Security. This strategy would be problematic, however. In short, the administrative structure of the program, including complicated eligibility procedures and an application process separate from Social Security, makes it very difficult for the program to be effective. The administrative structure is in large part responsible for the low take-up rates. In contrast, Social Security has nearly 100 percent take-up. Because our MBP requires meeting the forty quarters of earnings eligibility criteria for Social Security, SSI should continue to play a valuable role as the ultimate backstop for the poor (and frequently disabled) elderly, especially those in need of nursing home care or other Medicaid-financed care, but its expansion may not be the best way to create a substantial reduction in elder income poverty. In fact, a new program that drew seniors from SSI to a more generous income benefit could be partially funded by a reduction in SSI benefits for the aged.

Although most are unaware of it, the Social Security program has a special minimum benefit, but the rules are so restrictive that, in 2014 for example, only fifty-three thousand beneficiaries, or far less than 1 percent, received it. In short, it requires many years of low earnings and the benefits linked to it are quite low. Few people actually have consistent numbers of work years with very low earnings. Approximately 4 percent to 6 percent of full-time earners had below minimum wages for more than twelve consecutive months (Olsen and Hoffmeyer 2002). Moreover, parameters in the minimum benefit calculation grow with Social Security's cost-of-living adjustment rather than with wages, as other Social Security benefits do. Craig Feinstein (2013) points out that, as a consequence, it is exceedingly and increasingly rare for people to qualify or benefit from the special minimum benefit.

A NEW OPTION FOR THE UNITED STATES: A MINIMUM BENEFIT PLAN

To reduce poverty among the elderly, we argue for a new minimum benefit within Social Security that expands benefits and eligibility standards much less strict than they are today, but still ensures that only the poorest individuals receive it.

The models for our proposal are the Canadian GIS and the United States' EITC. Canada has managed to achieve much greater poverty reduction among seniors while spending much less on social retirement programs than other rich countries, though slightly more than the United States. The reason is that Canada spends its public pension money differently. In particular, it spends a great deal on the near-universal Old Age Security and income-tested GIS programs, and apply no asset test and only a relatively simple annual application process (which permits an income test integrated with income tax filing). Over 90 percent of the eligible Canadian elderly participate in GIS (Battle 1997), compared to about 50 percent elder participation in SSI in the United States (U.S. House Ways and Means Committee 2004; McGarry 2000; McGarry and Schoeni 2015; Smeeding 1999).

The most similar U.S. welfare policy to the Canadian GIS, in terms of administration and benefit application procedures, is the Earned Income Tax Credit. The EITC delivers income supplements to poor working-age Americans. The EITC has no asset tests. Further, individuals apply for EITC benefits through the tax system on a basic 1040 form. The ease of EITC eligibility and application procedures means that around 80 percent of those eligible actually receive benefits (Jones 2014). This is a substantial improvement over SSI's 50 percent take-up rate.

Features of the Targeted Minimum Benefit Plan

This section details four features of the MBP proposal: eligibility, benefit levels and income exclusions, administrative structure and take-up, linking to other programs, and funding and costs. Before we detail the specifics of our policy proposal in each of these sections, we highlight key issues in these categories, such as the logic for including or excluding asset tests or whether to require individuals to reapply for the benefit every year.

Eligibility

The first feature of a targeted minimum is the program's *eligibility requirements*, which may include income, asset, residency, work history, and citizenship tests. Should the MBP include an asset test? No. Evidence is widespread that liquid asset tests in the United States reduce savings (Hubbard, Skinner, and Zeldes 1995; Powers 1998; Neumark and Powers 1998). The Canadian GIS and the EITC have no asset test. We discourage an asset test for the following reasons. First, it negatively affects savings. Second, it would substantially increase the administrative cost and complexity of managing the program. Third, asset income would be included in total income eligibility. Last, the EITC provides a precedent for not including an asset test.

Should the MBP require beneficiaries to meet the ten-year earning requirement? Yes. Approximately 2 percentage points of the poverty rate among the elderly include those who do not qualify for Social Security (Whitman, Reznik, and Shoffner 2011). If this were a requirement, these individuals would have access to SSI, but would not benefit from the MBP. We believe it is important to integrate the new MBP into the existing Social Security program, which entails abiding by the existing eligibility criteria. This choice has two justifications. First, it maintains employment incentives within Social Security. The second, and more important, reason to keep the ten-year eligibility requirement is that it strikes between the equity and adequacy that have always existed within the program. Maintaining a focus on equity has been key to Social Security's political resilience, and related success, because individuals feel that these benefits are "earned" (Harrington Meyer and Herd 2007). Maintaining the link between employment and the Social Security minimum benefit, then, is likely important to maintain the political resilience of the program.

Our proposal is that the MBP would be payable at the Social Security normal retirement age, which is currently undergoing a gradual increase from sixty-five to sixty-seven. Eligibility would require at least twenty years of residency in the United States as well as the standard OASI eligibility tests. Moreover, eligibility would be based on income adjusted for marital status as linked to poverty income thresholds. Single individuals would qualify if their income fell below 100 percent of the poverty level for a single-person household. Married individuals would qualify if their income fell below 100 percent of the poverty level for a two-person household.

Benefit Levels and Income Exclusions

A second critical feature of a targeted program is its *benefit levels and income exclusions (set-asides and phase-outs)*. Should the MBP include set-asides and phase-outs? Yes. Higher benefit levels obviously lead to greater expenditures but less poverty. A more generous phase-out range—for example, allowing individuals to exclude half of all earnings or income from savings—also leads to higher expenditure levels because the program reaches a broader clientele higher in the income distribution. However, they also may provide added incentives for low-income workers to save, if only modestly, for retirement, and for seniors with low earnings histories to continue working at least part-time to improve their living standards. Further, having seniors continue to work improves the overall financial strength of the program. Similar incentives may be created by excluding, or setting aside, some fixed amount of other retirement income. For instance, the SSI program allows eligible beneficiaries to set aside up to $20 per month ($240 per year) of other retirement income, like Social Security.

We would also discourage employment tests beyond the ten-year or forty-quarter work history requirement. Many minimum benefit proposals are premised on linking the number of earnings years to benefit size, that is, forty years of earnings being required to receive a 100 percent poverty level benefit (Herd 2005a). The problem, however, is that the people who most need a generous minimum have had numerous labor force exits (Favreault 2010). Individuals at the bottom of the labor market are the first to be laid off during recessions and have no mandatory paid sick leave; in the United States, they lack job protection if they or their children get sick, and more generally limited educational attainment puts them in employment categories that provide limited long-term job protection. All of these factors make it difficult to generate a continuous and consistent stream of earnings years across the life course. We note that though some might be concerned that the MBP could negatively affect labor force incentives, the reality is that younger people know little about how the program works and therefore are unlikely to change for employment based on programmatic rules. Indeed, a recent American Association of Retired Persons survey found that just 9 percent of consumers understood how the benefits work (AARP 2015). Moreover, individuals who qualify for this benefit rely almost completely on Social Security for their income. They tend to have almost no savings, so we anticipate this benefit would not meaningfully influence savings either.

We propose that the MBP should offer a minimum benefit guarantee of 100 percent of the poverty line. It would include a general income exclusion, or set-aside, of $125 per month for all other income sources (earnings, pensions, property income). Those achieving eligibility for Social Security, which requires at least ten years of earnings, would be eligible for the full minimum benefit. A full minimum guarantee should be available to those who have spent at least twenty years as residents of the United States since turning eighteen. For those who have not lived in the country that long, the income guarantee amount would be prorated based on the percentage of years that they have done so. The benefit would be adjusted based on marital status. The MBP would ensure income to 100 percent of the official poverty line for single and married couple recipients.

Administrative Structures and Take-Up

The program's administrative and eligibility structure, including how administrative practices influence take-up, is a third critical aspect of safety net pension programs. Take-up is affected by the stigma attached to the program; the accessibility of the program, including ease of application and reapplication; whether government mounts strong outreach efforts to ensure that all eligible persons enroll; and, assuming eligibility, the level of benefits expected (McGarry 2000; Moynihan, Herd, and Harvey 2014; Herd et al. 2013). As noted, only 40 percent to 60 percent of the eligible elderly apply for SSI, versus 90 percent or more for the Canadian system and around 80 percent for the EITC.

A key administrative issue for the MBP regards the frequency of eligibility redetermination. Should the beneficiaries be required to reapply for the benefit on an annual basis? No. The justification for annual enrollment is to ensure that only those eligible receive the benefit and that they are receiving the proper amount. The problem, however, is that this additional layer of administrative burden will likely lead some of those eligible to not receive the benefit. Particularly at very low income levels, it is rare for there to be a meaningful income change. Given the increasing risk for serious health and cognitive declines, we believe this provision is critical to ensure those who need this benefit the most will continue to receive it.

In our proposal, MBP payments would be combined with the Social Security benefit check in a single monthly payment. Eligibility redetermination should generally be automatic and assessed through the income tax system. Thus, every elderly person needs to file an income tax return to qualify—akin to the way that the EITC is currently administered, though we will not require that individuals refile the 1040 once they are deemed eligible for the benefit—unless they have a change in income. Given that only about half of all OASI recipients file income taxes, nonprofit and elder advocacy groups would need to help elders file a simple 1040, much the same way that Volunteer Income Tax Assistance sites have helped low-income families with children to apply for and claim their benefits from the EITC. Simple (EZ-1040-A) income tax forms would have to be filed by all older adults, the key information on other income sources and liquid asset levels being sent from the Internal Revenue Service (IRS) to the Social Security Administration (SSA) automatically. Essentially, the IRS would provide SSA with the information needed to determine the benefit size. In effect, the MBP check would simply "top up" the OASI check to the determined percentage of the poverty level—adjusting for other sources of income. We expect that the income tax form qualification process will raise MBP participation to 80 percent or above, based on the Canadian experience and the EITC in the United States, including recent experience with the stimulus payments during the Great Recession.

Linking to Other Social Safety Net Programs
A fourth important aspect of safety net pension programs is how they influence eligibility to other safety net programs, such as reduced-cost medical care or housing benefits. First, some programs allow for an automatic "passport" to eligibility to other programs. For example, those eligible for SSI are automatically eligible for Medicaid. This is sometimes done when eligibility rules align between two programs. It can prove decidedly beneficial because it reduces administrative burdens for beneficiaries and increases take-up rates. Should the MBP include such an automatic passport to programs like Medicaid? No. Although we support automatic passports, we do not include them because the eligibility rules for the MBP do not align with those for other safety net programs. Eligibility rules would need to be changed in other programs for an automatic passport to be implemented.

Second, should the MBP benefit count as income toward eligibility for programs such as Medicaid or SNAP? No. Indeed, cash income from the EITC benefit does not count toward income thresholds for programs like Medicaid and SNAP. Under prior minimum benefit proposals, the additional income would count toward eligibility for other safety net programs. This raised some thorny issues given that one in five older adults uses Medicaid to supplement their Medicare benefits. Without Medicaid, out-of-pocket costs could eat up nearly 50 percent of their income (Kaiser Family Foundation 2014). Without this provision, the MBP would likely make many beneficiaries worse off than had it never existed because their out-of-pocket health-care spending would mostly consume or exceed the increase in income associated with the MBP.

Our proposal includes no automatic passport from the MBP to other social welfare programs. Income from the MBP will also not count as income to eligibility for other programs. That said, we are concerned about the potential administrative barriers that might arise for people who have received SSI and would now receive the MBP. The delinking of the Temporary Assistance to Needy Families program from Medicaid during the 1996 welfare reform led to significant reductions in participation in the Medicaid program (Ellwood and Ku 1998). Given that the federal government is already coordinating closely with states regarding state-level Medicaid eligibility via the Affordable Care Act health insurance exchanges, individuals below income Medicaid eligibility levels could receive—at a minimum—notifications that they may be eligible for Medicaid as well as information as to how to apply for the Medicaid program. All individuals should receive an annual accounting of the size of the MBP so that they have documentation if needed for application to other social welfare programs.

A final issue with a targeted MBP regards funding and costs. The MBP could be financed by general revenue or trust funding. The virtues of general revenue finance are that it relieves any MBP-induced pressure on the trust fund balance, and it does not raise payroll tax contributions to fund a program targeted only to the otherwise poor. Just as Medicare Part B is partly financed by general revenue, the MBP would rely on general revenues to top up benefits paid from the OASI trust fund to poverty-line income levels. Moreover, as more elderly women and low earners accrue more complete lifetime work histories, the MBP outlays and participants will fall, as GIS outlays have in Canada (Myles 2000).

We propose that the MBP be funded through general revenues, similar to Medicare Part B. However, we want to be clear that the MBP is a part of Social Security, like Medicare Part B, which is also largely funded out of general revenues, is a part of Medicare. To address cost issues with this new program, we also propose a gradual reduction in auxiliary spousal benefits. This would not likely mean negative impacts for the poorest Americans because they would end up qualifying for the MBP. The likely individual receiving a reduction in Social Security benefits with the elimination of spousal benefits is the spouse of a relatively high earner who herself had a relatively limited earnings history.

SIMULATING THE BENEFIT COSTS AND DISTRIBUTION OF WHO BENEFITS

In addition to providing a general sense of the financial cost of this proposal, we also consider its effect on older adults' economic well-being. We do so in two ways. First, we evaluate the magnitude of the benefit for varying subgroups of older adults, which was on average $3,400 a year for recipients, or a roughly a 40 percent increase in income. The implications of this policy for improvements in economic well-being among older adults are quite large. Second, we consider changes in poverty rates associated with the policy change.[2] We highlight changes in poverty based on the official poverty measure employed by the federal government. The use of the supplemental poverty measure to analyze the policy impact of the MBP would produce relatively significant measurement error. The appendix details why changes in the official poverty measure provide a more robust estimate with considerably less measurement error.

In terms of overall costs, the proposal is estimated to raise spending on Social Security by approximately $9 billion, or 1 percent of total expenditures on Social Security, specifically the Old Age Insurance portion of the program. Over time, the costs would increase because of the rising number of individuals on the program. However, because the benefit is pegged to the official poverty line, which rises based on consumer inflation rather than wages, spending on the minimum benefit as a fraction of overall spending on Social Security would fall over time. The calculation of the Social Security benefit is linked to wages rather than consumer inflation.

Table 1 provides an overview of the distribution of who would receive the MBP, as well as average benefit sizes. Overall, 6.6 percent of Social Security recipients are projected to receive the benefit. The average benefit size would be approximately $3,600. Not surprisingly, women relative to men (7.4 percent to 5.6 percent), unmarried women relative to married women (11.6 percent to 1.9 percent), black and Hispanic Americans relative to whites (14.1 percent to 11.4 percent to 4.9 percent) and those with low edu-

---

2. These were estimated using the Urban Institute's Dynamic Simulation of Income Model (DYNASIM) (for details, see http://www.urban.org/policy-centers/cross-center-initiatives/program-retirement-policy/projects/dynasim-projecting-older-americans-future-well-being, accessed November 17, 2017). DYNASIM was designed to simulate changes to retirement policies specifically. It does not incorporate potential behavioral responses to those policies.

Table 1. People Older Than Sixty-Five Receiving the MBP and Average Benefit, 2017

	Percent Receiving Benefits	Average Annual Benefit for Recipients
All	0.066	$3,601
Sex		
Women	0.074	3,734
Men	0.056	3,384
Race-ethnicity		
Hispanic	0.114	4,230
Non-Hispanic black	0.141	3,801
Non-Hispanic white	0.049	3,296
Non-Hispanic other	0.082	3,945
Marital status and sex		
Unmarried women	0.116	3,715
Unmarried men	0.111	3,037
Married women	0.019	3,896
Married men	0.031	3,950
Age		
65–69	0.048	3,562
70–74	0.056	3,689
75–79	0.062	3,567
80–84	0.079	3,420
85–89	0.094	3,426
90+	0.141	3,965
Education		
Less than high school diploma	0.129	4,053
High school diploma	0.083	3,482
Some college	0.061	3,141
College graduate	0.039	3,541
More than college	0.018	2,534

Source: Authors' compilation based on DYNASIM model.

cational attainment would be far more likely to receive the benefit. Generally, these groups (with the exception of married individuals) also received larger benefits as well, reflecting their greater economic need. For example, the average benefit for women is $3,734 versus $3,384 for men and $3801 for black recipients versus $3,296 for white recipients.

The distribution of benefits by educational attainment further clarifies that those most disadvantaged are most likely to benefit from the policy. Although 2 to 4 percent of those with college degrees would benefit, 13 percent of those without a high school diploma would receive this benefit. Indeed, in analyses not presented here, more than 90 percent of beneficiaries do not have a college degree. Moreover, the benefit size varies by educational attainment; the small fraction of beneficiaries with more than a college degree receive a benefit that is 40 percent smaller than do those beneficiaries without a high school degree.

Finally, what are the implications for poverty rates? These were calculated from the Current

Population Survey (CPS).[3] The poverty rate among those age sixty-five and older dropped from 8.6 percent to 4.4 percent. Not all individuals sixty-five and older living below the poverty line were eligible for the benefit. For example, if a person had not lived in the United States for long enough or did not have ten years of earnings, they were not eligible. On the whole, however, the MBP was effective at reducing poverty among those eligible; the official poverty rate among MBP recipients after the reform dropped by nearly 90 percent, while deep poverty (below the 50 percent threshold) disappeared.

CONCLUSION

Social Security is arguably the most popular and effective U.S. social welfare policy. Nonetheless, a new minimum benefit plan would markedly lower poverty and increase economic security among older adults in a way that is efficient in its targeting.[4] One might question the spending of additional resources on older adults, given their relatively lower poverty rates compared with other groups. But this aggregate focus on all older adults ignores high levels of poverty among subgroups, such as a 30 percent poverty rate among black older single women. Moreover, the tight targeting of this benefit ensures that only the poorest will actually benefit from the proposal, and that they will see an approximate 40 percent increase in their income.

Several features of this plan distinguish it from prior proposals to include a minimum benefit in Social Security. First, it most tightly targets benefits to those with the lowest incomes—taking into account family income resources. Prior proposals have not taken total family or household income resources into account, weakening their targeted nature. Further, unlike some proposals that required many years of work, this minimum ensures that many of those most economically vulnerable—which are typically those who have not had consistent labor force participation (Favreault 2010, forthcoming)—are protected. The policy, however, because it applies only to those eligible for Social Security, will not benefit all older adults who fall below the poverty threshold. Indeed, although the MBP cuts the poverty rate in half, about 4 percent of older adults remain below the line. Most of this group do not have enough earnings years to qualify or have not lived long enough in the United States either to qualify for the benefit or to receive the maximum. For them, the Supplemental Security Income program will remain a critical source of protection.

The second key distinguishing feature of this proposal is that it is sensitive to program interactions, especially Medicaid. For many older adults, any income gains associated with a minimum benefit would likely be offset if they lost access to Medicaid, which provides substantial reductions in their out-of-pocket health costs.

The issues with program interactions, however, point to a critical issue with this proposal in terms of implementation. Many individuals who had received SSI in the past but who would receive the MBP instead would no longer automatically be eligible for Medicaid. They would need to apply for Medicaid separately. This could reduce the fraction of those eligible for Medicaid who actually receive these benefits. These individuals could face increased economic insecurity as a result. Although it is not feasible to implement an automatic passport

---

3. We generally note that the CPS, relative to estimates derived from DYNASIM, includes more measurement error. DYNASIM is based on data from the Survey of Income and Program Participation. First, the CPS is not as effective as the SIPP in its inclusion of social welfare program data, which is problematic for older adults because of their higher reliance on these programs (Czajka and Denmead 2008). Second, the CPS is also specifically problematic for older adults generally because of how it collects income related to pensions, which likely leads to underreporting of income among the elderly.

4. Aged poverty elimination would not be possible with mechanisms tied strictly to Social Security eligibility. Kevin Whitman, Gayle Reznik, and David Shoffner describe the characteristics of non-beneficiaries of Social Security ages sixty-two to eighty-four in 2010 (2011). This group is largely late-arriving immigrants and people with little work history. Those who do not receive Social Security have markedly high poverty rates and are often depend heavily on their family members' incomes.

between the MBP and Medicaid because the eligibility criteria are different, a guiding principle in implementing MBP is to use administrative mechanisms to reduce the potential for this unintended consequence. For example, the federal government could use data from income tax returns to assess the likelihood of eligibility for state-level Medicaid programs. Indeed, the federal government already did so in the Affordable Care Act health insurance exchanges. They could use the information to notify individuals—and even states—of the possibility that beneficiaries may be Medicaid eligible, along with information regarding how to enroll.

More generally, the effectiveness of the MBP proposal will hinge on take-up. As noted, take-up rates in the SSI program, which involves a far more complicated eligibility process with lower benefit levels, are 50 to 60 percent. Around two-thirds of older adults currently file taxes—and those whom this benefit targets are more likely to be nonfilers (Mortenson et al. 2009). A strong informational campaign would be needed to get all older adults to file a return so that they could become eligible. Given the ease of the tax forms for those with limited incomes, the take-up success of the EITC in the United States, and the nearly 100 percent take-up of the GIS in Canada (where tax filing is mandatory for social retirement recipients), we anticipate that, with effective outreach, the policy will benefit the large majority of those eligible for the benefit.

Last are the political and financial limits to redistribution within a mature contributions-financed, earnings-related pension program. Building in too much redistribution is likely to lead to exit by upper-income contributors, where it is permitted (as with the State Second Pension in the United Kingdom), or to declining political support for the pension system among high-earners when exit is not allowed, such as in the United States. The limitation of this policy, which is that it does not reach a fraction of vulnerable individuals without the required earnings history, is a trade-off to ensure that this proposal does not cross that line. Most of the world's largest and most effective poverty-reducing welfare states now include income-tested minimum benefits. Sweden, Canada, Finland, Norway, and numerous other countries with low poverty rates have successfully implemented and maintained targeted minimum benefits at modest cost. We can learn from them and add our own, U.S.-style plan.

APPENDIX

The supplemental poverty measure is different from the official poverty measure in terms of how it defines income. Income includes benefits such as housing supports and food stamps, but is subtracted by expenses, such as out-of-pocket health-care costs and work-related expenses. The supplemental poverty measure has been critical because the official poverty measure does not include benefits such as SNAP or the EITC. For changes to those policies, if you want to assess the impact of policy change on poverty, it does require the use of this alternative supplemental poverty measure. For changes to Social Security, however, because it is counted as income in the official poverty measure, it is easy to assess change in poverty with the official measure.

The use of the supplemental poverty measure for older adults is, however, problematic because of measurement issues. The SPM is especially vulnerable to measurement error because it requires precise estimates of each element of resources gained or resources used—from housing subsidies and food stamps to out-of-pocket health-care expenditures. The two largest value factors that could bias these estimates are out-of-pocket medical costs (MOOP) and housing subsidies. MOOP, which are substantially higher for older adults, and housing subsidies, from which older adults disproportionately benefit, are especially vulnerable to measurement error (Congressional Budget Office 2015; van Dalen et al. 2014). Average MOOP expenditures for older adults are approximately $4,700 annually and average housing subsidies about $4,400 annually (Kaiser Family Foundation 2014; Meyer and Mittag 2015). The inclusion of medical out-of-pocket costs raises poverty levels among older adults by 5 to 6 percentage points, or 50 percent. Research provides a cautionary perspective on the general quality of self-reported health-care data for older adults given their especially high usage, costs, and cognitive functioning issues older adults are more likely to face (van Dalen et al. 2014).[5]

The housing subsidy also poses a problem. Recent estimates are that 35 percent of those receiving housing subsidies do not report them in the CPS (Meyer and Mittag 2015). Moreover, questions remain about the measurement error in the value of these resources, even among those who report that they receive them (Meyer and Mittag 2015). Given that 1.9 million older adults received housing subsidies and 4.2 million older adults live below the poverty line, this would indicate that around 15 percent of those living below the official poverty line, and thus eligible for the benefit, would not have the housing subsidy included in supplemental poverty estimates (Congressional Budget Office 2015). A good proportion of those remaining in poverty, according to the supplemental poverty estimate, would therefore actually be above the supplemental poverty level if housing subsidies were properly measured.

To clarify precisely how poorly measured housing and health-care costs might affect the SPM estimates for the MBP, we provide an illustrative example. If the official poverty threshold is $12,000, an individual whose income is $8,000 will receive a $4,000 Social Security benefit increase. If their MOOP are $5,000 and the housing subsidy is worth $2,000, they would be poor under the supplemental poverty threshold prior to the reform, but in many cases (depending on factors such as where they live, as mentioned earlier) be lifted out of poverty by the $4,000 income supplement. Undercounting the housing support or overcounting MOOP, however, would lead one to believe that the policy had not moved that individual above the supplemental poverty threshold. We focus on this interaction because it is precisely older adults with more health problems who are likely to end up in concentrated older adult housing (not institutions) where things like home health care can be provided more efficiently (Congressional Budget Office 2015). Consequently, the changes in the official poverty measure provide a more robust estimate with considerably less measurement error.

REFERENCES

AARP. 2015. "Social Security Planning in 2015 and Beyond: Perspectives of Future Beneficiaries and Financial Planners." Washington, D.C.: AARP.

Argento, Robert, Victoria Bryant, and John Sabelhaus. 2015. "Early Withdrawals from Retirement Accounts During the Great Recession." *Contemporary Economic Policy* 33(1): 1–16.

Battle, Ken. 1997. "A New Old Age Pension." In *Reform of Retirement Income Policy*, edited by Kalman Banting and R. Boadway. Kingston, Ontario: School of Policy Studies, Queen's University.

Bianchi, Suzanne, John P. Robinson, and Melissa Milkie. 2006. *Changing Rhythms of American Family Life*. ASA Rose Series. New York: Russell Sage Foundation.

Budig, Michelle J., and Paula England. 2001. "The Wage Penalty for Motherhood." *American Sociological Review* 66(2): 204–25.

Bureau of Labor Statistics. 2016. "Employment Characteristics of Families, 2015." Economic News Release, USDL-17-0444. Accessed October 17, 2017. http://www.bls.gov/news.release/famee.nr0.htm.

Burkhauser, Richard V. 1982. "Earnings Sharing: Incremental and Fundamental Reform." In *A Challenge to Social Security: The Changing Roles of Women and Men in American Society*, edited by Richard V. Burkhauser and Karen C. Holden. New York: Academic Press.

Burkhauser, Richard V., and Timothy Smeeding. 1994. "Social Security Reform: A Budget Neutral Approach to Older Women's Disproportionate Risk of Poverty." *Center for Policy Research* Policy Brief No. 2. Syracuse N.Y.: Syracuse University.

Caswell, Kyle J., and Brett O'Hara. 2010. "Medical Out-of-Pocket Expenses, Poverty, and the Uninsured." Working Paper no. 2010-17. Washington: U.S. Census Bureau. Accessed October 17, 2017. https://www.census.gov/content/dam/Census/library/working-papers/2010/demo/SEHSD-WP2010-17.pdf.

Center on Budget and Policy Priorities. 2014. "Introduction to the Supplemental Security Income

---

5. Although Kyle Caswell and Brett O'Hara do find that the CPS MOOP compare favorably to a high quality health-care utilization study, they do no subgroup analyses of the elderly, despite extensive analyses of those younger than sixty-five (2010).

(SSI) Program." Washington, D.C.: CBPP. Accessed October 17, 2017. http://www.cbpp.org/sites/default/files/atoms/files/1-10-11socsec.pdf.

——. 2015. "Safety Net Against Poverty More Effective than Previously Reported." Washington, D.C.: CBPP. Accessed October 17, 2017. http://www.cbpp.org/research/safety-net-more-effective-against-poverty-than-previously-thought.

Cohn, D'Vera, Gretchen Livingston, and Wendy Wang. 2014. "After Decades of Decline a Rise in Stay-at-Home Mothers." Washington, D.C.: Pew Research Center. Accessed October 17, 2017. http://www.pewsocialtrends.org/files/2014/04/Moms-At-Home_04-08-2014.pdf.

Congressional Budget Office. 1986. *Earnings Sharing Options for the Social Security System*. January. Washington: Government Printing Office. Accessed October 17, 2017. https://www.cbo.gov/sites/default/files/99th-congress-1985-1986/reports/doc04b-entire_1.pdf.

——. 2015. "Federal Housing Assistance for Low-Income Households." Washington: Government Printing Office. Accessed October 17, 2017. https://www.cbo.gov/publication/50782.

Congressional Research Service. 2014. "Social Security Reform: Current Issues and Legislation Dawn Nuschler Specialist in Income Security." *Congressional Research Service* 7-5700 report no. RL33544. January 15.

Czajka, John L., and Gabrielle Denmead. 2008. "Income Data for Policy Analysis: A Comparative Assessment of Eight Surveys." *Mathematica* no. 6302-601. Washington, D.C.: Mathematica Policy Research.

Ellwood, Marilyn R., and Leighton Ku. 1998. "Welfare and Immigration Reforms: Unintended Side Effects for Medicaid." *Health Affairs* 17(3): 137–51.

Employee Benefit Research Institute (EBRI). 2015. "Private- and Public-Sector Retirement Plan Trends." In *Databook on Employee Benefits*. Washington, D.C.: EBRI. Accessed October 17, 2017. https://www.ebri.org/publications/books/index.cfm?fa=databook.

Engelhardt, Gary V., and Jonathan Gruber. 2004. Social Security and the Evolution of Elderly Poverty. *NBER* working paper no. 10466. Cambridge, Mass.: National Bureau of Economic Research.

Favreault, Melissa. 2010. "Why Do Some Workers Have Low Social Security Benefits?" *Retirement Policy Project* discussion paper. Washington, D.C.: The Urban Institute.

——. Forthcoming. "How Might Earnings Patterns and Interactions among Certain Provisions in OASDI Solvency Packages Affect Financing and Distributional Goals?" Boston, Mass.: Boston College Center for Retirement Research.

Favreault, Melissa, and Eugene Steuerle. 2007. "Social Security and Spouse and Survivor Benefits for the Modern Family." Discussion Paper 07-01. Washington, D.C.: The Urban Institute. Accessed October 17, 2017. http://www.urban.org/UploadedPDF/311436_Social_Security.pdf.

Feinstein, Craig A. 2013. "Diminishing Effect of the Special Minimum PIA." Actuarial Note no. 154. Baltimore, Md.: Social Security Administration Office of the Chief Actuary. Accessed October 17, 2017. https://www.ssa.gov/oact/NOTES/pdf_notes/note154.pdf.

Goldin, Claudia. 1977. "Female Labor Force Participation: The Origin of Black and White Differences, 1870 and 1880." *Journal of Economic History* 37(1): 87–108.

Goldstein, J. R., and C. T. Kenney. 2001. "Marriage Delayed or Marriage Forgone? New Cohort Forecasts of First Marriage for U.S. Women." *American Sociological Review* 66(4): 509–19.

Gustman, Alan, Thomas Steinmeier, and Nahid Tabatabai. 2011. "The Effects of Changes in Women's Labor Market Attachment on Redistribution under the Social Security Benefit Formula." *NBER* working paper no. 17439. Cambridge, Mass.: National Bureau of Economic Research.

Haider, Steven, Alan Jacknowitz, and Robert Schoeni. 2003. "The Economic Status of Elderly Women." *Michigan Retirement Research Center* research paper no. WP 2003–046. Ann Arbor: University of Michigan. Accessed October 17, 2017. http://papers.ssrn.com/sol3/papers.cfm?abstract_id=1090901.

Harrington Meyer, Madonna. 1996. "Making Claims as Workers or Wives: The Distribution of Social Security Benefits." *American Sociological Review* 61(3): 449–65.

Harrington Meyer, Madonna, and Pamela Herd. 2007. *Market Friendly or Family Friendly? The State and Gender Inequality in Old Age*. New York: Russell Sage Foundation.

Harrington Meyer, Madonna, Doug Wolf, and Christine Himes. 2006. "Declining Eligibility for Social Security Spouse and Widow Benefits in the U.S.?" *Research on Aging* 28(2): 240–60.

Herd, Pamela. 2005a. "Ensuring a Minimum: Social

Security Reform and Women." *The Gerontologist* 45(1):12–25.

———. 2005b. "Reforming a Breadwinner Welfare State: Gender, Race, Class and Social Security Reform." *Social Forces* 83(4): 1365–93.

———. 2006. "Crediting Care?: Gender, Race, Class and Social Security Reform." *The Journals of Gerontology: Social Sciences* 61B(1): S24–S34.

———. 2009. "Women, Public Pensions and Poverty: What Can the U.S. Learn from Other Countries?" *Journal of Women, Politics and Policy* 30(2-3): 301–44.

Herd, Pamela, Thomas DeLeire, Hope Harvey, and Donald P. Moynihan. 2013. "Shifting Administrative Burden to the State: The Case of Medicaid Take-Up." *Public Administration Review* 73(1):69–81.

Hubbard, Glenn, Jonathan Skinner, and Stephen P. Zeldes. 1995. "Precautionary Savings and Social Insurance." *Journal of Political Economy* 103(2): 360–99.

Hurd, Michael, and David Wise. 1997. "Changing Social Security Survivorship Benefits and the Poverty of Widows." In *The Economic Effects of Aging in the United States and Japan*, edited by Michael D. Hurd and Naohiro Yashiro. Chicago: University of Chicago Press.

Iams, Howard, Gail Reznik, and Chris Tamborini. 2010. "Earnings Sharing in the U.S. Social Security System: A Microsimulation Analysis of Future Female Retirees." *Gerontologist* 50(4): 495–508.

Institute for Women's Policy Research (IWPR). 2016. "The Gender Wage Gap and Public Policy." Briefing Paper no. D435. Washington, D.C.: IWPR. Accessed October 17, 2017. https://iwpr.org/publications/the-gender-wage-gap-and-public-policy/.

Jones, Maggie. 2014. "Changes in EITC Participation, 2005–2009." *CARRA* Working Paper Series #2014-04. Washington: U.S. Census Bureau. Accessed October 17, 2017. https://www.census.gov/srd/carra/Changes_in_EITC_Eligibility_and_Participation_2005-2009.pdf.

Kaestner, Robert, Darren Lubotsky, and Javaeria Qureshi. 2016. "Mothers' Employment by Child Age and Its Implications for Theory and Policy." Working Paper. Chicago: Society of Labor Economists. Accessed October 17, 2017. http://www.sole-jole.org/16113.pdf.

Kahn, Joan, Javier García-Manglano, and Suzanne Bianchi. 2014. "The Motherhood Penalty at Midlife: Long-Term Effects of Children on Women's Careers." *Journal of Marriage and Family* 76(1): 56–72.

Kaiser Family Foundation. 2014. *How Much Is Enough? Out-of-Pocket Spending Among Medicare Beneficiaries*. Menlo Park, Calif: Kaiser Family Foundation. Accessed November 9, 2017. http://files.kff.org/attachment/how-much-is-enough-out-of-pocket-spending-among-medicare-beneficiaries-a-chartbook-report.

Katz, Larry, and Alan Krueger. 2016. "The Rise and Nature of Alternative Work Arrangements in the United States, 1995–2015." *NBER* working paper no. 22667. Cambridge, Mass.: National Bureau of Economic Research.

Marchand, Joseph, and Timothy Smeeding. 2016. "Poverty and Aging." In *The Handbook of the Economics of Population Aging*, vol. 1B, edited by J. Piggott and A. Woodland. New York: Elsevier.

Marshall, Thomas H. 1950. *Citizenship and Social Class*, vol. 11. Cambridge: Cambridge University Press.

McGarry, Kathleen. 2000. "Guaranteed Income: SSI and the Well-Being of the Elderly Poor." *NBER* working paper no. 7574. Cambridge, Mass.: National Bureau of Economic Research.

McGarry, Kathleen, and Robert Schoeni. 2015. "Understanding Participation in SSI." Working Paper 2015-319. Ann Arbor: Michigan Retirement Research Center. Accessed November 17, 2017. http://www.mrrc.isr.umich.edu/publications/papers/pdf/wp319.pdf.

Meyer, Bruce D., and Nikolas Mittag. 2015. " Using Linked Survey and Administrative Data to Better Measure Income: Implications for Poverty, Program Effectiveness and Holes in the Safety Net." *NBER* working paper no. w21676. Boston, Mass.: National Bureau of Economic Research.

Mortenson, Jacob A., James Cilke, Michael Udell, and Jonathon Zytnick. 2009. "Attaching the Left Tail: A New Profile of Income for Persons Who Do Not Appear on Federal Income Tax Returns." Paper presented at the National Tax Association Proceedings, 102nd Annual Conference on Taxation, November 12–14, 2009, Denver, Colo.

Moynihan, Donald, Pamela Herd, and Hope Harvey. 2014. "Administrative Burden: Learning, Psychological, and Compliance Costs in Citizen-State Interactions." *Journal of Public Administration Research and Theory* 25(1): 43–69.

Munnell, Alicia H., and Dina Bleckman. 2014. "Is

Pension Coverage a Problem in the Private Sector?" Policy Brief no. 14-7. Boston, Mass.: Boston College Center for Retirement Research. Accessed November 17, 2017. http://crr.bc.edu/wp-content/uploads/2014/04/IB_14-7-508.pdf.

Myles, John. 2000. "The Maturation of Canada's Retirement Income System: Income Levels, Income Inequality, and Low Income Among the Elderly." *Statistics Canada* working paper no. 147. DOI: 10.2139/ssrn.229486.

Neumark, David, and Elizabeth Powers. 1998. "The Effects of Means-Tested Income Support for the Elderly on Pre-Retirement Savings: Evidence from the SSI Program in the U.S." *Journal of Public Economics* 68(2): 181-206.

Olsen, Kelly, and Don Hoffmeyer. 2002. "Social Security's Special Minimum Benefit." *Social Security Bulletin* 64(2): 1-15.

Powers, Elizabeth. 1998. "Does Means-Tested Discourage Savings? Evidence from a Change in AFDC Policy in the United States." *Journal of Public Economics* 68(1): 33-53.

Proctor, Bernadette, Jessica Semega, and Melissa Kollar. 2016. "Income and Poverty in the United States: 2015." *Current Population Report*, series P60, no. 256. Washington: U.S. Census Bureau.

Quadagno, Jill. 1984. "Welfare Capitalism and the Social Security Act of 1935." *American Sociological Review* 49(5): 632-47.

Renwick, Trudi, and Liana Fox. 2016. "The Supplemental Poverty Measure: 2015." *Current Population Report*, series P60, no. 258. Washington: U.S. Census Bureau.

Sass, Stephen. 2016. "How Work & Marriage Trends Affect Social Security's Family Benefits." Issue Brief no. 16-9. Boston, Mass.: Center for Retirement Research.

Smeeding, Timothy. 1999. "Social Security Reform: Improving Benefit Adequacy and Economic Security for Women." *Center for Policy Research Policy Series* paper no.16. Syracuse, N.Y.: Syracuse University.

Smeeding, Timothy, Carroll Estes, and Lou Glasse. 1999. "Social Security Reform and Older Women: Improving the System." *Center for Policy Research Policy Series* paper no. 22. Syracuse, N.Y.: Syracuse University.

Social Security Administration. 2015. "Social Security Administrative Statistical Supplement." Tables 5.A14 and 5.A15. Washington: Government Printing Office.

U.S. Government Accountability Office (GAO). 2007. *Retirement Security: Women Face Challenges in Ensuring Financial Security in Retirement.* GAO-08-105. Washington: Government Printing Office. Accessed October 11, 2017. http://www.investmentnews.com/assets/docs/CI305391018.PDF.

U.S. House Ways and Means Committee. 2004. *Green Book*. Washington: U.S. Government Printing Office.

van Dalen, Melissa, Jacqueline Suijker, Janet, MacNeil-Vroomen, Marjon van Rijn, Eric Moll van Charante, Sophia de Rooij, and Bianca Buurman. 2014. "Self-Report of Healthcare Utilization Among Community-Dwelling Older Persons: A Prospective Cohort Study." *PLoS ONE* 9(4): e93372.

Whitman, Kevin, Gayle Reznik, and David Shoffner. 2011. "Who Never Receives Social Security?" *Social Security Bulletin* 71(2): 17-24.

Winslow-Bowe, Sarah. 2009. "Husbands' and Wives' Relative Earnings: Exploring Variation by Race, Human Capital, Labor Supply, and Life Stage." *Journal of Family Issues* 30(10): 1405-32.

Zajacova, Anna, Jennifer Montez, and Pamela Herd. 2014. "Socioeconomic Disparities in Health Among Older Adults: Implications for the Retirement Age Debate." *Journals of Gerontology* 69(6): 973-78.

Reforming Policy for Single-Parent Families to Reduce Child Poverty

MARIA CANCIAN AND DANIEL R. MEYER

We argue that child support, the central program specifically targeting single-parent families, should increase financial resources for children living with a single parent, with a secondary goal of holding parents responsible for supporting their children. Current child support policy is substantially successful for divorcing families in which the noncustodial parent has at least moderate formal earnings. However, the system does not work well for lower-income families, especially unmarried couples: far too few children regularly receive substantial support and the system is sometimes counterproductive to encouraging parental responsibility. We propose: a public guarantee of a minimum amount of support per child, assurances that no noncustodial parent will be charged beyond their current means, and a broadening of child support services.

Keywords: child support, divorce, guaranteed income, nonmarital births, single-parent families

Recognition is widespread that single-parent families with children are economically vulnerable but less so on the policies and programs to address these vulnerabilities (see, for example, Maldonado and Nieuwenhuis 2015). Policies addressing custodial parent families (those who have children who are living with only one of their parents) confront the fundamental challenge of balancing the role of public benefits and private support from the noncustodial parent. Efforts to hold noncustodial parents responsible for their children encounter issues related to the relative importance of encouraging financial support and encouraging noncustodial parents' active engagement in their children's lives. The response to these challenges has varied over time, and in some cases, for divorced and never-married families, and for families who do or do not receive means-tested public benefits.

Maria Cancian is professor of public affairs and social work and affiliate of the Institute for Research on Poverty at the University of Wisconsin–Madison. **Daniel R. Meyer** is professor of social work and affiliate of the Institute for Research on Poverty at the University of Wisconsin–Madison.

© 2018 Russell Sage Foundation. Cancian, Maria, and Daniel R. Meyer. 2018. "Reforming Policy for Single-Parent Families to Reduce Child Poverty." *RSF: The Russell Sage Foundation Journal of the Social Sciences* 4(2): 91–112. DOI: 10.7758/RSF.2018.4.2.05. Paper presented at the Russell Sage Foundation Conference "Anti-poverty Policy Initiatives for the United States" and at the related session at the 2016 Association for Public Policy Analysis and Management Research Conference. We thank Chris Wimer and Sophie Collyer for the cost and poverty estimates, Maria Serakos and Veronique Yeo for research assistance, and the reviewers, the editors, and conference participants, especially Lawrence Berger, Robert Doar, Irwin Garfinkel, and Elaine Sorensen, for their helpful comments. Any opinions expressed here are our own. Direct correspondence to: Maria Cancian at maria .cancian@wisc.edu, 3436 Social Sciences Building, 1180 Observatory Dr., Madison, WI 53706.

Open Access Policy: *RSF: The Russell Sage Foundation Journal of the Social Sciences* is an open access journal. This article is published under a Creative Commons Attribution-NonCommercial-NoDerivs 3.0 Unported License.

Current policy includes general programs for low-income families and specific ones for custodial parent families. It prioritizes private support over public, economic support over other engagement, and generally makes no distinction in the financial responsibilities of noncustodial parents who have had different types of relationships with the other parent. Policy goals for custodial parent families include encouraging private support from both low-income and other noncustodial parents by trying to set an appropriate amount of economic support to be transferred, monitoring whether it is transferred, and then enforcing the transfer through a variety of threats and penalties. Public and private support schemes function as substitutes, rather than complements, so that when private support is paid on behalf of a single-parent family receiving public support, all or a part of those resources are typically retained by the government or public support is reduced, making custodial parent families no better off if private support is or is not paid (Cancian, Meyer, and Caspar 2008; Skinner et al. 2017).

In this article we highlight central policy challenges in meeting the needs of children in single-parent families and consider the role of the current U.S. child support system in responding to those challenges. We argue that the traditional approach to child support, though functional for many middle-income families facing divorce, fails to address key challenges for lower-income families facing divorce and for individuals who, regardless of income, did not have a stable romantic relationship. Unrealistic child support expectations can harm noncustodial parents, create additional barriers for noncustodial parents to be involved with their children, and may even yield less support to vulnerable families than an alternative scheme (for example, Waller and Plotnick 2001). The traditional child support system also fails these families because it does not address the risk children face when their noncustodial parents do not pay support, despite nonpayment, partial payment, and irregular payment being common. By enforcing financial support while ignoring never-married noncustodial parents' access to their children, the current system is particularly flawed and unsustainable for the growing number of children of lower-income never-married parents.

The traditional child support enforcement strategy is premised on an often inaccurate view of noncustodial fathers' economic resources and employment stability and of parents' relationships. We highlight the costs of ignoring the disjuncture between ideals and current reality, and some of the key challenges that must be confronted in developing an appropriate policy response. In the next sections, we describe and then evaluate the current system. We then recommend a set of changes to private and public child supports that aim to address the identified challenges.

THE LOGIC AND FUNCTIONING OF THE CURRENT SYSTEM

A number of programs and policies, many covered in other papers in this volume, address the resources available to poor individuals, and especially families with children. Custodial parent families are disproportionately poor and therefore disproportionately affected by these general poverty policies. However, our focus here is on policies designed to address the challenges of families with children in which parents live apart. Although many policies are means-tested and account for the resources provided and required by members of these separated-parent households, policy governing child custody and child support are the primary policies specifically addressing the additional challenges arising when parents live apart.[1] In particular, we argue that a child sup-

---

1. Although social policy discussions often presume that single parents are entitled to programs that they would not receive if they were to marry, we find little evidence of programs that are available only to (or provide extra benefits to) those who are single parents, per se, outside of the child support system. Single parents are entitled to (or eligible for) some programs because they are parents who have low incomes, but in most cases are not differentially eligible based on single-parenthood in and of itself. In fact, single parents who marry someone without income would be eligible for *more* of some benefits because their family size is larger. The federal income tax system does have a special filing status for those who are head of household (that is, single parents). How-

port guarantee is needed, even given a general children's allowance, as proposed elsewhere in this volume, which reduce the poverty rate for those in married-couple families more significantly than for those in single-parent families (Wimer, Collyer, and Kimberlin 2018). Children who live apart from a parent are at substantially greater risk given economic and other vulnerabilities that emerge when parents live apart. In addition, custodial parents, who typically must serve as both breadwinners and caretakers, face economic and other challenges beyond those faced by "intact" (two-parent) families.

Child support policy comes into play when parents with children divorce. Divorce is a legal process within the judicial system and each state has its own rules (or guidelines). In general, a divorce where children are present involves formalized decisions on who will make important decisions for the child (legal custody), with whom the child will live (physical custody), whether there will be financial transfers and at what level (child support), and how joint assets will be divided. Legal and physical custody are typically set based on the best interests of the child, though many states have stated preferences for both parents sharing responsibility and children spending substantial amounts of time with each parent, unless these arrangements are not feasible or determined to be not in the child's best interests (Cancian et al. 2014). If a child is to live with one parent most of the time, the other parent may have specified visitation privileges, even including a detailed parenting plan specifying which parent has responsibility at each time and how the transitions between parents are handled.

Child support obligations are set based on each state's guideline. Nearly all states have a guideline in which the central principle is *continuity of expenditures*, the idea that noncustodial parents should provide the level of support that they would have had the parents lived together (Garrison 1999). When a child support order is in place and the noncustodial parent is employed, policy requires that the employer automatically withhold the amount of support due and transfer it to a central processing agency that then records the amount paid and distributes it (Pirog and Ziol-Guest 2006). In addition to these services, which should be available to all parents, custodial parents can request the services of the child support agency in their state. This agency can help parents locate the other parent, establish an order for child support, actively monitor whether the order is being paid, and take enforcement actions if it is not, through such steps as taking away a driver's license, intercepting a tax return, or even bringing civil or criminal charges that may result in imprisonment. The child support agency can take aggressive steps to enforce child support orders, but no comparable enforcement of parenting time is practicable; a parent who does not follow the agreed plan can eventually be brought to court, but no public agency monitors this and enforcement of a parenting plan is quite difficult.

Divorce law and procedures are not available to unmarried parents regardless of whether they were living together. The same child support policy does apply, but an extra step is required before child support can be ordered: paternity needs to be formally established or voluntarily acknowledged. If paternity is formally established in a court proceeding, or if a child support order is established in a court proceeding, then an opportunity to formally establish custody and visitation, and to set the rights and responsibilities of each parent, is possible. But in some states, child support orders need not be established by a court, and can instead be done within the child support agency; if so, then an opportunity to formalize custody and visitation is not possible because these are not part of the child support agency's purview. The federal Office of Child Support Enforcement recently acknowledged that "there is currently no systematic, efficient mechanism for families to establish parenting time agreements for children whose parents

---

ever, the amount of tax assessed for those filing head of household is the same or more than those who are married filing jointly, and those married have more exemptions and higher standard deductions, all else equal. One exception relates to work requirements, which may be greater for married couples—for example, in the case of TANF.

were not married at the time of their birth" (2013, 1).

This lack of a systematic opportunity for unmarried parents to define roles and set rights and responsibilities is a key way that unmarried parents are disadvantaged relative to divorcing parents. This disadvantage is even greater for lower-income unmarried couples, who are particularly likely to be served by the child support agency. The overrepresentation of low-income families in child support enforcement efforts occurs because the agency serves those having difficulty with child support issues who apply for services (who are more likely to have low incomes) and because lower-income custodial parents are required to cooperate with the agency as a condition of receiving some public benefits and even to sign over their right to child support to the state during periods when they receive Temporary Assistance to Needy Family (TANF) benefits. These same low-income families are also less likely to have the resources to pursue separate legal hearings related to parenting time. The one-sided focus of the child support system thereby leaves low-income families facing potentially punitive enforcement of orders for financial support, without effective access to agreements for parenting time.

Lower-income families and individuals are more likely to encounter challenges in the child support system both because of their income and employment status, and because they are more likely to have children outside of marriage. One key difference is that lower-income noncustodial parents are often ordered to pay a higher proportion of their income in child support than middle-income noncustodial parents (for example, Meyer 1998). In part this regressivity is intentional: the guidelines used in most states are called *income shares* and require a smaller percentage of income as the couples' income increases, consistent with the lower proportion of total income typically spent on children as family income rises. But this is also the result of other factors: when there is no income information available for a noncustodial parent (or they have very low incomes), some states have set orders based on imputed income—though this practice is restricted by recently finalized federal regulations.[2] Imputed income often reflects expectations that the noncustodial parent can work full time all year, which many do not, resulting in orders that are a high percentage of actual income. Finally, lower-income fathers are less likely to be in stable marriages and more likely to have had children with multiple partners, so their resources are being stretched across multiple families (Cancian and Meyer 2011; Sinkewicz and Garfinkel 2009). In these ways the child support enforcement system may exacerbate, rather than manage, the inevitable tension between setting orders high enough to provide enough income for children, and low enough to impose a manageable burden on noncustodial parents. This tension is inevitable because noncustodial parents with very low incomes do not have sufficient resources to support their children, even less so if they live apart. On the one hand, even setting orders at a relatively high proportion of income, or assuming income based on full-time low-wage work, may fall short of providing enough resources to meet half of children's needs. On the other hand, some states have tried a variety of efforts to lower the burden on lower-income noncustodial parents, including allowing the noncustodial parent a certain amount of income for their own purposes before child support is assessed (a self-support reserve) or having a lower percentage requirement for lower-income noncustodial parents. But this comes at the cost of support to the parent caring for the child. And, although orders are often insufficient, and a minority of low-income custodial parents receive all the support due, an entitlement to alternative support is no longer in place.[3]

Based on this review of the child support system, what are its explicit and implicit goals

---

2. The "Flexibility, Efficiency, and Modernization in Child Support (CMS-2343-P) Enforcement Programs" Rule (CMS-2343-P) clarifies policies designed to ensure that orders are consistent with a noncustodial parent's ability to pay.

3. Another difference is that middle-class families are more likely to opt for shared physical custody, and this custody arrangement typically requires fewer financial transfers (lower child support orders, if any). Because

and what should they be? The federal legislation governing child support services (Title IV-D of the Social Security Act) states a multifaceted purpose:

> [E]nforcing the support obligations owed by noncustodial parents to their children and the spouse (or former spouse) with whom such children are living, locating noncustodial parents, establishing paternity, obtaining child and spousal support, and assuring that assistance in obtaining support will be available under this part to all children. (SSA 2000)

But these are more on the order of activities than goals. What is the problem that policy for single-parent families, and the child support program in particular, is trying to solve? There are a number of potential answers, and a research literature and legal and regulatory documents that seek to clarify the current state of affairs. Here we clarify a set of priorities that we then use to evaluate policy options.

We argue that the primary goal of the child support system is to increase the financial resources available to children living with a single parent. This goal is mostly consistent with an anti-poverty strategy, given that children living with single parents are more likely to be economically vulnerable, but this is also consistent with a recognition of the rights of the child.

The secondary goal is to hold parents responsible for the financial support of their children. There are at least two motivations for this goal, which justify different policy preferences. First, private support from parents is often preferred to public support because holding noncustodial parents responsible reduces the burden on taxpayers, and maintains the U.S. policy preference for private support of children (Meyer 2012). Many U.S. benefits to families with children are means-tested, and therefore available only to families who are judged unable to meet the need themselves. In qualifying for means-tested benefits the incomes of both parents are considered for two-parent families. Requiring noncustodial parents to pay child support, and considering child support received as an income source for custodial parents, may be seen as equivalent treatment for single-parent families.

A second motivation for requiring financial support from noncustodial parents is that it reduces the economic incentive to stop living with children that would exist if noncustodial parents were free of the obligation to support their children. If the couple made a shared decision to raise children together, but later change their minds, holding noncustodial parents financially responsible reduces the negative consequences for children, custodial parents, and taxpayers. In other words, it retains the right of adults to end their relationship with one another, but requires that they accept responsibility to support children to adulthood. It renders separation (what was called *abandonment* in an earlier era) an ineffective strategy for escaping the financial responsibilities of parenting. On the other hand, it makes it more attractive for a parent who would prefer to care for their child, but not live with the child's other parent.

Both these arguments—providing for continuity of contributions after relationship dissolution, and avoiding a financial incentive to become a noncustodial parent—are more difficult to apply to couples or sexual partners who do not have an affirmative interest in becoming parents, and noncustodial parents who have never lived with their child.[4] With respect to continuity of contributions, child support cannot restore what never existed; assessing contributions based on hypothetical living situations requires confronting a number of challenges. (For example, if a father has children with multiple partners, do we imagine him living and sharing resources with each child, neglecting the others, or living with all the children simultaneously, or sequentially?) In addition, avoiding financial incentives to dissolve a prior commitment is arguably quite dif-

---

the difference in support due is intended to reflect differences in expenses associated with physical custody, the implications for resources available to each parents are not clear.

4. We also note that these arguments, and our proposal, do not address the case of children with a deceased (rather than nonresident) parent.

ferent from creating incentives to form a partnership that was not otherwise intended. Holding noncustodial parents financially responsible increases the incentive for men to avoid a pregnancy or birth; without a child support requirement, a father with limited connections to the mother would otherwise potentially face few consequences. By the same logic, child support mitigates the financial burden of unintended motherhood, though given the significant consequences of a birth for custodial mothers the incentive effects of financial support might be expected to be relatively small.[5]

Providing institutional support to regularize never-married noncustodial parents' contact with their children is a potential policy goal; it is less directly connected to our focus on economic resources, but it is not unrelated. In recent years there has been a growing focus on the potential importance of father involvement, and concern about how fathers' involvement with other aspects of their children's lives is related to financial support (for example, Garasky et al. 2010). With respect to noncustodial parents' involvement, the formal child support system may increase noncustodial parents' nonfinancial support and involvement with their children when noncustodial parents comply (Garasky et al. 2010; Huang 2009; Koball and Principe 2002; Nepomnyaschy 2007; Peters et al. 2004). But, for noncustodial parents who do not pay, or whose payments do not benefit their children because they are used to offset public welfare costs, child support may be a barrier to involvement (Edin 1995; Gunter 2016; Nepomnyaschy and Garfinkel 2010; Waller and Plotnick 2001). Further, clarifying the rights and responsibilities of noncustodial fathers, for example, with respect to parenting time, is an important challenge largely unmet by the current system for never-married parents. As the dominance of marital childbearing declines, and the traditional pattern of caregiving mother and breadwinning father become less prevalent, the future relevance and success of the child support program may depend on addressing this challenge. Although we do not include support in navigating nonmarital parents' relationships as a primary goal of the current child support system, we come back to this issue in our recommendations.

A number of other goals have been articulated for the child support system. These include recovering public expenditures made in other systems (such as Medicaid), improving the equality of outcomes between custodial and noncustodial parents, and discouraging nonmarital births. These may be worthy goals, at least in some instances, but we do not prioritize these goals in evaluating alternative approaches to child support. We do not believe recovering public expenditures is an appropriate goal for the child support system. A set of policies focused on cost recovery has been found to be ineffective and is regressive, transferring resources from economically vulnerable noncustodial parents to taxpayers (Cancian, Meyer, and Caspar 2008); meanwhile, those most vulnerable—children in low-income custodial parent families—receive the least. Moreover, for the potential goals of equality of outcomes and discouraging nonmarital births, the implications are not straightforward. For example, with respect to improving equality between custodial and noncustodial parents, this is consistent with the other goals of child support when the noncustodial parent is relatively better off, because requiring support from the noncustodial parent is equalizing, but also increases resources for the child and enforces parental responsibility. However, these goals are at odds when noncustodial parents are relatively disadvantaged (Ha, Cancian, and Meyer 2016). Finally, enforcing child support shifts the burden of nonmarital births somewhat from custodial to noncustodial parents, rather than simply discouraging nonmarital births. In sum, we argue that designing policies that provide adequate resources to children and appropriately encourage parental responsibility across

---

5. We use gendered language and assume that children born to parents without a significant relationship will remain with the birth mother. Father custody has increased, but remains unusual for children born to never-married parents (Grall 2016). An additional complication arises outside a stable relationship when mothers have a legal option to terminate a pregnancy, and fathers cannot be expected to have had an influence on the decision. We address this issue in the final section.

a range of situations is a challenge that requires and deserves a focused response.

EVALUATING THE CURRENT SYSTEM

How well does the current system meet the twin goals of supporting children and enforcing parental responsibility? The answer is mixed, and substantially different for families eligible for child support due to divorce or nonmarital birth. Recent federal estimates suggest that more than one in four children under the age of twenty-one in the United States lived with one parent but not the other (Grall 2016). In most (more than 80 percent) cases, census data suggest that the child or children lived with their mother, but not their father, and that pattern has remained fairly stable over time. Other analyses, using more detailed data for select samples, such as court cases in Wisconsin, suggest that shared custody is becoming more common in divorce cases, only about half of cases living with only their mother (Cancian et al. 2014). However, shared custody is less common for low-income divorcing families, and, especially, for never-married couples (Cancian et al. 2012). Thus, although most children in single-parent families live only with their mother, differences by class and union status are substantial, children of lower-income and never-married parents being less likely to share time with each parent.

Children living with single parents are much more likely to be poor, and tend to have worse long-term social and economic outcomes, than children raised by married parents do (see, for example, Amato 2005; McLanahan and Sandefur 1994). In 2015, 11 percent of children living with both their married parents, relative to 43 percent of children living with just their mother, were in poor families (U.S. Census Bureau 2015). To the extent that these discrepancies are related to the reduced economic resources available from a single parent, requiring financial support from the noncustodial parent may seem an obvious solution.

About half of the thirteen million custodial parents have a formal child support order—53 percent of all custodial mothers but only 31 percent of custodial fathers (Grall 2016). The proportion of custodial parents with orders increased through 2003, but has declined since then (Grall 2016). The change could be due to declines in the number of TANF families who are required to cooperate with child support, the economic prospects of noncustodial parents, or increases in shared custody (Meyer, Cancian, and Chen 2015; Schroeder 2016). Orders are more common among white Non-Hispanic (56 percent) than Hispanic (44 percent) or African American (37 percent) parents, among college graduates (54 percent) than those with only a high school degree (46 percent) or less (38 percent), and among divorced (58 percent) than among never-married (42 percent) parents. For unmarried parents, paternity establishment is a prerequisite for a child support order. Many parents voluntarily establish paternity, often immediately following birth. However, establishing paternity creates legal and financial obligations for the father but extends relatively few rights; as discussed, child support agencies are tasked with enforcing the same financial expectations for divorced and never-married parents, but only divorcing parents typically have formal custody and visitation agreements. Moreover, for low-income families receiving means-tested assistance, formal child support payments may be used to reimburse government costs rather than to directly benefit children—undercutting the incentive for parents to engage with the system.

Even for those who have orders, payment is not ensured. Fewer than half of all custodial parents who were supposed to receive support received all the child support due, and a quarter received nothing in a given year (Grall 2016). Moreover, although national data do not provide detailed accounting on the timing of payments, an analysis of administrative records in Wisconsin showed that only about half of those who received some child support in a year received it regularly, that is, in at least ten months (Ha, Cancian, and Meyer 2011). This irregularity is another important limitation of the current system, and can cause uncertainty and stress and make it difficult for custodial parents to plan for the future. Nonetheless, national estimates suggest that average orders are substantial for those who have them ($6,772 in 2013 dollars for divorced parents, and $4,486 for never-married parents), as are average amounts received for those supposed to receive support, especially divorced parents ($5,209, twice the $2,538 average for never-married parents) (Grall 2016).

This brief review of the most current data and related research suggests that in many cases the current child support system can be judged a success in meeting our two primary goals, because it transfers significant support from some noncustodial parents to their children, thereby supporting children and enforcing parental responsibility. The system works best for families in which the noncustodial parent has stable formal employment—which gives the noncustodial parent the means to pay, and generally results in automatic wage withholding of the child support due. However, custodial parents whose children are most in need of assistance are less likely to be owed support, and when they are, they are disproportionately more likely to be owed support from noncustodial parents who also have limited resources (Sinkewicz and Garfinkel 2009). As a result, they are less likely to receive support and to receive less when they do receive it; for example, even when custodial parents below poverty received support, they received on average about $1,000 less than nonpoor custodial parents. Only one-quarter of custodial parents below poverty received any child support and only 13 percent received all the child support due to them in 2013 (Grall 2016). Further, although the data are limited, it appears likely that low-income custodial parents are also least likely to receive *regular* child support because the noncustodial parents owing this support are more likely to have irregular employment. Thus, with disadvantages at every point in the process, the imperfect system falls far short of what is required for those who need it most.

The first overall problem with the current child support system, then, is straightforward: far too few children receive child support, receive substantial amounts, or receive this regularly. What are some of the reasons that child support provides so little support, on average, to low-income custodial parents? First, under- or unemployment means many noncustodial fathers of low-income children do not have enough income to provide substantial or consistent support. To the extent that these fathers would have provided relatively little support even if they lived with their children, this is less a problem specific to the child support system than a limitation of general support for low-income families. (Other papers in this volume address related policy options—including a child allowance and employment programs.) Still, a policy regime that relies on the support of noncustodial parents will often fail if these parents do not have the resources to provide support. Second, mass incarceration leaves many noncustodial parents of economically vulnerable children unable to pay support while incarcerated, and with reduced earnings potential after they are released (Chung 2012; Geller, Garfinkel, and Western 2011). Moreover, child support enforcement is a contributing factor to high levels of incarceration: sometimes we incarcerate those who are behind in their child support payments, and unmanageable child support obligations can discourage formal employment (Cancian, Heinrich, and Chung 2013). Another contributing factor is the instability of marital and nonmarital relationships. A substantial proportion of noncustodial parents have had children with more than one partner, a more common phenomenon among those with the fewest resources (for example, Carlson and Furstenberg 2006; Cancian, Meyer, and Cook 2011).

We highlight the problems created by multiple-partner fertility here because they are common, cause payment difficulties, and challenge basic notions of fairness. Some research suggests that more than half of children who were their mother's first child born outside of marriage will have a half-sibling by their tenth birthday (Cancian, Meyer, and Cook 2011). Failing to account for noncustodial fathers' potential obligations to multiple families creates significant overestimates of how much child support could be collected (Sinkewicz and Garfinkel 2009). Moreover, multiple-partner fertility is most prevalent among lower-income couples, making it even more difficult for noncustodial parents to provide support across more than one custodial parent family. Finally, multiple-partner fertility creates classic trade-off problems for child support policy in that basic notions of fairness cannot all be simultaneously met (Meyer, Cancian, and Cook 2005; Meyer, Skinner, and Davidson 2011). In summary, a policy scheme that relies on private support cannot meet our first goal of providing financial support to children when a noncustodial parent's few resources are spread across multiple families.

Moreover, some of the cause of no, low, or irregular child support receipts is social policy itself. We noted that the policy scheme in the United States makes public benefits for low-income custodial parents and child support from noncustodial parents function as substitutes. The TANF program requires recipients to sign away their right to child support payments during their period of recipiency, and many states retain all child support paid on behalf of children receiving benefits and use these receipts to offset public expenditures rather than sending them to the children. As a result, children receiving TANF do not benefit from a noncustodial parent's payment. But this problem also occurs for non-TANF families (and TANF families in states that do pass through a portion of the child support) because child support counts as income in some means-tested programs (food stamps, housing vouchers).[6] Thus, even if child support goes to the custodial parent family, their other benefits may then be reduced, making child support function as a cost recovery mechanism rather than supporting children, our first goal.

Child support policy is limited in encouraging parental responsibility, especially for never-married families. The U.S. child support scheme tends to focus exclusively on private financial transfers, in which any benefit to one parent is taken from the other. Current policy also has a large divide between child support payments and other aspects of parenting for never-married parents, even though these other aspects could generate more parental agreement. We noted that the child support system includes no natural place in which unmarried parents decide custody and visitation, let alone to gain skills in co-parenting. In most jurisdictions, if parents are able to come to some agreement, few if any institutional supports and few ways to enforce them are available for maintaining the agreement, for both unmarried and divorcing parents. Thus, many noncustodial parents feel that the child support system does not support their concerns, does not help them with developing a relationship with their children, and sees them only as a financial resource (Waller and Plotnick 2001). This may undercut noncustodial parents' willingness to provide financially.

In our assessment, current child support policy is often ineffective because it is based on unrealistic assumptions. The enforcement system was designed to enforce notions of paternal financial responsibility that, even if somewhat idealized, were grounded in broadly held views of appropriate family structure (for example, parents should marry), and gender roles (for example, fathers, more than mothers, should work for pay). Increasing nonmarital births, declines in postconception marriage (and in marriage in general), and union instability, signal a disjuncture between these views and contemporary realities.[7] More than 40 percent of all children are now born to unmarried parents. Imposing paternal responsibility based on biology alone is now more contested. Moreover, although mothers (who remain the more likely custodial parent) still work and earn less than fathers, the gap has declined, and reversed for some subgroups, making fathers' expected contributions more contested (Cancian, Meyer, and Han 2011). Finally, changing patterns of contraception and abortion that give women more control over fertility, also make biological fathers' rights and responsibilities more contested.

As a result, the current child support system, which still prioritizes biological responsi-

---

6. Although child support generally counts as income in other means-tested programs, child support payments are not consistently subtracted from the income of noncustodial parents.

7. For example, the percent of premaritally conceived children born to married parents fell from more than half in the 1960s to just over a quarter in the late 1980s (DHHS 1995), and has continued to fall, even among those cohabiting at the time of conception. Daniel Lichter, Sharon Sassler, and Richard Turner, using data from the 2006–2010 National Survey of Family Growth, estimate that for couples in which the mother is at least twenty-five years old, 16 percent of those cohabiting, and 5 percent of those noncohabiting at the time of conception, marry before a birth (2014).

bility, assumes that a noncustodial parent had a relationship with a child before separation (and thus should continue to support that child financially), was designed for simple families with one noncustodial parent and one custodial parent who have had children with no one else, and assumes that fathers have advantages in the labor market, will increasingly confront challenges to its effectiveness. At the same time, changes in the structure of the U.S. safety net, especially the lack of entitlement to cash assistance and program rules that require that custodial parents provide for their children financially as well as providing caregiving, makes it essential that children with only one parent's financial support have additional resources. To effectively address these challenges, we need to reorient child support policy for low-income single-parent families.

A NEW APPROACH TO SUPPORTING CHILDREN AND ENCOURAGING PARENTAL RESPONSIBILITY

Even while maintaining a focus on providing economic support and encouraging parental responsibility, we argue for transforming the child support program and broadening its mission beyond the assessment, collection, and enforcement of financial transfers from noncustodial parents to custodial parent families. The more comprehensive child support program would provide guaranteed payments to custodial parents, essentially extending a combination of grants (that is, with no expectation of repayment) and loans (with repayment required) to noncustodial parents who are unable to meet their obligations. Although we focus on the agency's role in financial support (the core of the agency's mission), we also argue for a complementary set of agency activities supporting stronger family relationships.

Financial Support

At the core, our model of family support would achieve the two central goals of the current child support program—supporting children and encouraging parental responsibility—by balancing private responsibility and support, with public responsibility for both enforcement and support of parents' ability to meet their responsibilities. The essential elements of our proposal are a minimum monthly support amount per child, a maximum child support obligation for noncustodial parents, and a public guarantee to bridge the gap when the minimum support for children exceeds what the noncustodial parent can reasonably pay. We include a specific proposal, to illustrate and support estimates of costs and impact. In particular, we propose a guaranteed minimum child support of $150 per month per child, and a child support order standard of 12.5 percent of noncustodial parent income per child. Each noncustodial parent's total current contributions are capped at 33 percent of income. In our basic proposal, we also assume that child support income up to the amount of the guarantee (whether this comes from the noncustodial parent or the government) would not count in determining eligibility and benefits for means-tested programs; we also assume that noncustodial parents would accrue debt when they failed to pay the current support due, or when the 33 percent maximum cap reduced their current payments below 12.5 percent per child. We next detail the proposal and outline a set of potential variations, each of which have implications for the costs and benefits of the new system.

The minimum guarantee of $150 per month per child ensures a reliable income source for all children living apart from a parent, regardless of the noncustodial parent's income or payment status. We propose that the government guarantee support up to the minimum benefit, so that every child would receive the minimum benefit every month.[8] This minimum benefit would be available to all children covered by a child support order, whether they were receiving other benefits or not. Because it provides a

---

8. A guaranteed child support amount is not a new idea. We owe much to the work of Irwin Garfinkel, who has written extensively about how it might work (see especially Garfinkel 1992; Garfinkel et al. 1992). Note that an assured benefit would now be even easier to implement than when it was proposed by Garfinkel, because nearly all child support payments go through a central registry. The mechanism for collecting child support and distributing it (or the guarantee, if the amount collected is less than the guarantee) is basically in place.

reliable income stream, it would decrease the insecurity and stress currently associated with irregular child support payments. Although $150 per child is modest relative to continuity of expenditures for middle-income families, it is higher than that standard would provide in very low-income cases.

The per child minimum, the 12.5 percent per child order, and disregarding the minimum amount of child support in means-tested benefits all reflect a child's rights, which are not diminished when there are siblings nor when the custodial parent has a low income and is therefore receiving means-tested benefits. For noncustodial parents with very low incomes, the minimum benefit of $150 would be higher than their expected contribution of 12.5 percent, and the government would provide the difference.[9] If the noncustodial parent failed to pay their expected contribution the government would pay up to the minimum benefit and hold noncustodial parents responsible. By failing to account for economies of scale, a per child approach requires less of a contribution from noncustodial parents with only one child, and relatively more from noncustodial parents with multiple children with the same partner, relative to a continuity-of-expenditures approach.[10] While it does not account for differences in family size, it reduces inequities and complications that arise with complex families (Meyer, Cancian, and Cook 2005), which are estimated to be a majority of families of low-income never-married parents (Cancian, Meyer, and Cook 2011).

The maximum per noncustodial parent contribution of 33 percent would avoid clearly unmanageable child support burdens. At the values we propose—12.5 percent contribution per child, and 33 percent maximum total contribution—the expected contribution for noncustodial parents with more than two children would exceed the 33 percent maximum. This gap would be paid by the government up to the $150 per child minimum benefit level. In our base proposal, amounts above the maximum noncustodial parent contribution rate would be considered arrears to be paid (with minimal interest) after the children reach majority and the order for current support ends.

Figures 1 and 5 illustrate the implications of our base proposal for noncustodial parents with one child who pay all current support due (1) or who pay nothing (5). For each level of noncustodial parent income, the figure shows support owed by the noncustodial parent and received by the custodial parent. In the case of custodial parent receipt, we differentiate between support provided from the noncustodial parent, from a government subsidy (public support provided when 12.5 percent of the noncustodial parent's income is less than the $150 per month minimum), or from a government loan to the noncustodial parent (public support advanced by the government, but to be repaid). For example, on figure 1, for one child, the non-

---

9. A flat percentage of income has the advantage of simplicity. Current policy in many states calls for a lower percentage for high-income cases (reflecting continuity of expenditures). For lower-income noncustodial parents, policies in many states suggest a lower percentage (to reduce burden). This concern remains relevant, though less urgent given the 33 percent cap. Other policies call for a higher percentage for lower-income parents in order to reach a minimum level of support, but that concern is mitigated by the minimum guarantee.

10. The implications of family size for child support owed by noncustodial parents and due to custodial parents is complicated. Following the continuity-of-expenditures logic, child support guidelines for simple families—in which the mother and father have children together, and with no other partners—generally call for higher orders for larger families, with smaller increments for each additional child. For example, the Wisconsin guidelines call for 17 percent of the noncustodial parent's income for one child, 25 percent for two children (that is, 8 percent more than for one), and 29 percent for three (4 percent more than for two). However, whereas a father paying support for two children born to the same mother would owe 25 percent of his income, a father paying support owed to two children born to different mothers would owe 17 percent to the first born, and 17 percent of his remaining income (14 percent of total income) to the second, for a total of 31 percent. Similarly, a mother owed support for two children would be due 25 percent of the father's income if both children had the same father, and 17 percent of each father's income (net of any prior child support owed by those fathers) if there were two fathers.

custodial parent owes 12.5 percent of income, and the government guarantees up to $150 per month. Thus, the custodial parent receives $150 a month, from a combination of public subsidy and noncustodial parent payments, when the noncustodial parent income is below $1200 per month. When noncustodial income is higher, the custodial parent receives more than the minimum, all from the noncustodial parent (and there is a government guarantee, but no government payment). In contrast, as shown in figure 5, if the noncustodial parent fails to pay child support, the custodial parent will receive the $150 per month minimum at all income levels. For cases with a low-income noncustodial parent, the payment will include a subsidy and an advance (a loan from the government to the noncustodial parent), and no additional support will be owed to the custodial parent. For cases with higher-income noncustodial parents, the $150 minimum will all be an advance, and additional support will remain due from the noncustodial parent to the custodial parent.

The remaining figures (2 through 4 and 6 through 8) show the outcomes for noncustodial parents with additional children. For noncustodial parents with three or more children we distinguish *total support* owed, and *current* support owed—since noncustodial parents with more than two children will have some amount deferred, given the 33 percent maximum current support level. For example, for four children (figure 4) the noncustodial parent will owe a total of 50 percent of income (12.5 percent for each of four children), but current support will be capped at 33 percent. Thus, a custodial parent will receive $150 per month per child, or a total (across all children) of 33 percent of income, whichever is greater.[11] Noncustodial parents will pay 33 percent of income, and will owe the remaining 17 percent of income when current child support is no longer due, to the government (for the amount due toward the $150 minimum) or to the custodial parent (for the amount due over the $150 minimum). In the case of noncustodial parents who are not paying support (6), the custodial parent will receive $150 per month per child, and the noncustodial parent will owe 33 percent of income immediately, and the additional 17 percent of income when current support is no longer due.

Some of the potential costs and benefits of the minimum guarantee are included elsewhere in this double issue (see Wimer, Collyer, and Kimberlin 2018). Those estimates show a modest reduction in the overall poverty rate (1.3 percent), and a larger effect among those who receive it, decreasing their poverty rate by 5.2 percentage points (or by 22.7 percent), for an estimated cost of $8.2 billion.

These estimates, the best available in the current context, are limited in several ways. First, they are based on only one of our proposals, the guarantee; they do not consider the proposals for changing the child support formula and for setting a maximum amount of support required. These other parts of our proposal might be consequential. For example, a cap on the percentage of income required from noncustodial parents would lower the amount that some noncustodial parents pay, which would then increase their disposable incomes and lower their poverty according to the Supplemental Poverty Measure. The $150 minimum monthly support per child would exceed the support received by many low-income families, but those currently receiving both more than $150 per month and more than 12.5 percent, per child, would receive less support under this proposal, decreasing their disposable incomes. More generally, our proposal to switch to a fixed proportion of income per child would have implications for the disposable incomes of custodial and noncustodial parents. These effects could not be estimated with available data.

Second, the estimates do not incorporate any second-round effects (behavioral changes) induced by a minimum child support guarantee (or by the other changes we propose); sim-

---

11. We have not specified the distribution of support across multiple families, when support is owed to more than one custodial parent. As we discuss elsewhere, the appropriate distribution is complex (Meyer, Cancian, and Cook 2005; Cancian and Meyer 2011). However, the minimum monthly guarantee per child substantially improves the outcomes and options for the most complex cases.

(Text continues on p. 107.)

Figure 1. One Child, Full Payment

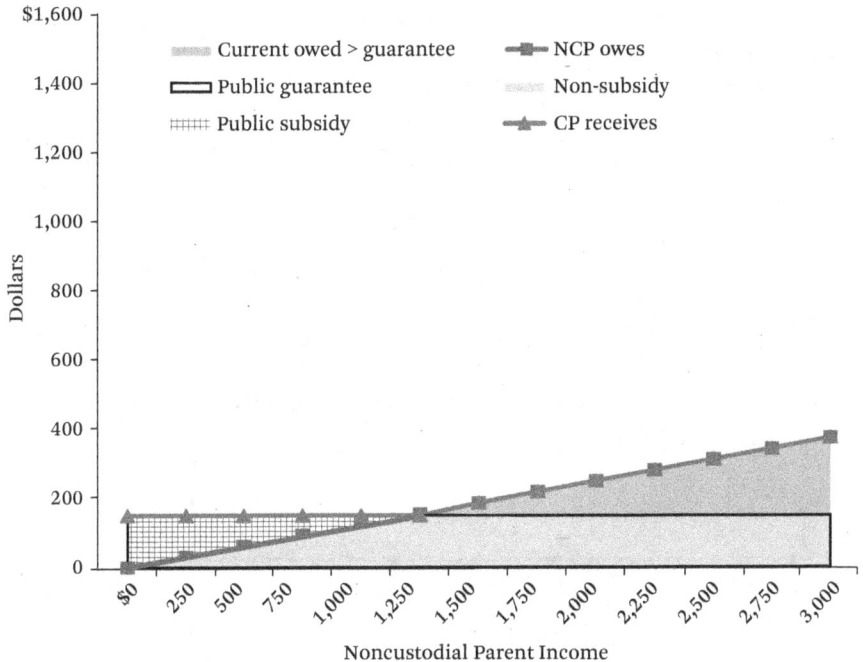

Source: Authors' representation of proposal.

Figure 2. Two Children, Full Payment

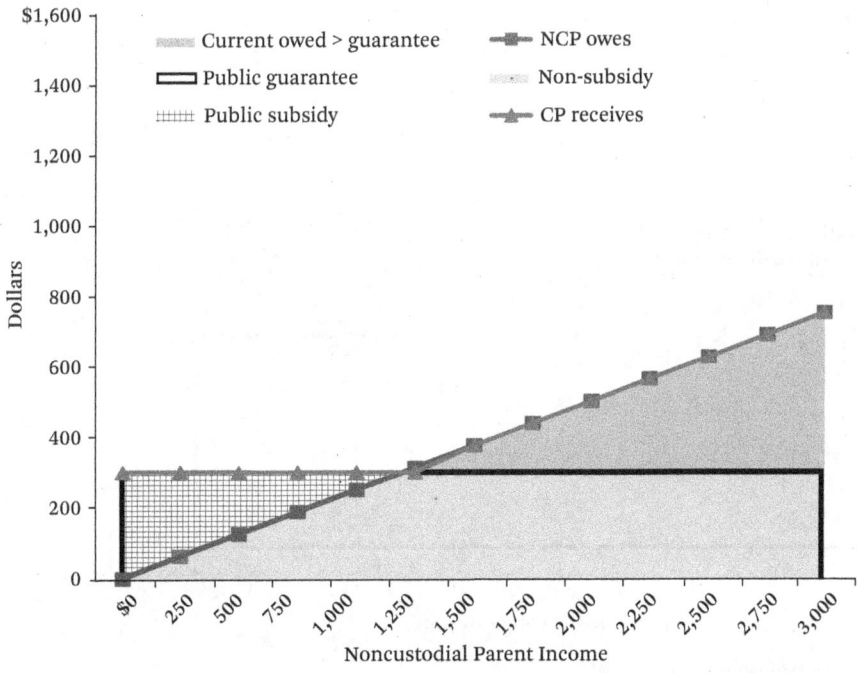

Source: Authors' representation of proposal.

Figure 3. Three Children, Full Payment

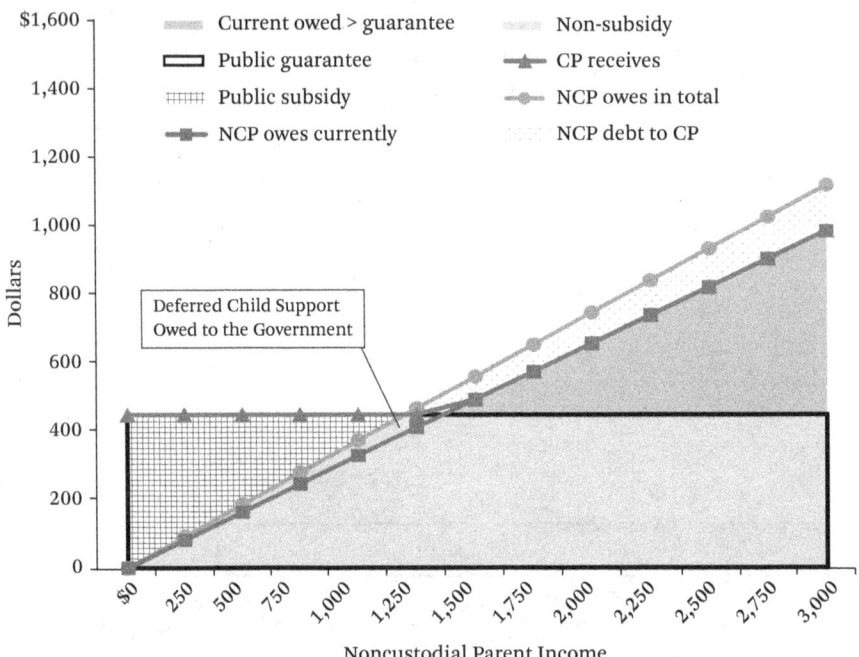

Source: Authors' representation of proposal.

Figure 4. Four Children, Full Payment

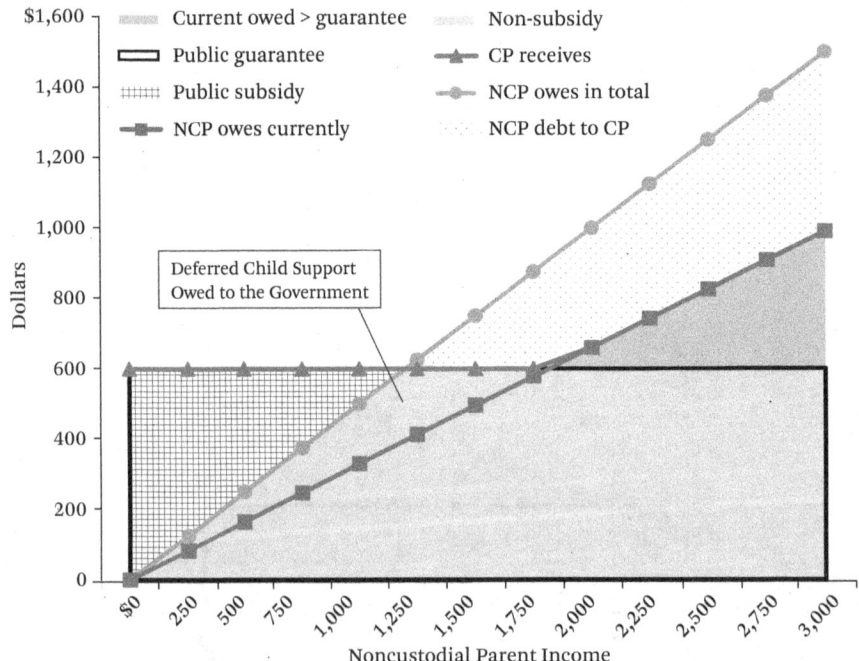

Source: Authors' representation of proposal.

Figure 5. One Child, No Payment

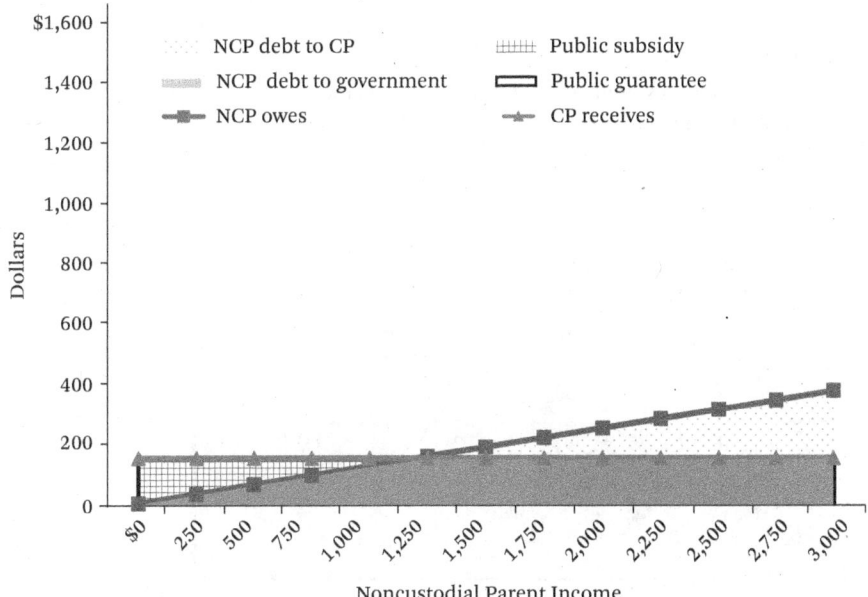

Source: Authors' representation of proposal.

Figure 6. Two Children, No Payment

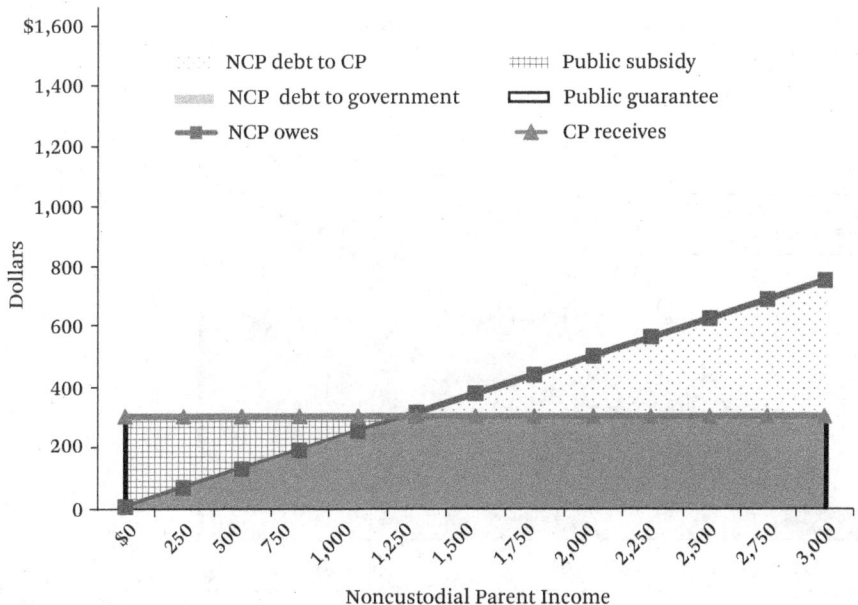

Source: Authors' representation of proposal.

Figure 7. Three Children, No Payment

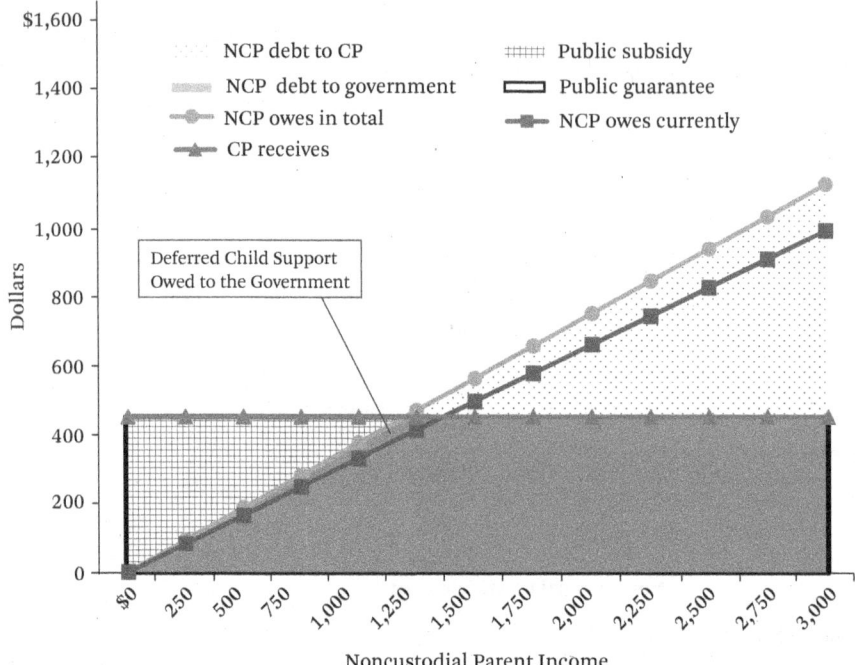

Source: Authors' representation of proposal.

Figure 8. Four Children, No Payment

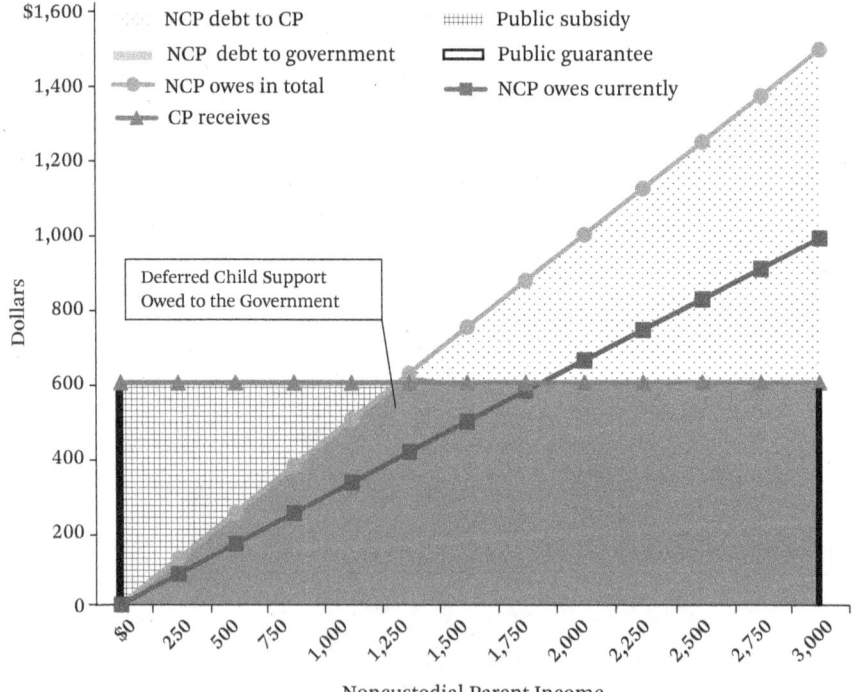

Source: Authors' representation of proposal.

ilarly, they do not consider changes that may take longer to emerge.[12] At the end of this section, we discuss what we view as the major concerns: changes in the incentives to have an order and to make payments. More minor limitations include not counting changes in TANF or SNAP, and the lack of a labor supply effect. For example, some custodial parents may be receiving TANF because of the regularity of income it provides; they might find the package of a guaranteed benefit and earnings better than continued TANF receipt. Some dated research has examined the sensitivity of cost estimates to incorporation of labor supply effects of a guarantee (Meyer and Kim 1998); this research shows that typical estimates of a labor supply response do not change overall cost and benefit estimates much because some welfare recipients are predicted to work more and some nonrecipients to work less.[13] The guarantee may also affect fertility, family dissolution, or custody, but none of these effects have been estimated.

It is difficult to compare these results with previous estimates, in part because the parameters differ and in part because the child support system, labor market, and policy regime has changed substantially from the 1980s to which previous estimates refer. Elaine Sorensen and Sandra Clark estimate a 1.2 percent poverty reduction among all children, at a cost of about $4.3 billion in 2016 dollars (1994). Daniel Meyer and Rebecca Kim, using a different model, different data, and a higher guarantee, estimate a decline in poverty among custodial parent families of 2.1 percent and net costs of $6.6 billion, also in 2016 dollars (1998).[14] These estimates are generally comparable to previous estimates: there would be a small reduction in poverty overall, a larger one among custodial parents, and particularly among those custodial parent families that were receiving the benefit. The current cost estimates are broadly consistent with the previous work, though they suggest somewhat higher costs because some savings are not considered and because the per child guarantee is more expensive than a guarantee that has marginal declines with the number of children.

We have outlined one approach to balancing private responsibility and public support with a guaranteed per child minimum support amount, a per child percent of noncustodial parent income due, and a maximum current per noncustodial parent contribution. The basic framework can be modified along a number of dimensions, altering the costs and benefits:

The minimum assured support could be set higher or lower than $150 per month per child. Our proposed guarantee of $150 per child per month is modest relative to some prior proposals.[15] A lower minimum would be less expensive for taxpayers, but would re-

12. For example, the current proposal calls for arrears to accumulate if the noncustodial parent's expected contribution of 12.5 percent of income is greater than the cap. The estimates do not consider eventual payments on these arrears.

13. The conclusion about limited effects of allowing labor supply responses come from their estimates of a guarantee of $1,500 per year (in 1988 dollars) for a one-child family; this is equivalent to $3,043 in 2016 dollars using the CPI-U (relative to the guarantee we propose here of $1,800 per year). Daniel Meyer and Rebecca Kim did not use a per-child model, so their benefit for a three-child family of $2,500 translates into $5,072 in 2106 dollars, similar to the $5,400 proposed here.

14. The estimates from Sorensen and Clark are for a guarantee of $2,491 for one child, $4,152 for two (both 2016 dollars), no reduction in AFDC benefits, and only families with child support orders being eligible. The estimates from Meyer and Kim are for a guarantee of $3,043 for one child and $4,058 for two (both 2016 dollars), a dollar-for-dollar reduction in AFDC benefits, and only families with child support orders being eligible. Meyer and Kim do show components of costs and savings, and the difference that including labor supply makes. In their model costs include the direct cost of the guarantee, and small increases in EITC benefits and other tax decreases; savings come from AFDC and food stamps. The labor supply module adds about $500 million to costs (2016 dollars).

15. A guarantee of $150 per child per month yields an annual minimum of $1,800 per year. In 1991 the National Commission on Children recommended a minimum annual benefit of $1,500 for one child; others proposed a guarantee of $3,000 (Sorensen and Clark 1994)—equivalent to about $2,650 to $5,300 today.

duce support to children of the lowest income noncustodial parents, for which the minimum benefit exceeds the percentage-of-income contribution expected from the noncustodial parent. A higher minimum benefit would increase costs but provide more to children of low-income noncustodial parents, and be a larger reliable income source for all children living apart from one of their parents.

The percentage of noncustodial parent income could be set higher or lower than 12.5 percent per child. A lower amount would yield orders below current guidelines in most cases with one or two children, but orders more consistent with current guidelines for larger families. A higher percentage standard would not affect current support due from noncustodial parents with more than two children, unless the maximum contribution were increased.

The maximum noncustodial parent contribution could be set higher or lower than 33 percent of noncustodial parent income, for all noncustodial parents, or for those noncustodial parents with higher incomes. In our base scheme, where support above the maximum contribution is to be paid by the noncustodial parent at a later date, and where support up to the $150 per child minimum is assured, a change in the maximum contribution would not affect the support received by children with low-income noncustodial parents, but would delay a greater share of the payments and allow the noncustodial parent additional income for current expenses. For higher-income noncustodial parents, a lower maximum would delay payments to the children. An alternative would be to provide for a noncustodial parent self-support reserve in calculating maximum current contributions.

Part of the minimum support payment could be contingent on the noncustodial parent's contribution. For example, given a minimum of $150 per month per child, guaranteed support could be reduced to $100 per month, with the remaining $50 per month per child provided only if the noncustodial parent paid at least $50 per month.[16] This would reduce the amount of reliable support for families of noncustodial parents who did not pay, but would increase the incentive for noncustodial parents to pay; children would receive more income if noncustodial parents paid support than if they did not pay—not otherwise the case for low-income noncustodial parents with orders below the $150 minimum.

Child support income up to the per child minimum could be considered in determining eligibility and benefits for means-tested programs. Although this is not consistent with child support being the right of the child and would result in a lowered value of the child support for single-parent families, who are arguably more vulnerable than two-parent families with comparable needs-adjusted incomes, it would be less expensive for taxpayers. Moreover, ignoring the benefit in these other programs generates inequities between families with parents living together and those living apart. We suggest minimizing the disregard to the per child minimum (proposed to be $150 per month) because the horizontal inequity generated by the disregard would be more problematic at higher levels.

The guarantee could be provided to all children living with a single parent, even without a child support order. This would be more consistent with guaranteed support as the right of the child, and also recognizes the vulnerability of many children who do not have a child support order on their behalf (and may not have legal paternity established). However, this would undercut the incentive for low-income families to establish an order, and would significantly raise costs. A more modest expansion would re-

---

16. If the noncustodial parent paid less than $50 per month, the child would receive less than the minimum of $150, if the noncustodial parent paid between $50 and $150 per month the child would receive $150, and if the noncustodial parent owed and paid more than $150 per month the child would receive the higher amount.

quire a child support order to qualify for the guarantee, except when there is good cause (for example, due to domestic violence) for not pursuing an order.

In addition to concerns regarding public costs, guaranteed minimum child support raises important concerns regarding the incentive for noncustodial parents to pay child support and to work. Because children would receive the minimum $150 per month per child support regardless of the noncustodial parents' payments, a child support guarantee would reduce the incentive for noncustodial parents to pay support. Some evidence indicates that noncustodial parents are more likely to pay support, or to pay more, when their children benefit (Cancian, Meyer, and Caspar 2008), but the estimated effects are relatively small and, we would argue, not enough to justify risking the minimum economic well-being of children. Moreover, although noncustodial parents working outside the formal economy may largely avoid child support enforcement efforts, their counterparts in the formal economy are subject to automatic withholding, largely making child support payments nondiscretionary (Bartfeld and Meyer 2003). To the extent that noncustodial parents are working so that they can support their children, a guaranteed payment means they have less incentive to work. However, previous analyses suggest that this potential effect is likely to be small (Freeman and Waldfogel 1998). Moreover, the minimum guarantee, available only to children with a child support order, would create a substantial positive incentive for custodial parents (and many noncustodial parents) to cooperate in establishing an order, which may reverse the decline in custodial parents participating in the child support system (Schroeder 2016).

Broader Supports for Parents

A new approach to assessing and ensuring financial support is at the core of our proposal. But policies enforcing noncustodial parents' financial responsibilities to their children will be most productive in a context that also supports parental responsibility more broadly, rather than focusing only on financial transfers. Addressing an array of issues for separating parents could improve co-parenting relationships, noncustodial parent-child relationships, and would rebalance the system from its overemphasis on finances. Although not directly focused on financial resources, improving these relationships might be expected to also lead to additional financial support. Moreover, putting these services in an agency that serves not only separating parents but also parents who are together would encourage a focus on child well-being and helping all parents. This model is similar to models being implemented in Australia (Moloney et al. 2013) and the United Kingdom (Skinner 2012).

Although married, cohabiting, and separating parents confront many related issues, effective policy must acknowledge and provide an institutional context for managing differences in biological parents' relationships with each other and with their children. Many children are born to parents who are not in a sustained or stable relationship, to parents who may not have intended to conceive a child, and even in circumstances in which the father may have had no part in the mother's decisions with respect to the pregnancy. Difficult policy challenges arise in a context where biological and social or emotional ties are inconsistent. Current policy largely ignores the inconsistency and imposes equivalent financial responsibilities on all noncustodial parents, but does not offer clear guidance or institutional support for managing noncustodial parents' rights or responsibilities with respect, for example, to time with their children. One step in resolving this tension would be to expand institutional supports for unmarried parents to resolve issues related to their relationship with each other and their children. Many unmarried mothers express an interest in their child's father's playing a role. The lack of formal institutional supports, including access to mediation and agency and court agreements related to visitation, may contribute to the challenges unmarried parents face in establishing and maintaining positive relationships. When both parents want to share responsibilities for their child, child support services should include efforts to establish both orders for financial support and parenting plans.[17]

When parents disagree about their roles and responsibilities, the appropriate policy response is considerably less clear. At present, pregnant women have a legal right to terminate a pregnancy, or, if they carry a child to term, to initiate termination of parental rights so that the child may be adopted. Unmarried mothers who do not rely on public benefits are largely free to decide whether to identify the biological father, establish paternity, and pursue a child support order. In contrast, low-income mothers are routinely required to cooperate with the child support agency as a condition of receiving Medicaid (including for childbirth), or other means-tested benefits. Once paternity is established, fathers are subject to the same child support responsibilities, regardless of their relationship with the mother, or their intentions or interests with respect to the birth. The current approach to child support, holding biological fathers responsible irrespective of their relationship to the mother or child, was once consistent with widely held attitudes and behaviors. But, as we have argued, declines in postconception marriage, increases in nonmarital childbearing, as well as increases in women's socioeconomic independence have undercut much of the logic for this approach. The contested nature of parental rights and responsibilities highlights the importance of institutional support for resolving issues related to parents' relationships with each other and their children.

SUMMARY

The United States has a variety of programs for low-income families with children, but current policy for single-parent families is primarily located in the child support system. We argue that the system's primary goal should be increasing the financial resources available to children living with a single parent, with a secondary goal of holding parents responsible for the support of their children. When assessed by this standard, current policy has been substantially successful for divorcing families in which the noncustodial parent has at least moderate earnings in the formal economy. But the current system clearly does not work well for lower-income families, especially those couples who were not married. The problems are clear: far too few children regularly receive substantial amounts of child support and, by being overly focused on financial transfers, the system is sometimes counterproductive to the broader mission of encouraging responsibility. We argued that a key part of the problem is unrealistic, outdated assumptions about separated parents. We propose a reformed system that includes a guaranteed minimum support per child and assurances that no noncustodial parent will be charged beyond their means. We also propose a new agency that focuses not only on these financial transfers, but also on supporting parents' relationships with their children. These reforms, aimed especially at addressing the challenges facing families with parents living apart, combined with other reforms supporting low-income families in general, would transform the resources available to economically vulnerable children and families.

REFERENCES

Amato, Paul. R. 2005. "The Impact of Family Formation Change on the Cognitive, Social, and Emotional Well-Being of the Next Generation." *The Future of Children* 15(2): 75–96.

Bartfeld, Judi, and Daniel R. Meyer. 2003. "Child Support Compliance among Discretionary and Nondiscretionary Obligors." *Social Service Review* 77(3): 347–72.

Cancian, Maria, Yiyu Chen, Eunhee Han, and Daniel R. Meyer. 2012. "Exploring Reasons for the Decline in Child Support Orders Among Paternity Cases." Report to the Wisconsin Department of Children and Families. Madison, Wisc.: Institute for Research on Poverty.

Cancian, Maria, Carolyn J. Heinrich, and Yiyoon Chung. 2013. "Discouraging Disadvantaged Fathers' Employment: An Unintended Consequence of Policies Designed to Support Families." *Journal of Policy Analysis and Management*. 32(4): 758–84.

Cancian, Maria, and Daniel R. Meyer. 2011. "Who Owes What to Whom? Child Support Policy Given Multiple-Partner Fertility." *Social Service Review* 85(4): 587–617.

---

17. For example, see the discussion of the Co-Parent Court program in Minnesota (Marczak et al. 2015).

Cancian, Maria, Daniel R. Meyer, Patricia R. Brown, and Steven T. Cook. 2014. "Who Gets Custody Now? Dramatic Changes in Children's Living Arrangements After Divorce." *Demography* 51(4): 1381–96.

Cancian, Maria, Daniel R. Meyer, and Emma Caspar. 2008. "Welfare and Child Support: Complements, Not Substitutes." *Journal of Policy Analysis and Management* 27(2): 354–75.

Cancian, Maria, Daniel R. Meyer, and Steven T. Cook. 2011. "The Evolution of Family Complexity from the Perspective of Children." *Demography* 48(3): 957–82.

Cancian, Maria, Daniel R. Meyer, and Eunhee Han. 2011. "Child Support: Responsible Fatherhood and the Quid Pro Quo." *Annals of the American Academy of Political and Social Science* 635(1): 140–62.

Carlson, Marcia J., and Frank F. Furstenberg Jr. 2006. "The Prevalence and Correlates of Multipartnered Fertility Among Urban U.S. Parents." *Journal of Marriage and Family* 68(3): 718–32.

Chung, Yiyoon. 2012. "The Effects of Paternal Imprisonment on Children's Economic Well-Being." *Social Service Review* 86(3): 455–86.

Edin, Kathryn. 1995. "Single Mothers and Child Support: The Possibilities and Limits of Child Support Policy." *Children and Youth Services Review* 17(1/2): 203–30.

Freeman, Richard B., and Jane Waldfogel. 1998. "Does Child Support Enforcement Policy Affect Male Labor Supply?" In *Fathers Under Fire: The Revolution in Child Support Enforcement*, edited by Irwin Garfinkel, Sara S. McLanahan, Daniel R. Meyer, and Judith A. Seltzer. New York: Russell Sage Foundation.

Garasky, Steven, Susan D. Stewart, Craig Gundersen, and Brenda J. Lohman. 2010. "Toward a Fuller Understanding of Nonresident Father Involvement: An Examination of Child Support, In-Kind Support, and Visitation." *Population Research and Policy Review* 29(3): 363–93.

Garfinkel, Irwin. 1992. *Assuring Child Support: An Extension of Social Security*. New York: Russell Sage Foundation.

Garfinkel, Irwin, Sara S. McLanahan, and Philip K. Robins, eds. 1992. *Child Support Assurance: Design Issues, Expected Benefits, and Political Barriers as Seen from Wisconsin*. Washington, D.C.: Urban Institute Press.

Garrison, Marsha. 1999. "Child Support Policy: Guidelines and Goals." *Family Law Quarterly* 33(1): 157–89.

Geller, Amanda, Irwin Garfinkel, and Bruce Western. 2011. "Paternal Incarceration and Support for Children in Fragile Families." *Demography* 48(1): 25–47.

Grall, Timothy. 2016. "Custodial Mothers and Fathers and Their Child Support: 2013." *Current Population Reports* series P60, no. 255. Washington: U.S. Census Bureau.

Gunter, Samara R. 2016. "Child Support Wage Withholding and Father-Child Contact: Parental Bargaining and Salience Effects." *Review of Economics of the Household*. DOI: 10.1007/s11150-016-9330-4.

Ha, Yoonsook, Maria Cancian, and Daniel R. Meyer. 2011. "The Regularity of Child Support and Its Contribution to the Regularity of Income." *Social Service Review* 85(3): 401–19.

———. 2016. "Child Support and Income Inequality." Working Paper. University of Wisconsin–Madison.

Huang, Chien-Chung. 2009. "Mothers' Reports of Nonresident Fathers' Involvement with Their Children: Revisiting the Relationship Between Child Support Payment and Visitation." *Family Relations* 58(1): 54–64.

Koball, Heather, and Desiree Principe. 2002. "Do Nonresident Fathers Who Pay Child Support Visit Their Children More?" *New Federalism: National Survey of America's Families*, series B, no. B-44. Washington, D.C.: The Urban Institute.

Lichter, Daniel T., Sharon Sassler, and Richard N. Turner. 2014. "Cohabitation, Post-Conception Unions, and the Rise in Nonmarital Fertility." *Social Science Research* 47 (September): 134–47.

Maldonado, Laurie C., and Rense Nieuwenhuis. 2015. "Family Policies and Single Parent Poverty in 18 OECD Countries, 1978–2008." *Community, Work & Family* 18(4): 395–415.

Marczak, Mary S., Emily H. Becher, Alisha M. Hardman, Dylan L. Galos, and Ebony Ruhland. 2015. "Strengthening the Role of Unmarried Fathers: Findings from the Co-Parent Court Project." *Family Process* 54(4): 630–38.

McLanahan, Sara, and Gary Sandefur. 1994. *Growing Up with a Single Parent: What Hurts, What Helps*. Cambridge, Mass.: Harvard University Press.

Meyer, Daniel R. 1998. "The Effect of Child Support on the Economic Status of Nonresident Fathers." In *Fathers Under Fire: The Revolution in Child Support Enforcement*, edited by Irwin Garfinkel, Sara S. McLanahan, Daniel R. Meyer, and Judith A. Seltzer. New York: Russell Sage Foundation.

———. 2012. "Child Maintenance Policies in the United States." *European Journal of Social Security* 14(4): 252–66.

Meyer, Daniel R., Maria Cancian, and Yiyu Chen. 2015. "Why Are Child Support Orders Becoming Less Likely after Divorce?" *Social Service Review* 89(2): 301–34.

Meyer, Daniel R., Maria Cancian, and Steven T. Cook. 2005. "Multiple Partner Fertility: Incidence and Implications for Child Support Policy." *Social Service Review* 79 (4): 577–601.

Meyer, Daniel R., and Rebecca Y. Kim. 1998. "Estimating a Proposed Family Policy's Effects: Incorporating Labor Supply Responses to an Assured Child Support Benefit." *Journal of Family Issues* 19(5): 534–55.

Meyer, Daniel, R. Christine Skinner, and Jacqueline Davidson. 2011. "Complex Families and Equality in Child Support Obligations: A Comparative Policy Analysis." *Children and Youth Services Review* 33(10): 1804–12.

Moloney, Lawrie, Lixia Qu, Ruth Weston, and Kelly Hand. 2013. "Evaluating the Work of Australia's Family Relationship Centres: Evidence from the First 5 Years." *Family Court Review* 51(2): 234–49.

Nepomnyaschy, Lenna. 2007. "Child Support and Father-Child Contact: Testing Reciprocal Pathways." *Demography* 44(1): 93–112.

Nepomnyaschy, Lenna, and Irwin Garfinkel. 2010. "Child Support Enforcement and Fathers' Contributions to Their Nonmarital Children." *Social Service Review* 84(3): 341–80.

Office of Child Support Enforcement. 2013. *Promoting Child Well-being & Family Self-Sufficiency*. Child Support Fact Sheet Series No. 13. Washington: U.S. Department of Health and Human Services, Administration for Children and Families, Office for Child Support Enforcement.

Organization for Economic Co-operation and Development (OECD). 2014. "Social Expenditure Update: Social spending is falling in some countries, but in many others it remains at historically high levels." Directorate on Employment Labour and Social Affairs. Accessed October 3, 2017. https://www.oecd.org/els/soc/OECD2014-SocialExpenditure_Update19Nov_Rev.pdf.

Peters, H. Elizabeth, Laura M. Argys, Heather Wynder Howard, and J. S. Butler. 2004. "Legislating Love: The Effect of Child Support and Welfare Policies on Father-Child Contact." *Review of Economics of the Household* 2(3): 255–74.

Pirog, Maureen A., and Kathleen M. Ziol-Guest. 2006. "Child Support Enforcement: Programs and Policies, Impacts and Questions." *Journal of Policy Analysis and Management* 25(4): 943–90.

Schroeder, Daniel. 2016. "The Limited Reach of the Child Support Enforcement System." Washington, D.C.: American Enterprise Institute.

Sinkewicz, Marilyn, and Irwin Garfinkel. 2009. "Unwed Fathers' Ability to Pay Child Support: New Estimates Accounting for Multiple-Partner Fertility." *Demography* 46(2): 247–63.

Skinner, Christine. 2012. "Child Maintenance in the United Kingdom." *European Journal of Social Security* 14(4): 231–51.

Skinner, Christine, Daniel R. Meyer, Kay Cook, and Michael Fletcher. 2017. "Child Maintenance and Social Security Interactions: The Poverty Reduction Effects in Model Lone Parent Families Across Four Countries." *Journal of Social Policy* 46(3): 495–516.

Social Security Administration (SSA). 2000. "Title IV: Grants to States for Aid and Services to Needy Families with Children and for Child-Welfare Services." Washington: U.S. Department of Health and Human Services. Accessed October 4, 2017. https://www.ssa.gov/OP_Home/ssact/title04/0400.htm.

Sorensen, Elaine, and Sandra Clark. 1994. "A Child-Support Assurance Program: How Much Will It Reduce Child Poverty, and at What Cost?" *American Economic Review* 84(2): 114–19.

U.S. Census Bureau. 2015. "America's Families and Living Arrangements: 2015: Children." Table 8. Washington: U.S. Department of Commerce.

U.S. Department of Health and Human Services (DHHS). 1995. *Report to Congress on Out-of-Wedlock Childbearing*. DHHS Pub. No. (PHS) 95-1257. Hyattsville, Md.: National Center for Health Statistics.

Waller, Maureen R., and Robert Plotnick. 2001. "Effective Child Support Policy for Low-Income Families: Evidence from Street Level Research." *Journal of Policy Analysis and Management* 20(1): 89–110.

Wimer, Christopher, Sophie Collyer, and Sara Kimberlin. 2018. "Assessing the Potential Impacts of Innovative New Policy Proposals on Poverty in the United States." *RSF: The Russell Sage Foundation Journal of the Social Sciences* 4(3): 167–83. DOI: 10.7758/RSF.2018.4.3.09.

Reconstructing the Supplemental Nutrition Assistance Program to More Effectively Alleviate Food Insecurity in the United States

CRAIG GUNDERSEN, BRENT KREIDER, AND JOHN V. PEPPER

Although the central objective of the Supplemental Nutrition Assistance Program (SNAP) is to reduce food insecurity in the United States, the majority of SNAP households are food insecure. Higher benefits may lead these households to food security. To evaluate this possibility, we use a question from the Current Population Survey that asks respondents how much additional money they would need to be food secure. Food insecure SNAP households report needing an average of about $42 per week to become food secure. Under a set of assumptions about the measurement of benefits and behavioral responses, we find that an increase in weekly benefits of $42 for SNAP households would lead to a 62 percent decline in food insecurity at a cost of about $27 billion.

Keywords: food insecurity, Supplemental Nutrition Assistance Program (SNAP), food stamp program, poverty

Food insecurity, described as "the uncertainty of having, or unable to acquire, enough food due to insufficient money or other resources" (Coleman-Jensen et al. 2016), has become a leading indicator of economic well-being in the United States for two central reasons. First, the extent of the problem is staggering—more than forty-two million Americans lived in food insecure households in 2015 (Coleman-Jensen et al. 2016). Second, a well-established set of negative health outcomes is associated with food insecurity (for a review, see Gundersen and Ziliak 2015), which lead to dramatically higher healthcare costs (Tarasuk et al. 2015). To reduce food insecurity, the U.S. Department of Agriculture (USDA) administers the Supplemental Nutrition Assistance Program (SNAP). Although a growing body of research has demonstrated that SNAP reduces food insecurity (see, for example, Gundersen, Kreider, and Pepper 2017),

Craig Gundersen is Soybean Industry Endowed Professor in Agricultural Strategy at the University of Illinois. **Brent Kreider** is professor of economics at Iowa State University. **John V. Pepper** is professor of economics at the University of Virginia.

© 2018 Russell Sage Foundation. Gundersen, Craig, Brent Kreider, and John V. Pepper. 2018. "Reconstructing the Supplemental Nutrition Assistance Program to More Effectively Alleviate Food Insecurity in the United States." *RSF: The Russell Sage Foundation Journal of the Social Sciences* 4(2): 113–30. DOI: 10.7758/RSF.2018.4.2.06. Direct correspondence to: Craig Gundersen at cggunder@illinois.edu, Department of Agricultural and Consumer Economics, University of Illinois, 324 Mumford Hall, 1301 West Gregory Dr., Urbana, IL 61801; Brent Kreider at bkreider@iastate.edu, Department of Economics, Iowa State University, 460C Heady Hall, Ames, IA 50011; and John V. Pepper at jvp3m@eservices.virginia.edu, Department of Economics, University of Virginia, 237 Monroe Hall, Charlottesville, VA 22904.

Open Access Policy: *RSF: The Russell Sage Foundation Journal of the Social Sciences* is an open access journal. This article is published under a Creative Commons Attribution-NonCommercial-NoDerivs 3.0 Unported License.

the majority of SNAP households are food insecure.

In this article, we provide new insights into the food insecurity of SNAP recipients. Whereas previous research studies the prevalence of food insecurity, our analysis focuses on the additional income households would require in order to become food secure. We label this measure the *resource gap*. Much of our analysis focuses on households participating in SNAP, but we also examine the resource gap for certain groups of currently ineligible low-income households. Throughout, we separately consider cases for all households and for the subset of households with children.

To measure the resource gap, we use questions in the 2014 Current Population Survey (CPS) that ask respondents how much more money they would need to become food secure. These self-reported amounts are subject to personal interpretation and potential mismeasurement. Nevertheless, such reports provide a useful starting point in assessing perceived food assistance shortcomings. After estimating the resource gap, we provide an exploratory analysis of the potential reductions in food insecurity rates that could result from different amounts of SNAP benefit increases. We then assess the resource gap for households with incomes just above the current eligibility threshold and consider potential reductions in food insecurity rates if eligibility was expanded.

This article contributes to our broader understanding of poverty and policies designed to reduce poverty. The prevalence of food insecurity is closely tied to household income and resources—poor households have substantially higher rates of food insecurity than non-poor households (Coleman-Jensen et al. 2016)—and many of the consequences associated with poverty are due, at least in part, to households being food insecure. As a result, anti-poverty policies in the United States have a direct impact on food security rates. Moreover, although the central goal of SNAP is to alleviate food insecurity (USDA 1999), the program also serves to mitigate the consequences of poverty. SNAP plays a role similar to cash in that it expands a household's budget opportunities. As such, SNAP leads to reductions in the depth and severity of poverty (Tiehen, Jolliffe, and Smeeding 2015).

BACKGROUND

We now turn to an overview of the two central concepts of this paper—SNAP and food insecurity. We then consider the relationship between them.

Supplemental Nutrition Assistance Program

SNAP began with the Food Stamp Act of 1964 and became a national program in 1974. Today, SNAP is the largest food assistance program in the United States. In 2015, more than forty-six million people received benefits totaling nearly $70 billion (for a broader view of the program, see Bartfeld et al. 2015). Though states have discretion over various aspects of SNAP, such as the gross income and asset eligibility tests, all benefits are funded by the federal government.

The program has undergone numerous changes over the years, but its basic structure has stayed the same. SNAP benefits can be used to buy food in authorized retail food outlets, which include virtually all food stores. Benefits are calculated by subtracting 30 percent of the household's net income from the value of the Thrifty Food Plan (TFP), a low-cost nutritionally adequate food plan that varies by household size and composition.

To be eligible for SNAP, households must first meet a monthly gross income test—the household's income (before any deductions) typically cannot exceed 130 percent of the poverty line, though some states have set more lenient thresholds.[1] Net income, which is calculated as gross income less certain deductions, cannot exceed the poverty line, even in states that have set a higher gross income threshold.[2] The net income test is binding, regardless of

---

1. There are some exceptions. For instance, households with at least one elderly or disabled member are not required to meet this test.

2. The allowable deductions include a standard deduction for all households, a 20 percent earned income deduction, a dependent care deduction when care is necessary for work, training, or education, a child support payments deduction, a medical costs deduction for elderly and disabled people, and an excess shelter cost deduction.

the gross income threshold. Historically, a household's total assets could not exceed $2,000 but most states now elect to waive this test.

Food Insecurity

Our central outcome of interest in this article is food insecurity. Food insecurity in the United States is measured through a series of questions in the Core Food Security Module (CFSM). The CFSM includes eighteen questions for households with children and a subset of ten questions for households without children. Examples follow. I worried whether our food would run out before we got money to buy more (the least severe item). Did you or the other adults in your household ever cut the size of your meals or skip meals because there wasn't enough money for food? Were you ever hungry but did not eat because you couldn't afford enough food? Did a child in the household ever not eat for a full day because you couldn't afford enough food (the most severe item for households with children)?[3] Each question is qualified by the stipulation that the problem was caused by lack of money.

Under the official definition established by the USDA, a response is labeled affirmative if the answer is yes (rather than no) or sometimes or often (rather than never). Based on these responses to the CFSM, households are placed into three food insecurity categories under the assumption that the number of affirmative responses reflects the level of food hardship that the family experiences. If a household responds affirmatively to two or fewer questions, it is labeled *food secure* under the premise that all household members had access at all times to enough food for an active, healthy life. If a household responds affirmatively to three to seven questions, it is labeled *low food secure* in that at least some household members were uncertain of having, or unable to acquire, enough food because they had insufficient money and other resources for food. If a household responds affirmatively to eight or more questions, it is labeled *very low food secure* in that one or more household members were hungry, at least sometime during the year, because they could not afford enough food. The measure we use in this article is *food insecure*, which holds if a household is either low food secure or very low food secure.

SNAP and Food Insecurity

The primary goal of SNAP is to alleviate food insecurity in the United States. Yet, the post–Great Recession increases in both the proportion of Americans receiving SNAP and the proportion residing in food insecure households have led some to question the efficacy of the program. In particular, from 2007 to 2013 the number of persons receiving SNAP increased from 26.3 million to a peak of 47.6 million in 2013.[4] Meanwhile, the number of food insecure persons rose from 36.2 million to 49.1 million over the same period (Coleman-Jensen et al. 2016, table 1A). Moreover, it is well known that SNAP recipients have higher rates of food insecurity than eligible nonrecipients. In 2015, for example, SNAP participants had a food insecurity rate above 50 percent, whereas those with incomes below 130 percent of the poverty line but did not receive SNAP had a rate of 25.3 percent (Coleman-Jensen et al. 2016, table 8).

These trends and associations between SNAP participation and food insecurity rates, however, are not causally indicative of the efficacy of SNAP. The decision to participate in SNAP presumably is based in part on whether a household expects to be food insecure, and SNAP is designed to reach those who are most at risk of food insecurity. In fact, the success of SNAP in meeting its central goal of reducing food insecurity has been demonstrated in numerous studies. After controlling for the nonrandom selection of households into SNAP, participants are approximately 20 percent less likely to be food insecure than eligible nonparticipants (see, for example, Kreider et al. 2012). Thus, the observed increase in food insecurity since the Great Recession likely would have been substantially higher in the absence of SNAP.

---

3. For a complete list of questions, see, Coleman-Jensen et al. 2016.

4. See https://www.fns.usda.gov/sites/default/files/pd/SNAPsummary.pdf

THE RESOURCE GAP

In this section, we introduce a measure we call the resource gap. For a food insecure household, we define this gap to be the amount of additional income the household reports needing in order to become food secure. Households are asked this question in the CPS, the official data source for poverty and unemployment rates in the United States, as well as the official source for national food insecurity rates (Coleman-Jensen et al. 2016). In particular, we estimate the resource gap across households using data from the December supplement of the 2014 CPS. We focus on two main samples: households classified as income-eligible for SNAP (income below 130 percent of the poverty line) and SNAP recipients.[5] These samples include 8,441 and 4,148 households, respectively. Within these samples, we also study the resource gap for the subset of households with children. The corresponding samples sizes are 3,225 and 2,147.[6]

For each household in the sample, we observe a rich set of socioeconomic indicators of well-being, including measures of income and SNAP receipt. Table 1 presents the SNAP participation rates by different socioeconomic factors using the 2014 CPS for each of the four samples described. Among households eligible for SNAP, the SNAP participation rate is 35 percent among all households (column 1) and 49 percent among households with children (column 3). The latter is roughly consistent with other studies using the CPS (for example, Gundersen et al. 2017). The SNAP participation rates are generally as expected across the categories. For example, it is not surprising that participation rates fall with income given the lower benefit levels that would be received. Perhaps contrary to expectations, participation rates are higher among households in nonmetro areas.

The second and fourth columns of table 1 display food insecurity rates among SNAP participants. Despite substantial variation in food insecurity rates within the broader low-income population (for example, food insecurity is less prevalent in higher income groups), these rates are quite similar across categories among SNAP recipients. The main areas where we see lower rates of food insecurity are among households headed by a married couple (versus a single parent) and those headed by someone with a college degree. Even in these cases, the differences are not large.

Importantly, the CPS also asks respondents how much additional money they would need to become food secure. Specifically, households responding that they need more money for food were asked the following question: "About how much more would you need to spend each week to buy just enough food to meet the needs of your household?" (for more on this question, see Gundersen and Ribar 2011). This question precedes the eighteen-item scale in the CFSM. We limit our attention to food insecure households.[7]

One important caveat with these data is that food insecurity is measured over the previous year rather than contemporaneously, while the question regarding the number of dollars necessary to become food secure is based on the respondent's perception from the previous week when they may or may not have been food

---

5. Because the CPS does not provide enough information to measure net income and assets, we focus on gross income eligibility. Virtually all gross income eligible households with incomes below the 130 percent of the poverty threshold are also net income eligible. For states that set a higher gross income threshold (such as, 200 percent), most households turn out to be ineligible based on net income. Income in the December CPS is defined only in ranges. Consistent with Craig Gundersen and his colleagues (2017), we measure income using the midpoint of the income category divided by the poverty line as defined for the size of the household.

6. The SNAP recipient sample is not a subset of the sample of households with income below 130 percent of the FPL. Some SNAP households, based on information in the CPS, have incomes above 130 percent of the poverty line. We include those households in our estimations involving samples of SNAP participants but not in our estimations that limit the sample to those with incomes below 130 percent of the poverty line.

7. Some food secure households also report needing more money to purchase food. Many of these households fall into the marginal food secure category—that is, responding affirmatively to one or two questions in the CFSM.

Table 1. SNAP Participation Rates and Food Insecurity Rates

	All Households		Households with Children	
	SNAP Participation Rates Among Eligible Households	Food Insecurity Rates Among SNAP Participants	SNAP Participation Rates Among Eligible Households	Food Insecurity Rates Among SNAP Participants
All	0.35	0.54	0.49	0.52
Income-poverty line				
0–0.50	0.44	0.54	0.65	0.53
0.51–1.00	0.37	0.56	0.48	0.54
1.01–1.30	0.22	0.56	0.30	0.53
Less than high school	0.40	0.54	0.51	0.53
High school	0.37	0.53	0.51	0.52
Some college	0.35	0.56	0.52	0.53
College	0.17	0.49	0.31	0.46
Married	0.27	0.50	0.36	0.47
Single	0.39	0.55	0.61	0.55
Own	0.23	0.52	0.33	0.48
Rent	0.43	0.55	0.57	0.54
Nonmetro	0.41	0.54	0.57	0.48
Metro	0.34	0.54	0.48	0.53
White	0.32	0.54	0.45	0.51
African American	0.48	0.53	0.63	0.53
Other (non-white, non–African American)	0.24	0.53	0.36	0.52
Hispanic	0.37	0.50	0.43	0.49
Non-Hispanic	0.35	0.55	0.53	0.53
Unweighted N	8,441	4,148	3,225	2,147

Source: Authors' calculations based on data from the 2014 December supplement of the CPS.
Note: Eligible households are those with incomes less than 130 percent of the poverty line. SNAP participants are those who report currently receiving SNAP. Sample estimates are weighted using the household-level weight defined for the December supplement.

insecure.[8] Consistent with this discrepancy, 42 percent of food insecure SNAP participants with children report not needing additional dollars in the previous week to become food secure. We do not attempt to account for the difference in timing between these two measures. Rather, we treat the self-reported measures of the resource gap in the previous week as informative about the resource gap during the previous year. In addition, we do not address the possibility that households may inaccurately perceive or report how many dollars they would actually need to become food secure. Some may underreport their need for assistance if ashamed to admit heading a food insecure household, while others may exaggerate their need for additional dollars if worried that doing otherwise could jeopardize the amount of SNAP benefits they receive. As such, our self-reported measure of the average resource gap among food insecure SNAP households may be biased in either direction. Future analyses of the resource gap is needed to address these issues.

As the resource gap has not been extensively studied, we provide some general background

---

8. SNAP participation is measured over the same time frame as food insecurity. That is, a household is defined as a SNAP participant if it received SNAP within the past twelve months.

Figure 1. Per Capita Dollars Needed for Food Security

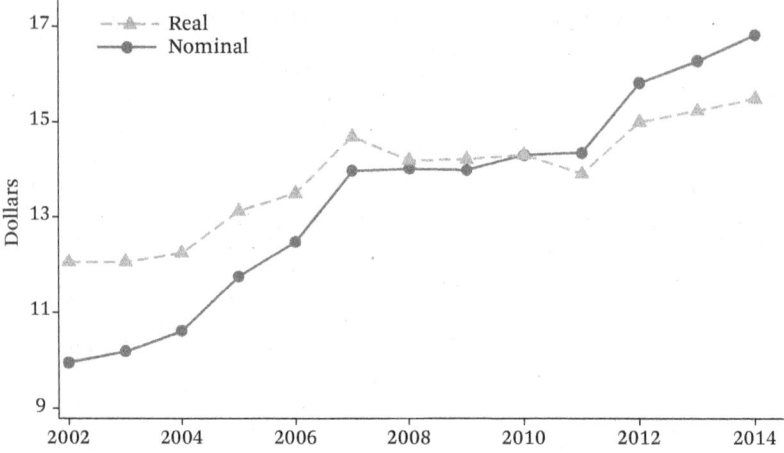

Source: Authors' calculations based on data from the 2002 to 2014 December supplements of the CPS.
Note: The sample from each year is composed of food insecure households.

Figure 2. Dollars Needed per Week for Food Security

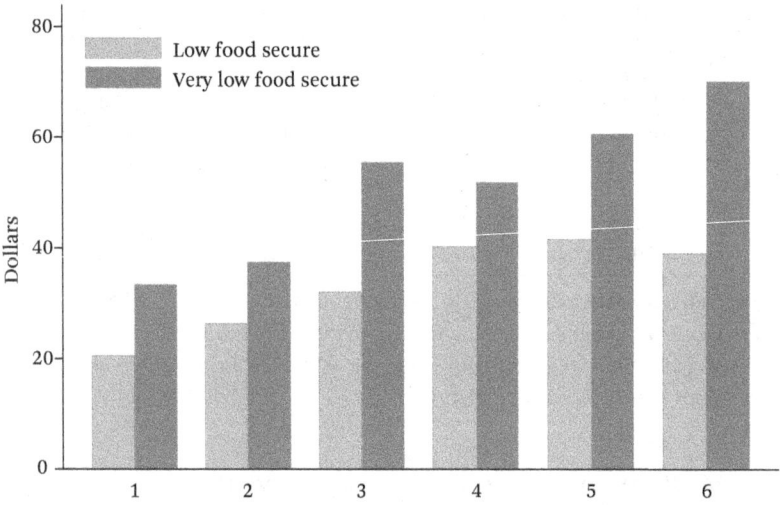

Source: Authors' calculations based on data from the 2014 December supplement of the CPS.
Note: The sample from each year is composed of food insecure households.

followed by information specific to SNAP participants. In figure 1, we display the average nominal and real (2010 dollars) per-capita average resource gaps when the sample is made up of all food insecure households, regardless of income or SNAP participation. These gaps increase markedly from 2002 to 2014 in real dollars (see Gundersen et al. 2013, figure 1). This is not a secular increase, however. Coinciding with the sharp increase in food insecurity rates from 2007 to 2008, reports of additional required dollars first fell, then stayed relatively constant through 2010, fell again from 2010 to 2011, and more recently have been on the rise again.

In figure 2, we show how the average resource gap for households with children, as reported in the 2014 survey, varies by the degree of food insecurity and household size. As might be expected, households reporting higher degrees of food insecurity (that is, very low versus low food security) report a larger average re-

Table 2. Average Additional Dollars per Week Needed to Become Food Secure Among Food Insecure SNAP Participants

	All Households		Households with Children	
	Dollars	Dollars as a Proportion of Maximum SNAP Benefits	Dollars	Dollars as a Proportion of Maximum SNAP Benefits
All	$41.62	0.42	$45.69	0.29
Income-poverty line				
0–0.50	47.39	0.39	50.39	0.31
0.51–1.00	37.13	0.42	40.64	0.27
1.01–1.30	44.92	0.48	50.30	0.31
Less than high school	45.15	0.45	46.99	0.29
High school	41.14	0.41	48.35	0.31
Some college	40.62	0.42	41.11	0.27
College	34.30	0.34	46.77	0.32
Married	44.42	0.31	46.23	0.25
Single	40.73	0.45	45.90	0.31
Own	39.34	0.38	43.32	0.26
Rent	42.43	0.43	46.38	0.30
Nonmetro	37.71	0.41	43.39	0.27
Metro	42.55	0.42	46.16	0.30
White	38.15	0.38	42.42	0.26
African American	48.82	0.52	50.69	0.35
Other (non-white, non–African American)	44.27	0.33	55.90	0.30
Hispanic	44.43	0.36	47.77	0.29
Non-Hispanic	40.87	0.43	44.93	0.29

Source: Authors' compilation based on data from the 2014 December supplement of the CPS.
Note: SNAP participants are those who report currently receiving SNAP. Sample estimates are weighted using the household-level weight defined for the December supplement.

source gap and, in general, reported levels of need increase as household size increases.

In table 2, the first and third columns display the resource gap among food insecure SNAP recipients for the same categories shown in table 1 for all households (N = 2,209) and households with children (N=1,099). The average resource gap is $41.62 per week across all households and $45.69 for households with children. In most categories, differences in the average resource gap are minimal, despite several exceptions. For example, the gap is substantially smaller for those with a college degree. In the second and fourth column, we normalize the number of dollars needed to become food secure by expressing them as a proportion of the maximum SNAP benefit level. This fraction is 0.42 among all households and 0.29 among households with children.

In table 3, we use a linear mean regression model to estimate how the average resource gap varies across the socioeconomic categories displayed in table 2. Columns (1) and (2) display the estimates for the sample of all households, and columns (3) and (4) those for households with children. For these regressions, household size and income are treated as separate variables rather than being combined as the income-to-poverty line measure presented in table 2. In columns (1) and (3), we include all of the variables in table 2. The coefficients are imprecisely estimated and statistically insignificant, with the exception of household size and, for households with children, households

Table 3. Mean Regressions of Additional Dollars Needed per Week to Be Food Secure Among SNAP Participants

	All Households		Households with Children	
	(1)	(2)	(3)	(4)
Income	0.013	−0.163	−0.666	−0.895
	(0.646)	(0.646)	(1.06)	(1.05)
Household size	5.24**	5.54**	6.91**	7.29**
	(0.70)	(0.69)	(1.24)	(1.23)
Less than high school	5.98	6.52	−8.20	−7.77
	(4.62)	(4.62)	(7.71)	(7.65)
High school	3.23	3.27	−2.44	−2.66
	(4.47)	(4.48)	(7.34)	(7.35)
Some college	1.47	1.49	−11.3	−11.6
	(4.53)	(4.54)	(7.41)	(7.43)
Married	−1.30	−2.22	−5.63	−6.50
	(2.69)	(2.68)	(3.81)	(3.78)
Homeowner	−2.25	−3.21	−1.04	−2.76
	(2.41)	(2.40)	(3.93)	(3.90)
Nonmetro	−0.25	−1.76	3.29	1.38
	(2.51)	(2.43)	(4.08)	(3.92)
White	−6.20		−13.8*	
	(4.77)		(6.80)	
African American	3.60		−3.37	
	(5.07)		(7.26)	
Hispanic	3.77		7.55	
	(3.03)		(4.32)	
Constant	26.3**	23.82**	35.4**	27.2**
	(6.50)	(4.54)	(10.6)	(8.13)
n	2,209	2,209	1,099	1,099

Source: Authors' compilation based on data from the 2014 December supplement of the CPS.
Note: Columns (1) and (3) include commonly used determinants of food insecurity drawn from the 2014 December supplement of the Current Population Survey. Columns (2) and (4) exclude race-ethnicity variables that are unlikely to be used in a restructuring of the SNAP benefit formula. Standard errors are in parentheses.
**p <.01, *p <.05

headed by a white person. For the household size variable, each additional household member is estimated to increase the resource gap by $5.24 among all households and by $6.91 among households with children. In columns (2) and (4), we restrict the set of variables that could be used to redirect benefits. In these restricted regressions, household size still has a statistically significant association with the expected resource gap with coefficients of 5.54 and 7.29.

In tables 2 and 3, we provide estimates for all SNAP participants regardless of income. In part to facilitate comparisons between SNAP participants and eligible nonparticipants, it is common in the literature to limit the sample to households with incomes below 130 percent of the poverty line.[9] For comparison purposes, then, we do so in table 4. The results are substantively similar to those in table 3. In particular, the estimated coefficients on household

9. In certain circumstances, a household is eligible for SNAP even if income exceeds 130 percent of the poverty line. The gross income criterion is waived, for example, if someone in the household has a disability. Other ex-

Table 4. Mean Regressions of Additional Dollars per Week Needed to Be Food Secure Among SNAP Participants, Incomes Less Than 130 Percent of the Poverty Line

	All Households		Households with Children	
	(1)	(2)	(3)	(4)
Income	−0.469	−0.927	−1.28	−1.65
	(1.77)	(1.77)	(2.20)	(2.19)
Household size	5.46**	5.91**	7.95**	8.41**
	(0.86)	(0.85)	(1.46)	(1.46)
Less than high school	9.76	10.39	−7.44	−6.72
	(5.74)	(5.74)	(9.32)	(9.29)
High school	7.08	7.08	−2.37	−2.51
	(5.65)	(5.66)	(9.09)	(9.10)
Some college	3.13	2.90	−13.3	−13.7
	(5.74)	(5.75)	(9.22)	(9.24)
Married	−2.23	−2.81	−9.80*	−10.1*
	(3.21)	(3.20)	(4.42)	(4.40)
Homeowner	−3.32	−4.54	−2.13	−3.75
	(2.89)	(2.87)	(4.64)	(4.60)
Nonmetro	0.38	−1.18	4.85	2.92
	(2.85)	(2.76)	(4.58)	(4.40)
White	−7.38		−15.6*	
	(5.51)		(7.68)	
African American	1.50		−6.35	
	(5.84)		(8.22)	
Hispanic	5.74		9.68*	
	(3.50)		(4.83)	
Constant	24.9**	21.2**	34.6**	24.7**
	(7.79)	(5.70)	(12.4)	(9.86)
n	1,683	1,683	866	866

Source: Authors' compilation based on data from the 2014 December supplement of the CPS.
Note: Columns (1) and (3) include commonly used determinants of food insecurity drawn from the 2014 December supplement of the Current Population Survey. Columns (2) and (4) exclude race-ethnicity variables that are unlikely to be used in a restructuring of the SNAP benefit formula. Standard errors are in parentheses.
**$p < .01$, *$p < .05$

size, at 5.91 for all households and 8.41 for households with children when estimated without race-ethnicity variables, are similar to the estimates in table 3.

Tables 5 and 6 are analogous to tables 3 and 4 except that household size is separated into discrete categories instead of a continuous measure of the number of household members.[10] These results suggest a nonlinear relationship between household size and the resource gap. For example, in column (2), a three-person household reports needing $12.60

---

amples include having net income below the poverty line while residing in a state with a gross income threshold above 130 percent of the poverty line, or having annual income above 130 percent but current monthly income below the threshold.

10. The sample for these tables is restricted to households with fewer than six people due to small sample sizes for larger households.

Table 5. Mean Regressions of Additional Dollars per Week Needed to Become Food Secure Among SNAP Participants

	All Households		Households with Children	
	(1)	(2)	(3)	(4)
Income	0.116	−0.063	−0.478	−0.726
	(0.664)	(0.664)	(1.13)	(1.13)
Two-person household	6.87*	6.92*		
	(3.04)	(3.05)		
Three-person household	11.7**	12.6**	8.53	9.08
	(3.29)	(3.28)	(5.57)	(5.58)
Four-person household	16.1**	17.2**	15.8**	16.8**
	(3.58)	(3.55)	(5.70)	(5.70)
Five-person household	18.5**	19.5**	19.6**	20.7**
	(4.19)	(4.16)	(6.24)	(6.23)
Six-person household	27.6**	29.1**	29.8**	31.7**
	(5.51)	(5.48)	(7.38)	(7.35)
Less than high school	5.28	5.97	−9.71	−9.10
	(4.60)	(4.59)	(7.71)	(7.65)
High school	2.42	2.54	−3.75	−3.84
	(4.43)	(4.44)	(7.31)	(7.31)
Some college	1.71	1.80	−10.8	−10.9
	(4.50)	(4.51)	(7.40)	(7.41)
Married	0.007	−0.93	−3.69	−4.63
	(2.74)	(2.74)	(3.95)	(3.93)
Homeowner	−2.56	−3.46	−1.24	−2.81
	(2.43)	(2.42)	(4.03)	(4.00)
Nonmetro	−0.85	−2.56	1.88	−0.418
	(2.52)	(2.44)	(4.17)	(3.99)
White	−3.14		−9.31	
	(4.84)		(7.04)	
African American	6.71		1.07	
	(5.14)		(7.49)	
Hispanic	4.00		7.70	
	(3.06)		(4.41)	
Constant	28.4**	29.1**	44.3**	41.0**
	(6.50)	(4.52)	(10.6)	(8.17)
n	2,209	2,209	1,099	1,099

Source: Authors' compilation based on data from the 2014 December supplement of the CPS.
Note: Columns (1) and (3) include commonly used determinants of food insecurity drawn from the 2014 December supplement of the Current Population Survey. Columns (2) and (4) exclude race-ethnicity variables that are unlikely to be used in a restructuring of the SNAP benefit formula. Standard errors are in parentheses.
**$p < .01$, *$p < .05$

Table 6. Mean Regressions of Additional Dollars Needed to Become Food Secure Among SNAP Participants, Incomes Less Than 130 Percent of the Poverty Line

	All Households		Households with Children	
	(1)	(2)	(3)	(4)
Income	−1.11	−2.25	−2.59	−2.85
	(1.91)	(1.30)	(2.41)	(2.41)
Two-person household	5.76	7.97**		
	(3.61)	(2.50)		
Three-person household	11.5**	12.4**	6.55	7.70
	(3.81)	(2.60)	(6.47)	(6.46)
Four-person household	14.7**	14.3**	14.6*	16.3*
	(4.18)	(2.87)	(6.63)	(6.61)
Five-person household	19.0**	18.1**	21.5**	23.2**
	(4.93)	(3.38)	(7.30)	(7.28)
Six-person household	27.9**	28.3**	31.1**	33.2**
	(6.523)	(4.45)	(8.67)	(8.62)
Less than high school	8.37	6.62	−10.1	−9.04
	(5.69)	(3.86)	(9.30)	(9.25)
High school	5.63	3.90	−4.98	−4.86
	(5.60)	(3.80)	(9.05)	(9.06)
Some college	3.13	3.64	−13.3	−13.4
	(5.70)	(3.89)	(9.21)	(9.23)
Married	−0.219	−0.51	−7.06	−7.55
	(3.28)	(2.26)	(4.60)	(4.58)
Homeowner	−3.65	−3.88*	−2.26	−3.78
	(2.91)	(1.98)	(4.76)	(4.73)
Nonmetro	−0.29	−2.58	3.78	1.29
	(2.86)	(1.90)	(4.67)	(4.48)
White	−3.02		−9.38	
	(5.60)		(7.96)	
African American	5.96		−0.310	
	(5.92)		(8.46)	
Hispanic	6.16		10.3*	
	(3.53)		(4.94)	
Constant	27.9**	20.6**	49.2**	45.3**
	(7.83)	(3.95)	(12.6)	(10.1)
n	1,683	1,683	866	866

Source: Authors' compilation based on data from the 2014 December supplement of the CPS.
Note: Columns (1) and (3) include commonly used determinants of food insecurity drawn from the 2014 December supplement of the Current Population Survey. Columns (2) and (4) exclude race-ethnicity variables that are unlikely to be used in a restructuring of the SNAP benefit formula. Standard errors are in parentheses.
**$p < .01$, *$p < .05$

more than a one-person household, a four-person household reports needing $17.20 more, and a five-person household reports needing $19.50 more. The respective gaps in households with children, compared with a two-person household, are $9.08, $16.80, and $20.70. When the sample is restricted to households with incomes below 130 percent of the poverty line (table 6), the results are closer to a linear relationship for households with children but are similar to table 5 for the sample of all households.

REDUCING FOOD INSECURITY BY CHANGING THE SNAP BENEFIT FORMULA

In this section, we provide an exploratory analysis of how changes to the SNAP benefit formula might lead to further reductions in the food insecurity rate. We do not undertake a formal benefit-cost analysis of the impact of changing the SNAP benefit formula. Instead, we present a descriptive exploration of the potential links between the resource gap, SNAP, and food insecurity. In doing so, we use information on the reported resource gap to study how changes in the SNAP benefit formula might reduce food insecurity rates. We assume that additional SNAP benefits reduce the resource gap dollar for dollar; for example, $50 in extra benefits is assumed to reduce the resource gap by $50. Thus, in this model, an extra $50 in SNAP benefits would result in all households reporting resource gaps of less than $50 to become food secure. Households with resources gaps in excess of $50 would remain food insecure.

Although the basic idea is simple, intended and actual effects may differ for several practical and theoretical reasons. Basic microeconomic theory tells us that any increase in benefit levels would likely lead SNAP recipients to spend more on nonfood items and may induce changes in the participation decisions of nonparticipants. Modeling these behavioral changes is beyond the scope of this article. On a more practical level, the resource gap is a self-reported measure that may not accurately measure the resources households need to become food secure. Respondents may not have a clear idea how to answer this question, the answer might change over time and, as noted, the questions about the resource gap are asked for a different period than questions about food insecurity.

In table 7, we present the potential reduction in food insecurity if SNAP benefits were to be strategically increased along with the costs associated with doing so. We consider three scenarios. The first involves giving each recipient the exact number of dollars they report needing to become food secure. In this first scenario, we assume all food insecure households would use these resources to become food secure; the food insecurity rate among SNAP recipients would drop to zero. Although this case is a useful benchmark, it would not be practical from a policy perspective to simply augment each household's SNAP benefits by whatever deficit amount a household reported. Among other issues, households would likely learn to modify their responses to maximize their benefits.

Scenario 2 provides an across-the-board increase in SNAP benefit levels that is equal to the average reported resource gap, $41.62 for all households and $45.69 for households with children, as found in table 2.[11] Under this proposal, both food secure and insecure households receive additional benefits. Moreover, some food insecure households might receive sufficient funds to become food secure while others would not.

The third scenario provides an increase in SNAP benefits equal to the adjustment based on household size from the estimates in tables 3 and 5. In particular, we use the predicted resource gap for each household size when the other variables are set at the average values for the sample.[12] We confine our attention to using

---

11. One could consider other uniform increases in the benefit level, ranging from zero dollars where the food insecurity rates would not change, to the maximum resource gap where the food insecurity rates might fall to zero.

12. Consider a comparison of a one-person household and a three-person household when the results for the full population of food insecure SNAP recipients are used. Based on the information from column (2) in table 3,

Table 7. Potential Impacts and Costs of Increases in SNAP Benefits, Households Receiving SNAP

	All Households		Households with Children	
	Percent Decline in Food Insecurity Rate Among SNAP Recipients	Additional Benefits (Billions of Dollars)	Percent Decline in Food Insecurity Rate Among SNAP Recipients	Additional Benefits (Billions of Dollars)
Scenario 1				
Exact dollars to be food secure for all participants	100.0	20.1	100.0	12.0
Scenario 2				
Average dollars to be food secure	61.8	27.0	56.6	16.1
Scenario 3				
Benefits directed by household size	61.7	26.9	58.7	16.3
Benefits directed by household size categories	60.4	25.2	58.5	14.6

Source: Authors' calculations from the 2014 December supplement of the CPS.
Note: The dollar values for scenario 2 are found in the first row of table 2. The dollar values for the two cases under scenario 3 are found in columns (2) and (4) from table 3 and columns (2) and (4) from table 5. The costs are based on the assumption that SNAP recipients would receive these increases in benefits for the full year.

household size and not other variables for several reasons. First, across all of the models, household size is the only variable that has statistically significant effects and, in each case, the estimated effect is large. Second, the SNAP benefit formula already takes into consideration household size, rendering this change in the benefit formula relatively straightforward. Finally, it may be problematic to alter the benefit formula based on characteristics like marital status, even though the effects may be statistically significant in some specifications. While marital decisions are unlikely to be influenced by small benefit changes, the public at large may have a negative reaction to this type of modification to the benefit formula.

As seen in table 7, the most effective way to reduce food insecurity among SNAP recipients—give each household the exact amount of money reportedly needed to become food secure—is naturally the least expensive option: $20.1 billion and $12 billion for all households and households with children, respectively.[13] These benefits would be provided, respectively, to 6.7 million food insecure SNAP households and 3.5 million food insecure SNAP households with children. Based on total SNAP expenditures of about $80 billion, this policy change would amount to a substantial increase in the cost of SNAP.

If the average value needed to become food secure is offered as a lump sum transfer—scenario 2—the estimated reductions in food security and associated costs are 61.8 percent and $27.0 billion for all households, or 56.6 percent and $16.1 billion for households with children. For scenario 3, when benefits increase linearly with respect to household size, the costs and reductions in food insecurity are similar to scenario 2. When household size is entered in a

---

this results in increases in SNAP benefit levels of, respectively, $30.50 and $41.59. When the information from column (2) in table 5 is used, the values are similar: $30.13 and $42.74.

13. The estimated costs of these scenarios are based on the assumption that households would receive SNAP for the full year.

categorical way, the impacts on food insecurity are roughly similar to the linear case. However, the costs decline to $25.2 billion (versus $26.9 billion) and $14.6 billion (versus $16.3 billion).

The previous analyses considered increases in benefit levels as a path to reducing food insecurity through SNAP. A substantial number of food insecure households, however, are not far from the eligibility threshold. For example, among households with gross income between 130 and 185 percent of the poverty line, the food insecurity rate was 25.3 percent in 2015 (see Coleman-Jensen et al. 2016, table 2). Using methods identical to those just cited, we consider providing SNAP benefits to those with incomes between 130 and 185 percent of the poverty line.[14]

As before, we provide separate results for households with children, a particularly relevant subpopulation. There have been recent proposals to distribute benefits to children who receive subsidized school meals during the summer (when they are not in school) through mechanisms similar to those used in SNAP. These benefits are primarily designed for children who are not currently eligible for SNAP—that is, those with incomes between 130 and 185 percent of the poverty line.

The average resource gap among all food insecure households with incomes between 130 and 185 percent is $30.91. For food insecure households with children, this value rises to $39.67. The potential costs and benefits of expanding SNAP are displayed in table 8 and are akin to those presented in table 7.[15] Under scenario 1, in which only food insecure households receive SNAP benefit levels which are set at the reported resource gap, the costs are $7.1 billion for all households and $3.5 for households with children. These benefits would be given, respectively, to 2.4 million food insecure households and 0.9 million food insecure households with children, substantially fewer than the numbers for SNAP recipients noted above. These estimates are substantially smaller than the increases in SNAP costs estimated in table 7 resulting from both fewer food insecure households and smaller resource gaps.

Under scenario 2 for the full population in this income category, however, the costs slightly more than triple compared with scenario 1, but only a relatively small increase when considering the population of food insecure SNAP recipients (see table 7). The comparative increase for households with children is also high—it more than doubles. Scenario 3, which adjusts benefit levels to account for family size, looks roughly similar to scenario 2. The relatively large costs in scenarios 2 and 3 reflect, in part, our assumption that all households in the income-ineligible population would take up these new SNAP benefits—13.8 million households and 4.2 million households with children. In contrast, the primary analysis summarized in table 7 is restricted to SNAP recipients, not all eligible households. The take-up rate among eligible households is only 35 percent for all households and 49 percent for households with children (see table 1).

DISTRIBUTION OF IMPACTS ON FOOD INSECURITY

The impacts of anti-poverty programs are often distributed unevenly throughout the population. This unevenness may also hold for changes to the SNAP benefit formula. In table 9, we consider how the lump sum increase in benefits proposed in scenario 2 might be associated with declines in food insecurity across various socioeconomic categories. For the sample of all households, the projected decline in food insecurity among SNAP participants in column (1) is similar across nearly all demographic groups. A notable exception is households headed by an African American, which would see an estimated 56.1 percent decline in food insecurity versus households headed by whites (64.3 percent) or racial groups other than white or African American (64.1 percent). Given that household size is one of the key indicators of the resource gap, it follows that a

---

14. As discussed, we included all SNAP participants in our calculations in table 7 even if their incomes exceeded 130 percent of the poverty line. In what follows, we only include SNAP nonparticipants, even if their income falls between 130 and 185 percent of the poverty line.

15. The regression results used to generate this table are available on request.

Table 8. Potential Impacts and Costs of Expanding Eligibility, Households Not Receiving SNAP

	All Households		Households with Children	
	Percent Decline in Food Insecurity Rate	Additional Benefits (Billions of Dollars)	Percent Decline in Food Insecurity Rate	Additional Benefits (Billions of Dollars)
Scenario 1				
Exact dollars to be food secure for new participants	100.0	7.1	100.0	3.5
Scenario 2				
Average dollars to be food secure	63.5	22.2	58.1	8.7
Scenario 3				
Benefits directed by household size	62.5	20.6	59.3	8.2
Benefits directed by household size categories	58.3	25.2	60.3	7.3

Source: Authors' calculations from the 2014 December supplement of the CPS.
Note: For scenario 2, the average dollars are $30.91 for all households and $39.67 for households with children. The costs are based on the assumption that currently non-SNAP recipients would receive benefits for the full year. The results for scenario 3, estimated in a manner similar to table 7, are available from the authors upon request.

uniform benefit increase is likely have a larger impact on smaller households. For example, single-person households would see a 74.1 percent decline and six-person households would see a 47.3 percent decline.

Estimated variation across demographic categories is higher if benefits are given to non-SNAP recipients with incomes within 130 to 185 percent of the poverty line. Hispanic households, for example, would see a 53 percent decline in food insecurity, and those headed by a non-Hispanic would see a 68 percent decline. Households in nonmetro areas would see a 76.7 percent decline, and those in metro areas would see a 62.8 percent decline. The results are broadly similar for households with children, a few exceptions notwithstanding. For example, among food insecure SNAP recipients, those with some college would see a 61 percent decline in food insecurity and those with a high school degree 52.9 percent (62.0 percent and 61.4 percent for all households). Among currently ineligible households, those with less than a high school education would see a 67.2 percent decline and those with some college 53.3 percent (62.1 percent and 62.8 percent for all households).

CONCLUSION

SNAP is a critical component of the social safety net, primarily because of its demonstrated impact on reducing food insecurity in the United States. Yet a majority of SNAP participants remain food insecure. One way to decrease food insecurity rates among these participants would be to raise the benefit level. In this article, we study an underutilized measure of need we call the resource gap. Based on their self-assessments, food insecure SNAP households would require an additional $41.62 per week in income, on average, to become food secure. This amounts to a 42 percent increase in benefits for a household currently receiving the maximum SNAP benefit level (that is, a household with zero net income), proportional increases for those with positive net incomes being larger.

In an exploratory analysis, we find that targeted increases in SNAP benefits could eliminate food insecurity at a cost of about $20 bil-

Table 9. Percent Declines in Food Insecurity Rates Under Scenario 2

	All Households		Households with Children	
	SNAP Participants	SNAP Nonparticipants with Incomes Between 130 and 185 Percent of the Poverty Line	SNAP Participants	SNAP Nonparticipants with Incomes Between 130 and 185 Percent of the Poverty Line
All	61.8	63.5	56.6	58.1
Income-poverty line				
0–0.50	57.1		54.6	
0.51–1.00	66.0		58.8	
1.01–1.30	61.8		56.8	
Less than high school	60.8	62.1	57.2	67.2
High school	61.4	67.8	52.9	59.7
Some college	62.0	62.8	61.0	53.3
College	67.6	71.0	53.6	61.5
Married	58.5	60.8	56.0	59.9
Single	62.9	68.5	56.8	55.8
Own	64.6	63.8	59.0	55.3
Rent	60.8	66.6	55.9	60.5
Nonmetro	63.1	76.7	55.3	78.3
Metro	61.5	62.8	56.9	52.8
White	64.3	65.6	58.4	59.6
African American	56.1	62.6	52.7	54.1
Other (non-white, non–African American)	64.1	73.8	57.3	57.1
Hispanic	58.6	53.0	54.8	52.2
Non-Hispanic	62.7	68.0	57.2	60.0
Household size				
1	74.1	74.8		
2	64.2	67.7	67.2	59.7
3	59.6	56.2	62.1	59.0
4	55.9	65.3	56.6	64.6
5	51.9	53.9	51.7	51.7
6	47.3	46.6	46.0	48.7

Source: Authors' calculations from the 2014 December supplement of the CPS.
Note: SNAP participants are those who report currently receiving SNAP. Scenario 2 refers to tables 7 and 8 in which the increase in SNAP benefits is assumed to be the same for all participants.

lion, whereas an across-the-board increase of SNAP benefits of $41.62 per week for all households could lead to a 62 percent decline in food insecurity among SNAP participants at a cost of about $27 billion. James P. Ziliak considers a related policy change that would increase the maximum SNAP benefit level from 100 to 120 percent of the Thrifty Food Plan (2016). Compared with the proposal evaluated in Ziliak's analysis, our scenario 2 increase in SNAP benefits (across-the-board increase equal to the average reported resource gap) is substantially greater, whereas our scenario 1 increase (personalized adjustments equal to the reported resource gap) is smaller. We also consider expansions of eligibility to those with incomes between 130 and 185 percent of the poverty line and find that giving these households SNAP benefits of $30.91 per week could lead to a 63.5 percent decline in food insecurity among this near-eligible group at a cost of slightly more than $22 billion.

Our analysis should be viewed as a starting point for future discussions and analyses of a policy to increase SNAP benefits to reduce food insecurity. Scenario 1 is useful as a baseline consideration but, for moral hazard and other reasons, it would not be practical to implement. Among the other two scenarios, one strength of scenario 3 is that it would limit leakage of benefits to single-person households and undercoverage of larger households; therefore either of the scenario 3 variants based on household size would seem more promising than the lump sum transfer considered in scenario 2. A more refined scenario might adjust the additional benefits to account for the observed heterogeneity revealed in table 9.

In any case, much additional research needs to be undertaken to understand the full impact that increasing benefits would have on food insecurity and other health outcomes, accounting for a host of measurement issues along with potential behavioral responses to changes in policy. At least four key issues are unresolved:

Labor supply effects of a notch. Each of our scenarios entails increases in benefit levels that are independent of household income. As a result, this would generate notch effects where losing eligibility would result in a discrete loss in these extra benefits. The resulting high marginal tax rate would presumably have labor supply implications for those near the threshold (for a discussion of marginal tax rates in SNAP plus other taxes, see Kosar and Moffitt 2016). The size of the labor supply distortions would need to be studied.

Take-up and participation rates. An increase in benefits is likely to lead to increases in participation and take-up rates in SNAP, all else equal. This would lead to an increase in expenditures on SNAP and, depending on the composition of households entering the program, a change in the proportion of SNAP recipients who become food secure. We have not modeled this change in participation rates.[16]

Marginal propensity to consume food. Our analysis assumes that all additional benefits are used to reduce the resource gap. However, it may be that households use some of the additional benefits on nonfood items.

Measuring the resource gap. Our estimates of the impact of benefit increases rely on households' self-reports of the resource gap. The accuracy of these reports should be studied along with a consideration of the influences of differences in timing of the food insecurity and reporting of the resource gap.

REFERENCES

Bartfeld, Judith, Craig Gundersen, Timothy M. Smeeding, and James P. Ziliak, eds. 2015. *SNAP Matters: How Food Stamps Affect Health and Well-Being.* Palo Alto, Calif.: Stanford University Press.

Coleman-Jensen, Alisha, Matthew P. Rabbitt, Christian A. Gregory, and Anita Singh. 2016. "Household Food Security in the United States in 2015." Economic Research Report no. 215. Washington: U.S. Department of Agriculture, Economic Research Service.

Gundersen, Craig, Brent Kreider, and John V. Pepper. 2017. "Partial Identification Methods for Evaluating Food Assistance Programs: A Case Study of the Causal Impact of SNAP on Food Insecurity." *American Journal of Agricultural Economics* 99(4): 875–94.

Gundersen, Craig, Brent Kreider, John V. Pepper, and Valerie Tarasuk. 2017. "Food Assistance Programs and Food Insecurity: Implications for Canada in Light of the Mixing Problem." *Empirical Economics* 52(3): 1065–87.

---

16. In contrast, the costs of expanding benefits to ineligible households is likely to be overestimated as some of these households would choose not to participate in an expanded SNAP.

Gundersen, Craig, and David Ribar. 2011. "Food Insecurity and Insufficiency at Low Levels of Food Expenditures." *Review of Income and Wealth* 57(4): 704–26.

Gundersen, Craig, Elaine Waxman, Emily Engelhard, Amy Satoh, and Namrita Chawla. 2013. "Map the Meal Gap 2013: Technical Brief." Chicago: Feeding America.

Gundersen, Craig, and James P. Ziliak. 2015. "Food Insecurity and Health Outcomes." *Health Affairs* 34(11): 1830–39.

Kosar, Gizem, and Robert A. Moffitt. 2016. "Trends in Cumulative Marginal Tax Rates Facing Low-Income Families, 1997–2007." In *Tax Policy and the Economy*, vol. 31, edited by Robert A. Moffitt. Chicago: University of Chicago Press. 2017.

Kreider, Brent, John V. Pepper, Craig Gundersen, and Dean Jolliffe. 2012. "Identifying the Effects of SNAP (Food Stamps) on Child Health Outcomes When Participation Is Endogenous and Misreported." *Journal of the American Statistical Association* 107(499): 958–75.

Tarasuk, Valerie, Joyce Cheng, Clare DeOliveira, Naomi Dachner, Craig Gundersen, and Paul Kurdyak. 2015. "Association Between Household Food Insecurity and Annual Health Care Costs." *Canadian Medical Association Journal* 187(14): E429–36.

Tiehen, Laura, Dean Jolliffe, and Timothy M. Smeeding. 2015. "The Effect of SNAP on Poverty." In *SNAP Matters: How Food Stamps Affect Health and Well Being*, edited by Judith Bartfeld, Craig Gundersen, Timothy M. Smeeding, and James P. Ziliak. Palo Alto, Calif.: Stanford University Press.

U.S. Department of Agriculture (USDA). 1999. *Annual Historical Review: Fiscal Year 1997*. Washington: Government Printing Office.

Ziliak, James P. 2016. *Modernizing SNAP Benefits*. The Hamilton Project, policy proposal 2016-06. Washington, D.C.: Brookings.

A Renter's Tax Credit to Curtail the Affordable Housing Crisis

SARA KIMBERLIN, LAURA TACH, AND CHRISTOPHER WIMER

To address the housing affordability crisis for low-income Americans, we argue for a refundable renter's tax credit. The proposed credit would be delivered through the tax code, reach a broad segment of renters, and target those with high housing cost burdens. We simulate the effects of the credit using Current Population Survey data. The credit would reach nearly 60 percent of poor renters and more than 70 percent of renters facing severe housing cost burdens, the credit amount averaging $2,059. Among recipients, the credit reduces the poverty rate by 12.4 percentage points and the deep poverty rate by 8.8 percentage points. For those who remain poor, it reduces the poverty gap by nearly a third. The annual cost is $24.1 billion.

Keywords: housing policy, renters, poverty, tax credits

The housing affordability crisis has reached historic levels in the United States amid rising rents, low wages, and an inadequate supply of housing. Fully half of renters face housing cost burdens, devoting more than one-third of their income to rent; one in four face severe cost burdens, handing over more than half of their income to rent (Joint Center for Housing Studies 2015). In 2015, a worker needed $19.35 per hour to afford the average two-bedroom rental in the United States, or two and a half times the federal minimum wage (National Low Income Housing Coalition 2016).

Problems of affordable housing are felt more acutely among the poor and near-poor, who do not earn enough to meet basic needs such as housing. Indeed, high housing costs are a primary driver of poverty because housing expenses represent such a large share of most families' budgets. Under the Census Bu-

---

Sara Kimberlin is an affiliate of the Stanford Center on Poverty and Inequality and a senior policy analyst at the California Budget and Policy Center. **Laura Tach** is assistant professor of policy analysis and management at Cornell University. **Christopher Wimer** is co-director of the Center on Poverty and Social Policy at Columbia University.

© 2018 Russell Sage Foundation. Kimberlin, Sara, Laura Tach, and Christopher Wimer. 2018. "A Renter's Tax Credit to Curtail the Affordable Housing Crisis." *RSF: The Russell Sage Foundation Journal of the Social Sciences* 4(2): 131–60. DOI: 10.7758/RSF.2018.4.2.07. We thank Meaghan Mingo for superb research assistance and the conference participants, reviewers, and editors for helpful feedback on earlier drafts of this manuscript. Direct correspondence to: Sara Kimberlin at skimber@stanford.edu, 450 Serra Mall, Bldg. 370, Stanford, CA 94305; Laura Tach at lauratach@cornell.edu, 253 Martha van Rensselaer Hall, Cornell University, Ithaca, NY 14853; and Christopher Wimer at cw2727@columbia.edu, 1255 Amsterdam Ave., New York, NY 10027.

Open Access Policy: *RSF: The Russell Sage Foundation Journal of the Social Sciences* is an open access journal. This article is published under a Creative Commons Attribution-NonCommercial-NoDerivs 3.0 Unported License.

reau's Supplemental Poverty Measure (SPM)—which measures the typical spending of low-income families on the basic needs of food, clothing, shelter and utilities—housing expenses make up approximately half of the total poverty threshold (Bureau of Labor Statistics 2017).

In addition to stress on families' current budgets, the lack of affordable housing has other negative ramifications, for communities as well as families. Families that pay too much for housing spend significantly less on food, health care, and retirement savings than those living in housing that is affordable (Joint Center for Housing Studies 2015). They are more likely to live in housing of substandard quality, to be evicted, and to go homeless (Desmond 2016). It comes as no surprise, then, that unaffordable housing negatively affects children's health and school performance, and interferes with parents' employment, parenting, and civic engagement (HUD 2014).

The United States has no entitlement program for housing, and public provision of affordable housing reaches only a fraction of all who are in need: only one in four families who are eligible for government subsidized housing receives it (Joint Center for Housing Studies 2015). This dearth of subsidized rental housing is inequitable, given the generous subsidies the United States provides to homeowners through mortgage interest and property tax deductions. Homeowners receive more than three-quarters of all federal housing subsidy allocations, and those making over $100,000 per year receive more than half of those dollars (Center on Budget and Policy Priorities 2017). Renters—who are excluded from this generous redistribution via the tax system—are much more likely to be poor than homeowners: from 2013 to 2015, the SPM poverty rate for homeowners stood at just 10 percent, versus 26 percent for renters.[1] As a result, our nation's existing portfolio of housing subsidies offered through affordable housing programs and the tax system fail to reach a majority of poor Americans.

In this article, we argue for a refundable renter's tax credit for families facing high rental housing costs relative to their income. The credit is designed to reflect geographic variation in housing costs and delivers the largest subsidies, proportional to income, to those with the greatest housing cost burdens. The proposed credit builds on existing programs delivered through the tax code, but it reaches a much broader segment of the population than existing housing assistance programs: the proposed credit would reach one-fifth of all renters and more than 70 percent of severely housing cost–burdened renters. Using the SPM as a framework to simulate the effects of the proposed policy change, we find that among beneficiaries the credit reduces the poverty rate by 12.4 percentage points and the deep poverty rate by 8.8 percentage points. For beneficiaries who remain poor, it reduces the poverty gap by nearly one-third, at an annual cost of $24.1 billion. We argue that a renter's tax credit harnesses the efficiencies of the tax system while targeting those who bear the brunt of the housing affordability crisis in the United States. The credit achieves a meaningful reduction in poverty for poor families while bringing overall federal housing expenditures into a more equitable equilibrium.

EXISTING HOUSING SUBSIDIES: INEQUITABLE AND INADEQUATE

Existing housing subsidy programs in the United States leave many poor families unassisted and have a number of administrative inefficiencies. The two largest sources of subsidized rental housing in the United States—the Low Income Housing Tax Credit (LIHTC) and the Housing Choice Voucher (HCV) program—have been successful in many ways. We argue, however, that scaling up these two programs would be inefficient and would not target poor families with the largest housing cost burdens.

The LIHTC is currently the largest project-based rental subsidy program in the United States, credited with the creation of more than two million rental units since its inception in 1986 (HUD 2017a). The program currently gives about $8 billion per year to states to issue tax credits to developers who build or rehabilitate rental housing and commit to reserving a certain share of units for lower-income house-

---

1. Per authors' calculations of Current Population Survey data 2012–2014 (Flood et al. 2016).

holds (those with incomes below 50 to 60 percent of the area median) for at least 15 years.[2] The LIHTC has grown over time to become the most significant revenue source for the production of affordable housing. These tax credits are available only for *new* housing construction or rehabilitation, however, not to subsidize existing housing. Moreover, because the credits go only to developers, their success in reducing housing burden and poverty among intended beneficiaries is more diffusely realized than through policy mechanisms that target renters more directly.

Though LIHTC is successful in producing new housing, LIHTC developments are out of reach for the poorest households. Rents at LIHTC properties are typically set to be affordable for those with incomes around 50 to 60 percent of the area median, which means that the properties are typically too expensive for poor families with incomes below half the area median. The rental rates are also fixed in LIHTC developments, meaning they do not vary based on a household's income. As a result, LIHTC housing can become unaffordable if a household's income falls. In practice, very-low-income households are only able to live in LIHTC units by using a housing voucher; more than 60 percent of LIHTC properties include residents with housing vouchers (O'Regan and Quigley 2000; Climaco et al. 2006). Doubly subsidizing units in this way limits the already-inadequate supply of subsidized housing units nationally.

Compared with the LIHTC, the Housing Choice Voucher program—the largest demand-side program for low-income families—offers a much deeper rental subsidy. Low-income households receive a voucher that can be used to rent units on the private housing market. A voucher holder pays 30 percent of the family's income toward rent, and the government makes up the rest. Low- and very-low-income families are given priority in the housing voucher program— public housing authorities must issue at least 75 percent of their vouchers to families with incomes less than 30 percent of the area median income.[3]

Despite the advantages of the deep subsidy, too few vouchers are issued each year to make the program widely accessible. In many large cities, the waitlists for housing vouchers are years—sometimes even decades—long.[4] A number of administrative barriers also limit voucher use by both landlords and tenants. First, voucher holders can only lease units with rents that are lower than the local fair market rent as established by the U.S. Department of Housing and Urban Development (typically the 40th percentile of rents for that area), making units in more desirable areas or with higher-quality amenities inaccessible to voucher holders. Second, voucher holders typically have just sixty days to locate a unit and sign a lease. As a result, a substantial share of families who do receive housing vouchers cannot "lease up" and use the vouchers (Smith et al. 2015). Finally, tenants must find landlords who are willing to accept vouchers. Landlords report being reluctant to participate in the program because of the administrative hassles involved, including having the unit inspected before being able to rent it to a voucher holder, limits on rent that may be charged, and managing payments from both housing authorities and tenants (Rosen 2014). Once a landlord accepts a voucher, he or she may decide to stop accepting vouchers at any time.

The lack of affordable housing in the United States has adverse consequences for families and children. High housing costs are a direct driver of poverty. Families facing high housing costs must restrict expenditures on other basic necessities, such as food or health care, and the economic stress associated with financial

---

2. Developers must commit to reserving at least 20 percent of their units for households with incomes less than 50 percent of AMI (known as the 20-50 rule), or at least 40 percent of their units for households with incomes less than 60 percent of AMI (known as the 40-60 rule).

3. "Housing Choice Vouchers Fact Sheet," http://portal.hud.gov/hudportal/HUD?src=/program_offices/public_indian_housing/programs/hcv/about/fact_sheet (accessed October 6, 2017).

4. "Open Public Housing Waiting Lists by State," *Affordable Housing Online*, http://affordablehousingonline.com/public-housing-waiting-lists/ (accessed November 17, 2017).

insecurity undermines mental health and parenting resources (Harkness and Newman 2005; Leventhal and Newman 2010). Families in unaffordable housing are also more likely to live in substandard housing and to experience eviction or homelessness (Desmond 2016). Not surprisingly, unaffordable housing has negative effects on the health and school performance of children, and interferes with parents' employment, parenting, and civic engagement (HUD 2014). Increasing access to affordable housing has been shown to improve children's short- and longer-term outcomes (Newman and Harkness 2002).

EXISTING ANTI-POVERTY POLICIES: ONE SIZE FITS ALL

Existing anti-poverty policies play an undeniable role in improving the fortunes of low-income Americans. Nationally, programs like the Earned Income Tax Credit (EITC) and the Supplemental Nutrition Assistance Program (SNAP, or food stamps) reduce poverty rates significantly (Renwick and Fox 2016). Despite these laudable effects, existing means-tested programs exclude large segments of the poor population, such as those who do not work or do not have dependent children. Additionally, existing federal means-tested programs rarely account for the vastly different costs of living across the United States. In fact, fair market rents in the continental United States for a two-bedroom apartment varied from less than $600 per month to more than $3,000 per month in 2017. In effect, most federal anti-poverty programs treat families living in these different areas the same, ignoring the vastly different expenses they face, so that benefits received by families in high-cost areas have lower purchasing power and do less to mitigate economic hardship than the same amount of benefits received by families living in low-cost areas. Some states offset high costs of living by offering more generous benefits or tax credits, but these efforts are uneven and sensitive to state budgets.

Because housing is the single largest expense for most families, a housing subsidy that reflects local cost variations would offer significant relief for those in high cost-of-living areas. Homeowners already receive some federal tax relief that accounts for variation in housing costs, as those who face higher property taxes and home prices receive comparatively more from tax deductions. Moreover, renters have a substantially higher SPM poverty rate than homeowners (25.7 percent versus 9.8 percent) and make up more than half of the overall SPM poor population.[5] They also typically face higher housing cost burdens than homeowners; nearly one-third have an expected housing cost burden of 50 percent or more, versus only 10 percent of homeowners. Thus poor renters are a particularly appropriate target population for both anti-poverty and housing affordability policy.

Renter households receiving federal housing subsidies via LIHTC or HCV programs already receive subsidies that account for local cost of housing because the value of these credits rises with housing costs. Thus, unsubsidized renters in high-cost areas stand out as receiving the least relief from both federal anti-poverty policy and existing housing programs.

ADVANTAGES OF A RENTER'S TAX CREDIT

Given these limitations of existing housing subsidy programs, we argue for a renter's tax credit that targets families facing high rental housing cost burdens relative to their incomes. The tax system offers an advantageous way to deliver such a subsidy. The United States already has a generous quasi-entitlement program that subsidizes homeownership, in the form of mortgage interest and property tax deductions. These deductions are inequitable, however, because they are limited to homeowners, and affluent homeowners receive the lion's share of the subsidies. Although no federal tax subsidy is in place for renters, several states have small renter's tax credits, some of which are refundable (see table A6).

Additionally, tax credits are used to deliver the largest anti-poverty cash program in the United States, the EITC. In 2013, more than 27 million tax filers received about $61 billion from the federal EITC, lifting 6.2 million out of

---

5. Homeowners make up 43.6 percent of the SPM poor population in our data; renters make up 56.4 percent.

poverty, including about 3.2 million children (Center on Budget and Policy Priorities 2016b). For all its successes as an anti-poverty program, however, we argue that several features of the EITC limit its ability to tackle housing affordability directly. First, several key populations are excluded from receiving it, including those who do not work and those without custodial children (the latter receive a much smaller credit). Second, the federal EITC offers a uniform benefit amount that does not adjust for geographic variation in housing costs, which means that some EITC-eligible households face housing cost burdens while others do not.

A renter's credit administered through the tax code also overcomes some of the programmatic limitations of the existing housing assistance programs described. Delivery via the tax code allows for lower administrative costs and reduced barriers to securing assistance. A tax credit to renters complements the tax subsidies that already go to developers via the LIHTC. Unlike the LIHTC, which sets rents too high for the poorest families and uses tax credits only for new housing construction, the renter's tax credit is targeted to those most in need, with the largest benefits, proportionate to income, going to those with the greatest housing cost burdens, and it applies to all forms of unassisted rental housing rather than just new housing construction. By offering a shallower subsidy than vouchers, with parameters that can be modified to respond to availability of federal funds, a tax credit can also be made available to all renters who meet specified eligibility criteria, avoiding the arbitrary rationing that results from housing voucher waitlists and the uneven spatial distribution of subsidized project-based rental units.

HOW THE PROPOSED RENTER'S TAX CREDIT WORKS

The credit is a refundable income tax credit designed to cover the gap between rent paid and 40 percent of a household's after-income-tax cash income. HUD identifies an affordable housing cost burden as paying no more than 30 percent of income toward rent, and categorizes households paying more than 50 percent of income toward rent as severely housing cost burdened. The 40 percent target for the renter's tax credit thus represents a middle ground between these two federal standards of housing affordability. (For simulations of credits based on a more stringent 50 percent housing cost burden eligibility threshold instead, see figure A1.)

The credit is calculated based on the amount of gross rent (cost of rent plus utilities) paid annually by a tax filer. Tax filers may claim rent paid at an amount that is the lowest of actual gross rent paid, assigned fair market rent (FMR), or 80 percent of after-tax tax unit income.

The amount of claimable rent is capped at the tax filer's FMR to target the credit to renters in the bottom half of the rental market: tax filers may only claim rent paid up to the average FMR in their state and metropolitan or nonmetropolitan area, adjusted for household size. Table 1 lists the average monthly gross rent paid by credit recipients and the average monthly FMRs for tax filers from 2013 through 2015 by state and metropolitan status. Capping claimable rent at the FMR amount ensures that the credit subsidizes housing consumption only up to the level identified by HUD as adequate, and does not subsidize "overconsumption" of housing.

Claimable rent paid is also capped at 80 percent of cash income for all family members, net of federal income taxes and credits, under the assumption that most households cannot sustainably pay more than 80 percent of total after-tax cash income toward rent. Note that this means that households with zero or negative after-tax income for the year are not eligible for a credit, even if they paid rent. We assume that tax filers with rent paid in excess of 80 percent of annual after-tax income would be likely to be either receiving additional unreported income, or are facing a temporary major income shortfall, which this policy is not intended to address. Limiting the claimable rent paid to 80 percent of income also incentivizes households to seek housing with a rent burden that does not exceed the very minimal sustainability threshold of 80 percent of income.[6]

---

6. The primary purpose of this policy is to assist households facing ongoing high rent burdens, not to serve as an emergency safety net for households whose incomes have dropped dramatically due to a short-term crisis,

Table 1. Average FMR and Credit Recipient Gross Rent Paid Amounts for Tax Units, by State and Metropolitan Status

State	Mean Tax Unit FMR, Metro	Mean Recipient Tax Unit Rent Paid, Metro	Mean Tax Unit FMR, Nonmetro	Mean Recipient Tax Unit Rent Paid, Nonmetro	High-Cost State
Alabama	$650	$522	$577	$354	0
Alaska	1,041	820	929	678	1
Arizona	810	604	614	250	0
Arkansas	641	515	543	336	0
California	1,182	848	839	668	1
Colorado	819	764	739	559	1
Connecticut	1,103	827	860	605	1
Delaware	951	719	833	596	1
Washington, D.C.	1,188	958	n/a	n/a	1
Florida	882	705	680	459	1
Georgia	747	586	582	448	0
Hawaii	1,588	1,108	1,100	848	1
Idaho	626	556	610	367	0
Illinois	818	647	593	507	1
Indiana	664	521	584	360	0
Iowa	641	552	528	342	0
Kansas	679	522	556	346	0
Kentucky	629	564	539	351	0
Louisiana	727	554	624	372	0
Maine	766	578	636	602	0
Maryland	1,141	857	881	653	1
Massachusetts	1,055	790	n/a	n/a	1
Michigan	682	508	574	445	0
Minnesota	784	606	594	441	0
Mississippi	699	582	588	374	0
Missouri	683	520	567	414	0
Montana	613	547	620	432	0
Nebraska	672	542	563	415	0
Nevada	885	664	742	674	0
New Hampshire	954	706	863	601	1
New Jersey	1,133	837	n/a	n/a	1
New Mexico	692	506	643	469	0
New York	1,120	813	659	650	1
North Carolina	688	557	601	404	0
North Dakota	578	533	639	480	0
Ohio	642	536	579	389	0
Oklahoma	649	504	556	299	0
Oregon	760	651	650	428	0
Pennsylvania	795	609	626	464	0
Rhode Island	805	589	n/a	n/a	0
South Carolina	666	503	628	368	0
South Dakota	638	502	544	363	0
Tennessee	674	556	526	400	0
Texas	783	607	652	476	0
Utah	740	602	n/a	n/a	0

(continued)

Table 1. (*continued*)

State	Mean Tax Unit FMR, Metro	Mean Recipient Tax Unit Rent Paid, Metro	Mean Tax Unit FMR, Nonmetro	Mean Recipient Tax Unit Rent Paid, Nonmetro	High-Cost State
Vermont	1,102	794	760	590	1
Virginia	1,012	802	619	632	1
Washington	904	720	715	496	1
West Virginia	597	489	542	380	0
Wisconsin	683	550	593	361	0
Wyoming	684	536	680	441	0

Source: Authors' calculations from 2013–2015 CPS data (Flood et al. 2016), gross rent paid imputed from 2015 ACS data (Ruggles et al. 2016).
Note: Missing data for nonmetro areas indicate no renter's credit recipients for those areas in 2013–2015 CPS data. High-cost state defined as average rental costs in the top third nationally. Note that sample sizes for some state-metro areas are small, making corresponding estimates less reliable.

The capped rent paid amount is then compared with the tax unit's income, the income including all taxable and nontaxable cash income for the tax filer, spouse, and dependents, net of federal income tax liabilities and credits. Tax filers would need to report their nontaxable income and the income of their dependents for this calculation. (Similar income reporting is currently required on the tax form used to calculate individual responsibility penalties for not having insurance coverage under the Affordable Care Act.) Linking the credit amount to after-tax income is highly feasible as the credit is claimed at the same time as the filing of annual income taxes. Moreover, using after-tax income better accounts for the resources available to pay for basic needs among low-income households by excluding income tax liabilities that reduce discretionary income and by including tax credits such as the EITC, which represent a large share of income for many low-income households.

A tax filer's credit is equal to the difference between capped rent paid and 40 percent of the family's total after-tax cash income. The credit as presented in this analysis is equal to the full *rental cost gap*—the difference between (capped) rent paid and 40 percent of a tax unit's income—but the credit could easily be adjusted to cover only a portion of the rental cost gap (for example, half) if desired to reduce the policy cost. The final credit amount for tax unit i is thus calculated as

$$Credit\ Amt_i = Capped\ Rent\ Paid_i - (0.4 \times After\text{-}Tax\ Income_i)$$

The maximum credit is available to tax filers with extremely high housing cost burdens, of 80 percent or more, and those living in areas with high rental prices, as represented by assigned FMRs. From there, the credit gradually phases out to zero for tax filers for whom capped rent paid equals between 80 percent and 40 percent of after-tax income (for an illustration of the proposed structure of the rent-

---

hence the cap on claimable rent at 80 percent of after-tax income (which includes taxable and nontaxable unemployment benefits, disability benefits, and retirement income as well as refundable tax credits, over the course of a full year). Capping the claimable rent paid minimizes incentives to misreport rent paid or take on an unsustainable ongoing rent burden, and allows the renter's credit resources to be focused on the primary target problem. Other policies such as homelessness assistance, homelessness prevention programs, public housing, and income support programs are better suited to address short-term housing crises or the chronic inability to secure enough ongoing income to achieve a rent burden of 80 percent or less. For this simulation of the renter's tax credit in CPS data, capping the allowable rent paid at 80 percent of after-tax income also helps to minimize potential distortions of the estimated policy costs and poverty impact that could be introduced by our imputation of rent paid, as necessitated by the lack of reported rent paid in the CPS data.

Figure 1. Simulated Renters' Tax Credit Schedule

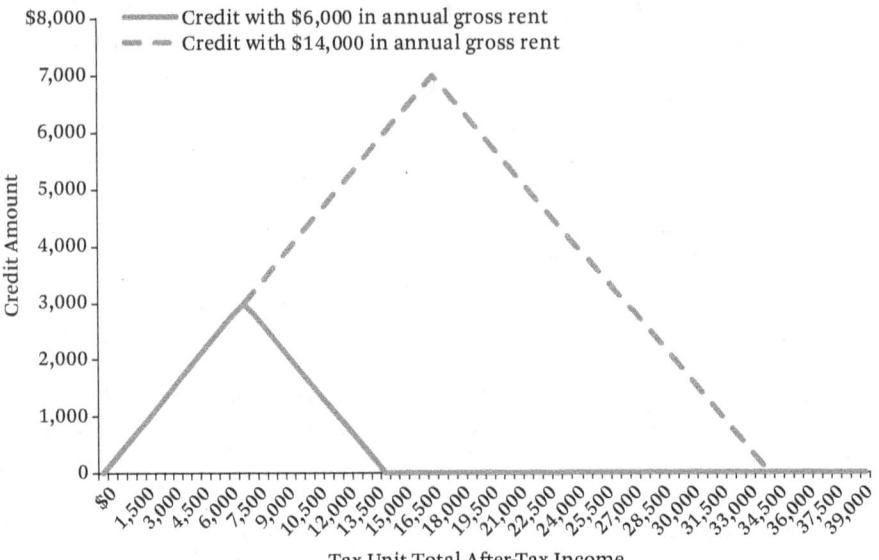

Source: Authors' compilation.
Note: Annual gross rent of $6,000 is equivalent to approximate average Fair Market Rent (FMR) for tax filers in nonmetro Iowa. Annual gross rent of $14,000 is equivalent to approximate average FMR for tax filers in metro California. Assumes tax filer's annual gross rent does not exceed FMR cap (set to average FMR by state and metropolitan status, adjusted to family size).

er's credit schedule, see figure 1). The credit amount is then applied to any tax liability, and anything left over is refunded to the tax filer. Tax filers may apply to receive their refund as deferred payments on a quarterly basis, or in a lump sum when they file their annual tax return.

Tax filers are not eligible for the credit if they are already receiving a housing subsidy, or if they are not paying rent. Tax filers who receive a housing subsidy via the public housing program or housing voucher program already pay no more than 30 percent of their income toward rent, so their rental expenses are too low to qualify for the credit. Homeowners are categorically excluded from the renter's tax credit. Although homeowners make up approximately 44 percent of the SPM poor, poor homeowners as a group are more advantaged than poor renters, having more assets and more housing security than poor renters, and existing tax structures address housing-related costs of homeowners. Thus they are not targeted for assistance through the renter's tax credit. Poor nonhomeowners who pay no rent (including those living with friends or family, and those who are incarcerated or institutionalized) have no housing cost burden and so are appropriately excluded from the credit as well.

Compared with traditional housing vouchers, the proposed renter's tax credit provides a shallower subsidy but is available to a much broader segment of the housing cost-burdened population—anyone with nonzero income who pays more than 40 percent of income to afford an adequate rental unit qualifies. No approval by the landlord or inspection of the housing unit is required to receive the credit. Compared with the LIHTC, the proposed credit is adjusted progressively, based on the tax unit's housing cost burden, larger subsidies being proportional to income for those with higher housing cost burdens. The credit is not restricted to new construction or rehabilitation; that is, it can be used for any existing rental housing. The application process is highly accessible, because most households file tax returns anyway, and administrative costs are low, because it takes advantage of the existing (and relatively low-cost) tax processing infrastructure.

Compared with proposals to add cost-of-living adjustments to existing anti-poverty programs, such as the EITC, the renter's credit provides more targeted assistance to those truly housing cost burdened, and it also reaches those left out of many contemporary anti-poverty programs such as SNAP or Supplemental Security Income (SSI), where benefit generosity is driven by the presence of children in the household or extreme levels of deprivation.

METHODOLOGY

To estimate the likely anti-poverty effects of the proposed renter's tax credit, we use the Census and Bureau of Labor Statistics' SPM as a framework in which to simulate the proposed policy scenarios. Importantly for our purposes, the SPM uses a broad definition of resources, which include not only cash income but tax subsidies and in-kind assistance like housing subsidies (Renwick and Fox 2016). In so doing, the measure provides a suitable context for assessing the effectiveness of government policies and programs in reducing the poverty rate, as well as comparing the potential effectiveness of policy alternatives.

For our main analysis, we use data from the Current Population Survey's March Supplement from 2014 to 2016 (corresponding to calendar years 2013 to 2015). These data are the primary source of both official and supplemental poverty statistics in the United States (n=583,693).[7] We use the individual and household microdata to construct tax units and simulate those eligible for the renter's tax credit, assuming full take-up among those eligible, using the criteria spelled out above to define eligibility parameters and benefit amount parameters. We identify gross rent paid by each tax unit.[8] We assign an FMR cap for claimable rent paid based on each tax filer's place of residence and number of dependents.[9]

With these data, we examine the reach and cost of the program and the demographics of

---

7. Sample size for renters, our focal population, is n=187,181. We use a three-year sample (2013 to 2015) to maximize sample size for individual states and for demographic subgroups. In contrast, estimates of costs and poverty impact for this renter's credit proposal presented elsewhere in this double issue use a one-year CPS sample, for 2015 only (Wimer, Collyer, and Kimberlin 2018).

8. Because the CPS does not collect information on rental costs, we impute rental cost values from the American Community Survey based on the following characteristics: number of adults, any young adults, any elderly adults, number of children, race of household head, any foreign-born household members, highest educational attainment in household, any household member receiving TANF, SNAP, SSI, or SS household income, FMR, state, metro or nonmetropolitan status, and survey year. Rent paid is imputed to the household or housing unit. We prorate the amount of rent paid by each tax unit as follows. First, we prorate rent paid to SPM family units within each household based on the number of individuals in each SPM family unit relative to the total number of individuals in the household (most households include only one SPM family unit, which includes all individuals related by blood or marriage as well as cohabiters and their relatives). Next, we prorate rent paid to tax units within SPM family units based on the share of after-tax income represented by each tax unit relative to the SPM family unit total income. This approach assumes that within SPM family units, family members will share rent expenses proportionate to their income.

9. FMR amounts are calculated as the population-weighted average FMRs for a two-bedroom apartment across all metropolitan areas and all non-metropolitan areas by state. FMR amounts are then adjusted for units with one, three, and four or more bedrooms based on the ratio of FMR costs for other size units relative to two-bedroom FMRs. For example, to calculate the FMR for a three-bedroom unit, the two-bedroom apartment FMR amount is multiplied by 1.3, which represents the mean ratio of FMRs for three-bedroom apartments to FMRs for two-bedroom apartments. The number of tax dependents is used to assign the number of bedrooms for the tax filer's FMR, with the one-bedroom FMR assigned to filers with no dependents, two-bedroom to filers with one dependent, three-bedroom to filers with two dependents, and four-bedroom to filers with three or more dependents. This method of assigning FMRs thus utilizes only two FMR amounts for each state—the population-weighted average two-bedroom FMR for metro areas and nonmetro areas—simplifying administration of the credit. In addition, specific geographic location is not identified for more than half of the CPS sample, necessitating FMR assignment based on broader location data for the analysis.

beneficiaries. We estimate changes in poverty status for credit recipients, and then assess the overall impact a renter's credit would have on poverty rates for the total population, all renters, and credit beneficiaries, nationally and by state. We also explore other dimensions of economic hardship, including the poverty gap, as well as housing cost burden (calculated as gross rent paid divided by total family SPM resources). In the appendix, we also explore options for targeting the credit more narrowly to specific subgroups (for example, to families with children, or families with seniors, or renters in high housing-cost states).

The design of the credit allows for modification of the credit parameters (such as share of rental gap covered, maximum rent amount allowed to be paid, phase-out level and rate) to target particular households or adjust the cost or depth of subsidy. In the appendix, we present results for a version of the credit with parameters modified to target households with more severe housing cost burden (those expected to spend at least 50 percent of income on housing).

To put the projected impact of the credit in context, we compare the reach and poverty reduction of the credit with three other safety net programs: SNAP, EITC, and existing housing subsidies. We calculate reach using reported program participation in Current Population Survey (CPS) data. To present a consistent measure of poverty reduction across these programs, we calculate the SPM poverty rate with and without each of these programs included in families' resources, after adding the renter's tax credit for eligible families. Note that safety net program participation is known to be underreported in survey data such as the CPS (Meyer, Mok, and Sullivan 2015), thus these estimates likely underestimate program impact for SNAP and housing subsidies, less so for EITC.[10]

Throughout our analysis, we focus primarily on the impact of the renter's credit on the population of renters, given that homeowners are categorically ineligible for the credit.

RESULTS

We begin by presenting descriptive information on the impact of our proposed credit. Table 2 presents estimates of the number of beneficiaries and cost of the credit, its reach, and the demographics of simulated beneficiaries. More than 11.5 million tax filers would receive the simulated credit, which translates into more than 20 million total beneficiaries whose family incomes would see a boost from the program. The total cost of the program would be roughly $24 billion. The average amount of these credits would be about $2,100, and would be of more value for poor families (roughly $2,300) than to nonpoor families (roughly $1,500).[11]

The credit would also reach a wide swath of American renters. Approximately 20 percent of all renters and nearly 60 percent of poor renters would benefit from the proposed credit. By

---

10. EITC receipt is fully imputed in CPS data and thus not subject to the same level of underreporting.

11. As noted, the renter's credit is designed to reduce rent burden from a maximum of 80 percent of after-tax income, and claimable rent paid is capped at 80 percent of income (out of consideration of both policy goals and simulation practicalities). That said, it would be possible to modify the renter's credit to provide larger credits to households paying rent in excess of 80 percent of income, and to provide credits to households paying rent that have no after-tax annual income. A total of 4.74 million tax filers with nonzero income who were found to be eligible for renter's credits had imputed rent paid (after capping rent at the appropriate FMR) equal to more than 80 percent of income. Allowing these filers to claim rent paid up to 100 percent of after-tax income, rather than capping the allowable rent at 80 percent of income, would increase the estimated annual cost by $2,844 million. Providing these filers with a refundable credit equal to their total imputed rent paid (after capping at the appropriate FMR), even if that amount exceeded total after-tax income, would increase the estimated annual cost by $12,232 million, a substantial increase. In addition, 3 percent of renter tax filers, or 1.86 million filers, had no reported after-tax income for their entire household (and did not report a housing subsidy). Providing these filers with a refundable credit equal to their imputed rent paid (after capping at the appropriate FMR) would increase the estimated annual cost by an additional $12,356 million.

Table 2. Beneficiaries and Cost of the Proposed Renters' Tax Credit

Total tax filers receiving credit per year (M)	11.681
Total beneficiaries[a] per year (M)	20.821
Total cost per year (M)	$24,051
Mean credit amount per tax filer	$2,059
Per poor tax filer[b]	2,258
Per nonpoor tax filer[b]	1,547
Median credit amount per tax filer	$1,742
Per poor tax filer[b]	2,040
Per nonpoor tax filer[b]	1,143
Proportion of renters receiving the credit	
All renters	19.9%
Poor renters[b]	59.6
Renters with housing burden[c] >40 percent	54.4
Renters with housing burden >50 percent	70.2
Renters with housing burden >70 percent	75.2

Source: Authors' calculations from 2013–2015 CPS data (Flood et al. 2016).
[a]Total beneficiaries includes all individuals in families receiving credit.
[b]Poverty status for tax filers determined based on Supplemental Poverty Measure (SPM), before the credit is received.
[c]Housing burden calculated as gross rent paid (imputed from 2015 ACS data) divided by total SPM family resources (cash income plus near-cash benefits net of taxes, work expenses, and out-of-pocket medical expenses).

design, renters with high housing cost burden—who are the majority of all poor renters—would stand to gain the most. More than 70 percent of severely cost-burdened renters and more than three-quarters of renters spending 70 percent or more of their income on housing would benefit from the credit.

Table 3 shows the demographics of those simulated to receive the renter's credit. More than half of beneficiaries are in families with children, and more than a quarter in families with very young children. Because a growing literature suggests that low income and poverty are detrimental to children's short- and long-term outcomes, that so many beneficiaries would include children suggests that this credit would have a positive impact on child well-being (see, for example, Duncan, Morris, and Rodrigues 2011). The credit would also enhance the resources of a diverse group of Americans by race-ethnicity. Approximately half of beneficiaries would be in families with the highest educational attainment of a high school degree or less, and they would be most concentrated in the South, where incomes tend to be low, and West, where housing costs tend to be high.

Poverty Reduction Effects of the Renters' Tax Credit

Table 4 presents our key results for the impact of the proposed renters' tax credit on poverty. We find that, overall, the credit would reduce poverty among renters by 2.5 percentage points, a 10 percent relative reduction (see also figure 2), and would reduce deep poverty by 1.7 percentage points, a 22 percent relative reduction. For the full U.S. population (including homeowners categorically ineligible for the credit), the credit would reduce the poverty rate by 0.8 percentage points, a 5 percent relative reduction, and would reduce the deep poverty rate by 0.6 percent, a 12 percent relative reduction. The anti-poverty effects of the proposal are of course larger among beneficiaries. These families, who are more likely to be poor

Table 3. Demographic Characteristics of Renter's Credit Beneficiaries

Family composition of beneficiaries	
Families with children	54.4%
Families with young children (under five years old)	26.5
Families with seniors	14.3
Race-ethnicity of beneficiaries	
Non-Hispanic white	38.0
Non-Hispanic African American	21.0
Hispanic	32.8
Non-Hispanic Asian	7.0
Non-Hispanic other race	1.2
Highest level of education in beneficiary families	
Less than high school	17.2
High school graduate	31.7
Some college but no four-year degree	32.4
College graduate with four-year degree	18.7
Beneficiary region of residence	
Northeast	20.6
Midwest	12.1
South	32.8
West	34.5

Source: Authors' calculations from 2013–2015 CPS data (Flood et al. 2016).

and facing a housing cost burden before the credit, would see a drop in poverty rate of 12.4 percentage points, a 16 percent relative reduction, and a decline in the deep poverty rate of 8.8 percentage points, a 35 percent relative reduction. In total, 2.6 million people would be lifted out of poverty by the credit (for results by state and for versions of the credit targeting only families with children, families with seniors, or residents of high housing cost states, as well as a credit that targets more severely housing-burdened households, see the appendix).

Of course, the credit's effects would extend beyond simply lifting some people over the poverty line. In the second half of table 4, we show that another 13.4 million Americans would see a decline in their poverty gap, or the gap between their level of resources and the poverty threshold. This reduction would be substantial. The median poverty gap among poor beneficiaries was more than $7,700 before the simulated credit, which is reduced to roughly $5,100 after the credit. The median decline in the poverty gap for poor credit beneficiaries is 32 percent. In addition, more than 4 million individuals who start out somewhat above the poverty line, but still face high housing cost burdens, would also benefit from the credit.[12]

Effects of Renter's Credit on Housing Cost Burden

We also examine the projected effects of the credit on housing cost burden (gross rent divided by total family SPM resources). Figure 3 shows that that the share of renters who are severely housing cost burdened (paying 50 percent or more of income toward housing) declines by 2.1 percentage points, a 9 percent relative reduction, and the share of renters with an expected housing cost burden of 70 percent or more declines by one quarter (3.1 percentage points). Among credit beneficiaries, the impacts are larger: severe housing cost burden

---

12. Beneficiaries who start out above the poverty line have median family resources equal to only 127 percent of the poverty threshold.

Table 4. Anti-poverty Effects of Renter's Credit

Full population	
Poverty rate before credit	15.1%
Poverty rate after credit	14.2
Change in poverty rate	0.8
Deep poverty rate before credit	5.1
Deep poverty rate after credit	4.5
Change in deep poverty rate	0.6
All renters	
Poverty rate before credit	25.7%
Poverty rate after credit	23.2
Change in poverty rate	2.5
Deep poverty rate before credit	7.9
Deep poverty rate after credit	6.2
Change in deep poverty rate	1.7
All beneficiaries	
Poverty rate before credit	76.9%
Poverty rate after credit	64.5
Change in poverty rate	12.4
Deep poverty rate before credit	25.4
Deep poverty rate after credit	16.6
Change in deep poverty rate	8.8
Total beneficiaries (M)	20.821
Beneficiaries lifted out of poverty (M)	2.581
Beneficiaries remaining poor but poverty gap reduced (M)	13.421
Beneficiaries lifted out of poverty or poverty gap reduced (M)	16.002
Median poverty gap among poor beneficiaries[a]	
Before credit	$7,749
After credit	$5,083
Change in median poverty gap	$2,666
Median share of poverty gap closed	32.2%

Source: Authors' calculations from 2013–2015 CPS data (Flood et al. 2016).
Note: All poverty rates refer to SPM poverty rates. Deep poverty defined as resources less than half the poverty threshold. Beneficiaries include all individuals in families receiving the credit.
[a] Poverty status for beneficiaries prior to receiving the credit.

declines by 10.3 percentage points, a relative reduction of 13 percent, and housing cost burden of 70 percent or more declines by 15.5 percentage points, a 33 percent relative reduction.

Renter's Credit Relative to Other Anti-poverty Programs

To put the poverty reduction impact and reach of the credit into perspective, we compare the credit with SNAP, the EITC, and existing housing subsidies. At an estimated cost of $24.1 billion, the credit would be substantially less expensive than the EITC (approximately $67 billion in 2016), SNAP (approximately $71 billion in 2016), and existing housing subsidy programs (approximately $55 billion in 2016, including approximately $37B for HUD rental assistance and public housing programs) (Center on Budget and Policy Priorities 2016a). Comparison of poverty reduction for these programs is presented in figure 4. (As noted, these results rely on safety net program participation as reported in CPS data; because participation is known to be underreported, these estimates

Figure 2. Poverty Rate Before and After Credit

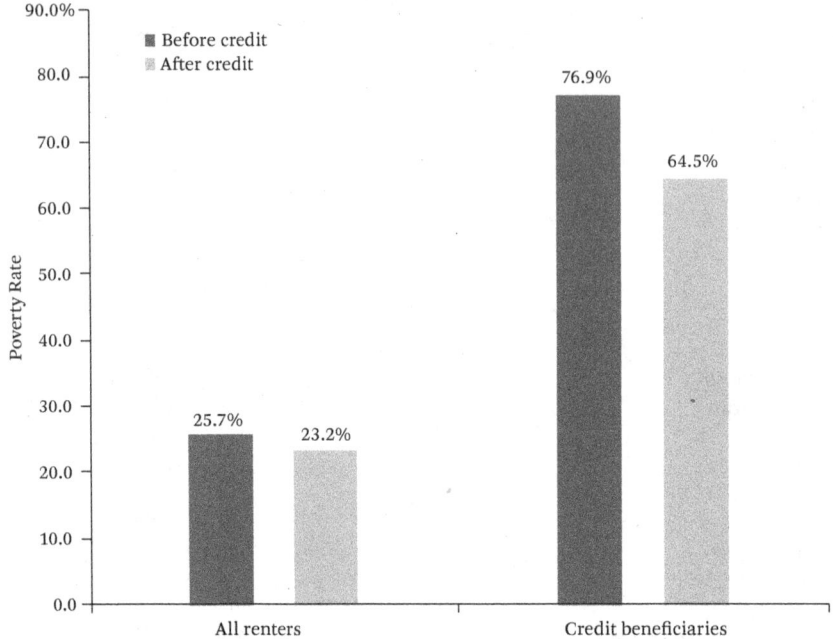

Source: Authors' calculations from 2013–2015 CPS data (Flood et al. 2016).
Note: Poverty rate determined by Supplemental Poverty Measure.

Figure 3. Housing Cost Burden Before and After Renter's Credit

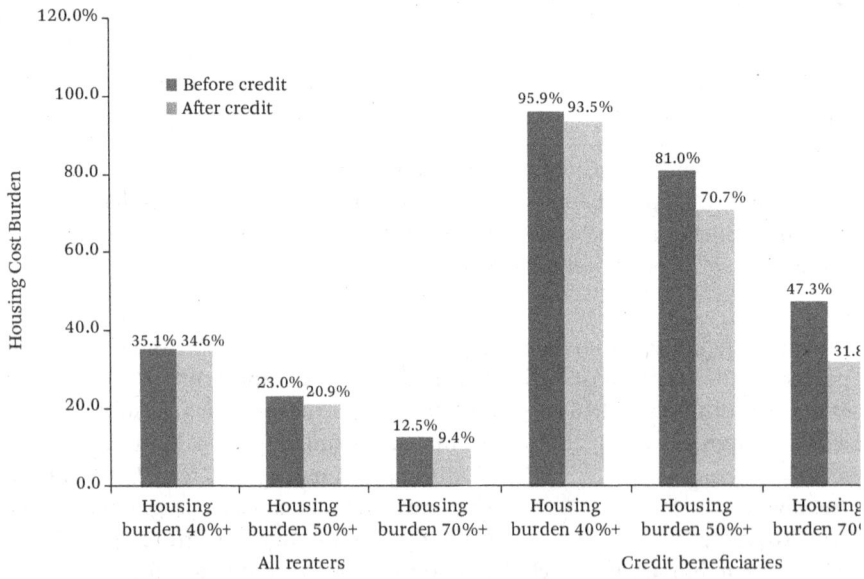

Source: Authors' calculations from 2013–2015 CPS data (Flood et al. 2016).
Note: Housing burden calculated as gross rent paid (imputed from ACS data) divided by total Supplemental Poverty Measure family resources (cash income plus near-cash benefits net of taxes, work expenses, and out-of-pocket medical expenses).

Figure 4. Poverty Rate Reduction from Safety Net Programs

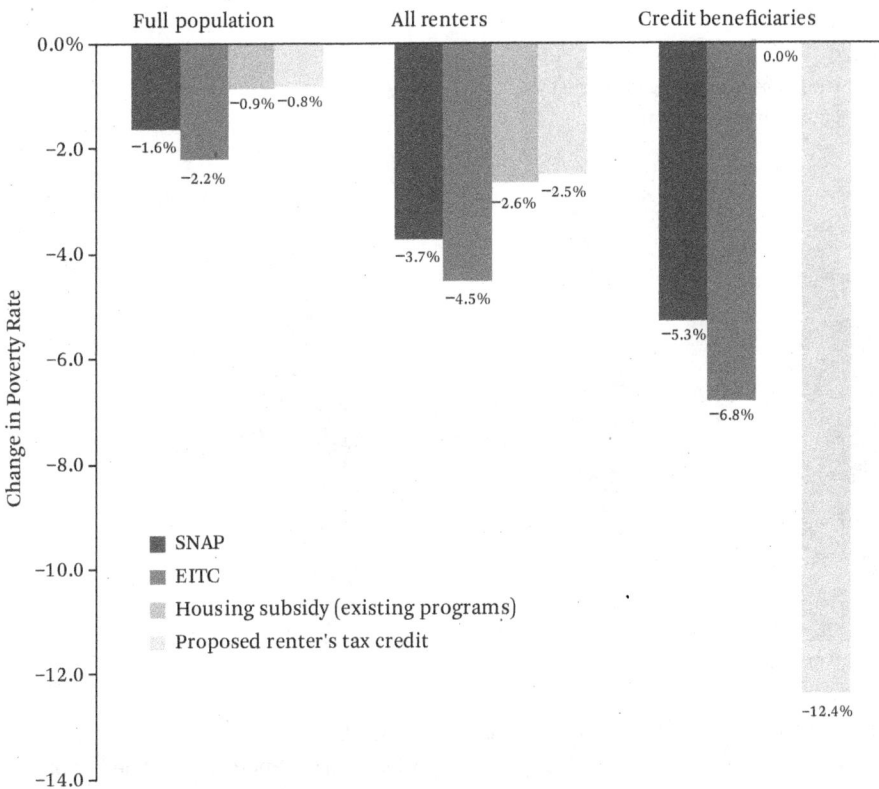

Source: Authors' calculations from 2013–2015 CPS data (Flood et al. 2016).
Note: All poverty rates refer to Supplemental Poverty Measure. Poverty rate reduction calculated by subtracting SNAP, EITC, housing subsidy, or renter's credit after adding renter's credit to family resources. Individuals already receiving housing subsidies are not eligible for the proposed renter's tax credit.

are conservative.) For the full population, the credit reduces poverty a similar amount as existing housing subsidies, less than the EITC, and somewhat less than SNAP. Among renters, the credit again reduces poverty a similar amount to existing housing subsidies, less than the EITC and somewhat less than SNAP. Among credit beneficiaries, the credit reduces poverty substantially more than either the EITC or SNAP (and more than housing subsidies, by definition, because individuals already receiving housing subsidies are ineligible for the credit).

Reduction in the poverty rate is not the only relevant measure of impact on poor families, however, because it captures only the number of individuals moved across the poverty line by the benefits, and not the total number of poor individuals assisted (many of whom benefit from increased resources yet remain below the poverty threshold). We present a comparison of the reach of these programs to vulnerable households in figure 5. In comparing the reach of the credit with other safety net programs, we find that the credit assists nearly 1.4 times as many severely cost-burdened renters as EITC and more than twice as many severely cost-burdened renters as report receiving SNAP, suggesting that a significant share of renters who struggle with housing affordability and would be eligible for the credit may not already be participating in these other safety net programs. The credit also assists nearly two and a half times as many poor renters and more than

Figure 5. Poor and Housing Cost-Burdened Assisted by Other Safety Net Programs

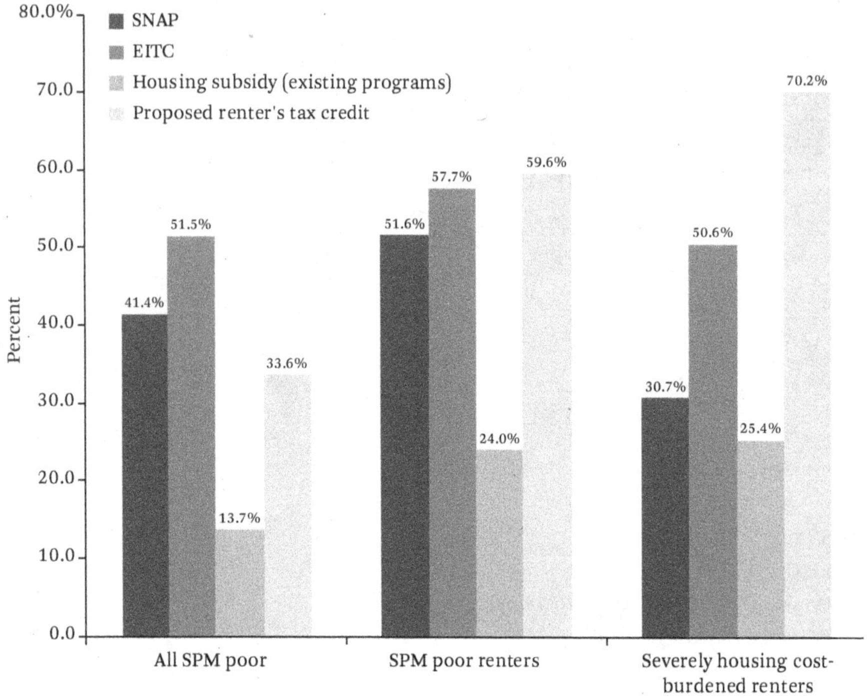

	All SPM poor	SPM poor renters	Severely housing cost-burdened renters
SNAP	41.4%	51.6%	30.7%
EITC	51.5%	57.7%	50.6%
Housing subsidy (existing programs)	13.7%	24.0%	25.4%
Proposed renter's tax credit	33.6%	59.6%	70.2%

Source: Authors' calculations from 2013–2015 CPS data (Flood et al. 2016).
Note: Poor refers to Supplemental Poverty Measure. Severely housing cost-burdened defined as paid gross rent (imputed from ACS data) greater than or equal to 50 percent of Supplemental Poverty Measure family resources (cash income plus near-cash benefits net of taxes, work expenses, and out-of-pocket medical expenses). Percentages represent share of individuals who received SNAP, EITC, housing subsidy, or renter's credit out of all individuals who were poor or housing burdened before incorporating SNAP, EITC, housing subsidy, or renter's credit into family resources.

2.75 times as many severely housing cost-burdened renters as existing housing subsidy programs, suggesting that the credit would mitigate the extremely limited reach of the current system of housing-specific assistance.

Administrative data from HUD provide another point of comparison for the cost and reach of the proposed renter's credit. In fiscal year 2015, HUD's rental assistance and public housing programs had a budget of $35.9 billion and assisted 9.9 million individuals (HUD 2017b).[13] The proposed renter's credit would have an annual cost of $24.1 billion, equal to two-thirds of the HUD rental assistance and public housing budget, and assist 20.8 million individuals, more than twice as many as these HUD rental programs. The renter's credit would thus reach a substantially larger number of low-income renters than HUD's existing subsidies for renters, at a lower cost (and shallower subsidy) per assisted individual.

DISCUSSION

A refundable renter's credit stands to significantly curtail the current dearth of affordable housing in the United States. Our estimates suggest that more than 20 million individuals would benefit from the proposed credit, with an average benefit amount of $2,300 for poor families. We estimate that the credit would reach more than 70 percent of all severely cost-burdened renters, who spend more than half

13. These programs include tenant-based rental assistance, project-based rental assistance, Section 202 elderly housing, Section 811 housing for people with disabilities, and public housing.

of their incomes on rent. The credit has a significant impact on the poverty rates of beneficiaries, reducing their poverty rate by 12.4 percentage points and lifting 2.6 million people above the poverty line. Another 13.4 million poor Americans would be made less poor by the credit, reducing the gap between their incomes and the poverty line by nearly one third. A substantial number of near-poor individuals would also benefit from the credit.

Some might argue that we should incorporate cost-of-living adjustments to existing anti-poverty and housing subsidy programs, rather than create a new renter's credit. An example of such an approach is adjusting the size of credits for the EITC for local differences in the cost of living. The renter's credit reaches a different subset of the population than existing anti-poverty programs or existing housing subsidy programs, however, and seeks to accomplish a different goal. Our estimates show that the renter's credit assists more severely cost-burdened renters than the EITC or SNAP. Significant numbers of poor and nonpoor renters who struggle with housing affordability are not eligible for or may not participate in these other programs. As a result, a renter's credit would reach more poor renters than would a cost-of-living supplement to existing anti-poverty programs.[14] The credit also reaches more than twice as many poor and severely cost-burdened renters as existing housing subsidy programs, which are highly rationed. Administering the credit via the tax code also has the added benefits of greater administrative efficiency compared to existing housing programs like vouchers and developer tax credits, and reducing inequities between renters and homeowners in the existing tax code.

As a result of the distinct targeting to high-cost areas, the proposed renter's credit reaches a different segment of poor Americans than related proposals to address housing costs through the tax code, such as a proposal to add a housing supplement to the EITC (Dreier 2016). As noted, the proposed credit would reach substantially more severely cost-burdened renters than a housing supplement to the EITC, given that many poor and cost-burdened renters do not receive the EITC. Only half of the renter's credit beneficiaries in our simulation are in tax units eligible for the EITC. Even among tax filers who receive the EITC, the renter's tax credit differs from a EITC housing supplement in that it specifically targets renters, and 54 percent of tax filers receiving EITC are homeowners.[15] Because renters generally have higher poverty rates, fewer assets, less housing security, and fewer existing tax benefits than homeowners, targeting low-income housing assistance specifically to renters prioritizes the neediest households who are often excluded from existing safety net programs. To address housing need specifically, therefore, a renter's tax credit offers more efficient targeting to individuals with greater housing need than an EITC housing supplement.

The proposed renter's credit also serves a different anti-poverty purpose than a child allowance, such as the ones proposed elsewhere in this double issue (Shaefer et al. 2018; Bitler, Hines, and Page 2018). Whereas the child allowance addresses poverty among all children in all locations, the renter's credit targets poor renters in areas with high housing costs, regardless of whether they have children. As a result, the proposed credit offers an important complement to anti-poverty efforts that specifically target families with children (as much of the existing safety net does), reaching segments of the poor population that receive fewer benefits from existing anti-poverty programs, particularly individuals hardest hit by the growing crisis of housing affordability in the United States. The renter's credit is responsive to differences in cost of living across the United States, as it is based on rent paid, while the proposed child allowance is the same regardless of place of residence. The child allowance thus, in effect, provides smaller real benefits to families living in high-cost areas and larger real benefits to those in low-cost areas. The uni-

14. Among renters who are SPM poor in the CPS data before assigning any renter's tax credit, 43 percent are in families with reported SNAP, 49 percent are in families with reported EITC, 14 percent are in families with reported housing subsidies, and 60 percent are in families eligible for the renter's tax credit.

15. Figures are per authors' analysis of EITC receipt as imputed in CPS data.

versal design of the proposed child allowance—with benefit levels that are the same nationwide and serving both poor and nonpoor children—has specific benefits, particularly politically, though consequently it has a substantially higher cost, with a larger share of benefits directed to individuals with less economic need. The renter's credit is more targeted to the lowest-income households, which have a smaller share of nonpoor beneficiaries and thus lower costs, corresponding to a smaller number of individuals assisted, but this narrower targeting could also make it more vulnerable politically.

Why not simply expand existing affordable housing programs, such as the housing voucher program or the LIHTC? We believe that a renter's credit delivered via the tax system is the most efficient and equitable way to get the most money into the hands of the families who need the most help. The voucher program is stymied by the fact that landlords must consent to be in the program and limits are placed on eligible units based on cost and housing quality inspections. Although the voucher program offers the very deep subsidies needed for the lowest-income households, these restrictions also make the program extremely expensive per household served. Thus the program is far too limited in its reach. A renter's credit, by contrast, offers no restrictions on the housing units eligible for subsidies so it expands the supply of eligible units significantly. Because landlords and neighbors would not need to know who receives the credit, it may also be less stigmatizing than the voucher program.

Administration through the income tax system offers many advantages over the voucher administration system. Because most households file income taxes anyway, the administrative barriers to applying for and receiving the renter's credit are much lower than the barriers to applying for and successfully using housing vouchers. The renter's tax credit is also designed to function as a shallower subsidy that reaches a broader share of renters than existing housing vouchers. Indeed, largely replacing the existing highly rationed voucher program, which provides deep subsidies to some households while leaving the majority unassisted, with a wide-reaching refundable renter's tax credit that is more accessible, more administratively efficient, and distributes assistance more evenly across housing-burdened households could offer benefits. A final advantage to administering the renter's credit through the tax system is that subsidies offered through the renter's credit would not be subject to annual appropriations votes in the same way as other subsidized housing programs, making the credit less subject to budget cuts and political gridlock.

We also believe that a renter's credit delivered directly to cost-burdened renters is more advantageous than delivering a credit to landlords or to housing developers. The LIHTC is an important mechanism for increasing the supply of affordable housing via new construction and rehabilitation. But the housing it produces remains unaffordable to most low-income households and, even more significantly, a nontrivial share of the profits go to private investors, diverting funding that could be used to supply more affordable housing. We therefore argue that the proposed renter's credit channels more money directly to cash-strapped households and as a result serves as a more effective anti-poverty program. Targeting subsidies to renters directly also means that renters have more choice over the locations and characteristics of their housing, and are not limited to the units that developers or landlords have chosen for participation in subsidy programs. This might have the added benefit of promoting greater racial and socioeconomic integration, given that landlords in the housing voucher program have been known to concentrate units disproportionately in poor and high-minority neighborhoods (Rosen 2014). On the downside, any effort to subsidize low-income renters on a large scale runs the risk of contributing to rent inflation, with some of the credit captured by property owners in the form of higher rents. Capping renter's credits at FMR or a percentage of renters' incomes, however, should help mitigate this concern.

What would it take to implement a renter's credit like the one we have proposed here? Many of the administrative structures for delivering the credit are already in place, which is one key advantage of providing the credit via the tax system. The Internal Revenue Service (IRS) already requests most of the information needed to determine credit amounts; the only additional pieces of information that would need to be collected on tax returns are the tax unit's nontaxable cash income (such as SSI or Temporary Assistance to Needy Families payments) and income of dependents (similar to the income data currently collected on Affordable Care Act health insurance tax forms), and rent paid. The FMRs used to cap the base credit amounts are already collected by the Department of Housing and Urban Development routinely every year for use in other housing programs. There is precedent at the state level as well: many state tax systems already offer tax rebates or credits for renters, often framed as a way to recoup some of the cost of local property taxes that renters pay indirectly through their rent. However, these systems are uneven across states in terms of their presence and generosity (see table A6). Following the lead of other refundable tax credits, the proposed renter's credit would not need to be counted as income when determining eligibility for other means-tested programs. An additional benefit of administering the proposed credit via the tax system is that it would reduce the inequities in how homeowners and renters are treated under existing tax law.

Almost all families receive their tax rebates as a lump sum payment at the time they file their taxes. Rent payments are due on a monthly basis, however, which means that the timing of payment for the renter's credit at tax time may not align with the timing of need for households facing high housing costs. If the misalignment in the timing of the credit and rent payments is a concern, the disbursement of the credit payments could be handled several ways. One option would be to offer a deferred disbursement plan, where the credit is paid out quarterly, at the same time that estimated tax payments are due (for a related proposal for deferred disbursement of the EITC, see Shaefer et al. 2018). A second option would be to allow tax filers who have some tax liability to take a deduction for the credit on their W-4s, which would increase the amount of money they keep in their paycheck each week. A monthly disbursement plan via another federal agency, such as HUD or the Social Security Administration (SSA), might offer more regular rental support, but some of that benefit would be eroded because such monthly payments would be counted as income when determining eligibility for other means-tested programs, and administrative costs would likely be higher.

Finally, how might a renters' tax credit be funded? One possibility would be to fund the tax credit by reducing the subsidies that currently go to high-income homeowners. Currently, more than 75 percent of the tax expenditures devoted to homeownership via mortgage interest and property tax deductions go to homeowners who make more than $100,000 per year, at a cost of more than $70 billion per year (Center on Budget and Policy Priorities 2016b). Cutting these tax expenditures to fund a renter's credit would improve both the horizontal and vertical equity of our tax and transfer system by shifting resources from affluent homeowners to poor renters. Another option would be to tax profits from residential rental property income, or to tax capital gains from residential real estate sales; either would allow for sharing some of the profits of landlords and property owners with renters burdened by high rental costs, though landlords' passing on the taxes in the form of higher rents is a risk.

Overall, the proposed refundable renter's tax credit is a promising policy tool to address the affordable housing crisis and reduce poverty. It offers efficient targeting, broad reach, low administrative burden for beneficiaries, and low administrative costs for the government, and it would achieve a noteworthy reduction in poverty. The renter's tax credit can also be flexibly modified to achieve specific policy goals in terms of target households, depth of subsidy, and total cost. Innovative approaches such as this renter's credit are urgently needed to reduce the high housing cost burdens faced by low-income households and the resulting problems of poverty and housing instability and all of their negative consequences.

APPENDIX

Renter's Tax Credit Impact by State

Table A1. Credit Reach, Cost, and Poor Beneficiaries by State

State	Tax Filers Receiving Credit per Year (M)	Beneficiaries per Year (Individuals in Families Receiving Credit) (M)	Total Cost per Year (M)	SPM Poor Renters Benefiting from Credit	All Renters with Expected Housing Burden >50% Benefiting from Credit	Beneficiaries Lifted Out of Poverty per Year (M)	Beneficiaries Remaining Poor but with Poverty Gap Reduced per Year (M)
AL	0.076	0.147	$104.486	40.5%	59.6%	0.009	0.118
AK	0.015	0.030	30.036	62.1	73.7	0.003	0.019
AZ	0.242	0.455	388.751	61.0	65.6	0.032	0.352
AR	0.054	0.110	73.569	46.8	59.3	0.007	0.092
CA	2.606	5.210	6,759.454	73.7	81.0	0.749	3.098
CO	0.170	0.275	292.361	61.1	67.2	0.037	0.157
CT	0.125	0.202	284.048	53.2	67.9	0.033	0.099
DE	0.025	0.044	47.515	54.8	77.7	0.004	0.029
DC	0.057	0.089	147.676	55.5	74.3	0.015	0.045
FL	0.908	1.645	1,876.576	66.7	72.2	0.230	1.059
GA	0.331	0.617	507.261	54.0	63.3	0.058	0.451
HI	0.072	0.130	223.730	61.8	76.5	0.023	0.053
ID	0.032	0.047	36.179	47.5	50.5	0.003	0.037
IL	0.448	0.712	818.654	59.7	66.3	0.093	0.478
IN	0.110	0.177	153.976	39.4	53.2	0.015	0.138
IA	0.055	0.077	71.881	47.9	60.0	0.005	0.064
KS	0.050	0.086	63.214	49.4	57.9	0.007	0.067
KT	0.100	0.192	145.475	44.1	60.8	0.011	0.152
LA	0.127	0.225	192.199	50.1	60.7	0.019	0.176
ME	0.029	0.043	46.154	55.8	68.9	0.005	0.030
MD	0.220	0.388	552.249	60.1	68.9	0.074	0.203
MA	0.306	0.468	745.169	57.5	74.8	0.071	0.286
MI	0.241	0.422	347.952	58.5	67.0	0.019	0.322
MN	0.094	0.130	157.068	42.9	61.5	0.016	0.090
MS	0.057	0.123	85.419	54.4	63.8	0.007	0.106
MO	0.113	0.173	144.449	41.0	56.0	0.013	0.132
MT	0.018	0.027	26.137	45.8	61.0	0.002	0.022
NE	0.038	0.059	42.058	46.2	59.3	0.003	0.043
NV	0.147	0.254	271.510	62.5	71.8	0.034	0.164
NH	0.029	0.047	55.388	59.5	71.8	0.003	0.030
NJ	0.413	0.777	1,090.412	62.8	77.8	0.118	0.440
NM	0.062	0.111	97.654	60.0	62.6	0.008	0.088
NY	1.285	2.152	3,204.723	62.1	78.6	0.330	1.111
NC	0.283	0.471	415.628	51.3	53.6	0.031	0.375
ND	0.011	0.015	15.306	31.6	43.9	0.000	0.013
OH	0.262	0.425	352.195	48.9	57.3	0.044	0.317
OK	0.058	0.101	70.695	40.9	51.4	0.009	0.081

(continued)

Table A1. (*continued*)

State	Tax Filers Receiving Credit per Year (M)	Beneficiaries per Year (Individuals in Families Receiving Credit) (M)	Total Cost per Year (M)	SPM Poor Renters Benefiting from Credit	All Renters with Expected Housing Burden >50% Benefiting from Credit	Beneficiaries Lifted Out of Poverty per Year (M)	Beneficiaries Remaining Poor but with Poverty Gap Reduced per Year (M)
OR	0.133	0.212	202.735	56.0	58.1	0.025	0.138
PA	0.313	0.510	570.750	51.1	62.9	0.067	0.323
RI	0.035	0.058	56.428	57.4	60.6	0.010	0.036
SC	0.123	0.190	161.756	48.9	58.4	0.020	0.137
SD	0.010	0.014	10.227	26.7	50.4	0.001	0.010
TN	0.194	0.337	258.330	51.9	62.0	0.018	0.271
TX	0.851	1.583	1,446.116	59.5	66.3	0.156	1.172
UT	0.038	0.070	56.469	48.8	52.2	0.003	0.055
VT	0.015	0.022	28.242	63.3	71.5	0.002	0.013
VA	0.316	0.527	679.199	62.3	66.2	0.063	0.304
WA	0.205	0.351	384.686	54.3	68.6	0.048	0.195
WV	0.027	0.049	32.948	44.3	62.0	0.003	0.041
WI	0.140	0.225	212.394	51.5	60.4	0.020	0.177
WY	0.010	0.015	13.077	49.3	55.1	0.002	0.011

Source: Authors' calculations from 2013–2015 CPS data (Flood et al. 2016).
Note: Sample sizes for some state-metro areas are small, making corresponding estimates less reliable.

Table A2. Credit Impact on Poverty Rate and Severe Housing Burden by State

	All Renters			Beneficiaries		
State	SPM Before Credit	SPM After Credit	Change in SPM	SPM Before Credit	SPM After Credit	Change in SPM
AL	25.4	24.7	0.7	86.1	80.3	5.8
AK	16.9	15.4	1.6	75.5	64.3	11.2
AZ	26.5	25.2	1.4	84.5	77.4	7.1
AR	23.7	22.9	0.8	90.3	83.7	6.6
CA	30.9	26.5	4.4	73.8	59.5	14.4
CO	17.7	15.6	2.1	70.6	57.1	13.5
CT	24.2	21.0	3.2	65.8	49.3	16.5
DE	25.1	23.5	1.5	73.9	65.6	8.3
DC	28.3	24.3	4.0	67.7	50.7	17.0
FL	28.6	25.2	3.4	78.3	64.4	14.0
GA	27.6	25.9	1.7	82.5	73.0	9.5
HI	23.2	18.9	4.3	58.1	40.7	17.4
ID	18.1	17.6	0.6	84.4	78.7	5.7
IL	24.9	22.5	2.4	80.3	67.2	13.1
IN	22.8	21.9	0.9	86.8	78.0	8.7
IA	19.2	18.6	0.6	89.2	82.9	6.3
KS	17.8	17.0	0.8	86.7	78.8	8.0
KT	27.1	26.2	0.8	85.0	79.1	6.0
LA	27.8	26.4	1.4	86.7	78.1	8.6
ME	20.5	18.9	1.5	79.6	68.9	10.8
MD	24.9	20.9	4.0	71.5	52.3	19.1
MA	27.0	23.9	3.1	76.3	61.1	15.2
MI	25.6	24.8	0.9	80.8	76.2	4.6
MN	19.2	18.0	1.3	82.0	69.4	12.5
MS	27.2	26.3	0.9	91.6	86.0	5.6
MO	22.1	21.3	0.8	84.0	76.3	7.7
MT	17.9	17.2	0.7	87.6	79.8	7.8
NE	18.8	18.2	0.6	77.8	72.7	5.2
NV	24.5	21.9	2.6	78.0	64.8	13.2
NH	20.0	18.8	1.2	70.1	63.1	7.0
NJ	29.7	25.8	3.9	71.8	56.6	15.2
NM	24.3	23.0	1.2	86.2	78.9	7.3
NY	27.2	23.3	3.9	66.9	51.6	15.3
NC	26.1	25.1	1.0	86.2	79.6	6.7
ND	17.7	17.5	0.2	90.5	87.1	3.4
OH	21.7	20.4	1.3	84.8	74.5	10.3
OK	20.1	19.3	0.8	88.7	79.9	8.8
OR	20.4	18.6	1.7	77.0	65.2	11.8
PA	24.2	22.1	2.1	76.5	63.3	13.2
RI	22.3	19.5	2.8	79.6	62.1	17.5
SC	24.9	23.3	1.6	82.9	72.2	10.8
SD	18.1	17.8	0.3	78.9	73.8	5.1
TN	27.7	26.8	0.9	85.7	80.4	5.2
TX	24.0	22.3	1.7	83.9	74.0	9.9
UT	15.9	15.6	0.3	81.5	77.9	3.6
VT	16.4	14.8	1.6	71.9	61.0	10.9
VA	23.5	21.0	2.5	69.7	57.8	12.0
WA	18.8	16.8	2.0	69.2	55.5	13.7
WV	26.2	25.5	0.8	89.5	83.7	5.9
WI	24.0	22.7	1.3	88.0	78.8	9.1
WY	18.3	17.1	1.2	87.7	76.4	11.3

Source: Authors' calculations based from 2013–2015 CPS data (Flood et al. 2016).
Note: All figures in percentages. Sample sizes for some state-metro areas are small, making corresponding estimates less reliable.

	All Renters			Beneficiaries	
Individuals with Burden 50%+ Before Credit	Individuals with Burden 50%+ After Credit	Change in 50%+ Burden	Individuals with Burden 50%+ Before Credit	Individuals with Burden 50%+ After Credit	Change in 50%+ Burden
16.2	14.3	1.9	81.0	65.2	15.8
15.8	14.8	1.0	83.5	76.4	7.1
22.9	20.9	1.9	78.3	68.3	10.0
14.3	13.9	0.4	68.7	65.5	3.2
31.4	28.3	3.1	82.5	72.4	10.1
19.4	18.2	1.2	84.9	77.3	7.7
23.3	20.9	2.3	80.8	69.0	11.8
18.6	17.6	1.0	77.9	72.3	5.5
28.1	25.1	3.0	90.0	77.1	12.9
28.1	25.1	3.0	83.5	71.0	12.5
21.6	20.0	1.6	75.7	66.6	9.1
26.9	25.1	1.8	83.5	76.1	7.4
15.6	15.0	0.6	77.4	71.4	5.9
23.1	21.7	1.4	82.6	74.9	7.7
14.5	13.5	0.9	74.4	65.4	8.9
13.9	13.5	0.3	80.5	77.4	3.1
13.4	12.3	1.1	76.7	66.0	10.7
14.8	13.3	1.5	64.2	53.5	10.7
19.9	17.7	2.2	75.1	61.6	13.5
16.6	14.9	1.6	79.8	68.3	11.5
24.4	21.8	2.6	80.4	67.9	12.5
24.7	22.8	1.9	90.6	81.3	9.3
19.7	18.4	1.3	71.2	64.0	7.2
14.3	13.4	0.9	87.7	78.7	9.0
17.1	16.3	0.8	67.5	62.3	5.2
14.8	14.0	0.9	77.0	69.0	8.0
13.1	12.4	0.6	84.9	78.1	6.7
14.2	13.6	0.6	75.5	70.3	5.2
22.4	20.5	1.9	81.7	72.1	9.6
18.3	16.3	2.0	77.4	65.9	11.5
28.3	25.3	3.0	84.8	73.3	11.6
21.2	19.1	2.1	78.6	66.3	12.3
26.5	23.3	3.2	82.6	70.1	12.5
21.8	21.0	0.8	75.3	70.0	5.4
12.5	12.4	0.2	89.3	86.4	2.9
16.2	14.8	1.4	74.2	62.9	11.3
13.0	12.1	0.9	72.4	62.2	10.2
20.6	19.4	1.2	80.7	72.7	8.0
19.8	18.1	1.7	76.8	66.6	10.3
20.5	18.5	1.9	77.2	65.2	12.0
20.5	19.3	1.2	81.8	73.5	8.2
9.4	9.4	0.0	77.3	77.3	0.0
20.2	18.0	2.2	74.5	61.4	13.1
21.2	19.1	2.1	82.9	70.4	12.5
14.1	13.5	0.6	77.2	71.1	6.1
15.5	13.1	2.5	77.0	59.9	17.1
28.5	26.8	1.7	89.8	81.6	8.2
16.6	15.8	0.8	77.2	71.5	5.7
15.5	14.6	0.9	73.8	67.0	6.8
16.8	15.9	0.9	72.3	66.0	6.3
15.1	13.9	1.2	81.1	69.1	12.0

Credit Results Targeting Children, Seniors, Residents of High Housing Cost States

Table A3. Reach, Cost, Poverty Impact, and Housing Burden Impact for Credits Targeting Subpopulations

Number of Beneficiaries and Cost	Subpopulation Targeted by Credit		
	Tax Units That Include Children Only	Tax Units That Include Elderly Only	Residents of High Housing Cost States Only (State-Average FMR in Top Third Nationally)
Total tax filers receiving credit (M)	2.931	1.894	7.214
Total beneficiaries[a] (M)	10.292	2.385	13.068
Total cost (M)	$6,938	$4,609	$17,220
Proportion of renters receiving the credit			
Poor renters[b]	59.8%	65.4%	66.0%
Renters with expected housing burden >50%	74.2	76.7	75.9
Anti-poverty effects			
All renters in target subpopulation			
Poverty rate before credit	27.1%	26.8%	27.4%
Poverty rate after credit	25.1	21.6	23.8
Change in poverty rate	2.0	5.2	3.6
All beneficiaries			
Poverty rate before credit	81.7	64.9	72.8
Poverty rate after credit	71.7	45.6	58.3
Change in poverty rate	10.0	19.3	14.5
Beneficiaries lifted out of poverty (M)	1.028	0.462	1.897
Beneficiaries remaining poor but poverty gap reduced (M)	7.378	1.087	7.619
Housing burden effects			
All renters in target subpopulation			
Housing burden 50%+ before credit	19.1%	31.7%	27.2%
Housing burden 50%+ after credit	16.3	29.8	24.6
Change in 50%+ housing burden	2.8	1.9	2.6
All beneficiaries			
Housing burden 50%+ before credit	71.5	90.2	83.2
Housing burden 50%+ after credit	57.2	83.2	72.6
Change in 50%+ housing burden	14.3	7.0	10.6

Source: Authors' calculations from 2013–2015 CPS data (Flood et al. 2016).
[a]Total beneficiaries includes all individuals in families receiving credit.
[b]Poverty status for tax filers determined based on Supplemental Poverty Measure, before filer receives the credit.

Modified Renter's Tax Credit Targeting Households with Severe Housing Burden

The design of the renter's tax credit allows for modification of the credit parameters to adjust the population targeted, the depth of the subsidy, and the total cost of the credit. Here we present an alternative version of the credit with modified parameters to target households with more severe housing burden.

The credit follows the same formula as that presented as our main results, except that a tax unit is eligible for the credit if they are expected to spend more than 50 percent of their total after-tax cash income on the average rental unit rather than 40 percent. The final credit amount for tax unit i is calculated as

$$\text{Credit Amt}_i = \text{Capped Rent Paid}_i - (0.5 \times \text{After-Tax Income}_i)$$

This modified version of the credit, then, targets a narrower population of households with more severe housing cost burden. Results for this modified credit are presented in the tables.

Table A4. Alternate Credit Reach, Cost, and Beneficiary Demographics

Number of beneficiaries and cost			**Race-ethnicity of beneficiaries**[a]	
Total tax filers receiving credit (M)	7.689		Non-Hispanic white	38.0%
Total beneficiaries[a] (M)	13.403		Non-Hispanic African American	22.0
Total cost (M)	$12,653		Hispanic	31.7
Mean credit per receiving tax filer	$1,646		Non-Hispanic Asian	7.1
Per poor tax filer[b]	1,696		Non-Hispanic other race	1.1
Per nonpoor tax filer[b]	1,335		**Highest level of education in beneficiary families**[a]	
Median credit per receiving tax filer	$1,458		Less than high school	18.2%
Per poor tax filer[b]	1,530		High school graduate	32.0
Per nonpoor tax filer[b]	999		Some college but no four-year degree	31.6
Proportion of renters receiving the credit			College graduate with four-year degree	18.3
All renters	12.8%		**Beneficiary region of residence**[a]	
Poor renters[b]	44.8		Northeast	20.9%
Renters with housing burden >40%	36.0		Midwest	12.1
Renters with housing burden >50%	51.6		South	33.2
Renters with housing burden >70%	67.9		West	33.8
Beneficiary demographics				
Family composition of beneficiaries[a]				
Families with children	51.4%			
Families with young children (under five years old)	24.6			
Families with seniors	14.6			

Source: Authors' calculations from 2013–2015 CPS data (Flood et al. 2016).
[a]Total beneficiaries includes all individuals in families receiving credit.
[b]Poverty status for tax filers determined based on Supplemental Poverty Measure, before filer receives the credit.

Table A5. Anti-Poverty Effects of Alternate Renter's Credit

All renters	
Poverty rate before credit	25.7%
Poverty rate after credit	24.7
Change in poverty rate	1.0
Deep poverty rate before credit	7.9
Deep poverty rate after credit	6.6
Change in deep poverty rate	1.3
All beneficiaries	
Poverty rate before credit	89.7%
Poverty rate after credit	82.2
Change in poverty rate	7.5
Deep poverty rate before credit	37.6
Deep poverty rate after credit	27.5
Change in deep poverty rate	10.1
Total beneficiaries (M)	13.403
Beneficiaries lifted out of poverty (M)	1.008
Beneficiaries remaining poor but poverty gap reduced (M)	11.015
Beneficiaries lifted out of poverty or poverty gap reduced (M)	12.023
Median poverty gap among poor beneficiaries[a,b]	
Before credit	$9,211
After credit	$7,224
Change in median poverty gap	$1,987
Median share of poverty gap closed	21.6%

Source: Authors' calculations from 2013–2015 CPS data (Flood et al. 2016).
[a] Total beneficiaries includes all individuals in families receiving credit.
[b] Poverty status for tax filers determined based on Supplemental Poverty Measure, before filer receives the credit.

Table A6. State-Level Renter's Tax Credits

State	Any Renter Credit?	Refund-able	Available to Nonelderly or Nondisabled	Credit Calculation	Max Income (2015) Single Married/Household	Max Credit (2015) Single Married/Household	Rent Documentation Required
Arizona	Y	N	N	renter income + landlord property taxes	$3,751 5,501	$502	landlord certification
California	Y	N	Y	income	39,062 78,125	60 120	flat statewide credit not based on actual rent paid
Colorado	Y	Y	N	rent + income + heat	13,234 17,839	792	Self-reported; no proof required
Connecticut	Y	Y	N	rent + income + utilities	35,200; 42,900	700 900	evidence of rent and utilities paid. If renting from family member, copy of landlord form 1040.
District of Columbia	Y	N	Y	rent + income	20,000	750	self-reported; no proof required
Hawaii	Y	N	Y	rent	30,000	50 per person	self-reported; no proof required
Indiana	Y	N	Y	rent	None	3,000	self-reported; no proof required
Iowa	Y	Y	N	rent + income	22,584	1,000	self-reported; no proof required
Maine	Y	Y	Y	rent + income + exemptions	33,333 53,333	600	self-reported; no proof required
Maryland	Y	N	Y	rent + income	24,230	750	self-reported; no proof required

(continued)

Table A6. (continued)

State	Any Renter Credit?	Refund-able	Available to Nonelderly or Nondisabled	Credit Calculation	Max Income (2015) Single Married/Household	Max Credit (2015) Single Married/Household	Rent Documentation Required
Massachusetts	Y	N	Y	rent	None	3,000	self-reported; no proof required
Michigan	Y	N	Y	rent + income	50,000	1,200	self-reported; no proof required
Minnesota	Y	Y	Y	rent + income	58,880	2,060	landlord certification
Missouri	Y	N	N	rent + income	27,500 29,500	750	rent receipts or signed statement from landlord
Montana	Y	Y	N	rent + income	45,000	1,000	rent receipts or signed statement from landlord
New Jersey	Y	N	Y	rent	None	Deduction: $10,000 Credit: Flat $50	self-reported; no proof required
New Mexico	Y	Y	N	rent + income	16,000	250	self-reported; no proof required
New York	Y	Y	Y	rent + income	18,000	75	self-reported; no proof required
North Dakota	Y	Y	N	rent + income	42,000	400	self-reported; no proof required
Pennsylvania	Y	Y	N	rent + income + area of residence	15,000	975	landlord certification
Rhode Island	Y	N	N	rent + income	30,000	335	lease, rent receipts, or HUD Statement
Utah	Y	Y	N	rent + income + utilities	32,101	951	self-reported; no proof required
Vermont	Y	Y	Y	rent + income	47,000	3,000	landlord certification
Wisconsin	Y	Y	Y	rent + income	24,680	1,168	landlord certification

Source: Author's compilation.

Figure A1. Expected Housing Cost Burden Before and After Alternate Credit

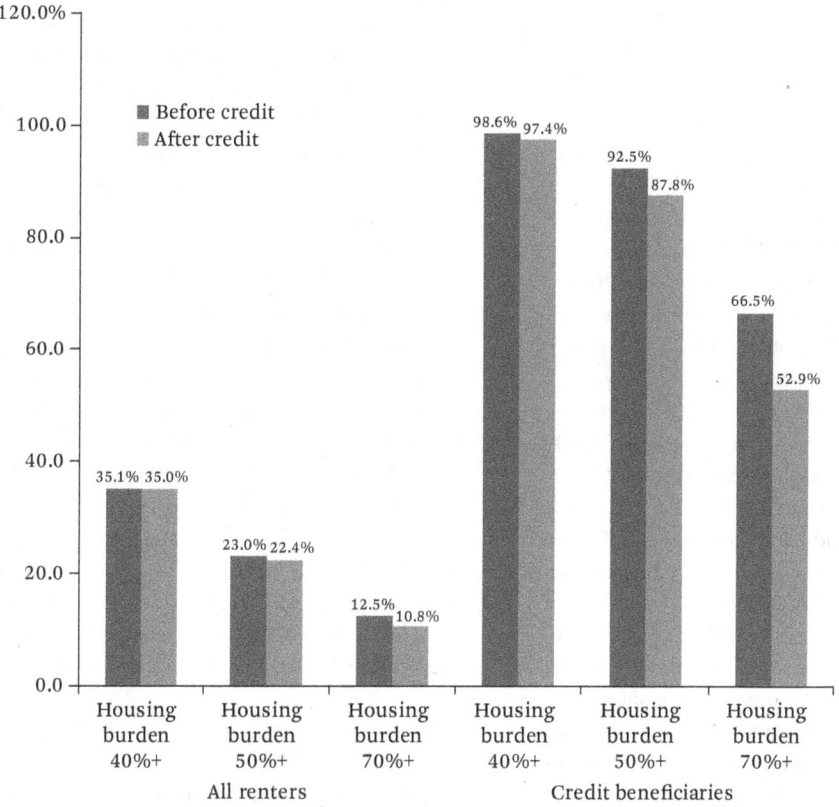

Source: Authors' calculations from 2013–2015 CPS data (Flood et al. 2016).
Note: Housing burden calculated as gross rent paid (imputed from ACS data) divided by total Supplemental Poverty Measure family resources (cash income plus near-cash benefits net of taxes, work expenses, and out-of-pocket medical expenses).

REFERENCES

Bitler, Marianne P., Annie Laurie Hines, and Marianne Page. 2018. "Cash for Kids." *RSF: The Russell Sage Foundation Journal of the Social Sciences* 4(2): 43–73. DOI: 10.7758/RSF.2018.4.2.03.

Bureau of Labor Statistics. 2017. "Research Experimental Poverty Thresholds." *Price and Index Number Research*. Last modified August 29, 2017. Accessed October 6, 2017. https://www.bls.gov/pir/spmhome.htm.

Center on Budget and Policy Priorities. 2016a. "Most Federal Housing Expenditures Benefit Homeowners." Accessed October 6, 2016. https://www.cbpp.org/most-federal-housing-expenditures-benefit-homeowners.

———. 2016b. "Policy Basics: The Earned Income Tax Credit." Accessed September 28, 2016. http://www.cbpp.org/research/federal-tax/policy-basics-the-earned-income-tax-credit.

———. 2017. "Chart Book: Federal Housing Spending Is Poorly Matched to Need." Accessed October 6, 2017. https://www.cbpp.org/research/chart-book-federal-housing-spending-is-poorly-matched-to-need.

Climaco, Carissa, Sandra Nolden, Meryl Finkel, and Karen Rich. 2006. *Updating the Low Income Housing Tax Credit (LIHTC) Database*. Washington, D.C.: Abt Associates.

Desmond, Matthew. 2016. *Evicted: Poverty and Profit in the American City*. New York: Crown.

Dreier, Peter. 2016. "Housing and the Working Poor." *Democracy Journal*. Accessed September 15, 2017. https://democracyjournal.org/arguments/housing-and-the-working-poor/.

Duncan, Greg J., Pamela A. Morris, and Chris Rodrigues. 2011. "Does Money Really Matter? Estimating Impacts of Family Income on Young Children's Achievement with Data from Random-Assignment Experiments." *Developmental Psychology* 47(5): 1263–79.

Flood, Sarah, Miriam King, Steven Ruggles, and J. Robert Warren. 2016. Integrated Public Use Microdata Series, Current Population Survey: Version 5.0. [dataset]. Minneapolis: University of Minnesota. DOI: 10.18128/D030.V5.0.

Harkness, Joseph, and Sandra J. Newman. 2005. "Housing Affordability and Children's Well-Being: Evidence from the National Survey of America's Families." *Housing Policy Debate* 16(2): 223–55.

Joint Center for Housing Studies. 2015. "America's Rental Housing." Accessed September 28, 2016. http://www.jchs.harvard.edu/sites/jchs.harvard.edu/files/americas_rental_housing_2015_web.pdf.

Leventhal, Tama, and Sandra Newman. 2010. "Housing and Child Development." *Children and Youth Services Review* 32(9): 1165–74.

Meyer, Bruce D., Wallace K. C. Mok, and James X. Sullivan. 2015. "The Under-reporting of Transfers in Household Surveys: Its Nature and Consequences." *NBER* working paper no. 15181. Cambridge, Mass.: National Bureau of Economic Research. Accessed November 17, 2017. http://harris.uchicago.edu/sites/default/files/AggregatesPaper.pdf.

National Low Income Housing Coalition. 2016. "Out of Reach." Accessed September 28, 2016. http://nlihc.org/oor.

Newman, Sandra J., and Joseph M. Harkness. 2002. "The Long-Term Effects of Public Housing on Self-Sufficiency." *Journal of Policy Analysis and Management* 21(1): 21–43.

O'Regan, Katherine, and John M. Quigley. 2000. "Federal Policy and the Rise of Nonprofit Housing Providers." *Journal of Housing Research* 11(2): 297–318.

Renwick, Trudi, and Liana Fox. 2016. "The Supplemental Poverty Measure: 2015." *Current Population Survey* series P60, no. 258. Washington: U.S. Census Bureau. Accessed September 4, 2017. https://www.census.gov/content/dam/Census/library/publications/2016/demo/p60-258.pdf.

Rosen, Eva. 2014. "Rigging the Rules of the Game: How Landlords Geographically Sort Low-Income Renters." *City & Community* 13(4): 310–40.

Ruggles, Steven, Katie Genadek, Ronald Goeken, Josiah Grover, and Matthew Sobek. 2016. Integrated Public Use Microdata Series: Version 7.0 [dataset]. Minneapolis: University of Minnesota. DOI: 10.18128/D010.V7.0.

Shaefer, H. Luke, Sophie Collyer, Greg Duncan, Kathryn Edin, Irwin Garfinkel, David Harris, Timothy M. Smeeding, Jane Waldfogel, Christopher Wimer, and Hirokazu Yoshikawa. 2018. "A Universal Child Allowance: A Plan to Reduce Poverty and Income Instability Among Children in the United States." *RSF: The Russell Sage Foundation Journal of the Social Sciences* 4(2): 22–42. DOI: 10.7758/RSF.2018.4.2.02.

Smith, Robin E., Susan J. Popkin, Taz George, and Jennifer Comey. 2015. "What Happens to Housing Assistance Leavers?" *Cityscape* 17(3): 161–92.

U.S. Department of Housing and Urban Development (HUD). 2014. "Housing's and Neighborhoods' Role in Shaping Children's Future." Accessed September 28, 2016. https://www.huduser.gov/portal/periodicals/em/fall14/highlight1.html.

———. 2017a. "Low-Income Housing Tax Credits." Updated July 10. Accessed October 6, 2017. https://www.huduser.gov/portal/datasets/lihtc.html.

———. 2017b. "Picture of Subsidized Households, 2015." Accessed February 3, 2017. https://www.huduser.gov/portal/datasets/assthsg.html.

Wimer, Christopher, Sophie Collyer, and Sara Kimberlin. 2018. "Assessing the Potential Impacts of Innovative New Policy Proposals on Poverty in the United States." *RSF: The Russell Sage Foundation Journal of the Social Sciences* 4(3): 167–83. DOI: 10.7758/RSF.2018.4.3.09.

The Rainy Day Earned Income Tax Credit: A Reform to Boost Financial Security by Helping Low-Wage Workers Build Emergency Savings

SARAH HALPERN-MEEKIN, SARA STERNBERG GREENE, EZRA LEVIN, AND KATHRYN EDIN

Financial stability depends on emergency savings. Low-wage workers regularly experience drops in income and unexpected expenses. Households with savings absorb these financial shocks but most low-income Americans lack rainy day savings. Therefore, even a small shock, like car repairs, can result in a cascade of events that throws a low-income family into poverty. Nonetheless, existing policies address emergency savings only indirectly. However, the Earned Income Tax Credit (EITC) already functions as an imperfect, makeshift savings tool. This lump sum refund at tax time gives workers a moment of financial slack, but many EITC recipients lack emergency reserves later in the year. By creating a "Rainy Day EITC" component of the existing EITC, policymakers can help low-wage workers build up emergency savings.

Keywords: EITC, emergency savings, financial instability, income volatility

Financial stability depends on emergency savings. Low-wage workers regularly experience large drops in income and unexpected expenses (Farrell and Greig 2015; Hannagan and Morduch 2015; Morduch and Schneider 2013). A household with accessible savings can absorb the impact of these financial shocks (Cramer, King, and Schreur 2015; Gjertson 2014; Holt

---

Sarah Halpern-Meekin is associate professor in human development and family studies at the University of Wisconsin–Madison. **Sara Sternberg Greene** is associate professor at Duke University School of Law. **Ezra Levin** is president of the board of directors at the Indivisible Project. **Kathryn Edin** is Bloomberg Distinguished Professor in Sociology and Public Health at Johns Hopkins University.

© 2018 Russell Sage Foundation. Halpern-Meekin, Sarah, Sara Sternberg Greene, Ezra Levin, and Kathryn Edin. 2018. "The Rainy Day Earned Income Tax Credit: A Reform to Boost Financial Security by Helping Low-Wage Workers Build Emergency Savings." *RSF: The Russell Sage Foundation Journal of the Social Sciences* 4(2): 161–76. DOI: 10.7758/RSF.2018.4.2.08. The authors benefited from the input of Miren Beitia (Community Tax Aid), Maria Cancian (University of Wisconsin–Madison), Michal Grinstein-Weiss, Janie Oliphant, and Phillip Poirier (Center for Social Development), Steve Holt (HoltSolutions), Chye-Ching Huang (Center on Budget and Policy Priorities), Clint Key (Pew Charitable Trusts), Justin King and Rachel Black (New America), Yuri Kim (United Way of King County), David Marzahl and Dylan Bellisle (Center for Economic Progress), Robin McKinney (Maryland CASH Campaign), and David Sieminski (Consumer Financial Protection Bureau). Note that the recommendations made in this paper are the authors' alone and do not necessarily reflect the recommendations of these reviewers. Direct correspondence to: Sarah Halpern-Meekin at sarah.halpernmeekin@wisc.edu, School of Human Ecology, 1300 Linden Dr., University of Wisconsin–Madison, Madison, WI 53706; Sara Sternberg Greene at greene@law.duke.edu, Duke University School of Law, 210 Science Dr., Durham, NC 27708; Ezra Levin at ezra@indivisibleguide.com, 924 Spring Rd NW, Washington, D.C. 20010; and Kathryn Edin at kathy_edin @jhu.edu, Department of Sociology, 533 Mergenthaler Hall, 3400 N. Charles Street, Baltimore, MD 21218.

Open Access Policy: *RSF: The Russell Sage Foundation Journal of the Social Sciences* is an open access journal. This article is published under a Creative Commons Attribution-NonCommercial-NoDerivs 3.0 Unported License.

2016; Mills and Amick 2010), but a near majority of Americans lack even modest rainy day savings (Pew Research Center 2015d; Wiedrich et al. 2016). Further, evidence indicates that this short-term financial insecurity has long-term negative consequences, such as health deterioration, adverse early schooling outcomes, and reduced postsecondary educational attainment (Cramer et al. 2009; Holt 2016).

Despite its importance to both short-term financial security and long-term economic opportunity, existing public policies address emergency savings only indirectly. The Earned Income Tax Credit (EITC) program has one of the most significant impacts among low-wage workers, raising labor force participation, health outcomes, and children's educational attainment (for a summary, see Marr et al. 2015). Although it was not created to boost savings, it can function as an imperfect, makeshift savings tool (Greene 2013; Halpern-Meekin et al. 2015). For some EITC-eligible workers, the U.S. Treasury effectively serves as a savings account that is accessible once a year at tax time. The lump sum refund gives workers a rare moment of financial slack, but many EITC recipients nonetheless lack emergency reserves later in the year (Greene 2013; Halpern-Meekin et al. 2015; Romich and Weisner 2000).

To address low-income workers' absence of rainy day savings outside of tax time, this article proposes a "Rainy Day EITC" addition to the existing EITC.[1] This reform would allow taxpayers to defer 20 percent of their EITC for six months and receive a modest savings match for doing so. By taking advantage of the savings moment made possible by the lump sum refund at tax time, the Rainy Day EITC would allow low-wage workers to build emergency savings for use later in the year. The proposal would increase EITC costs by roughly 1.3 percent. The goals of this proposed policy are, primarily, to provide greater liquidity to lower-income families, allowing them to better cope with financial shocks—guarding against the risk of poverty, and, secondarily, to facilitate their pursuit of their expressed savings goals. The intention is to add an option to the set of financial management strategies low-income families deploy to avoid material hardship.

EMERGENCY SAVINGS AND FINANCIAL INSECURITY

A near majority of Americans have little to no money saved for emergencies. Measures of *liquid asset poverty* illustrate the precarious financial state of millions of Americans. Liquid assets include funds held in bank accounts, as well as in quasi-liquid accounts like IRAs. It excludes illiquid assets, such as vehicles and homes. A household is liquid asset poor if it lacks enough accessible savings to remain above the federal poverty line for three months without any income. Given a nationwide liquid asset poverty rate of 44 percent, a lack of liquid savings is an issue for a much larger percentage of the population than income poverty is (Wiedrich et al. 2016).[2] Data on liquid asset poverty reveal that a large percentage of the population is in a precarious financial situation—one unanticipated car repair or job loss away from economic crisis. Because income and consumption volatility is so common among low-wage workers, their lack of emergency savings can be a key driver of their financial insecurity (Chase, Gjertson, and Collins 2011). Household incomes are complex and often vary month to month, causing financial distress even for middle-class households with adequate annual incomes (Hannagan and Morduch 2015; Morduch and Schneider 2013). A 2015 poll found that 60 percent of Americans surveyed had experienced a substantial income drop or unexpected expense in the previous twelve months (Pew Research Center 2015a). Over the past thirty years, the lifetime risk of individuals experiencing poverty has risen, suggesting that the financial volatility families are facing puts them at risk of material hardship (Sandoval, Rank, and Hirschl 2009). Evidence also exists

---

1. The basic structure of this proposal was described in *It's Not Like I'm Poor* (Halpern-Meekin et al. 2015); a similar proposal was published in the *New York University Law Review* (Greene 2013).

2. Other estimates find even higher rates of this type of short-term financial insecurity (Financial Industry Regulatory Authority 2013; Grinstein-Weiss, Comer et al. 2014; Morduch et al. 2015; Pew Research Center 2015b).

that income volatility is growing, indicating that this problem is expected to only become more pressing (Hacker 2006; Nichols and Zimmerman 2008; Pfeffer, Danziger, and Schoeni 2014; Western et al. 2012).

When more affluent families experience a surprise income drop or expense, they tap into liquid assets or cut back on nonessential consumption. In contrast, when low-wage workers lack liquid savings and experience an economic shock, they cut back on essential expenses or take on debt to make ends meet (Mullainathan and Shafir 2009; Seefeldt 2015). Behavioral science researchers have described this precarious financial situation—little savings and unstable income—as a lack of "financial slack" (Lusardi et al. 2011; Mullainathan and Shafir 2009).

Despite families increasingly taking on consumer debt, consumption volatility has been rising (Dogra and Gorbachev 2016), indicating that they are unable to compensate adequately to smooth out the consequences of their income volatility. These rises in consumption volatility have been most marked for people of color and those with a high school degree or less (Gorbachev 2011). Reasons are sound to expect that volatility in family finances will have negative consequences for children's well-being because family functioning is likely disrupted (Hill et al. 2013).

In line with this expectation, research has found that, controlling for a wide set of factors, income volatility is predictive of adolescent school disengagement, suspensions, and expulsions (Gennetian et al. 2015). The negative consequences of financial volatility for family and individual well-being are also shown by the fact that negative income shocks are predictive of food insecurity, and especially so for those with liquidity constraints (Leete and Bania 2010). Especially among those with low incomes, holding assets is protective against food insecurity (Chang, Chatterjee, and Kim 2014; Guo 2011). These consequences indicate that families are often not able to adequately cope with volatility given the current set of financial tools available to them, but that holding additional assets could help provide a bulwark against such hardships.

In their interviews with a Boston-area sample of EITC recipients, Sarah Halpern-Meekin and her colleagues found that low-income households relied heavily on earned income to meet their families' needs: 80 percent of these households' monthly income comes from wages (2015). This is often from administrative and service industry jobs—for example, an auto shop receptionist, Head Start staffer, fast food worker, office supply salesperson, housekeeper, or nurse assistant. The remaining 20 percent of household income comes from government benefits, help from family members, and child support payments.

Despite their dedication to work, financial uncertainty is the rule for these families. Most report experiencing substantial surprise expenses or income drops over the course of a given year, or even a given month; more than three-quarters describe such a financial shock occurring in the past three years (Tach et al., forthcoming). These financial shocks often have a ripple effect: a broken down car—and the inability to pay for repairs—precipitated a job loss, for example; the implication is that the inability to cope with a small financial problem could raise a very real risk of poverty for a working family. Similarly, in the 2013 Household Financial Survey—a survey of approximately 8,500 TurboTax users, more than 65 percent of respondents report a household member had experienced unemployment, a major car repair, or hospitalization in the six months after receiving their tax refund (Grinstein-Weiss et al. 2015). Further, nationally representative data show that rising income volatility for men appears to be driven by both growing volatility in wages and number of work hours, meaning that families must be prepared to deal with financial instability due to changes in both incomes and expenses (Dynan, Elmendorf, and Sichel 2012).

As a result, there is no average financial month for many families, but rather periods of financial slack punctuated by regular financial shortfalls. When expenses in a given month outweigh available income, families often rely on high-interest credit cards and other forms of debt. As a consequence, debt is almost universal among low-income workers, evident in both national surveys and qualitative interviews (Despard et al. 2015; Halpern-Meekin et al. 2015; Seefeldt 2015; Weller 2006; Wiedrich et al. 2016).

In the past few decades, consumer debt has grown dramatically, especially among low-wage workers. Of the 115 EITC-recipient families Halpern-Meekin and colleagues interviewed, only five had no debt (2015). The Household Financial Survey found that credit card debt was the highest-interest source of debt among EITC-eligible workers, who held an average of $5,082 in credit card debt (Despard et al. 2015). In addition, many families also owed for missed utility payments, car loans, education loans, medical costs, mortgages, or loans from family and friends (Halpern-Meekin et al. 2015; Seefeldt 2015). Every one of the forty-five low- and moderate-income women Kristin Seefeldt interviewed in the Detroit area between 2006 and 2011, carried debt at some point (2015). Nationally, the average family spends nearly one in five income dollars on debt-related expenses each year (Weller 2006).

Halpern-Meekin and colleagues describe how families also often have delinquent debt, causing both financial and psychological stress, with the pressure of being repeatedly contacted by creditors seeking repayment (2015). Many families report having accrued these debts years earlier when they were young adults, inexperienced with financial products. For one working mother, a $100 debt owed to the bank for an overdraft charge turned into over $700 after years left unpaid. This story is typical—about half of all debt carried by interviewed families is long-term debt that accumulated over the years. In national data, among all individuals with a credit file, more than 30 percent have a mark of a debt going into collections on their credit reports (Ratcliffe et al. 2014). When families lack the wherewithal to address small financial problems in the short term, the problems can turn into major issues over the long term, affecting credit scores and the access to loans, employment, and ability to meet needs that accompany them. Further, Kristin Seefeldt found that many of the low- to moderate-income women she interviewed had delinquent debts that resulted in their wages being garnished (2015). This, in turn, led to problems covering everyday expenses. Seefeldt's respondents are not alone. An estimated one in ten Americans between the ages of thirty-five and forty-four have their wages garnished for debt payment (Arnold and Kiel 2014).

For low-income families, facing the demands of debt repayment is a regular, pressing issue. In interview data, families regularly report relying on low-limit, subprime credit cards with high interest rates to make ends meet, juggling multiple cards, and paying a little here and there to avoid penalties (Halpern-Meekin et al. 2015; Seefeldt 2017; Tach and Greene 2014). Although these cards can work well for building a credit history and covering expenses in a pinch, this approach to gaining liquidity is a double-edged sword. Buying on credit smooths consumption for the moment but can entail the accumulation of additional debt, and missed credit card payments are disastrous for credit scores. Plus, juggling card payments to cover monthly obligations is not always enough to get by. When families are unable to cover debt payments—a common dilemma evident in both national and interview data—they are forced to prioritize which payments to make and which debts to leave unpaid (Draut and Silva 2003; Halpern-Meekin et al. 2015; Lyons 2003; Seefeldt 2015, 2017; Tach and Greene 2014).

THE ROLE OF TAX TIME IN PROMOTING FINANCIAL SECURITY

For many families, tax time is a unique opportunity to begin paying off debt. Nationally, more than 120 million individuals receive a refund, worth an average of $3,050, each year.[3] The average tax refund for lower-income families (counting the EITC, other credits, and any overwithholding) is $4,686—the equivalent of about 20 percent of annual earned income—in one Boston-area study (Halpern-Meekin et al. 2015). This tax refund provides a much-needed financial boost to families who are typically unable to fully cover expenses every month. Between a quarter and half of tax refund dollars are estimated to go to debt repayment (Despard et al. 2015; Halpern-Meekin et al. 2015). The remainder typically is divided among current expenses such as groceries, rent, and childcare

---

3. Authors' calculations based on Internal Revenue Service 2016a.

(24 percent of refund dollars), durable goods such as a washing machine or a bed (21 percent), and savings, so often spent down in the months following tax time (17 percent). Approximately one in ten refund dollars is spent on extras, such as a meal at a sit-down restaurant (Halpern-Meekin et al. 2015).

The EITC is described as an income subsidy, but it often functions as a type of savings tool. During the year, families aspire to save, but the pressures on their budgets from regular income and consumption volatility often leave them coming up short (Halpern-Meekin et al. 2015), and so they hope that tax time will bring an essential boost. Notably, families are not just passive recipients of the refund. Although their knowledge of tax code is often fuzzy, parents can be deliberate in how they file their taxes (Tach and Halpern-Meekin 2014). For example, many opt to withhold extra income tax from each paycheck to guard against the risk of owing taxes and to boost their future tax refund (Tach and Halpern-Meekin 2014; see also Barr and Dokko 2006).

This strategy of increasing paycheck withholdings will lead to a larger tax refund, but it also directly reduces income in the months before tax time. Some evidence indicates that the lump sum structure of the EITC is associated with greater debt accumulation over the course of the year, with tax filers smoothing consumption by taking on debt earlier in the year, and paying off the debt at tax time (Jones and Michelmore 2016). Smoothing consumption via taking on debt can carry risks, such as the need to cover interest payments and the hit to credit scores if these debts are not repaid in full and on time.

In short, tax filers are using the EITC's lump sum structure to build savings, address debt, or both. This indicates that EITC recipients are already treating tax time as part of their financial toolkit, which provides support for our proposal to offer further tools to families at tax time.

EVALUATIONS OF TAX-TIME SAVINGS PROGRAMS

The lump sum tax refund is often the largest single payment a low-income household receives in a given year. The average 2014 EITC was more than $2,400, and the total tax refund—which can include the refundable portion of the Child Tax Credit and the return of any overwithholding—is often even higher (Internal Revenue Service 2016b). Two recent randomized control trials explore the possibility of using the tax system to promote emergency savings: SaveUSA and Refund2Savings. Evaluations of each of these innovations find modest but statistically significant and positive impacts on low-wage workers in terms of savings rates and amount of liquid savings.

The SaveUSA pilot was launched in 2008 in New York as $aveNYC and expanded as SaveUSA to several cities between 2011 and 2013. The program partnered with Volunteer Income Tax Assistance sites, at which low-income filers can have their taxes prepared for free, to boost emergency savings. Tax filers at these sites were given the option to participate in the program, which supported savings accumulation. In two sites, New York City and Tulsa, participants who were interested in participating in the tax-time savings program were randomly assigned to either the SaveUSA or control group. SaveUSA group members were required to open a SaveUSA savings account, and nearly 100 percent did so. These group members pledged to save at least $200 of their tax refund into their SaveUSA account, and they were also asked to retain a portion of their deposit until the following year. Those who fulfilled the pledges received a 50 percent savings match of up to $500. Control group members did not have access to a SaveUSA account but were free to save their tax refund in other accounts (Azurdia and Freedman 2016).

Participants in the SaveUSA group were significantly more likely to save and to save more than tax filers in the control group who were not offered access to the SaveUSA account. At the forty-two-month follow-up, individuals in the treatment group with short-term savings in any account increased roughly 8 percentage points over the savings rate in the control group; the average total savings was $522 (30 percent) higher in the treatment group. The evaluation found positive effects on some aspects of financial security, such as level of emergency savings, but it found no effects on debt holdings, material hardship (such as food insecurity), or other indicators of financial security. Some analysts argue that these results support the pursuit of increased tax-time savings options (Black and Cramer 2011).

Refund2Savings (R2S) is the largest savings experiment conducted in the United States, with a sample of about nine hundred thousand tax filers (Grinstein-Weiss, Comer, et al. 2014; Key et al. 2015). Researchers partnered with Intuit to use TurboTax to overcome the "psychological, behavioral and institutional barriers that limit the accumulation of savings" (Grinstein-Weiss et al. 2015, 11). The intervention was low-cost and low-touch. Low-income TurboTax users were randomly assigned to a control group with no intervention or a treatment group, which was nudged to split their tax refunds so that at least a portion was directed into a savings account. The experiment tested the impact of various defaults and messages on savings behavior.

The R2S intervention significantly increased the rate of savings, the amount of savings, the rate of splitting refunds between accounts, and the amount of tax refund savings held for at least six months when compared with the control group. Though statistically significant, the effect sizes were modest. In the highest impact iteration, those depositing their refund into a savings vehicle increased by two percentage points (8 percent in the control made a deposit versus about 10 percent in the treatment group). The intervention nearly doubled the rate of splitting refunds into savings for those in the treatment group, but this represents an increase from 1.3 percent to 2.5 percent. Average savings were higher in the treatment group as well ($224 versus $197); among those who chose to save, the difference was larger between the control and treatment groups ($387 versus $695). The likelihood of retaining some savings six months later was 5 percentage points higher in the treatment group (25 percent versus 30 percent).

In short, evaluations of past tax-time savings programs have found that low-income tax filers are more likely to choose to save at tax time with incentives and nudges, though the impact from these programs has been modest and the data are not nationally representative. Two reasons may explain these modest impacts. First, in the case of the SaveUSA experiment, both the treatment and control groups were composed of tax filers who had indicated interest in the SaveUSA tax-time savings program. The measured impact of the SaveUSA program therefore represents the difference between offering tax filers who intend to save the option of a matched savings SaveUSA account and offering them more traditional savings options. SaveUSA did not measure the impact of offering matched savings accounts to a broader population. Second, in the case of R2S, although the program targeted a broader population, the intervention was limited to low-touch, behavioral nudges, with no additional incentive to participate in the program. R2S demonstrated that simply offering savings options to a general population of low- and moderate-income tax filers can increase the number of people who are saving and the total amount of savings. A program targeted to a broader population, like R2S, that provides a matched savings account, like SaveUSA, may achieve a positive impact at a greater scale than seen in either experiment separately. Such a program would combine a financial incentive similar to SaveUSA's while encouraging participation among a broad group of tax filers.

THE RAINY DAY EITC PROPOSAL

Federal policymakers and researchers have proposed several tax-based policies to address budget volatility and the lack of emergency savings among low-wage workers. In general, these proposals pursue one of three strategies: rewarding workers with a credit *after* they have developed emergency savings; allowing workers to access a portion of their expected future tax refund early; or encouraging workers to defer a portion of their refund in order to build emergency savings (Holt 2015). However, these strategies have potential limitations.

First, for the cash-strapped, deferring resources to savings—especially when done via set-asides from paychecks—can mean that present expenses are unmet, thereby accumulating debt or incurring material hardship. Therefore, facilitating the development of emergency savings during times of financial slack is essential. Second, asking low-wage workers to bank on a future tax refund by necessity requires that either they or the government take on some risk; if the amount they receive as an advance exceeds their actual refund, either they must make up the difference or the government must take the loss. Among other reasons, this is why the Advanced EITC was not widely used and the policy ended (Holt 2009, 2015; U.S. Government Accountability Office 2007). Finally, the tax system feels opaque to many, including low-income filers (Tach and Halpern-Meekin 2014); therefore, the easier and more straightforward it is to pursue savings goals, the more likely they should be able to act on them. Our proposed Rainy Day EITC policy follows this third approach and seeks to make the process of choosing to build emergency savings at tax time simple.

Structure of the Rainy Day EITC
The proposed reform builds on the existing EITC structure, providing an option for families to defer a portion of their EITC for use later in the year. We describe the key features of the Rainy Day EITC as well as the reasoning behind these key features.

Opt-In
Workers will be able to opt into the program on their tax returns. Although an automatic, opt-out program would likely achieve higher take-up rates, take-up is not the only determinant of a successful program. Deferring a portion of the EITC may not be the optimal financial strategy for some tax filers, such as those who depend on their tax refunds to pay past due bills or reduce costly debt (Despard et al. 2015). In addition, an opt-in approach is less paternalistic because it does not assume that saving via this government-provided mechanism is the best choice for tax filers. For these reasons, providing the option to defer, rather than making it a default, was preferable, even at the expense of take-up. To increase the take-up rate, policymakers should invest in adequate education and outreach about the Rainy Day EITC to tax preparers, taxpayers, and tax software companies.

Standardized Deferral Percentage
Those who opt in would receive 80 percent of their EITC at tax time and save 20 percent of their EITC as a deferred payment. We considered but rejected two alternatives: allowing multiple pre-set deferred amounts or allowing taxpayers to choose their own deferred amount. These options would increase program flexibility, but they would also increase both administrative complexity and difficulty in explaining the program to potential participants. Because policy success is contingent on the buy-in of relevant administrative entities, such considerations are essential (see, for example, Kettl 2006; McLaughlin 1987), especially given that the Internal Revenue Service (IRS) is already stretched in its capacities (National Taxpayer Advocate 2013, 2014; GAO 2014).

We arrived at the 20 percent deferral because we wanted to maintain a substantial lump sum refund, given that recipients express a desire for this feature (Barr and Dokko 2006; Halpern-Meekin et al. 2015). Further, as we explain, this would put many families within reach of covering the median expense shock—$1,000—faced by low-income households (Pew Research Center 2015c), and, for most, this would easily replace the cost of the average size payday loan (just under $400; Pew Research Center 2012).

Fifty Percent Savings Match
For every EITC dollar deferred, the taxpayer would receive fifty cents in additional benefits when the Rainy Day payment was received later in the year. The 50 percent match is in line with SaveUSA's incentive, and evidence shows that using larger savings match rates to increase participation has diminishing returns (Duflo et al. 2005). This is also an attempt to balance the desire to provide a savings incentive against the necessity of limiting program costs. Further, the savings match puts additional dollars in the pockets of low-income families, providing additional protection against material hardship.

Single Lump Sum Deferred Payment
Households will receive the remaining 20 percent of their EITC plus their 50 percent savings match as a single payment six months after the tax return is filed. To avoid predatory practices by for-profit tax preparers or other organizations, policymakers should enact regulations ensuring that actors charging high fees to front

the deferred payment early do not victimize low-income tax filers. Even in the absence of a Rainy Day EITC program, such predatory tax-preparer practices are common, such as in the form of "Refund Anticipation Loans" and, more recently, "Refund Anticipation Checks" (Rothstein and Black 2015). The proposal also addresses this concern by providing an "escape hatch" to allow families to access their deferred money early, with no penalties.

We considered but rejected two alternatives: providing the Rainy Day payment in monthly installments, and spreading it across a more limited number of periodic payments (for example, quarterly). Given the existing volatility of low-income household budgets, we expected that monthly payments would be so small as to not cover many of the financial shocks families experience. The option of periodic payments was rejected in the interest of administrative simplicity. Similarly, the six-month deferral period was deemed the simplest way to split the two EITC payments over time. With most EITC recipients filing their taxes in February (Goodman-Bacon and McGranahan 2008), the Rainy Day portion of the EITC will therefore be disbursed in August, just as parents are paying for back-to-school expenses.

Delivery Via Direct Deposit
The Rainy Day payment will be deposited into the same account used for the initial direct deposit of the filer's tax refund. Roughly 90 percent of EITC recipients receive their refund through direct deposit transfers (Perantie, Oliphant, and Grinstein-Weiss 2016). Using tax filers' existing method for receiving their tax refund transfer is the simplest way to disburse the new deferred payment. To further increase both take-up and bank account ownership, the Rainy Day EITC could be coupled with an option to open an eligible account, such as a Treasury-run prepaid card, directly on the tax form at tax time.

In some cases, the Rainy Day program participant's direct deposit account will become inactive before receiving the Rainy Day payment. Administrators can address this issue using existing processes for handling direct deposit accounts made inactive between filing a tax return and receiving a refund; this could include sending a paper check to the tax filer if a direct deposit fails.

Escape Hatch
Participants who opt in at tax time but require their funds before the Rainy Day EITC payment later in the year could choose to receive their deferred amount early, but they would forgo some or all of the 50 percent match if they did so.[4] Given budget volatility, Rainy Day EITC participants must have the option of accessing their deferred refund early if emergency needs arise. This feature should also increase take-up because participants will know they can still access their EITC dollars in the event of an emergency.

Benefits of the Rainy Day EITC
As discussed, low-wage workers often experience volatile income and expenses, causing financial stress and material hardship. Without emergency savings to cover financial shocks, these workers regularly build up costly debt over the course of the year. This financial cycle is expensive, making it difficult for low-wage workers to move beyond living paycheck to paycheck (Gjertson 2014). Breaking out of this cycle, therefore, offers possibilities for the comforts of firmer financial footing and upward mobility.

Currently, no federal program aims at boosting emergency savings. For some families, the EITC functions as a makeshift savings tool but an imperfect one. Families use much of their tax refund to pay off debt, invest in long-term assets, and build savings (Despard et al. 2015). But within a few months of receiving the refund, most have exhausted much of the emergency savings they built up at tax time (Halpern-Meekin et al. 2015). The following months see a familiar pattern of unexpected expenses or income shocks, ballooning debt and missed bill payments. These workers need support to

---

4. To avoid creating a benefit cliff, policymakers may want to ensure that the amount of match forfeited is proportional to the amount of time it has been deferred. For instance, if a filer opts out of the program three months after tax time—halfway through the six-month deferral—she would receive half of the full match amount.

maintain a financial cushion beyond tax time; such a cushion is essential as part of a safety net to protect working families from being economically crippled by a financial shock.

The Rainy Day EITC would take advantage of the tax time moment. Low-income taxpayers view tax time as an opportunity to create a more secure future (Halpern-Meekin et al. 2015; Tufano, Schneider, and Beverly 2008). The program is targeted at the optimal period for this sort of financial decision making, when scarcity has just been relieved (Mullainathan and Shafir 2013). The Rainy Day EITC takes advantage of this moment by giving households a tool to hedge against future expenses and income fluctuations. It is most likely to have poverty alleviation functions for lower-earning filers among the EITC-recipient population, because their larger EITC benefits mean they will be able to set aside a larger dollar amount (plus a 50 percent match) than their higher-income counterparts in the phase-out section of the EITC benefit structure.[5]

For those who opt in to the program, the Rainy Day EITC guarantees that they will have some emergency savings that lasts beyond their initial tax refund. Using the average EITC as a base, the deferred portion would be $480; adding the 50 percent match means that the amount would grow to $720 in a Rainy Day EITC six months after tax time. Given that nearly half of Americans report that they would not have enough liquid savings to cover a $400 emergency expense (Larrimore, Dodini, and Thomas 2016), this Rainy Day payment represents a sizable emergency fund that could be used to make ends meet. As described, this amount could more than replace the size of the average payday loan and covers nearly three-quarters of the median expense shock that low-income families face.

Current private market solutions to the problem of inadequate emergency savings tend to come in the form of payday loans and similar financial products. They do offer a way to combat food insecurity (Fitzpatrick and Coleman-Jensen 2014), but they cost lower-income Americans billions of dollars annually (Standaert and Davis 2016). Although some workers may avoid relying on these predatory financial products by splitting their tax refunds themselves or building emergency savings without new tax-time interventions, the ongoing use of these products indicates an existing need. Because the introduction of regulations limiting the availability of payday loans may increase food insecurity, such regulations could be paired with other avenues to liquidity—such as the Rainy Day EITC—for low-income families (Fitzpatrick and Coleman-Jensen 2014). By buoying low-income workers' financial security, the Rainy Day program could help them avoid predatory lending products. In short, to the extent that government has an interest in reducing the negative externalities associated with budget volatility and the use of predatory financial products, it should consider using tax time to boost emergency savings.

DEMAND FOR RAINY DAY EITC AND ESTIMATED COST

Estimates of the Rainy Day EITC program cost depend on take-up rates. Workers who do not opt into the program would receive no savings match and so would not contribute to the cost of the proposed program expansion. A generous rough estimate of the initial cost, based on reasonable administrative costs and with a take-up rate based on the SaveUSA program, would be roughly 1.3 percent of the current cost of the EITC. We arrived at this estimate using the upper end take-up rate of the SaveUSA program, 13 percent.[6] We assumed that the typical

---

5. A single parent with two children earning $18,000 would receive an EITC worth $5,572 (in 2016); this would mean $4,458 received at tax time and $1,114 deferred for six months, with a $557 match. The family would be below the poverty line before EITC receipt. With the EITC and match, the family would then be at 118 percent of the federal poverty line. In contrast, a single parent with two children earning $36,000 would receive an EITC worth $1,816 ($1,453 received at tax time and $363 received six months later, plus a $182 match); her EITC receipt would not affect this higher-earning parent's poverty status, though it would influence her family's material well-being.

6. The take-up rates in the four SaveUSA experiment cities ranged from 6 to 13 percent.

Rainy Day EITC participant would have an average-sized EITC. For each participant, the cost of the program would be 10 percent of the cost of their EITC benefit—50 percent of the 20 percent of the EITC deferred. We further assumed administrative costs equal to 1 percent of Rainy Day EITC expenditures, comparable to administrative costs of the current EITC (Internal Revenue Service 2008). In 2015, given an EITC expenditure of $66.7 billion, a Rainy Day EITC in that year would have cost roughly $867 million (1.3 percent of EITC benefit expenditures).[7]

However, the take-up rate for the Rainy Day EITC may be higher than other tax-time savings programs targeted at low-income workers in the past. A survey of 2,675 EITC-eligible tax filers found that the overwhelming majority (82 percent) said they would choose to participate in a program with the Rainy Day EITC's features were it available (Perantie, Oliphant, and Grinstein-Weiss 2016). If this level of interest corresponds to a similar level of participation, it would represent a more than five-fold increase in participation rate over the SaveUSA program. At this high level of participation, the Rainy Day EITC in 2015 would have increased EITC expenditures by roughly 8.2 percent over 2014 expenditures. Although substantially larger than the 1.3 percent estimate described, such an increase in EITC expenditures would not be historically extraordinary. Between 1985 and 2011, there were fourteen instances of year-on-year increases in EITC expenditures in excess of 8 percent (Tax Policy Center 2014).

DISCUSSION AND ALTERNATIVES

The Rainy Day EITC proposal is designed to address a specific liquidity problem: millions of lower-income tax filers receive a substantial refund payment early in the year but find themselves without emergency savings later in the year. The proposal addresses this problem by creating a short-term, subsidized savings tool that will be appropriate for some, but not all, of these tax filers. The Rainy Day EITC is not the only potential solution to this problem. We considered several alternatives or amendments, along with practical and political concerns for each. This type of policy tool cannot erase the occurrence of many of the underlying forces that create financial shocks in the lives of low-income families, like the need for car repairs, a divorce, or the loss of wages; rather, the Rainy Day EITC seeks to offer a way of dealing with these shocks when they occur. In this section, we consider three alternatives and amendments to the proposed Rainy Day EITC: increasing the base EITC and converting the Rainy Day EITC to an opt-out enrollment system; expanding eligibility for the program to tax filers who are not eligible for the EITC; and expanding the scope of the program to support medium- and long-term savings.

Alternative 1: Increase the Base EITC and Make the Rainy Day EITC Opt-Out

One potential alternative to the proposal would be to convert the program from opt-in to opt-out enrollment while increasing the size of the base EITC by 10 percent. Such a program would hold harmless all existing EITC participants by preserving their existing benefit levels (and then providing higher benefits in the form of a match for those who do not opt out); we would expect this to increase Rainy Day EITC participation.

For example, an EITC recipient who would have received a $2,000 EITC before the new program was implemented would have two choices under the new regime. She could choose to opt out of the program and receive $2,200 at tax time, a 10 percent increase. Or, she could take no action, be automatically enrolled in the deferral program, receive $2,000 at tax time, and receive a $300 Rainy Day payment six months after filing.

Such a program would have two benefits and a downside. Using an opt-out enrollment system, the program would presumably result in a higher take-up rate than an equally generous opt-in program. Furthermore, by increasing the size of the baseline EITC, no participants would see a reduction in their tax-time refund payment relative to prior years. However, the opt-out enrollment system would be more pater-

---

7. This amount would be lower, depending on the use of the escape hatch among those who opt in but then withdraw their Rainy Day EITC early, forfeiting some or all of the match money.

nalistic than the opt-in model. Rather than providing an optional tool that low-income workers could use if attractive, an opt-out model presumes that EITC-eligible workers are best served by deferring a portion of their tax refund. Nonetheless, this approach does overcome the need for tax preparers and tax filers to have a strong understanding of the program necessary to choose to participate under an opt-in system.

Because of its higher take-up and the increase in the size of the baseline EITC, the program would be significantly more expensive. Increasing the size of the EITC by 10 percent would have amounted to $6.56 billion in 2015. Assuming an increased participation rate of between 20 and 90 percent as a result of the opt-out enrollment, the entire reform would cost between $8 billion and $13.05 billion—an increase over existing EITC expenditures of between 12.2 and 20 percent.

Alternative 2: Expand the Rainy Day EITC to All Filers

Another alternative structure for the program would be to expand access to all tax filers, rather than limiting the program only to EITC-eligible tax filers. In 2016, across the general tax filer population, approximately 73 percent of tax filers received a refund, worth an average of $2,860 (Internal Revenue Service 2016c). Such a program would have several benefits and at least one downside depending on how it was structured.

An expanded Rainy Day program would benefit low-income workers who are ineligible for the EITC, as well as moderate-income workers who could still benefit from assistance in building emergency savings. An expanded Rainy Day program would also be simpler to administer, eliminating the need for the IRS to distinguish between the EITC and non-EITC portions of participants' refund, while also simplifying the experience of participants. Finally, a universal approach would avoid the possibility of creating stigma for participants by ensuring all tax filers, regardless of income, can participate. In part for these reasons, Senators Cory Booker (D-NJ) and Jerry Moran (R-KS) introduced the Refund to Rainy Day Savings Act in 2016, legislation modeled on the Rainy Day EITC concept, but expanded to allow all tax refund recipients to participate.

There are two main concerns with expanding the Rainy Day program in this way: distribution and cost. The extent of the concerns depends on the granular structure of the program. If, for instance, a 50 percent savings match were made available to all refund recipients, we would expect the new program to be highly regressive, given that higher-income households are more likely to save (because they are less likely to have pressing current needs) and more likely to have large tax refunds. Likewise, expanding the program to all tax filers would multiply its cost.

However, both concerns could be addressed with relatively simple structural tweaks to the program. For instance, by limiting the 50 percent match to EITC-eligible or other low-income households, policymakers could reduce program costs and ensure financial support remains targeted to lower-income tax filers while still offering the program's structure to all. Under such a program, higher-income tax filers could participate, but would simply receive interest on their savings rather than a government-subsidized match.

Alternative 3: Support Longer-Term Savings and Asset-Building

As designed, the proposal focuses on short-term savings; it includes no options to maintain that savings over the longer term or to direct the withdrawn savings to an account other than the standard direct deposit account. However, policymakers may wish to expand the scope of the program to support long-term savings and asset development, such as higher education and homeownership. An amendment to the Rainy Day EITC could allow participants to maintain their deferred funds in a Treasury-held account on an ongoing basis instead of having those funds deposited in their direct deposit account. Alternatively, policymakers could allow direct deposits into longer-term savings accounts, such as tax-preferred higher education or retirement accounts.

Expanding the Rainy Day EITC to support such long-term savings would not be a simple tweak to the proposal. Such an amendment would convert a relatively simple program focused squarely on a liquidity problem, to a much more complicated program designed to address both liquidity and long-term asset development. In addition to increasing the complexity of administration, potential participants may have difficulty understanding the purpose of the program, which could reduce the take-up rate.

CONCLUSION

Financial insecurity is a fact of life for low-wage workers (Wiedrich et al. 2016). Millions of working Americans have trouble developing any kind of personal emergency savings fund, so they often manage the irregularity of their financial lives by taking on costly debt (Draut and Silva 2003; Weller 2006). As an escape from this perpetual financial insecurity, many workers rely on the tax system to function as a savings account of sorts—relying on their tax refund to deliver some financial cushion once a year (Halpern-Meekin et al. 2015; Tufano, Schneider, and Beverly 2008). This approach is not without its downsides, however. Financial volatility and a lack of liquidity raises families' risk of food insecurity and negative child outcomes, among other measures of well-being (Chang, Chatterjee, and Kim 2014; Gennetian et al. 2015; Guo 2011; Hill et al. 2013; Kainz et al. 2012).

The Rainy Day EITC can help some workers better maintain financial security throughout the year. The benefits of these lump sum tax refund payments are well documented (for a summary, see Marr et al. 2015), but the EITC was not designed to function as a savings program. A Rainy Day EITC option would change this, allowing workers to develop a personal emergency savings account for use later in the year. This proposal is a relatively modest expansion of the EITC, increasing current EITC expenditures by only about 1.3 percent.

A version of the Rainy Day EITC was introduced as bipartisan legislation: Senators Cory Booker and Jerry Moran introduced the Refund to Rainy Savings Act in 2016. The legislation would allow all tax filers, not just EITC recipients, to defer a portion of their tax refund for six months, and the deferred amount would accrue interest. Low-income tax filers would be eligible to participate in a new pilot program that would provide savings matches for these deferrals. The legislation would also reengineer the federal Assets for Independence matched savings program to invest in local, matched, tax time savings innovations.

The Rainy Day EITC, either as proposed in this article or as introduced in the proposed pilot form, is not a silver bullet. Without further reform of the EITC, childless workers will benefit little because they are often ineligible for the EITC and therefore receive smaller, if any, tax refunds. In addition, even for those with dependent children, this tool will be of little use to those with earnings too low to qualify them for a substantial EITC. Further, many low-income workers will need immediate access to their full tax refund and so will decline to defer a portion of their tax refund. But for those low-wage workers who regularly find themselves flush with resources at tax time and scraping to get by later in the year, the Rainy Day EITC could help them take more control of their financial lives. A tool of this type, rooted in research and provided at a modest cost, could expand economic well-being for millions of working Americans. Financial volatility is common, especially among low-income families, and it has negative consequences, including increased material hardship and poorer outcomes for children, thereby risking the future of the next generation. By providing liquidity, the Rainy Day EITC offers an additional way for families to cope with the volatility they face, putting them on stronger financial footing.

REFERENCES

Arnold, Chris, and Paul Kiel. 2014. "Millions of Americans' Wages Seized over Credit Card and Medical Debt." National Public Radio, September 15. Accessed October 19, 2017. http://www.npr.org/2014/09/15/347957729/when-consumer-debts-go-unpaid-paychecks-can-take-a-big-hit.

Azurdia, Gilda, and Stephen R. Freedman. 2016. *Encouraging Nonretirement Savings at Tax Time*. New York: MDRC. Accessed October 19, 2017. https://www.mdrc.org/sites/default/files/SaveUSA_FinalReport%202015.pdf.

Barr, Michael S., and Jane Dokko. 2006. "Tax Filing Experiences and Withholding Preferences of Low- and Moderate-Income Households: Preliminary Evidence from a New Survey." In *Recent Re-*

search on Tax Administration and Compliance: Selected Papers Given at the 2006 IRS Research Conference, edited by Justin Dalton and Beth Kliss. IRS Research Bulletin no. 1500. Washington: U.S. Department of the Treasury, Internal Revenue Service.

Black, Rachel, and Reid Cramer. 2011. "Incentivizing Savings at Tax Time: $aveNYC and The Saver's Bonus." Washington, D.C.: New America Foundation.

Chang, Yunhee, Swarn Chatterjee, and Jinhee Kim. 2014. "Household Finance and Food Insecurity." *Journal of Family and Economic Issues* 35(4): 499–515.

Chase, Stephanie, Leah Gjertson, and J. Michael Collins. 2011. "Coming Up with Cash in a Pinch: Emergency Savings and Its Alternatives." Madison: University of Wisconsin–Madison, Center for Financial Security.

Cramer, Reid, Justin King, and Elliot Schreur. 2015. "Flexible Savings: The Missing Foundation for Financial Security and Economic Mobility." New America.

Cramer, Reid, Rourke O'Brien, Daniel Cooper, and Maria Luengo-Prado. 2009. "A Penny Saved Is Mobility Earned: Advancing Economic Mobility through Savings." Washington, D.C.: Pew Charitable Trusts.

Despard, Mathieu, Dana Perantie, Janie Oliphant, and Michal Grinstein-Weiss. 2015. "Do EITC Recipients Use Tax Refunds to Get Ahead? New Evidence from Refund to Savings." *CSD* research brief no. 15–38. St. Louis, Mo.: Washington University in St. Louis, Center for Social Development.

Dogra, Keshav, and Olga Gorbachev. 2016. "Consumption Volatility, Liquidity Constraints, and Household Welfare." *Economic Journal* 126(597): 2012–37.

Draut, Tamara, and Javier Silva. 2003. "Borrowing to Make Ends Meet: The Growth of Credit Card Debt in the '90s." New York: Demos. Accessed October 19, 2017. http://www.demos.org/sites/default/files/publications/borrowing_to_make_ends_meet.pdf.

Duflo, Esther, William Gale, Jeffrey Liebman, Peter Orszag, and Emmanuel Saez. 2005. "Saving Incentives for Low- and Middle-Income Families: Evidence from a Field Experiment with H&R Block." *NBER* working paper no. 11680. Cambridge, Mass.: National Bureau of Economic Research. Accessed October 19, 2017. http://www.nber.org/papers/w11680.

Dynan, Karen, Douglas Elmendorg, and Daniel Sichel. 2012. "The Evolution of Household Income Volatility." *B.E. Journal of Economic Analysis and Policy* 12(2). DOI: 10.1515/1935-1682.3347.

Farrell, Diana, and Fiona Greig. 2015. "Weathering Volatility: Big Data on the Financial Ups and Downs of U.S. Individuals." New York: JP Morgan Chase Institute.

Financial Industry Regulatory Authority. 2013. "Financial Capability in the United States: Report from the 2012 National Financial Capability Study." FINRA Investor Education Foundation.

Fitzpatrick, Katie, and Alisha Coleman-Jensen. 2014. "Food on the Fringe: Food Insecurity and the Use of Payday Loans." *Social Service Review* 88(4): 553–93.

Gennetian, Lisa A., Sharon Wolf, Heather D. Hill, and Pamela A. Morris. 2015. "Intrayear Household Income Dynamics and Adolescent School Behavior." *Demography* 52(2): 455–83.

Gjertson, Leah. 2014. "Emergency Saving and Household Hardship." *Journal of Family and Economic Issues* 37(1): 1–17. DOI:10.1007/s10834-014-9434-z.

Goodman-Bacon, Andrew, and Leslie McGranahan. 2008. "How Do EITC Recipients Spend Their Refunds?" *Economic Perspectives* 32(2Q): 17–32.

Gorbachev, Olga. 2011. "Did Household Consumption Become More Volatile?" *American Economic Review* 101: 2248–70.

Greene, Sara. 2013. "The Broken Safety Net: A Study of Earned Income Tax Credit Recipients and a Proposal for Repair." *New York University Law Review* 88(2)(May): 515–88. Accessed October 19, 2017. http://www.nyulawreview.org/sites/default/files/pdf/NYULawReview-88-2-Greene.pdf.

Grinstein-Weiss, Michal, Krista Comer, Blair Russell, Clinton Key, Dana Perantie, and Dan Ariely. 2014. "Refund to Savings: Evidence of Tax-Time Saving in a National Randomized Control Trial." St. Louis, Mo.: Washington University in St. Louis, Center for Social Development.

Grinstein-Weiss, Michal, Dana Perantie, Blair Russell, Krista Comer, Samuel Taylor, Lingzi Luo, Clinton Key, and Dan Ariely. 2015. "Refund to Savings 2013: Comprehensive Report on a Large-Scale Tax-Time Savings Program." *CSD* research report no. 15–06. St. Louis, Mo.: Washington University in St. Louis, Center for Social Development.

Guo, Baorong. 2011. "Household Assets and Food Security: Evidence from the Survey of Program Dynamics." *Journal of Family and Economic Issues* 32(1): 98–110.

Hacker, Jacob. 2006. "Universal Insurance: Enhancing Economic Security to Promote Opportunity." Washington, D.C.: Brookings Institution.

Halpern-Meekin, Sarah, Kathryn Edin, Laura Tach, and Jennifer Sykes. 2015. *It's Not Like I'm Poor: How Working Families Make Ends Meet in a Post-Welfare World*. Berkeley: University of California Press.

Hannagan, Anthony, and Jonathan Morduch. 2015. "Income Gains and Month-to-Month Income Volatility: Household Evidence from the US Financial Diaries." *U.S. Financial Diaries* working paper no. 1. Accessed October 19, 2017. http://www.usfinancialdiaries.org/paper-1.

Hill, Heather D., Pamela Morris, Lisa A. Gennetian, Sharon Wolf, and Carly Tubbs. 2013. "The Consequences of Income Instability for Children's Well-Being." *Child Development Perspectives* 7(1): 85–90.

Holt, Steve. 2009. "Beyond Lump Sum: Periodic Payment of the Earned Income Tax Credit." *Community Investments* 21(1): 26–40. Accessed October 19, 2017. http://www.frbsf.org/community-development/files/Holt_Steve.pdf.

———. 2015. "Periodic Payment of the Earned Income Tax Credit Revisited." Washington, D.C.: Brookings Institution.

———. 2016. "Income Volatility: A Primer." Washington, D.C.: Aspen Institute.

Internal Revenue Service. 2008. "IRS Earned Income Tax Credit (EITC) Initiatives." Washington: U.S. Department of the Treasury. Accessed September 28, 2016. https://www.irs.gov/pub/irs-utl/poc_summary_addendum_121708_final.pdf.

———. 2016a. "Internal Revenue Service Data Book, 2016." Publication 55B. Washington: U.S. Department of the Treasury. Accessed October 19, 2017. https://www.irs.gov/pub/irs-soi/16databk.pdf.

———. 2016b. "Statistics for Tax Returns with EITC." Washington: U.S. Department of the Treasury. Accessed September 14, 2016. https://www.eitc.irs.gov/EITC-Central/eitcstats.

———. 2016c. "2016 Filing Season Statistics for Week Ending December 30, 2016." Washington: U.S. Department of the Treasury. Accessed October 19, 2017. https://www.irs.gov/uac/newsroom/filing-season-statistics-for-the-week-ending-december-30-2016.

Jones, Lauren Eden, and Katherine Michelmore. 2016. "Timing Is Money: Does Lump-Sum Payment of Tax Credits Induce High-Cost Borrowing?" SSRN Scholarly Paper ID 2712849. Social Science Research Network. Accessed October 19, 2017. http://papers.ssrn.com/abstract=2712849.

Kainz, Kirsten, Michael T. Willoughby, Lynne Vernon-Feagans, and Margaret R. Burchinal. 2012. "Modeling Family Economic Conditions and Young Children's Development in Rural United States: Implications for Poverty Research." *Journal of Family and Economic Issues* 33(4): 410–20.

Kettl, Donald F. 2006. "Managing Boundaries in American Administration: The Collaboration Imperative." *Public Administration Review* 66(1): 10–19.

Key, Clinton, Jenna N. Tucker, Michal Grinstein-Weiss, and Krista Comer. 2015. "Tax-Time Savings Among Low-Income Households in the $aveNYC Program." *Journal of Consumer Affairs* 49(3): 489–518. DOI:10.1111/joca.12070.

Larrimore, Jeff, Sam Dodini, and Logan Thomas. 2016. *Report on the Economic Well-Being of U.S. Households in 2015*. Washington: Board of Governors of the Federal Reserve System. Accessed October 19, 2017. https://www.federalreserve.gov/2015-report-economic-well-being-us-households-201605.pdf.

Leete, Laura, and Neil Bania. 2010. "The Effect of Income Shocks on Food Insufficiency." *Review of Economics of the Household* 8(4): 505–26.

Lusardi, Annamaria, Daniel J. Schneider, and Peter Tufano. 2011. "Financially Fragile Households: Evidence and Implications." *NBER* working paper no. 17072. Cambridge, Mass.: National Bureau of Economic Research. Accessed October 19, 2017. http://www.nber.org/papers/w17072.

Lyons, Angela C. 2003. "How Credit Access Has Changed Over Time for U.S. Households." *Journal of Consumer Affairs* 37(2): 231–55. DOI:10.1111/j.1745-6606.2003.tb00452.x.

Marr, Chuck, Chye-Ching Huang, Arloc Sherman, and Brandon Debot. 2015. "EITC and Child Tax Credit Promote Work, Reduce Poverty, and Support Children's Development, Research Finds."

Washington, D.C.: Center on Budget and Policy Priorities.

McLaughlin, Milbrey W. 1987. "Learning from Experience: Lessons from Policy Implementation." *Educational Evaluation and Policy Analysis* 9(2): 171–78.

Mills, Gregory, and Joe Amick. 2010. "Can Savings Help Overcome Income Instability?" Washington, D.C. Urban Institute.

Morduch, Jonathan, and Rachel Schneider. 2013. "Spikes and Dips: How Income Uncertainty Affects Households." *U.S. Financial Diaries*, issue 1. Accessed October 19, 2017. http://www.usfinancialdiaries.org/issue1-spikes/.

Morduch, Jonathan, Rachel Schneider, Timothy Ogden, Anthony Hannagan, and Julie Siwicki. 2015. "Emergency Savings." *U.S. Financial Diaries*, issue 4. Accessed October 19, 2017. http://www.usfinancialdiaries.org/issue4-emersav/.

Mullainathan, Sendhil, and Eldar Shafir. 2009. "Savings Policy and Decisionmaking in Low-Income Households." In *Insufficient Funds: Savings, Assets, Credit and Banking Among Low-Income Households*, edited by Rebecca M. Blank and Michael S. Barr. New York: Russell Sage Foundation.

——. 2013. *Scarcity: Why Having Too Little Means So Much*. New York: Henry Holt.

National Taxpayer Advocate. 2013. *Annual Report to Congress 2013*, vol. 1. Washington: Government Printing Office. Accessed October 19, 2017. http://www.taxpayeradvocate.irs.gov/2013-Annual-Report/downloads/Volume-1.pdf

——. 2014. *Annual Report to Congress 2014*, vol. 1. Washington: Government Printing Office. Accessed October 19, 2017. http://www.taxpayeradvocate.irs.gov/Media/Default/Documents/2014-Annual-Report/Volume-One.pdf.

Nichols, Austin, and Seth Zimmerman. 2008. "Measuring Trends in Income Variability." Washington, D.C.: Urban Institute.

Perantie, Dana, Janie Oliphant, and Michal Grinstein-Weiss. 2016. "Support for a Tax-Time Savings Policy: Interest in Deferring Tax Refunds with Matched Incentives." St. Louis, Mo.: Washington University in St. Louis, Center for Social Development.

Pew Research Center. 2012. "Payday Lending in America: Who Borrows, Where They Borrow, and Why." Washington, D.C.: Pew Charitable Trusts. Accessed July 14, 2017. http://www.pewtrusts.org/~/media/legacy/uploadedfiles/pcs_assets/2012/PewPaydayLendingReportpdf.pdf.

——. 2015a. "Americans' Financial Security: Perception and Reality." Washington, D.C.: Pew Charitable Trusts.

——. 2015b. "The Precarious State of Family Balance Sheets." Washington, D.C.: Pew Charitable Trusts.

——. 2015c. "The Role of Emergency Savings in Family Financial Security: How Do Families Cope with Financial Shocks?" Washington, D.C.: Pew Charitable Trusts. Accessed July 14, 2017. http://www.pewtrusts.org/~/media/assets/2015/10/emergency-savings-report-1_artfinal.pdf .

——. 2015d. "What Resources Do Families Have for Financial Emergencies?" Washington, D.C.: Pew Charitable Trusts. Accessed November 1, 2017. http://www.pewtrusts.org/~/media/assets/2015/11/emergencysavingsreportnov2015.pdf.

Pfeffer, Fabian, Sheldon Danziger, and Robert Schoeni. 2014. "Wealth Levels, Wealth Inequality, and the Great Recession." New York: Russell Sage Foundation. Accessed November 1, 2017. http://www.stanford.edu/group/scspi/_media/working_papers/pfeffer-danziger-schoeni_wealth-levels.pdf.

Ratcliffe, Caroline, Signe-Mary McKernan, Brett Theodos, Emma Kalish, John Chalekian, Peifang Guo, and Christopher Trepel. 2014. "Delinquent Debt in America. An Opportunity and Ownership Initiative Brief." Washington, D.C.: Urban Institute. Accessed October 19, 2017. https://www.encoreccri.org/wp-content/uploads/2014/07/Delinquent-Debt-in-America_final.pdf.

Romich, Jennifer L., and Thomas Weisner. 2000. "How Families View and Use the EITC: Advance Payment versus Lump Sum Delivery." *National Tax Journal* 53(4)(Part 2): 1245–65.

Rothstein, David, and Rachel Black. 2015. "Improving the Tax Preparation Experience." Washington, D.C.: New America Foundation. Accessed December 15, 2017. https://static.newamerica.org/attachments/1678-improving-the-tax-preparation-experience/PaidTaxPrep-Report-FINAL.pdf.

Sandoval, Daniel A., Mark R. Rank, and Thomas A. Hirschl. 2009. "The Increasing Risk of Poverty Across the American Life Course." *Demography* 46(4): 717–37.

Seefeldt, Kristin S. 2015. "Constant Consumption Smoothing, Limited Investments, and Few Repayments: The Role of Debt in the Financial Lives of Economically Vulnerable Families." *Social Service Review* 89(2): 263–300. DOI:10.1086/681932.

———. 2017. *Abandoned Families: Social Isolation in the Twenty-First Century*. New York: Russell Sage Foundation.

Standaert, Diane, and Delvin Davis. 2016. "Payday and Car Title Lenders Drain $8 Billion in Fees Every Year." Washington, D.C.: Center for Responsible Lending.

Tach, Laura, and Sara Greene. 2014. "'Robbing Peter to Pay Paul': Economic and Cultural Explanations for How Lower-Income Families Manage Debt." *Social Problems* 61(1): 1–21. DOI :10.1525/sp.2013.11262.

Tach, Laura, and Halpern-Meekin, Sarah. 2014. "Tax Code Knowledge and Behavioral Responses Among EITC Recipients: Policy Insights from Qualitative Data." *Journal of Policy Analysis & Management* 33: 413–39.

Tach, Laura, Sarah Halpern-Meekin, Kathryn Edin, and Mariana Amorim. Forthcoming. "As Good as Money in the Bank: Building a Personal Safety Net with the Earned Income Tax Credit." *Social Problems*.

Tax Policy Center. 2014. "Spending on the EITC, Child Tax Credit, and AFDC/TANF, 1975—2011." Washington, D.C.: Urban Institute and Brookings Institution.

Tufano, Peter, Daniel Schneider, and Sondra Beverly. 2008. "Leveraging Tax Refunds to Encourage Saving." Washington, D.C.: Brookings Institution.

U.S. Government Accountability Office (GAO). 2007. "Advance Earned Income Tax Credit: Low Use and Small Dollars Paid Impede IRS's Efforts to Reduce High Noncompliance." GAO-07-1110. Washington: Government Printing Office. Accessed October 19, 2017. http://www.gao.gov/products/GAO-07-1110.

———. 2014. "Internal Revenue Service: Absorbing Budget Cuts Has Resulted in Significant Staffing Declines and Uneven Performance." GAO-14-534R. Washington: Government Printing Office. Accessed November 19, 2017. http://www.gao.gov/assets/670/662681.pdf .

Weller, Christian. 2006. "Drowning in Debt." Washington, D.C.: Center for American Progress. Accessed October 19, 2017. https://www.americanprogress.org/issues/regulation/news/2006/05/11/1961/drowning-in-debt/.

Western, Bruce, Deirdre Bloome, Benjamin Sosnaud, and Laura Tach. 2012. "Economic Insecurity and Social Stratification." *Annual Review of Sociology* 38(1): 341–59. DOI:10.1146/annurev-soc-071811-145434.

Wiedrich, Kasey, Lebaron Sims, Holden Weisman, Solana Rice, and Jennifer Brooks. 2016. "The Steep Climb to Economic Opportunity for Vulnerable Families." Washington, D.C.: Corporation for Enterprise Development.